Motor Fleet
Safety Manual

Motor Fleet Safety Manual

A GUIDE TO BUILDING
AND MAINTAINING AN EFFECTIVE
ACCIDENT CONTROL SYSTEM

National Safety Council, Chicago, Illinois 60611

SECOND EDITION

SECOND EDITION, 1972

ISBN: O-87912-046-0

LIBRARY OF CONGRESS CATALOG CARD NO. 72-81117

PRINTED IN THE UNITED STATES OF AMERICA

25M107208   Stock No. 221.02

Contents

psychological testing, employment interview, checking references, physical examination, acceptance interview   Legal and social restrictions

Preface

This Manual discusses the establishment and operation of a loss prevention program. It is designed to help fleet management set up a system of accident prevention or to strengthen a program that needs help. It is based on the belief that it is short-sighted to try to maximize profit from a commercial operation, only to scatter the profits all over the road.

Control of losses associated with motor vehicle collisions is a day-to-day responsibility of all management personnel, just as is responsibility to control other business losses and to maintain top-quality performance. Intelligent planning and supervision is the hallmark of a valuable fleet executive.

The size of the vehicle operation will determine the extent of authority for maintaining adequate loss control that can be delegated through management. In a fleet of five or less vehicles, the owner or local manager himself may do the selection, training, and supervision. In larger fleets (or in the scattered small fleets of a large organization), this authority can be delegated to specialists who will organize, plan, and institute measures to safeguard vehicles, employees, and both company and noncompany property and the public. This Manual provides information for an effective program, no matter what the fleet size.

However, these recommendations must be adapted to the specific circumstances of each fleet operation. Ultimate responsibility for selection of the methods to improve any given situation rests with individual fleet management.

Many persons contributed to this Manual by offering technical advice, counsel, and direction to Staff of the National Safety Council. Thus the Manual reflects fleet operations as they exist today. Although suggestions are drawn from past experiences of successful operations, it is hoped that improvements will take place in the future. It is with this hope that both the Council's Motor Transportation Conference and its members will review this *Motor Fleet Safety Manual* periodically to keep it up to date through revisions. But, it is emphasized, this Manual is not an official code or standard.

Staff of the National Safety Council is deeply indebted for the help and encouragement from its family of fleet members, especially the Publications Committee of the Motor Transportation Conference and the many others who contributed to and reviewed this Manual.

NATIONAL SAFETY COUNCIL

FOUNDED SEPTEMBER 24, 1913
INCORPORATED IN ILLINOIS OCTOBER 1, 1930
INCORPORATED BY ACT OF CONGRESS AUGUST 13, 1953

Purposes and Powers. Certain essential provisions of the Act of Congress which incorporated the National Safety Council are as follows:

Objects and Purposes

"The objects and purposes of the corporation shall be --

to further, encourage, and promote methods and procedures leading to increased safety, protection, and health among employees and employers and among children in industries, on farms, in schools and colleges, in homes, on streets and highways, in recreation, and in other public and private places;

to collect, correlate, .. and disseminate educational and informative data, .. relative to safety methods and procedures;

to arouse and maintain the interest of the people of the United States, its Territories and possessions in safety and in accident prevention, and to encourage the adoption and institution of safety methods by all persons, .. and .. organizations;

to organize, establish, and conduct programs, .. for the education of all persons, .. in safety methods and procedures;

to cooperate with, enlist, and develop the cooperation of and between all persons .. and .. organizations .. both public and private, engaged or interested in, .. any or all of the foregoing purposes .."

Powers

"The corporation shall have power --

to establish and maintain offices for the conduct of its business, and to charter local, State, and regional safety organizations, .. in appropriate places throughout the United States, its Territories and possessions;

to charge and collect membership dues, subscription fees, and receive contributions or grants of money or property to be devoted to the carrying out of its purposes;

to choose such officers, directors, trustees, managers, agents, and employees as the business of the corporation may require.;

to adopt, amend, and alter a constitution and bylaws, ..

to organize, establish, and conduct conferences on safety and accident prevention;

to publish magazines and other publications and materials, .. consistent with its corporate purposes;

to adopt, alter, use, and display such emblems, seals, and badges as it may adopt."

Nonpolitical Nature

"The corporation and its officers, directors, and duly appointed agents as such, shall not contribute to or otherwise support or assist any political party or candidate for office."

No Stock or Dividends

"The corporation shall have no power to issue any shares of stock nor to declare nor pay any dividends."

Audit and Congressional Report

The financial transactions shall be audited annually, .. by an independent certified public accountant .. A report of such audit shall be made by the corporation to the Congress not later than six months following the close of such fiscal year for which the audit is made."

Exclusive Right to Name and Emblem

"The corporation, and its subordinate divisions and regional, state, and local chapters, shall have the sole and exclusive right to use the name, National Safety Council. The corporation shall have the exclusive and sole right to use, or to allow or refuse the use of, such emblems, seals, and badges as it may legally adopt .."

Transfer of Assets

"The corporation may acquire the assets of the National Safety Council, Incorporated, a corporation organized under the laws of the State of Illinois, upon discharging or satisfactorily providing for the payment and discharge of all of the liability of such corporation and upon complying with all laws of the State of Illinois applicable thereto."

Congressional and Presidential Approval. The Act which incorporated the National Safety Council was passed during the First Session of the 83rd Congress and was designated Public Law 259. Leadership in the Congress was as follows:

	Bill introduced by	Approved by the Sub-Committee on Federal Charters of the Judiciary Committee,	Approved by the Judiciary Committee,	Passed by the Senate, President of
In the Senate	Arthur V. Watkins, Senator from Utah	John Marshall Butler, Senator from Maryland	William Langer, Senator from North Dakota	the Senate, Richard M. Nixon, Vice President of the United States
In the House of Representatives	Bill introduced by Clifford Davis, Representative from Tennessee	Approved by the Sub-Committee on Federal Charters of the Judiciary Committee, Chairman John M. Robsion, Representative from Kentucky	Approved by the Judiciary Committee, Chairman Chauncey W. Reed, Representative from Illinois	Passed by the House, Speaker of the House, Joseph W. Martin, Jr., Representative from Massachusetts

The Act was signed by the President of the United States, Dwight D. Eisenhower, on August 13, 1953.

Transfer of Operations to the Federal Corporation. At the time the Act was passed granting the National Safety Council a federal charter, the Council was functioning as an Illinois corporation. This arrangement continued until on which date the Council's assets, operations and organizational structure were transferred from the Illinois corporation to the federal corporation.

THE NATIONAL SAFETY COUNCIL is the only national nonpolitical and nonprofit organization established solely for accident prevention. In 1953, the 83rd Congress of the United States issued a Federal charter for the Council. This recognized it as an integral part of the American way of life.

1

Why accident prevention?

The need for teaching safety (as a means of self preservation) is always with us. This need doesn't end when we leave school. In fact, it increases. On-the-job hazards must be discovered by each individual, either "the hard way" (by bitter experience), or "the easy way" (by being pointed out and warned against). If employees know their job hazards and avoid them, they seldom get hurt.

Across-the-board safety education has not always been recognized as a real need for efficient fleet operation. Although few persons will disagree about teaching a new driver how to handle his vehicle safely, all too often, they forget that fleet shop and garage employees should also be trained, and that all employees should be made conscious of off-the-job safety.

Not only do we have a moral obligation to help safeguard our fellow man, but we have a financial obligation as well. The economic-minded business man learned long ago that it is far less expensive to set up and maintain a program for *preventing* personal injuries to employees, than it is to trust to luck that no one will get hurt.

The soap-bubble idea that people get hurt only through their own carelessness or stupidity goes "poof" when we understand that accidents and accidental injuries are *caused*. Actually, an entire organization can be trained to recognize and to correct or avoid physical-mechanical and personal behavior hazards that could ultimately result in someone's getting hurt.

This *Motor Fleet Safety Manual* points out these hazards, and discusses ways to minimize them through proper selection, training, and supervision. Both general and specific fleet hazards are covered.

Employee Injury Statistics

Since 1948, the National Safety Council has ranked the forty major industries in this country according to their disabling injury and severity rates. Of the entire Motor Transportation Industry, only the Transit Industry portion has compiled sufficient data on its employee injuries to warrant inclusion in the NSC publication *Accident Facts.* Commercial vehicle, bus, and other groups have not.

The employee on-the-job safety record of the Transit Industry does not compare favorably with that of other industries. Since 1948 the fleets have never ranked higher than the lower third for injury frequency rate nor higher than the middle third in severity rate standing when compared with the experience of other major industries. The *average* ranking of the Transit Industry during this period has been in the *lower third for frequency* and also in the *lower third for severity*—not a very enviable record for fleets.

Costs of Accidents

The three main areas of fleet accidents are those arising from (1) vehicle accidents, (2) employee injury accidents, and (3) off-the-job accidents.

In the case of passenger carriers, there is a fourth area, namely passenger accidents, not resulting directly from vehicle accidents.

Before discussing each of these, let's look at some estimates of what accidents, in general, cost our industry.

The American Trucking Associations' *Trucking Trends* estimates accidents (including insurance) cost common carrier fleets slightly less than 5 per cent of gross revenue for Class I, II, and III carriers. This alone would amount to over $600,000,000, and is slightly more than profit before taxes.

The Interstate Commerce Commission fully regulates about 15,600 carriers who operate over 350,000 trucks in intercity service. The I.C.C. estimates there are probably more than 1,000,000 private trucks engaged in intercity commerce. (There are also some 23,000 buses in intercity service and about 50,000 in local transit service, plus an undetermined number of vehicles in taxi fleets and local truck services, and nearly 300,000 school buses.) Thus the total industry cost of accidents is way over a billion dollars a year.

Accident costs are difficult to determine because so many factors

2

enter into the calculation. A specific example is given in Appendix A. Here, E. J. Emond, former safety director for Armour and Company, documents a total loss of $5,611.16 that resulted from an accident that amounted to "a mere $200" to the other vehicle, and involved no personal injury.

Let's look at each area of fleet accidents.

1. VEHICLE ACCIDENTS

In a typical fleet, *vehicle accidents* (especially those involving injury) will usually represent one of the largest dollar losses. Every time a company vehicle moves on or off the premises, it runs the risk of becoming involved in an accident. It matters little whether the vehicle comes from a large or small fleet, from a common or private carrier, whether the vehicle is a passenger car or a semi-trailer truck, or who is driving it. If it becomes involved in an accident, the company may be held liable—the actual cost will depend on many variables over which the company now has little control, such as illustrated in Appendix A.

Although a fleet may buy insurance to cover such contingencies, the fact is that in the long run every fleet pays for its own accidents. When an insurance company pays for a vehicle accident, it does so with fleet money (from premiums paid)—and, in addition, the insurance company gets paid for overhead costs, taxes, and its profit.

Insurance, however, is not only a method of distributing accident costs over a period of years (in other words, budgeting to meet them), it is also a means of obtaining expert claims and legal service which serves as a valuable buffer between the fleet owner and claimants. Depending upon the accident experience of the fleet, however, the insurance premium can be modified. Therefore, the best way to reduce insurance premiums is to reduce accident experience.

In addition to the insurance premium and other direct costs of vehicle accidents, there are many indirect costs. These result from disruption of service, downtime of damaged vehicles, supervisory time and expense involved in cleaning up after the accident, overtime, and many other expenses. Total indirect costs are often many times the direct costs, as illustrated in Appendix A.

2. EMPLOYEE ACCIDENTS

Injuries incurred on the job by the company's own employees are another very significant accident cost. Another form of insurance—known as Workmen's Compensation—is designed to compensate an injured worker

3

for (a) loss of wages while recovering from an injury or (b) any permanent bodily impairment resulting from the injury.

Here again, regardless of the type of insurance carried, the premiums over the years are about in proportion to the fleet's own employee injury costs, and, in addition, the fleet must pay the indirect costs. Although often difficult to assess in dollars and cents, these indirect costs drain an organization's resources and efficiency.

Examples of this indirect cost drain are:

a. Production time lost by other employees leaving their regular job to assist the injured employee;

b. Cost of equipment repairs;

c. Value of material spoiled or damaged, or the cost of reprocessing;

d. Extra labor and supervisory cost to straighten out or cleanup after the accident;

e. Cost of investigating and reporting the accident by supervisors and management personnel.

3. OFF-THE-JOB ACCIDENTS

Injuries to employees while off the job are another fleet expense that is seldom calculated. The principal cost to the fleet of such accidents is absenteeism—lower production through loss of skilled and experienced manpower. Another cost is wages paid for nonproductive time or for below-standard work, such as done by a person returning from an injury. If replacement workers must be hired, there are personnel department costs, medical fees, and training costs.

One thing is certain: when accidents are avoided, accident costs are also avoided.

Preventability of Vehicle Accidents

To what extent, then, are accidents controllable? Let's look at examples.

Some fleets fail to control accidents to such a degree that their insurance rates became almost prohibitive. In order to survive, such fleets must institute accident prevention programs to reduce their accident frequency rates and their premiums.

The Bureau of Motor Carrier Safety reports many fleets allow their level of compliance with its regulations to fall so low that operating rights are in jeopardy. To forestall this, carriers must institute far-reaching safety programs and give safety the priority required. Most fleets admit that if they had started a safety program earlier, they could have saved

ACCIDENT AFTERMATH. More than service gets disrupted when vehicle crashes.

many dollars. Some single-fleet savings have totaled millions of dollars. The National Safety Council's National Fleet Safety Contest records tell the story of many individual fleet improvements. Frequency rates over the past decade have shown substantial reductions. The all-contest rate for 1932 was over 30 reportable accidents per million vehicle miles. Today, this accident rate had been reduced to about 12.

Preventability of Employee Injuries

Work injuries, too, can be controlled. National Safety Council records show that the steel industry, once very hazardous (with a frequency rate of 32.09 disabling injuries per million man hours in 1926), has reduced its rate to less than 4 and ranks now as the fourth safest industry in the United States.

The disabling injury frequency rate for all industry in the United States was 31.87 in 1926. Today, it has dropped to less than 9. This shows how successfully industry has worked to prevent accidents.

Even rudimentary accident prevention efforts can be successful. When the construction superintendent of a large building project became alarmed at the rise in accidents, he called his foremen and supervisors together and stated in no uncertain terms that he wanted accidents

5

stopped. He repeated this order several times. Responsibility was placed and records were kept. This alone resulted in a 30 per cent reduction in accident frequency during the remainder of the project.

Preventability of Off-the-Job Injuries

Another dimension of accident prevention, off-the-job accident losses, has also been controlled. One company reduced its off-the-job injury rates from 6.34 to 4.89 per million man hours of exposure over a four-year period. (This compares favorably to the current national average of about 10. Off-the-job motor vehicle fatalities for this company also declined during the same period from about the national rate of 5.5 per 100,000,000 miles of travel to 40 per cent less. Another company was able to reduce its off-the-job injury rate over a three-year period from 15.05 to 11.7.

Further evidence of management influence over off-the-job injuries is evidenced by the record of a company that reduced days lost to off-the-job injuries from 1,138 per year to 695—or by almost 40 per cent.

Human and Social Cost of Accidents

Although cost saving provides strong motivation for management to strive for maximum accident prevention effectiveness, there are higher motivations: management's moral obligations.

1. A disabling injury sustained by an employee, or a member of his family, inevitably involves loss to the employee—reduced income while away from work, as well as pain and suffering. If a permanent bodily impairment is involved, the worker must always live with it and no amount of financial compensation will actually offset the loss.

2. Deaths and disabling injuries due to accidents have a social cost which affects the worker's family and the whole community. When a family loses a father and breadwinner, it loses many other things as well, including emotional security and many plans for the future.

3. Management also has a civic obligation because company vehicles travel on the public streets and highways. Not only should such vehicles be operated so as not to endanger the lives of other highway users and pedestrians, but, in fact, career drivers should set an example of exemplary traffic safety.

Management Rewards

Management will find that although accident prevention techniques must be learned, the time spent in learning and applying them provides personal satisfaction as well as contributing to the welfare and profits of the company.

1. One of the first of these is pride in executive skill. Managerial skill has many components: certainly the ability to make accident prevention work and work well is one of them. Stockholders often look at a company's accident rate as an index to the overall efficiency and the skill of the manager. The good executive should be expected to be good at controlling vehicle accident and personal injury loss. As one fleet manager put it, "You can't separate management effectiveness into good and bad. If the top man is good at marketing, but loses money through a poor accident record, he's still a poor manager. A good manager is good all the way around: he includes accident prevention as one of his top responsibilities."

2. One of the basic management functions is to provide leadership. For this, the safety program offers many opportunities. Through it, employees see the chief executive in the role of inspirer and persuader, reconciling the interests of the employee and that of the enterprise in an area where mutuality of interest is easy to see. Having accepted management leadership in this role, the average employee will more readily respond to the same leadership in working toward the other goals of the fleet.

3. Improved supervision is another fringe benefit of the safety program. Enforcement of safety rules by the supervisor is merely a reflection of the company's interest in the personal welfare of employees. This provides the basis for improved communications between the supervisor and his subordinates whether they be drivers, mechanics, dock workers, or other employees.

4. The safe company is a better place to work than the company that pays little attention to safety. A worker not only has less chance to be injured, but he finds his work easier because there is evidence of concern for his dignity and worth. The safety program thus contributes to good morale, company loyalty, and improved job performance.

Safety and Public Relations

Safety is not limited to the production function of the fleet; it also can contribute to the marketing function. A reputation for safety is a definite asset.

The motor vehicle fleet operates in the public eye and the public expects it to be operated by drivers with high professional ability. Because of this expectation, it is news when a company vehicle has an accident. But it can also be news when the fleet wins an award for safety

7

or its drivers earn safety awards. (See Appendix B, "Getting Publicity from 'Safe Driver Awards.' ")

Any company would like an attractive billboard in the high-traffic areas of a city—and a well-maintained, politely driven vehicle can provide just that. (See Chapter 13 and Appendix E.)

The fleet manager is justified in actively seeking a reputation for excellence in traffic safety since this is a definite public relations asset not only for his company, but very often for the industry. It should never be forgotten, however, that in the long run, the public judges a company for what it is rather than what it pretends to be.

Any bid for public recognition for safe operation should be based on sincere effort and on achievement by all members of the fleet.

2

Elements of a fleet safety program

What is a fleet safety program? What are its main elements? What and whom does it involve? How is it done, anyway?

The fleet safety program encompasses all that the fleet does systematically to prevent accidents, all accidents: vehicle accidents, work injury accidents, and off-the-job accidents. This chapter discusses the main elements of a fleet safety program. Later chapters will detail the more complex parts of the program, and its application to specialized fleets.

Management Leadership

The cornerstone of any company activity—and especially of a safety program—is management. The success of the fleet safety program depends largely upon the top manager—what he knows about safety, what he thinks and feels about safety, what he expects from the safety program, and how much money, people, and personal participation he will invest in it.

The fleet manager must be convinced that accident prevention is a good investment. Ideally, he should also know the basics of accident prevention and should know when his fleet is doing well and when it is falling short. He should be willing to provide leadership through face-to-face talks with other top management, supervisors, and employees, and through policy statements and safety policy. He should radiate enthusiasm and determination for safety and, above all, he should set a good example. He should work well with his safetymen.

His interest in accident prevention should be sincere because employees can sense this attitude. If it is insincere, it can harm the entire program. A former chief of staff of the United States Army once said, "The leader must be everything that he desires his subordinates to become. Men think as their leaders think, and know unerringly how their leaders think."

Perhaps fleet management has not placed sufficient emphasis on employee injury prevention because they have not clearly understood the problem they face. Here is a summary of steps that must be taken when starting a program:

1. Arrange for reports that truly reflect the total costs of accidents. Such reports should reflect not only the direct costs of accidents—such as workmen's compensation, fleet insurance, and medical costs—but also reflect at least an estimate of the indirect costs (responsible studies show these average three to four times the amount of the direct costs).

2. Publish a clear, easily understood company safety policy. One of the classic policy statements is that of the Bell Telephone System:

"No job is so important and no service is so urgent—
that we cannot take time to perform our work safely."

3. Employ a professional safety specialist to set up and administer the program. A person already in the employ of the company may be chosen. If he is not already a professional safety engineer, he can be trained to administer the safety program. There are many opportunities for a person to be trained in accident prevention techniques (discussed later in this chapter).

4. Make it clear to all levels of supervisory management that (a) they have responsibility for preventing employee injuries, and (b) the safety specialist works with them and through them.

5. Budget sufficient funds to provide all necessary safety equipment— for employees, vehicles, and garages and terminals. Supplies such as eye, face, head, and body protective equipment, and all necessary respiratory equipment should be included.

6. Budget sufficient funds for training foremen, supervisors, and superintendents in employee safety practices.

7. Budget sufficient funds to cover the cost of holding employee safety committee meetings, and at least one or two general employee safety meetings annually, the latter to be scheduled for the presentation of safety record awards such as safety cards or certificates or plaques, or for other reasons.

8. Budget sufficient funds to permit a reasonable investigation of each personal injury. Nondisabling injuries may require only a little extra time of a foreman or supervisor. Serious injuries will probably require a full-dress investigation. This is not a responsibility that can be shifted

THE SUCCESS OF THE FLEET SAFETY PROGRAM depends largely upon the top manager—what he knows about safety, what he thinks and feels about safety, what he expects from the safety program, and how much manpower, money, and personal participation he will invest in it. He must believe that accident prevention is a good investment.

11

to a workmen's casualty insurance company.

9. Budget sufficient funds to permit a periodic inspection of plant, tools, and equipment. The hours spent on such activities are usually considered as "nonproductive time." Let it be counted as such, because a comparison of the total of all injury prevention costs *vs.* uncontrolled injury costs will stand the spotlight of realistic cost accounting.

10. Plan to personally attend, as often as practical, safety meetings and safety committee meetings to show personal interest in these activities, and to compliment outstanding safety records achieved by departments, divisions, sections, or the company as a whole. Re-emphasize top management's sincere concern for the personal safety of each and every employee. Endeavor to instill group pride in what has been accomplished, and also to establish even more impressive safety goals.

This list can be adjusted to fit the size of and to cope with the accident experience of each fleet.

The Safety Policy

Management's attitude toward safety should be carefully phrased in the form of a written safety policy made known to all employees, supervisors, and top management. A written policy serves as a checkpoint whenever a conflict arises between safety and expediency, and is useful in enforcement of safety rules by the supervisors. The precise form of the written policy is not important, so long as it is a clear and forceful statement of management's desires.

• A large fleet expressed its belief in safety in a policy manual for all employees:

"Why do we have an accident prevention program? Because we know that money spent to pay for property damage or for personal injuries resulting from accidents is a direct loss to our company—a direct charge against our profits. Accidents can be prevented. Through such prevention, these costs are reduced with a resulting increase in profits. It makes no difference whether the cost is in the form of insurance premiums or direct payment by our company through any of several forms of self-insurance, since in either case it is our money that is spent. Accordingly, it is the policy of the company that every effort be made to prevent accidents. It is the responsibility of all personnel—from top management, through all ranks of employees—to comply with this policy."

• One of the first policy statements on safety was issued in 1906 by

Judge Elbert Gary, President of the United States Steel Corporation. It has now become an historic safety document.

> "The United States Steel Corporation expects its subsidiary companies to make every effort practicable to prevent injury to its employees. Expenditures necessary for such purposes will be authorized. Nothing which will add to the protection of the workmen should be neglected."

- Sometimes the safety policy can be expressed in a very short form, almost in the nature of a motto. An example is the policy of the Bell Telephone System, cited earlier, which reads "No job is so important and no service is so urgent—that we cannot take time to perform our work safely." This policy is shown on dashboard decals, desk mottos, posters, and in so many other places throughout the company, that it is probable that any Bell employee could repeat it verbatim if asked.

Assigning Safety Responsibility

Top management has the ultimate responsibility for the safety performance of the fleet, but this responsibility must be extended, as authority is delegated, in a direct line through the operating departments to the drivers and other employees. Management must see to it that this responsibility is fully accepted, and then—in turn—hold supervisors and foremen accountable for the safety performance of their respective departments.

SAFETY DIRECTION

Every supervisor in the organization has a responsibility for accident prevention, but some one person should be assigned special responsibility for directing the accident prevention effort through line management. The job title of this person may be "Safety Director," "Safety Manager," "Safety Counselor." Whatever the title, it is important that the position be one of responsibility, authority, and respect.

In larger fleets, safety direction will be a full-time assignment. Often additional personnel are needed to carry on departmental and specialized functions. In smaller fleets, safety direction may be a part-time responsibility, carried on in addition to an employee's other duties. Where such an arrangement is necessary, the safety duties of the job should be carefully spelled out to make sure that sufficient time is allotted for accident prevention work and that the press of other duties does not divert him from accident prevention work. In the very small fleet, the owner or manager can direct the activity himself. The

FLEET SAFETY TRAINING includes maintenance instruction as well as class-room and field work. This class at North Carolina Truck Driver Training School is taught different methods of assisting mechanics and other shop personnel.

important point is that one person in the organization should assume this special responsibility.

DUTIES

The safety director's duties shall be to organize and administer an effective safety program through line management, along the lines described in this manual. He must study all hazards existing in any part of the fleet operation and formulate practical plans for their elimination, control, or for protection against them. His recommendations in this regard are submitted to management for approval, after which they become the official directives of management. (This is why management interest is important to success.) The safety director should keep records of the fleet's safety performance (see Chapter 5 for details) and keep management informed as to the degree of success of the program.

Considering the amount of money that can be saved through a carefully planned and administered safety program, the selection of a qualified person to direct the program is as important as the selection of a good sales manager, or superintendent of transportation or maintenance. The person selected should—in addition to being knowledgeable and sincerely interested in safety—be a good administrator, a sound

14

technician, and one who can sell ideas equally well to the newest driver or to the boss himself.

More details are given in the next chapter.

PART-TIME

When the fleet must assign safety as a part-time job, the person must be capable of learning the basic techniques. There are, unfortunately, few schools or colleges that provide complete courses in fleet safety engineering. The National Committee for Fleet Supervisor Training conducts a number of one-week courses at colleges and universities throughout the United States.

More information on these courses may be obtained by writing to:

> Motor Transportation Department
> NATIONAL SAFETY COUNCIL
> Chicago, Illinois 60611

These courses can provide a new man with the fundamentals of the job. He will have to increase his knowledge of accident prevention by reading manuals such as this one, by participating in regional and national motor vehicle safety conferences and by keeping posted on current information from safety periodicals and trade magazines.

Accident Reports

Every accident prevention program must include (1) a careful gathering of information about the fleet's accidents and (2) putting this information to work in the prevention of future accidents. The accident reporting system also plays an important role in the handling of claims. A good system with good accident reporting discipline is absolutely necessary. More details are given in Chapters 4 and 5.

Driver Selection

When a new employee is added to the payroll, the selection procedure should be designed to properly evaluate—in terms of safety and loss prevention—the employee's past experience and his potential.

It is the responsibility of safety direction to guide employment personnel in screening for physical disabilities as well as determining, insofar as possible, the ability of each prospect to work and drive safely. In many instances this search should even carry over into the prospect's ability to be safe away from work. More details are given in Chapter 6, "Driver Selection."

Driver Training

Every organization conducts a certain amount of training for new employees: company policy, work rules and conditions, and job essentials. In some cases, this is accomplished by assigning the worker to an experienced employee; in other cases, the supervisor does the training. In larger fleets, training the new employee may involve formal classroom training. One of the primary functions of the safety program is to make sure that the training program, in addition to teaching the employee what to do, teaches him how to do it safely. Details in Chapter 7.

Vehicle Safety

The safety director should be consulted in the selection, painting, purchase, and maintenance of vehicles. The selection of color or color combinations should be considered with safety in mind (see Appendix E, "Protective Coloring for Commercial Vehicles"). Vehicles must be kept in a safe condition and provided with all needed safety and emergency equipment. Adequate pretrip inspections, en route reporting of difficulties, and procedures for reporting and correcting mechanical defects should be instituted. Details in Chapter 13.

Employee Safety

The fleet safety program is not complete unless it concerns itself with the prevention of work injuries to all employees. Drivers, clerical staff, dock help, maintenance employees, outside sales force, and all others should be covered in the overall safety programing.

Buildings, grounds, and all other physical facilities should be planned to control accidents. Interiors should be well lighted, heated, and ventilated. The selection of pleasing color schemes for interiors not only makes pleasanter places in which to work, but it aids safety. Poor housekeeping, especially at garages and terminals, should not be tolerated. Safety thrives in an environment that has the "look of safety," that says "management cares about safety."

The employee safety program should include good injury reporting with corrective followup to assure that a repetition of the accident cannot occur. Hazardous job operations should be carefully studied and safe practices devised to guard against the hazards. Machine guards and protective clothing should be provided and used wherever needed. Details in Chapter 11.

16

Off-the-Job Safety

The safety program should also include activities designed to encourage workers to practice safety while off the job. In this area there are a number of effective things management can do. A safety program animated with the spirit of "Safety Everywhere—All the Time" reinforces all safety work in the three areas—safe driving, safe work practices, safety off the job. Details in Chapter 12.

Safety Supervision

Supervision has two aspects: positive and negative. The first is concerned with inspiring workers to a high quality and quantity of output; the negative, with checking and correcting substandard performance.

There is also a safety aspect of supervision: safety standards are to be met in every job. The supervisor's positive task is to inspire total compliance with safety rules (policies) and high safety performance among drivers. Negatively, he must correct unsafe acts and conditions.

Good safety supervision is animated by top management support. It also depends upon the safety training of supervisors. They should be taught that safety is *a part of* every job, not *apart from* every job. See Chapter 8 for details.

Interest-Sustaining Activities

Every successful safety program includes activities aimed at arousing employee interest in safety and keeping it at a fairly high pitch. The inexperienced safety director is apt to think that a safety program is solely concerned with this objective. This, of course, is not true. Interest-sustaining activities, while important, cannot have any great effect unless they are effectively coordinated with all the other elements that make up a sound safety program.

It is sometimes difficult to separate interest-sustaining activities from some of the other elements such as training, but they can be classified as being of three main types.

    1. Informative activities cover such things as safety meetings, special-emphasis campaigns, posters, dash cards, driver letters, bulletins, and magazines. Their function is to provide information as well as to remind and inspire. Their effect is cumulative.

    2. Competitive activities include various contests and awards based on group and individual safety performance. These appeal to the competitive spirit.

EXPRESSION OF NATIONWIDE INTEREST in fleet safety is shown at annual awards luncheon for National Fleet Safety Contest winners. Information and contest forms can be obtained from the Motor Transportation Department of N.S.C.

3. Expressions of management interest. These include award presentation ceremonies, safety banquets, rallies, carnivals, and special events attended by the top manager himself for the purpose of expressing his personal appreciation for successful group and individual safety effort. The scale of such events, the care with which they are planned, and the sincerity of the top manager's participation will be regarded by employees as management's true feeling of the importance of safety.

The objective of all three types of interest-sustaining activities is to keep alive the employee's interest in safety, maintain his desire to achieve a good safety performance record, and still keep an element of fun in the whole thing. See "Maintain Interest in Accident Prevention" in Chapter 11.

Integrating Safety With the Job

Is safety something that is superimposed over the work-a-day functions of the fleet? Or should it be an integral part of the job?

Certainly one can think of a job as having a functional aspect—achieving the job objective, whether it be grinding a valve or driving a vehicle through an intersection. One can also think of safety as being those additional precautions added to the job, because of a recognized hazard present, to make sure that the job objective is achieved without accident.

In the training of employees and supervisors, it might be helpful to separate the safety content of the job from the functional aspect and hold it up for inspection. But in actual performance and supervision, however, any distinction between the two disappears: safety blends in with the functional part of doing the job.

This blending in of safety should apply to the whole safety program. As time goes on, the safety program becomes less and less obtrusive. It is accepted and becomes part of the day-to-day activities of the fleet.

It is to this fundamental objective that this entire Manual is dedicated.

3

Safety direction

Regardless of who administers the fleet loss-control program—whether he be the boss himself or a highly skilled specialist—he must include in the program certain elements that are, to a degree, dictated by local circumstances.

When fleet operation is the sole concern of a business (such as a for-hire common carrier), it is often easier to systematize the loss-control program. Nevertheless, the fleet operation of any business or agency must contain these basic elements of control if it is to be efficient and successful.

As a guide to organizing the work of safety direction, this chapter provides a step-by-step approach to the basic elements of a safety director's work.

Background Required

It has often been said that a safety director must be a "Jack-of-all-Trades." In many respects this is so. There are, unfortunately, no "Jack-of-all-Trades" finishing schools. A fleet safety director is often a person of varied backgrounds and education—none of which was originally intended to prepare him for the task.

Although the past several decades have produced much information on which to build a workable program of safety direction, unfortunately there are too few courses. Perhaps, some day fleet management will endow schools of higher learning to investigate and prepare a thorough academic approach to fleet loss-control manage-

SUCCESSFUL SAFETY DIRECTION includes these seven steps: preparation, investigation, planning, selling, training, followup, and reporting. Close identification with management and close work with the fleet, coupled with enthusiasm and knowledge, are basic to safety direction if it is to be efficient and successful.

ment. But for the most part, such training now consists of short courses presented by industry safety directors guided through the work of the National Committee for Fleet Supervisory Training. A few scattered colleges and universities offer degree instruction in elements of loss prevention. Most of these are in the engineering schools.

A background that includes either education or work experience in business administration, human relations, traffic, or law enforcement has proved valuable to present-day safety directors. The most successful directors have supplemented this type background with short courses in management, safety engineering, writing, speaking, and other valuable subjects.

Typical Job Descriptions

Two examples of typical job descriptions provide some insight into the many, varied talents needed for effective management of loss-prevention programs. These start on the next page.

The first description represents the suggestions of a prominent safety director and winner of the Marcus A. Dow Memorial Award. The following Job Description was prepared to fit the loss-control program of his company, a well-known for-hire carrier:

Position Described: Director of Safety and Personnel

DEPARTMENT: "Operations" (division of)
REPORTS TO: Vice President of Operations
SCOPE: Entire system
FUNCTION: Initiate general and specific safety programming, and oversee operation for compliance with management's safety policies. Provide top management and supervision with information and techniques for the prevention of motor vehicle accidents, personal injuries, and fires. Inspect all locations for potential accident situations including buildings, grounds, vehicles, tools, and work areas. Maintain liaison with outside agencies to bring new knowledge back to improve our present program.

Specific Duties

I. Reports and Recording

1. Properly report all accidents to company officers, and state and federal agencies. (Also see paragraphs 7 and 9.)
2. Keep individual accident and injury reports on all employees.
3. Analyze this statistical information to recommend corrective action.
4. Receive driver violations and/or arrest notifications and forward to proper supervisor for action.
5. Prepare monthly recap for each terminal listing persons who had accidents during the month. Classify all reports as to "preventability."* Keep the information up to date on terminal bulletin boards.
6. Maintain individual safety award (safe driving and no work injury) records. Procure and present awards.
7. Prepare required Bureau of Motor Carrier Safety (BMCS) reports of accidents and fires. Also certain reports of same to state agencies. Keep detailed BMCS Accident Register up to date.
8. Process any BMCS driver equipment compliance reports arising out of BMCS road inspections.
9. Prepare reports of investigation of motor vehicle accidents involving injuries to Automotive Crash Injury Research of Cornell Aeronautical Laboratories, Inc., PO Box 235, Buffalo, N.Y. 14221.
10. Check on trailer interchange policies and techniques to make

* *Explained in Chapter 7 under "Defensive Driving."*

22

certain they are in compliance with BMCS Regulations.

11. Maintain perpetual inventory of all fire extinguishers in terminals and in vehicles, and check their servicing periods.

II. Investigations

1. Investigate serious accidents, injuries, and fires. Direct investigations by local supervision of others.

2. Investigate all instances of rough handling or reported abuse of equipment.

III. Personnel Practices

1. Personally interview all prospective employees after initial screening by the local terminal manager. This is done prior to the individual's being employed or before the 30-day probationary period has expired.

2. Review all references returned from previous employers, public agencies, and other sources. Check information and review against original application for accuracy.

3. Make decision from this information and notify the manager concerning the desirability of retaining applicant.

4. Periodically check employee files in various terminal locations to ascertain information being retained.

5.   **a.** Personally interview employees to compliment them for unusual or outstanding conduct or service.

      b. Attend and occasionally chair meetings of local supervisors to determine disciplinary action to be taken.

6. Process all physical examination reports.

7. Maintain master personnel file in general office.

IV. Services

1. Prepare and distribute information pertaining to new or revised company safety rules or personnel policies.

2. Prepare and distribute information about new or revised laws that relate to drivers or their activities.

3. Distribute bulletins and literature furnished by National Safety Council, American Trucking Associations, and insurance companies.

4. Followup with drivers and supervisors concerning the regular use of seat belts by the road drivers. [All road power units are furnished with appropriate seat belt brackets.—Ed.]

5. Order safety equipment and process information for payroll deductions.

6. Maintain a tickler file and provide notification to terminal personnel to keep drivers' BMCS physical examinations up to date.

7. Make available current issues of BMCS Regulations to all interested personnel along with information on handling and transport of dangerous articles.

8. Conduct safety meetings with drivers, supervisors, and other employees.

9. Counsel employees through personal interviews.

JOB DESCRIPTION—II

The safety director of a large utility fleet which also operates the transit system for its community, indicates the additional burden of direction required in such a complex organization. Arthur Naquin, former safety counselor for the New Orleans Public Service Company, lists the following requirements to succeed in safety:

Position Described: Staff Safety Specialist in Prevention of Employee Injuries

In the motor fleet activity, a staff safety specialist has as his primary responsibility the prevention of mishaps to motor vehicles, passengers, merchandise, and the general public. This is as it should be, for it is in this area that sizeable savings can be made.

If the staff safety specialist must also set up and administer a productive employee injury-prevention program, he will probably do the following:

1. Keep informed about employee accident-prevention techniques, including industrial health hazards and their control.

2. Teach accident prevention to both employees and supervisors. This will require some classroom instruction and the use of visual aids.

3. Help foremen, supervisors, and superintendents set up effective safety programming within their jurisdiction.

4. Provide continuous help to foremen, supervisors, superintendents, and safety committee chairmen so that they can direct such activities effectively.

5. Encourage the attendance of foremen, supervisors, superintendents, and safety committee chairmen at the Annual National Safety Congress in Chicago, and at regional, state, and local safety conferences and safety equipment exhibitions. This will help to keep them apprised of the latest techniques and safety aids.

The staff safety specialist should obtain approval from management and provide for rotation attendance of key persons at safety meetings. He should coordinate transportation, hotel reservations, pre-conference registrations, and other details. He should suggest a list of conference sessions to attend, and he should encourage a daily critique of what was usefully learned. He should prepare or coordinate the preparation of a joint activity report upon the return from safety conferences.

6. Develop a schedule of mutually agreeable meeting dates for safety committee meetings in departments, divisions, sections, shops, stations, or garages.

7. Attend all company safety committee meetings in the role of counselor or advisor. (He should neither preside nor serve as secretary or reporter to the committee. He should assist in the preparation of meeting agenda only.)

8. Attend general safety meetings. At such meetings, he will:

> **a.** Give a brief summary of the safety record of the company. Include any outstanding record of manhours worked without a disabling injury or extended fleet records.
>
> **b.** Assist members of top management and others in the presentation of safety awards. Prepare fact sheets to assist in the preparation of remarks to be made by management.
>
> **c.** Report the facts concerning any employee injury or motor vehicle accident that is of particular interest and to be discussed at the meeting.
>
> **d.** Exhibit and demonstrate new items of safety equipment.
>
> **e.** Introduce safety films and provide background information.

9. Coordinate use and purchase of safety posters for the safety department, and foremen, supervisors, or safety committee chairmen.

10. Procure safety training materials used, such as motion pictures, filmstrips, slides, Safetygraphs, and exhibits.

11. Maintain an up-to-date library of safety reference publications such as the National Safety Council's *Accident Prevention Manual for Industrial Operations,* pertinent selected lists of "Industrial Safety Data Sheets," "Fleet Safety Memos," and all "Fleet Safety Manuals." (See the Bibliography on pages 397 and 398.)

12. Advocate membership in the National Safety Council. Include purchase of suitable administrative units for key personnel.

13. Keep management informed of progress—or lack of it—made in preventing accidents.

14. Prepare suggestions to determine hazardous conditions, and/or unsafe acts related to employee injuries or motor vehicle accidents.

15. Prepare a guide for the safety inspection of plant and equipment.

16. Encourage setting up an effective employee safety suggestion system.

17. Prepare articles for publication in a company magazine or newspaper relative to off-the-job accidents. If no company magazine is published, safety information can be prepared in bulletin or memorandum form for distribution to all concerned.

18. Prepare publicity concerning safety awards. The articles should emphasize the number of times such awards have been earned, their significance in terms of injuries avoided, and the safety-minded teamwork that was required to earn the awards.

19. Prepare material suitable for the company's annual report. Such material could include a photographic reproduction of any safety achievement awards received during the preceding calendar year, and a brief summary of the company's safety record—both motor vehicle and employee.

20. Arrange for suitable "Safe Worker" and "Safe Driver" recognition, including certificates and emblems. Provide rules governing the awarding of such forms of recognition.

21. Apply for, on behalf of eligible employees, membership in the Wise Owl Club of America (eyesight saved), and the Turtle Club of America (head injuries avoided).

22. Apply for, on behalf of eligible employees, life saving awards such as the National Safety Council's "President's Medal" for resuscitation, or the Carnegie Hero Fund Medal.

23. Counsel employees on personal accident prevention problems. For example: arrange for the purchase of safety glasses ground to the individual's prescription.

24. Represent the company with the National Safety Council, state and local safety councils, the American Society of Safety Engineers, industry associations, and other groups.

25. Work with the company's casualty insurance carrier.

26. Cooperate with the company medical office.

27. Coordinate safety matters between the safety department and the training department.

28. Provide safety liaison between the safety department and all other departments of the company.

29. Assist in selection of first-aid equipment. Assist in setting up a replacement material control program to make sure first-aid kits are correctly stocked.

30. Coordinate the selection of adequate fire-fighting equipment.

31. Supervise and direct the work of safety subordinates.

32. Prepare the annual budget for expenses of the safety department and approve such expenditures.

33. Stimulate interest in accident prevention work throughout the company. Stimulate pride in group safety achievements at all levels. For example: The American Transit Association will issue to member companies a "Gold," "Silver," or "Bronze" Certificate of Safety Achievement to company, department, division, section, shop, station, or garage groups that attain no-lost-time injury records of 1,000,000, 500,000, or 250,000 man-hours. The safety specialist should handle the necessary paper work and apply for such awards. He will maintain an up-to-date record of man-hours worked safely by the company and by each subordinate group. He will arrange to display awards, plaques, and trophies in a prominent location and to get maximum publicity concerning them (Appendix B).

34. Participate as much as possible in community safety work. Provide outside leadership as an authority on accident prevention.

From these two job descriptions, we see that safety direction, contrary to popular opinion, is not hit-or-miss. The techniques of loss prevention are sound and are as demanding of academic preparation as any of the other arts, sciences, or professions.

For maximum effectiveness, the techniques of loss prevention must be channeled through line supervision to every element of a business. The time-worn but erroneous statement, "That's the safety director's responsibility," has merely been buck-passing by poorly qualified line supervisors. If accidents occur, such failure is usually his. He has not directed supervisors in their safety responsibilities.

Seven Steps to Safety Direction

To sum up, the job of safety direction includes seven factors. These will shift in importance at various stages in the creation or maintenance of an accident loss-prevention program.

1. PREPARATION

The safety director's preparation or qualifying period will consist of his formal education, special safety training and prior pertinent work experience.

Preparation, just as in many professions, is a continuing endeavor. All available means of keeping up-to-date must be used by the safety director. These could include the use of professional journals and trade publications, attendance at conferences and seminars, and participation in the activities of various safety organizations.

Preparation may even consist of going back to school to study special subjects required by peculiar conditions or problems.

Preparation will be a continuing consideration of the industrious safety director to allow him to cope with changing science and new products and procedures.

2. INVESTIGATION

In every safety program, new or old, there is a time when the safety director must dig for facts. Whether establishing a new program or

INVESTIGATION—AN IMPORTANT FACTOR OF SAFETY DIRECTION.
Check of steering mechanism, for example, may reveal clues to an accident.

revitalizing a going program, such investigative work should be thorough. Time spent in checking out a problem is well invested.

Investigation may involve many facets. Most likely it will start by a thorough examination of accident records. Analysis of past accidents (for several years, when available) should indicate high-frequency types, locations, causes, and other factors.

Quite often, accident reports will not reveal all pertinent information. It may be necessary to interview the involved parties and personally examine the evidence.

Plant, building, dock, and similar facilities should be visited, and work methods, job instruction and routine supervision should be examined.

It is extremely important that key information be logged for future reexamination. (This preliminary work is known as "fact finding.")

3. PLANNING

Once he is armed with information from accidents, inspections, and personal interviews, the safety director can now analyze the pieces and assemble a suggested plan of action. This may require changing procedures, work habits, supervision, plant and facilities. The plan is the blueprint to obtain management consent for action, therefore suggestions must be complete, understandable, and practical. The more carefully prepared the plan, the better the prospects for success.

Plans must also be flexible. Not only must they include alternate courses of action, they should be designed to allow revision. Frequently, changes are dictated by experience or new procedures or practices.

At this point, it would pay to verify conclusions by sampling opinions or seeking the advice of other experts. Veterans in the business (within, or outside of the organization if necessary) can help avoid costly mistakes.

4. SELLING

Once convinced that the most effective action has been planned, the safety director must sell management on embarking on such a program. Whether the safety administrator reports to the chief executive of the organization or not, he must insist that the chief executive be apprised of the program and concur in the recommendations.

Management can best be sold on supporting a safety program when the case is presented in a factual and businesslike manner. Too often, a safety program is expected to be bought because it's the "right or moral obligation" of management to do so. Actually, this is the weakest reason for management to support any business function. Any manager worthy of his job will examine any proposal on the basis of its anticipated cost and its relative value to the organization. He decides whether to go ahead or not. He can then leave the work to subordinates.

The cost of the safety program, or any part of the program, together with the possible dollar return in savings, should therefore be first examined by the safetyman and included with proposals presented to management. (See pages 31 to 35.)

5. TRAINING

Training for accident prevention starts with line supervision. All too often the first-line supervisor is the "forgotten man" in the training effort. As the vital link between management and the employee, the supervisor must be carefully trained if there is to be any measure of success with the employee.

Supervision must be given a chance to examine all new safety procedures and plans and be allowed ample time to question these and to become thoroughly familiar with them. "Sell the supervisor and you sell the employee" is an axiom of successful safety programming.

Not only must the supervisor be "kept informed" of all programs, he should be instructed how to best present accident prevention information to his employees, and how to coordinate it with other training the employee may receive.

No matter who does safety training—the line supervisor or a training specialist—it must be checked by the safety administrator. In fact, from a practical viewpoint, such training will undoubtedly originate with the safety group.

All job training, job specifications, and work methods should be reviewed by the safety director to make sure no opportunity is lost in incorporating safe methods in the employee instructions.

Indoctrination training is usually done by the training specialist. Sometimes the safety director handles it. The training of drivers, including those employees whose driving is incidental to their regular employment, must be adequately planned and outlined in training procedures.

In most companies the safety specialist advises top management, executive staff, and line supervision. As an advisor, he must institute training plans, either directly for the classroom or as a guide for management.

6. FOLLOWUP

A safety program, once set into motion, requires periodic followup. Such followup can be simple or soul-searching.

- For example, a monthly memo report of accident absentees may be obtained from payroll records to make sure injury or vehicular accident reports are being submitted.
- Safety inspection by committees on a regular schedule will determine how well supervisors comply in such matters as housekeeping, personal protective equipment usage, and vehicle upkeep.

Return incomplete accident reports for additional information. When remedial action is indicated, check on compliance after a reasonable time.

7. REPORTING

Report to management and to all employees at regular intervals. Management reports should be informative and business-like, and prepared in accepted accounting methods.

Employee reports should emphasize the object lesson. It is not as important, for instance, that employee Bill Smith was involved in an intersection collision as it is that the accident resulted from Smith's failure to approach the intersection carefully.

TRAIN EMPLOYEES—then follow up to make sure they practice safety.

The "How to" of Safety Direction

So far we have merely indicated the highlights of the job of safety direction. Suggested plans, reports, and procedures that illustrate the principles discussed are included to illustrate elements of safety direction.

An example of how a proposal can be made follows.

Proposal to Start a Safety Program

I. Problem

1. Average of 1,500 man days lost through disabling injuries during each of the last three years: Salary loss equivalent to about $25,000 a year.

2. Five permanent disabilities in current year, four in previous year, and three in year before that. [Describe these such as lost eye, finger amputation, 30 per cent loss of use of left arm.]

3. Two employees killed in motor vehicle accidents. [Tell where and how.]

4. Casualty insurance premium $750 per vehicle, compared with rate of $485 per comparable vehicle in competitive operations.

5. Workman's compensation premium $1.50 per hundred dollars of payroll, compared with industry rate of $1.00 per hundred.

6. Cargo losses $80 per ten thousand dollars of revenue [or per thousand dollars of product transported] compared with industry average of $55.

7. Estimated excess cost of accidents compared to industry average—

Casualty insurance (100 vehicles @ $265 each):	$26,500
Workman's compensation (200 employees @ $0.40/ $100 payroll):	5,200
Cargo claims ($3,000,000 gross revenue @ $25 per ten thousand):	7,500
8. Direct Costs:	$39,200
9. Estimated indirect costs (experts indicate a 4 to 1 ratio, but to be conservative, use of 2 to 1 ratio):	78,400
TOTAL COSTS:	$117,600

II. Cause

1. Lack of a system to select, train and supervise workers and drivers. EXAMPLE: Selection system does not include check of previous driving experience or examination of driving ability.

2. Drivers put right to work without indoctrination training.

3. Supervisors lack accident prevention know-how.

III. Solution

1. Reorganize selection system. Provide one additional clerk to check references, state vehicle department, and license revocation records. He will also process and analyze accident reports and records. Salary approximately:	$ 4,000
2. Employ full-time safety specialist to organize and develop loss control program, including training of drivers and key supervisory personnel. Salary approximately:	10,000
3. Secretary-clerk in safety department. Salary:	4,500
4. Provide facilities for safety department and training program (furniture, office supplies, etc.). Annual charges:	3,000
5. Staff time (average 20 hours per employee for first year):	10,000

32

6. Provide transportation for safety specialist (car purchase or lease): 3,500

7. Outside services, memberships, material: 2,000

TOTAL COSTS: $37,200

8. Estimated direct dollar reduction in accident losses anually: 39,200

$ 2,200

9. Estimated savings in indirect losses (same ratio as costs—2 to 1): 78,400

10. ANTICIPATED NET ANNUAL SAVINGS: $80,600

NOTE: The above is based on the premise of reaching an industry average with 1 to 2 years. It should be explained that better-than-average results could be obtained over a longer period.

In actual practice, this proposal would be more detailed and would include a step-by-step description of the program including suggested training materials, training schedules, and other details.

Annual Reports

Following is an annual report, typical of one that might be sent management after three years' work. (Also see Appendix A.)

ANNUAL REPORT OF ACCIDENT PREVENTION PERFORMANCE
Vehicles

	1st year	2nd year	3rd year
Total number of vehicular accidents	50	40	30
Average cost per accident	$585	$560	$510
Total cost of accidents	$29,250	$22,400	$15,300
Savings based on reduction in accident costs over previous year (using current year per-accident costs)		$5,600	$5,100
Current year's savings compared with base (1st) year (difference in accidents × $510)			$10,200
If a substantial increase in miles operated occurred, refer to cost rate per 1,000 miles, such as:	1st year: 9.75 mills/3,000,000 miles 2nd year: 6.40 mills/3,500,000 miles 3rd year: 3.82 mills/4,000,000 miles		
Savings (current mileage times saving over base year)		$11,725	$23,720
Savings (current mileage times saving over previous year)			$10,320

Safety Budgeting

Private carrier fleet operations, usually a part of an entire business operation, should be reported as a separate division and the cost of accidents related to a product, service, or other common denominator. For common carrier fleets, the most common reference of accident costs is made to gross revenue. For example, the American Trucking Association reports that the overall cost of accidents, insurance, and related expenses for vehicular, cargo and personnel accidents is slightly less than 5 per cent of gross revenues in the Class I, II, and III carriers. (See "Costs of Accidents" section of Chapter 1.)

One carrier reduced its ratio from 7.5 to 3.4 per cent of revenues, which were $40 million annually. Such a reduction saved the company $1,640,000 a year. The for-hire carrier industry during the early sixties had a net income of 2 per cent of gross revenue. Therefore, they were spending two and a half times their net income for accidents.

Progressive fleets have established budget costs relating to accidents. They hold the departmental or divisional manager just as responsible for excesses in this budget as they would for other items (such as salary, production costs, and maintenance). When accident losses are an integral part of a supervisor's or manager's operating efficiency (on which he is rated for salary increases and promotion), he cannot shift the responsibility to a safety director or other "scapegoat."

DO NOT OVERLOOK ANY COSTS

In order to provide accurate records for management's use and guidance it is necessary to set up cost controls which provide sufficient information to make valid comparisons. It is very easy to overlook pertinent items or to purposely omit costs that might be disguised in some other element of operating cost.

Many costs are revealed in a superficial examination of the records. Among these are salaries and wages lost to accident absenteeism. Doctor, hospital and other fees are also easily identified. The not-so-easy-to-see costs can be considerable, however, and often involve judgment and "guesstimates."

For example, when a capable employee is replaced by a novice (even temporarily) there is usually an appreciable difference in work output attributed to the accident as a loss. Lost time due to other employees stopping to help, watch, or discuss an accident is a factor difficult to measure.

34

All supervisory time spent in reporting and investigating an accident, as well as time spent in cleanup, and in ordering and obtaining replacement or repair of machinery, equipment, or vehicles, should be charged against the accident that triggered the series of events in the first place.

It is rare, however, that an organization will examine every accident (vehicular or occupational) in terms of its absolute cost. To do so would require an elaborate and costly investigative and clerical setup. It is easier to spot check periodically to determine fluctuations in the total costs of typical incidents. These costs, including hidden costs, can then be applied (by ratio) to the complete accident record. (Example of a cost study is given in Appendix A.)

Accident Prevention

Whether it be fleet loss control or any other managerial program, observing certain fundamentals will ensure success.

1. SET STANDARDS

Regardless of the activity—driving, production, service, or whatever—management must establish performance standards. Production standards must include work behavior as well as quality control. The most common standard used to judge professional driving performance is the ability to avoid *preventable* accidents (as defined in Chapter 4 under "The Post-Accident Interview," and in Chapter 7 under "Defensive Driving.") Other standards can be used.

The standard, once adopted, must be thoroughly explained to the employee. It must be upheld and administered both strictly and fairly. This will now be discussed. (Also see discussion in Chapter 8, "Driver Supervision.")

2. TRAIN EMPLOYEES

Once the standard has been announced, every effort must be made to train the employee so he can achieve it. Remember that a standard, by itself, cannot prevent accidents—it is but a goal to achieve through constant training and supervision. Training must be adequate.

In the training effort there should be safeguards to prevent preachment of rules as a poor substitute for job instruction. Rules as they exist must be obeyed out of respect and understanding. Principles must be given for guidance. Good driving is an art. It requires intelligence, not blind obedience.

THE PROFESSIONAL DRIVER must be motivated to police his own driving.

3. SUPERVISE AND CHECK

A regular system of checking driving performance includes adequate and factual accident reporting. Without such a system it is difficult and often impossible to ascertain training effectiveness and compliance to the standard.

Although the driver is often considered to be a company's most "unsupervised" employee, it is not impossible to check his performance. Usually only those drivers who are known to stretch the rules are checked extensively. Followup remedial and rehabilitation efforts can be extensive at the outset until there is evidence of satisfactory performance.

Spot checks for all drivers are occasionally needed to disclose "soft spots" in their performance, and to help in training and retraining.

4. MOTIVATE

Because he cannot be personally supervised every minute, the professional driver must be motivated to police his own driving. Although pride of workmanship, skill, and other factors lead to good performance, a driver has that added factor of self-preservation to provide a special reason to perform safely.

But even in spite of the constant threat of physical harm that can result from motor vehicle collisions, prolonged accident-free operation can provide a false sense of security. Therefore the added prestige of motivation through achievement must be included to complete the package of requirements for a successful fleet operation.

4

Organizing fleet accident data— motor vehicle

Accidents are caused. This is the first axiom of accident prevention.

Accidents can be prevented, then, by removing or controlling their causes. A large part of a fleet safety director's job is (1) identifying accident causes and (2) recommending ways to remove them or to guard against them by protecting the employee.

Many facts about accident causes are found in published motor vehicle accident statistics, in summaries and reports of the Bureau of Motor Carrier Safety, in reports of various turnpike authorities, and in special studies released by insurance companies, trade associations, and the National Safety Council. Use these as background when planning a safety program and accident-reporting system.

However valuable these reports may be, they can never reveal the exact distribution of accident causes in any one particular fleet. General reports cannot pinpoint specific accident causes or tell their relative importance. To get this information about accident causes—essential to any effective accident prevention program—a system of accident reporting, recording, and analysis must be carefully planned and intelligently used. This chapter analyzes accident causes, then tells how to organize accident-causing factors, and operate a system that will pinpoint causes and provide effective followup.

How Accidents Are Caused

When a vehicle collides with a person, another vehicle, or any object, this event is caused. Moreover, the accident usually results from several factors working together: the result of a chain of causal events. This is illustrated in the following example.

Bill Jones was dispatched to transport a load of freight to a distant city. He recognized that his tractor was hooked up to a trailer that was different from those he usually pulled. Bill noticed that this particular trailer had an unusually high center of gravity. The entire capacity of the trailer—from front to rear and from bottom to top—was loaded with knocked-down cardboard cartons. This elevated the center of gravity still further.

A rookie driver was assigned to Bill for the trip.

Seeking to impress this new driver, Bill negotiated a right turn faster than he should. To make matters worse the road was crowned. The combination of speed, load, crown of road, and centrifugal force worked together to create an accident situation. The accident was triggered by Bill's desire to "show off a little."

If this accident must be attributed to one factor, "Speed too fast for conditions" is usually recorded. Unfortunately, "speed too fast for conditions" by itself would not be a good subject on which to base corrective action unless the complete story were told. Bill's accident could trigger many changes, other than reducing speed. Some of these might be:

1. Use of a low center of gravity trailer for the type material hauled.
2. Rerouting to avoid the section of high-crowned road.
3. Establish a company rule to lower speeds at right or left turns.
4. Refresher training of driver who breaks in new drivers.
5. Vehicle or trailer design modification.

Organizing an Accident Record System

Accident prevention lists the factors that could cause an accident and then compensates for them by planning ahead. Although accidents usually result from several contributing factors, accident prevention activity is based on the premise that removal of one or more factors, in any accident situation, may have prevented the accident. Therefore, the primary purpose of an accident reporting, recording, and analysis system is to determine *all* the factors contributing to the accident, in order to eliminate as many of these causes as possible.

The organization and operation of such a system must include: (1) gathering accident data; (2) analyzing the data; and (3) using the data in the administration of an accident prevention program.

Gathering Accident Data

A carefully planned system for gathering all pertinent information about fleet accidents is essential not only for the determination and elimination of accident causes, but also for these additional reasons:

1. Court action: There is always the possibility that the employee operator of the vehicle will be cited to traffic court or indicted in a criminal action as a result of an accident. The thoroughness with which accident data has been gathered is, in many cases, the balance upon which any traffic court or criminal court action may hinge—complete data is the first line of defense in a civil court action. Many cases have been won because of the thoroughness with which a company obtained the facts about the particular accident.

2. Places responsibility where it rightfully belongs. When gathering information, never be concerned with "white-washing" the actions of the company driver. Any attempt at this nullifies the whole value of the process. Only by knowing the full facts, whether favorable or unfavorable to the company, can the necessary corrective action be taken.

3. Labor relations. The vehicle operator involved in an accident should know that his safety record, as well as his security of employment, will be treated fairly. Where discharge is indicated, labor unions will concur in such action only upon the presentation of factual evidence.

THE ACCIDENT REPORT FORM

The basic tool of an accident data gathering system—the accident report form—blueprints the information-gathering process. It lists the types of facts to be gathered for every accident in order to be available later for the analysis of the accident. Because it serves as a checklist for the person completing the form to assure that all the essential information is obtained, it should provide for accurate recording of important information about the accident, yet it should be as easy as possible to complete and to analyze. The person reading the report should be able to visualize exactly how the accident happened.

The National Safety Council's Form Vehicle 1 "Motor Transportation Driver's Accident Report" is suggested as a guide to an adequate report form. Various insurance company report forms may also prove adequate for company accident prevention administration. Any form may be modified to meet the needs of a particular organization.

Form Vehicle 1 is shown on pages 40–43. Text continues on page 44.

National Safety Council
Form Vehicle 1

MOTOR TRANSPORTATION
DRIVER'S ACCIDENT REPORT

READ CAREFULLY - FILL OUT COMPLETELY

(For office use)

FILE NO.........

☐ PREVENTABLE
☐ NOT PREVENTABLE
☐ REPORTABLE
☐ NOT REPORTABLE

COMPANY.................

ADDRESS.................

DIVISION.................

TIME

Date of
Accident ...., 19.... Day of
Week .... Hour .... a.m.
p.m.

LOCATION

PLACE WHERE ACCIDENT OCCURRED:

☐ CITY   County .... City, town
☐ SUBURBAN   or township
☐ RURAL

.... miles .... of ☐ limits of -
         north-south   ....
.... miles .... of ☐ Center of   City or Town
         east-west

If accident was outside city limits
indicate distance from nearest
town. Use two distances and two
directions if necessary.

ROAD ON WHICH ACCIDENT OCCURRED: Give name of street or highway number (U.S. or State)

☐ AT ITS INTERSECTION WITH: Name of intersecting street or highway number

     OR .... feet .... of ....
              north-south
☐ NOT AT INTERSECTION .... feet .... of
              east-west
(Check and complete one) Show nearest intersecting street or highway, house number, curve,
bridge, railroad crossing, alley, driveway, culvert, milepost, underpass,
numbered telephone pole, or other identifying landmark. Show exact
distance, using two directions and two distances if necessary.

TYPE

☐ HEAD ON   ☐ REAR END (☐ You hit ☐ You were hit) ☐ NON COLLISION (Describe)
☐ SIDESWIPE   ☐ OTHER (Describe)
☐ RIGHT ANGLE

ACCIDENT INVOLVED

MOVING
☐ Another com'l vehicle
☐ Passenger car
☐ Pedestrian
☐ ☐ ☐ (Specify other)

FIXED
☐ Building or fixture
☐ Parked vehicle
☐ ☐ ☐ (Specify other)

COMPANY VEHICLE NO 1   VEHICLE NO 2

DRIVER

☐ Chauffer   → Driver's Name ←
☐ Operator   → Address ←
☐ Beginner   → City And State ←
                  → Driver's Licence ←

.... Age .... Sex .... Driving experience .... yrs .... Age .... Sex

☐ Chauffer
☐ Operator
☐ Beginner

DRIVERS

Date employed .... month .... day .... year

Hours on duty since last period of 8 consecutive hours off duty ....   Actual hours of driving since last period of 8 consecutive hours off duty ....

Condition of Driver ....

(If vehicle driven by other than owner)

Owner's name ....
Address ....
City and State ....

COMPANY VEHICLE NO 1	VEHICLE NO 2

VEHICLES

Type of Vehicle →

← Make .... Year .... No. ....

← State .... No. ....

← License   → Make .... Year .... No. ....

← Vehicle Damage   → State .... No. ....

← Other Damage
(cargo loss, etc.)

INJURED

	Name	Address	Age	Sex	Describe Injuries
Driver vehicle 1					
Driver vehicle 2					
Passenger veh.					
Passenger veh.					
Pedestrian					
Pedestrian					
Others					

WITNESSES

	Name	Address	Remarks
Company representative			
Insurance representative			
Police	Badge no	Station	

TURN THE PAGE - COMPLETE BOTH SIDES!

Stock No. 229.31

MOTOR TRANSPORTATION DRIVER'S ACCIDENT REPORT, National Safety Council Form Vehicle 1—front page.

41

VEHICLES

MOVEMENT

	1	2
Going straight ahead	☐	☐
Passing	☐	☐
Being passed	☐	☐
Turning	☐	☐
Pulling from curb or loading zone	☐	☐
Pulling into curb or loading zone	☐	☐
Backing	☐	☐
Stopped in traffic lane	☐	☐

(Specify other) _____

DRIVERS And PEDESTRIAN

CONDITIONS

	1	2
Influenced by alcohol	☐	☐
Had not been drinking	☐	☐
Asleep or fatigued	☐	☐
Sick	☐	☐
Physical defects	☐	☐
Not known	☐	☐
No defects	☐	☐

VEHICLES

CONTRIBUTING

	1	2
Did not have right-of-way	☐	☐
Following too closely	☐	☐
Failure to signal intentions	☐	☐
Speed too fast for conditions	☐	☐
Disregarded traffic signs or signals	☐	☐
Improper passing	☐	☐
Improper turning	☐	☐

PEDESTRIAN

Walking with traffic	☐
Walking against traffic	☐
Coming from behind parked vehicle	☐
Crossing at intersection	☐
Crossing not at intersection	☐
Alighting from a vehicle	☐
Working in roadway	☐
Playing in roadway	☐

(Specify other)

VEHICLES

	1	2
Defective brakes	☐	☐
Defective steering	☐	☐
Defective lights	☐	☐
Defective tires	☐	☐
No defects	☐	☐

(Specify other)

VEHICLES

	1	2
Improper backing	☐	☐
Improper traffic lane	☐	☐
Improper parking	☐	☐
No improper driving	☐	☐

(Specify other)

PASSENGER

Boarding vehicle	☐
Alighting from vehicle	☐
Caught in doors	☐
Seated	☐
In motion in vehicle	☐
Other (describe)	☐

WEATHER

Clear	☐
Raining	☐
Snowing	☐
Sleeting	☐
Fog	☐

(Specify other)

ROADWAY

Under repair	☐
Holes or ruts	☐
Slippery	☐
Muddy	☐
Icy or snowy	☐
No defects	☐

VEHICLES

SPEED

	1	2
Exceeding legal limit	☐	☐
Too fast for conditions	☐	☐
Safe speed ___ MPH		
Estimated speed when danger noticed ___ MPH		
Estimated speed at moment of impact ___ MPH		

At what distance was danger first noticed?

INDICATE NORTH BY ARROW

INDICATE ON THIS DIAGRAM WHAT HAPPENED

Use one of these outlines to sketch the scene of your accident, writing in street or highway names or numbers.

1. Number each vehicle and show direction of travel by arrow.
2. Show pedestrian by: ———O
3. Show street and show
4. Show railroad by: ++++++++

42

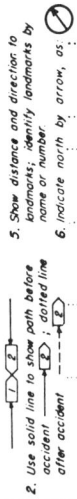

2. Use solid line to show path before accident ____; dotted line after accident ----

5. Show distance and direction to landmarks; identify landmarks by name or number.

6. Indicate north by arrow, as

DRIVER'S ACCOUNT OF ACCIDENT

(Refer to vehicles by number.)

Use this space for listing additional injured persons. Also explain questions not fully answered by checking in the boxes provided.

If more space is needed use another form or a sheet of paper the same size.

Suggestions for PREVENTING future accidents of this type:

★ SIGNATURE

Signature of person submitting report is required   Address   Date of report

☐ Driver
☐ Investigator
☐ Supervisor

PAGE 2 of "Motor Transportation Driver's Accident Report," Form Vehicle 1.

43

The fleet should spell out the details for the driver to complete an accident report on the designated report form for every incident coming under the following definition:

> Any incident in which a company vehicle is involved (whether in motion, temporarily stopped, parked, or being unloaded or loaded) that results in personal injury and/or property damage, regardless of who was hurt, what property was damaged, or who was responsible.

Most companies require that drivers also report any claims that they were involved in an accident, even if they were not. The company also may require drivers to report complaints, the witnessing of an accident, the rendering of aid, or any other unusual incident arising from the operation of their vehicle.

A company sometimes also spells out that failure to report an accident will be considered a cause for dismissal. The enforcement of this rule requires continuous attention. When strict compliance is obtained, the company is said to have "good accident reporting discipline." This is also a very good index to overall safety discipline.

Good accident reporting discipline requires not only the reporting of every incident, but also the submission of complete and well-written accident reports. To accomplish this, supervisors should be required to submit complete accident reports and to train their drivers how to conduct themselves at the accident scene, with emphasis on their data-gathering responsibilities. Incomplete reports should be returned to the supervisor if necessary to obtain complete reporting.

Devote sufficient time to accident reporting discipline during the driver and supervisor training and retraining sessions. Drivers who submit substandard reports should be counseled and warned about repeating incomplete reports.

Driver Conduct at Scene of Accident

At the scene of an accident, certain things must be done by the driver involved, prior to the arrival of the accident investigator, because he may be the only company representative there at the time. Therefore, all driving personnel should be trained in the procedure to be followed. Form Vehicle 2, "Accident Report Packet," lists on the envelope the sequence of events in the order of their importance. On the other side, an "Accident Memorandum" is printed.

A courtesy card is shown on page 47.

National Safety Council
Form Vehicle 2 REP. 10M 76103 Stock No. 229.32

ACCIDENT REPORT PACKET
KEEP THIS ENVELOPE IN YOUR VEHICLE
OPEN ONLY IN CASE OF ACCIDENT

FIRST —

Stop Immediately and determine damage. Avoid obstructing traffic if possible.

Place emergency flags or flares.

Aid the injured and see to it that they receive medical attention as soon as possible.

Report accident to local police and your company.

SECOND —

Get witnesses to sign courtesy cards.

Record information on reverse side of this envelope at scene of accident.

IMPORTANT —

Make no statement to anyone except:

A. An officer of the law.

B. Your company's representative.

C. Your insurance company's representative. Make no settlements. Do not argue about the accident.

If the accident involves an unattended vehicle or fixed object, take reasonable steps to locate and notify the owner. If the owner cannot be found, leave a notice in a conspicuous place on the vehicle or object, listing your name and address, the company name, and a brief description of the accident. Whenever possible get a witness signed statement.

TURN ENVELOPE — FILL IN INFORMATION

ACCIDENT REPORT PACKET, NSC Form Vehicle 2—Instructions.

ACCIDENT MEMORANDUM

Date of Accident.................................., 19...... Day of Week..................................Hour..........a.m. / p.m.

PLACE WHERE ACCIDENT OCCURRED	
☐ CITY ☐ SUBURBAN ☐ RURAL	County........................ City, town or township........................
If accident was outside city limits indicate distance from nearest town. Use two distances and two directions if necessary.	........miles............ north-south / ....miles............ east-west of { ☐ limits of ☐ center of } .... City or Town

ROAD ON WHICH ACCIDENT OCCURRED........................
Give name of street or highway number (U.S. or State)

☐ AT ITS INTERSECTION WITH........................
OR
☐ NOT AT INTERSECTION
(Check and complete one)
........feet............ north-south / ....feet............ east-west of........................

Name of intersecting street or highway number
Show nearest intersecting street or highway, house number, curve, bridge, rail crossing, alley, driveway, culvert, milepost, underpass, numbered telephone pole, or other identifying landmark. Show exact distance, using two directions and two distances if necessary.

OTHER DRIVER'S NAME		
ADDRESS		
CITY	STATE	DRIVER'S LICENSE No.
OTHER VEHICLE OWNER'S NAME		
ADDRESS		
CITY	STATE	VEHICLE LICENSE No.
TYPE VEHICLE	MAKE	YEAR No.

DAMAGE TO OTHER VEHICLE AND/OR PROPERTY

INJURED PERSONS	Age	Sex	Injuries
Name			
Address			
Name			
Address			
Name			
Address			

POLICE   Name   Badge No.

BE SURE WITNESS CARDS ARE COLLECTED   PLACE THEM IN THIS FOLDER

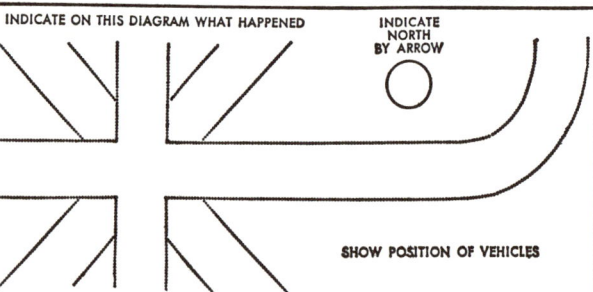

INDICATE ON THIS DIAGRAM WHAT HAPPENED   INDICATE NORTH BY ARROW

SHOW POSITION OF VEHICLES

DRIVER'S SIGNATURE

OTHER SIDE OF ENVELOPE is for recording accident memoranda.

BE SURE COURTESY CARDS are distributed, filled in, and collected. They help determine who saw the accident in case witnesses are needed later.

STEPS TO FOLLOW

1. The first step—protect the scene of the accident. The driver should try to keep the effects of the accident from becoming worse. He should immediately place warning signals and devices to permit, as nearly as possible, the uninterrupted normal flow of vehicular traffic.

2. Second—the driver should protect the injured. If possible, he should request medical assistance from authorized sources (police, fire, hospital, etc.)

3. Report the accident. Call the local police and state police, if warranted, and notify the designated company representative. A procedure should be established whereby the driver, telephoning a report of the accident, can talk to the person who will be responsible for the accident investigation. A previously prepared telephone check list is invaluable in recording the information reported by a driver. With the information obtained from the telephone check list, the company can decide whether to dispatch additional equipment, another driver, a mechanic, or additional manpower to the scene of the accident. Arrangements for whatever additional help will be needed can thus be made with a minimum of delay and confusion. Place a prominent notice somewhere on the dashboard of the vehicle to indicate who should be notified in the event the driver is incapacitated as a result of the accident (see sample on next page).

47

IN CASE OF ACCIDENT

CALL COLLECT

DAY OR NIGHT
CHICAGO, ILLINOIS
AREA CODE 312
345-2822

REVISED SEPTEMBER, 1971

DASHBOARD STICKER tells who should be notified in case of accident. *Courtesy Allied Van Lines, Chicago.*

4. Obtain information. To assist the driver in gathering information at the scene of the accident, he should be supplied beforehand with an accident report packet. Outside are printed instructions and inside an accident memorandum for the driver to record the details. In addition to the accident memorandum, the packet should contain a sharp pencil, paper, courtesy cards, a piece of chalk, a couple of dimes for phone calls, and other materials as needed. The driver should review the steps mentioned on the outside of his accident packet and follow the instructions. He should take "courtesy cards" (Form Vehicle 12) from the packet and pass them out. Whether or not a person actually saw the accident occur will have no bearing as to whether or not he should fill out the card. Use of the cards will help determine who actually saw the accident. Although these cards are often referred to as "witness cards," it is known that people do not like to be "witnesses." Therefore, these should always be called "courtesy cards" in order to remove the stigma associated with the word "witness." Every person who was in the area at the time of the accident should be asked to fill out one of these cards.

At this point, the operator is in a position to fill out the "Accident Memorandum" (on the back of the Form Vehicle 2 envelope). When properly filled out, this will assure getting information which may not be available later, and will provide the necessary information for the driver to report the accident to his company.

A few things need to be emphasized about filling out the accident report:

1. It should be filled out completely and legibly, because it may ultimately serve as evidence in court.

2. Facts should be definite and specific.

3. There should be no question as to the accuracy.

4. This report should identify all vehicles involved.

5. The report should supply the names of persons involved correctly and fully, so as to identify the specific person(s) intended.

6. Addresses of all persons involved in the accident should be included.

7. Date, day of week, and exact time of day should be recorded.

8. The location of the accident should be designated so specifically that someone else could take this memo at a later date and go to the exact spot where the accident occurred.

9. The diagram of the accident should indicate direction of travel, and show the exact location of the vehicles on the street or roadway, obstacles, traffic signs, signals, and other pertinent objects. The diagram should show exactly what happened and where it happened.

10. All accident memorandum, courtesy cards, and other pertinent data should be carefully secured and preserved.

This memorandum report of an accident is usually all of the information that a company can expect its drivers to obtain at the scene of an accident. Some companies require their drivers to fill out a "Driver's Accident Report," a much more detailed accident investigation report. Other companies prefer that this report be filled out later, under the supervision of a company official. (Typical report—Form Vehicle 1— was shown on pages 40–43).

The Accident Investigator

Because financial liability could be high, and accident prevention must be effective, every company should have available a trained accident investigator who can be dispatched to the scene of an accident, take charge of the company's interests, direct the activities of the driver, and gather additional data concerning the accident which will supplement the data gathered by the driver.

The availability of the trained accident investigator is essential. If the company driver involved was killed or disabled in the accident, a responsible company representative must show up promptly to take charge. Even if the driver is not disabled, the company should not rely solely on the driver's account of what happened. Also, a good driver has an accident so infrequently that he does not have the opportunity to acquire experience in dealing with an accident situation. The accident investigator who has presided over the cleanup of a number of accidents should have the skill and poise necessary to deal with such situations effectively.

Aside from gathering useful accident prevention information, the trained accident investigator can:

1. **Keep costs at a minimum.** If the investigator arrives promptly at the scene of the accident, he can prevent further damage from occurring and can protect company property and prevent looting.

2. **Expedite the movement of traffic** by capable handling at the scene of an accident.

3. **Prevent excess costs.** Efficient investigation and handling of an accident provides efficient management and reduction of fraud.

4. **Preserve vital information.** Complete investigation of the situation is necessary for claims protection.

Accident Investigation

The accident investigator needs to be trained in the specifics of conducting a detailed investigation. He needs to use the "Drivers Accident Report" (Form Vehicle 1), or a similar form, as a checklist to determine whether or not he has obtained all of the necessary data during the course of his investigation to not only protect the company, but to help complete the required accident reports, the Bureau of Motor Carrier Safety report, and any other records that may be required. Because each accident situation is unique, it may not be practical for the investigator to follow the checklist item by item. The particular situation may necessitate entering data as it presents itself. However, as many items as possible should be completed before the investigator leaves the accident scene.

An accident investigation is a search for facts. The investigator should have an open mind and an unbiased attitude. It is his responsibility to determine the factors which may have contributed to the accident, as opposed to merely filling out an accident report. His job is not complete until he has determined:

50

1. All of the factors that contributed to the accident.
2. How the accident occurred.
3. All the physical evidence which might have a bearing on the case.
4. Sufficient information, details, and data to record and preserve so that he can reconstruct the entire accident at any subsequent time.

What To Investigate

Ideally, all accidents involving vehicles operated by the motor carrier should be investigated to determine the basic causes behind them. In practice, limitations of time and manpower, the scope of the company's operations, or other factors may preclude the complete investigation of every accident. However, an investigation should be made of every accident sufficiently serious to require a report to the Bureau of Motor Carrier Safety and/or state regulatory authorities.

Accidents involving the following should be thoroughly investigated:

1. Fatalities and/or personal injuries.
2. Extensive property damage.
3. Transportation of explosives and other dangerous articles, particularly where the nature of the cargo might have contributed to the seriousness of the accident.
4. Vehicles or loads of abnormal dimensions and/or weight.
5. Unusual circumstances.

A series of accidents involving common factors or circumstances which indicate a pattern should also be investigated. Such a pattern would include but not be limited to those involving:

1. A single driver, particularly in a relatively short period of time or under recurrent circumstances.
2. A particular locality.
3. Special types of cargo.
4. Certain types or makes of vehicles (or combinations of same).
5. Factors in common, such as a particular type of accident.

Tools for Investigation

Each investigator should have adequate equipment to do a thorough job of investigation. His equipment should include the following:

1. Recording device (tape or dictating unit) for witness and driver statements.
2. Metallic measuring tape (100 ft).
3. Camera and accessories.

51

4. Accident investigation reports, checklists, pencils, paper, clip board (with light), chalk, dimes for telephone calls, and other such items.
5. Auxiliary floodlights.
6. Emergency type firefighting equipment (10 lb capacity, multi-purpose dry chemical agent extinguisher).
7. Flags, flares, fuses, and other approved warning devices.
8. First-aid kit and blankets.
9. Tow cable and similar emergency tools.
10. Accident diagraming template.

Investigation Procedure

Upon arriving at the scene, the investigator should park his car where it will not obstruct traffic or contribute to another accident. If it is nighttime, he may want to park so that his headlights illuminate the scene but do not blind on-coming motorists. He should make sure the accident scene will not contribute to additional accidents, and that flags, flares, fusees, or other approved warning devices have been placed in accordance with regulations and in such a manner as to ensure maximum protection. He should then:

1. Identify himself to the police at the scene, or when they arrive, and give them his full cooperation.
2. If necessary, assist in the protection of the injured until medical aid arrives. (Here he should use a good deal of caution and judgment—lest he inadvertently aggravate an injury.)
3. Check the bystanders for possible witnesses and volunteer helpers.
4. Insure that steps are taken to protect company property from theft or damage.
5. Examine the area carefully for any possible hazards, such as spilled gasoline, flammables, or broken electrical cabling.
6. Look for any evidence that may be associated with the accident and have it guarded until it can be properly examined.
7. Locate the driver of the company vehicle, properly identify himself, and assume charge of the situation. The investigator should then take possession of all reports, data, and any information the driver may have.

Pursuing a step-by-step accident investigation (such as shown on the "Driver's Accident Report") requires the investigator to bear in mind the following:

1. **Time.** Record the exact date, day of the week, and hour of the day. If the vehicle is equipped with a Tachograph, the chart would show

these. If not, every effort should be made to determine the exact time the accident occurred.

2. Accident location. Be specific enough so that a complete stranger could take the report at any time subsequent to the accident and go directly to the scene where the accident occurred. In most cases, it is insufficient to say "accident occurred in the county of Fulton, ten miles north of Atlanta on U.S. Route 29." This does not tell exactly where the accident occurred. It is better to give the above mentioned designation, then add more specific information such as "355 feet south of utility pole No. 647328" or "550 feet north of the north end of a bridge abutment where U.S. Highway 29 crosses Rising Creek," or some similar, specific designation. Notation should likewise be made on the diagram to reference these specific points. (Data should agree with that of the "Accident Memorandum," previously filled out.)

3. Accident involved. The investigator should tell exactly what was involved in the accident. If it be another vehicle, a determination should be made as to (1) its type, and (2) whether the vehicle itself (as contrasted with the action of the operator) contributed anything to the accident, by virtue of its type or color, or other characteristic. The investigator should indicate when one or more pedestrians are involved and indicate the contribution made by each to the accident. If there be a fixed object involved, a detailed description of it is necessary: location, size, shape, marks, and any other pertinent data.

4. Type of accident. The accident type (see "Driver's Accident Report" form) should be determined and recorded in the accident report. Any information with regard to type, not covered specifically in the accident report, should be described completely so as to avoid doubt or indecision.

5. Drivers. The driver of each vehicle must be definitely identified by complete name, exact address, operator's or chauffeur's license number, and any other information necessary.

6. Vehicles. All vehicles involved in the accident must be definitely identified by type, make, year model, company number (if any), and state and number of the license. A description of the damage to the vehicles and the damage to cargo or other property should be noted. Any estimates should be as accurate as possible.

7. Injured. List the exact name and the exact address, age, and sex of every injured person. However, do not antagonize an injured person by persistent questioning in public. Wait until a better time presents itself, such as at the hospital, or at the person's home. Describe the injuries as completely as it is possible to do. Then, upon the investigator's visit to the doctor's office or hospital where the injured were taken, he should verify the injuries and make any necessary changes to his notes. It is important to specify whether the injured persons were

53

drivers of vehicles, or were passengers or pedestrians. Their relation to the accident must be given.

8. Witnesses. Seek out witnesses as soon as possible. They are not obligated to remain at the scene and may leave before you have a chance to question them. Accordingly, record the license numbers of the cars parked at the accident area. Through the license numbers, other possible witnesses may be contacted at a later date if needed. Also, frequently witnesses may be found talking to a driver, discussing the acident among themselves, or examining the damage caused by the accident. The investigator should check the courtesy cards which were turned over to him by the driver. The exact spelling, and the complete name and address of any witness is important. In addition to the address, the investigator should make a notation as to how these persons might be contacted at their office, place of business or employment, or any other place where they might be temporarily. Any interest the witness may have in the accident should be indicated—such as investigating police officer, bystander, passenger in a company vehicle, passenger in the other vehicle involved, or any other designation. Many times the driver of a vehicle which has escaped damage has somehow been involved in the situation leading to the accident. The investigator should get statements from such persons. All passengers involved should be interviewed, especially in serious accidents. *While questioning passenger(s)*, it may be helpful to establish the relationship of the passenger to the driver to detect a possible reason for bias in his statements. In addition, establish the position of the passenger in the vehicle to determine if the passenger could actually have seen the accident occur. *When interviewing witness(es)*, make sure that a witness actually saw the accident happen. The investigator should note only *facts* and not the opinions of witnesses. In addition, it is wise to determine exactly what the witness is saying. For instance, if the witness says that a vehicle was traveling "fast" determine what he or she considers as "fast." Similarly, if the witness says "a long distance" determine approximately how "long" is long. The *reliability* of witness testimony will be enhanced if the investigator observes the following:

• Each witness should be shown courtesy and consideration at all times.
• Each witness should be interviewed separately with no other witnesses present, whenever practical.
• The investigator should get the *full* story of one witness before he asks any questions about or cites any contrary or conflicting statements made by other witnesses.
• If it serves a useful purpose, the statement obtained from one witness may be quoted to another, but the names of any witnesses should never be used.

- The investigator should make no attempt to coerce witnesses who refuse to make a statement.
- The investigator should not engage in any controversies with witnesses.
- There should be no retaliation against hostile witnesses.

9. Movement.

a. An indication should be made as to the exact movement of each **vehicle** at the time of the accident. In many cases more than one box should be checked for each vehicle involved.

b. Pedestrian. Indicate in this section exactly what any pedestrian(s) was doing. Then in the diagram, make an effort to show exactly where any pedestrian was in relation to the accident.

c. Passenger. Identify any passengers who were involved in the accident. It makes no difference whether or not the passengers were injured—we are concerned because they were involved.

10. Conditions.

a. Drivers and pedestrian(s). Use this section of the report to indicate completely the condition of any person involved in the accident. Check all appropriate boxes in an effort to show more completely the condition of each person involved, use additional space in an effort to properly describe the conditions, if necessary. The investigator should make an effort to determine any evidence of intoxication or physical defects. In attempting to determine the driver's condition prior to the accidents, take into account such items as prior delays, coffee stops, arguments, fatigue, schedules, or other factors. Such information helps to establish the driver's mental alertness and disposition just prior to the accident and may suggest future remedies for the particular type of accident. In addition, it may be helpful to establish the amount of sleep the driver had one to four days prior to the accident. *Upon returning to the office,* the following information, as it pertains to the driver, should be secured from the fleet's personnel files:

- Length of employment.
- Training.
- Overall driving experience, and experience in driving the particular type of vehicle involved in the accident.
- Attitude toward job.
- Record of physical examination.
- Illnesses and personal problems.

- Accident record.
- Record of traffic violations.
- Commendations or disciplinary actions.

b. Vehicles. Investigation should be made to determine the extent to which the mechanical condition of each vehicle involved may have been a contributing factor in the accident. The thoroughness of the check at the accident scene should be governed by the extent of damage to the vehicle. If possible, a road test should be made to determine brake performance, including a test of the braking system for leakage or inoperative parts. In addition, the steering mechanism, noticeable damage to wheel alignment, engine performance, and any other mechanisms affecting the safe operation of the vehicle should be thoroughly checked to determine if it may have been a factor. If, as a result of the accident, the condition of the vehicle does not permit a road check at the accident scene, a thorough investigation should be made of the vehicle upon its return to the storage or repair location. *Extreme care should be used when attempting to determine whether a vehicle part or system was inoperative before the accident or as a result of the accident.*

c. Weather. Weather conditions at the time of the accident should be noted. In addition, indicate whether any previous weather condition may have contributed to the accident. Weather conditions may reduce visibility. For instance, sun glare can blind a driver and affect his viewing of signals, pedestrians, and other vehicles.

d. Roadway. The roadway itself contributes to a number of accidents, yet in many cases this is not noted. The proper indication should be made on the accident report; then a more detailed description should be recorded on extra paper so as to give a complete description of the roadway.

11. Contributing factors. At this point, the investigator should be aware that there are usually several factors which contribute to any accident. This means that in most cases more than one box should be checked for each vehicle involved.

a. Speed. Speed is a contributing factor to many accidents; speed, therefore, is considered of sufficient importance to warrant special consideration. Every effort should be made to fill out this section of the report carefully and accurately. Here again, if the report does not have sufficient space to properly describe the existing situation, the description should be made on extra paper.

b. The trip. The origin, destination, and related distances of the trip on which the accident occurred should be investigated. If the total trip extends over more than one day, the point at which driving began should be noted, as well as the origin and destination of the entire trip. In addition, the distance from the point of origin to the accident scene should be noted. List stops en route, time spent at each, and determine the activities of the driver at each stop. *Retrace the driver's activities* for at least 24 hours prior to the accident, showing time spent on and off duty. Investigation of driver's activities over a longer period of time preceding the accident should be conducted when it appears desirable. A copy of the driver's log record for the same period should be made a part of the company's accident file and record. If the vehicle was equipped with an operations recorder, the chart should be examined with special attention to speed and stops en route, and its correlation with the driver's log. This chart, or a facsimile, should be a permanent part of the accident file. Insofar as possible, the activities of other drivers, or persons involved, should be reconstructed in the effort to determine the extent to which their actions or their physical and mental condition may have contributed to the accident. Such investigation should also cover at least 24 hours prior to the accident, and a longer period, if such appears fruitful. Information relative to the activities of other persons will generally have to be developed through direct inquiry.

12. Accident diagram. The accident diagram should be sufficiently comprehensive to show at a glance exactly what happened. Graph paper might be used to enhance the accuracy of the diagram. In drawing the accident scene, various factors should be recorded.

a. Primary factors. The following primary factors should be considered:

• Width of roadway, including condition and type of pavement. Indicate whether new, slippery from oil deposits, or covered with deposits of sand, gravel, stones, or full of holes, or ruts.
• Width and number of traffic lanes, with numbers assigned to each lane.
• Width and condition of shoulder of road, including the measurement of any drop-off from the pavement edge to the shoulder. Depth and running length of this "lip" should be accurately identified.

• Point of impact as indicated by physical evidence and what the physical evidence was.

• Dimensions of any intersecting street, roadway, alley, or driveway.

• Location and direction of travel of each vehicle prior to impact, at impact, and after impact.

• Pinpointing the exact location of the accident in order that its site can be definitely relocated at a later time. This may be done by identifying a number on an adjacent utility pole such as: "three feet east of center line, 50 feet northeast of utility pole number 16847," or it may be done by designating any permanent object such as: "three feet east of center line, 300 feet north of the north side of Cain Creek Bridge, Highway 41, six miles north of Citizensville, Home State."

b. **Secondary factors.** The following secondary factors should be considered:

• Length of skid mark for *each* wheel.

• Exact position and physical description (for example, size and height) of any objects which might have obstructed the vision of any driver, such as buildings, trees, embankments, billboards.

• Exact location of debris, spilled liquids, marks, scratches, or gouges in the pavement made by any of the vehicles involved.

• Exact location of any traffic sign, signal, or other traffic control device. Indicate whether or not devices were working at the time of the accident. If view of device was obstructed by foliage or other object, or defaced by markings, or obliterated by road film. Note this on the diagram (and report).

• Location of fixed objects near the accident scene, debris, which appear in the photographs as well as any measurements related to these objects.

• Exact positions of points from which photographs were taken.

Two diagrams may be necessary if a large number of the above items must be noted.

c. **What should be measured.** Measurements usually are needed of:

• Skid marks.
• Sight distances.

- Location and position of point of impact and final resting position of the vehicle.
- Location of dead or injured.
- Point at which vehicle ran off the road.
- Distance to fixed objects from which photographs were taken.

d. **How to make measurements.** All measurements should be made with a metallic measuring tape to ensure accuracy. The investigator should have witnesses who, if called upon, can verify the accuracy of these measurements. In locating ob-

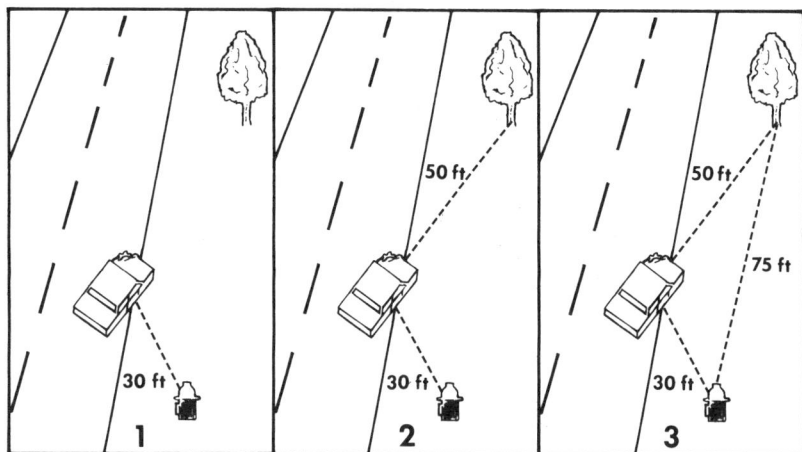

THREE STEPS IN TRIANGULATION. **1.** Measure from debris to a fixed object (in this illustration, a fire hydrant). **2.** Measure the distance to another fixed object (a tree). **3.** Measure the distance between the fixed objects.

jects in the accident diagrams, such as spilled liquids, debris at the point of impact, or injured persons, the best method of measurement is "triangulation." This can be done by simply locating two fixed points, such as a utility pole or tree, and a manhole cover on or near the road. Then measure from the object to be located to each of these points. To finish the triangle, measure the distance between the fixed points. See accompanying illustration.

To relocate the exact spot at which the accident occurred, use the distances measured and swing two arcs from the fixed points.

59

13. Driver's account of accident. This section of the investigation requires the driver's own statement as to how the accident occurred. The investigator should carefully interview the company driver to obtain the driver's detailed account of the accident. This should be done while the facts are still fresh in the mind of the driver. Find out how the driver attempted to avoid involvement. Establish whether or not the driver could have possibly avoided the accident. Obtain his observations and a statement of his actions leading up to the accident. Through tachographs, logs, and schedules, establish the driver's approximate operating speed prior to the time the accident situation developed. Learn when and how the accident situation was first noticed.

14. Suggestions. This portion of the report asks for the driver's opinion as to how he should be able to prevent future accidents of this type. This part of the report will be discussed in Chapter 10 (under "Safety Suggestion Systems").

15. Photographs. Photography is an excellent way to record facts and preserve evidence that may be needed in the future. It can also record things you may fail to notice. Photographs should be made of the accident scene as soon as possible in order to: (1) record the position of the vehicles before they are moved; (2) record debris, such as broken glass, oil stains, hubcaps, before they are moved or obliterated; and (3) record skid marks.

Here are some suggestions.

• Take several photographs of the accident scene: (1) in each direction *from* the point of impact; (2) from each approach to the point of impact, showing the view each driver had approaching the key point of the accident, as well as road alignment; (3) a closeup of the scene, showing the point of impact; and (4) an overall view of the scene.
• For each vehicle, show the extent of damage. Try to establish the angle of collision and the movement of each while in contact.
• Photograph debris, skid marks, or any other physical evidence of vehicular movement prior to and after impact.
• Photograph any broken vehicle parts. Try to establish whether the accident caused the damage or whether the damage preceded the accident.
• Take any other photographs which will preserve data such as road defects, obstructions, foliage which blocks the view, or other physical conditions that may have been a factor in the accident. Identify each photograph as to time and date taken, direction in which taken, and location from which taken—use measurements to pinpoint the location.

A photo report of an accident is shown in Chapter 16, "The Utility Fleet."

Followup

The next step in the investigation involves clearing the accident scene. This should be done as quickly and completely as possible, even to the extent of sweeping the roadway to remove all debris.

Followup also involves removing damaged cargo to a place where it can be salvaged or recouped; transporting undamaged cargo to its destination (in case of a bus accident, this would be passengers, baggage, and any express); and making arrangements for disabled vehicles to be removed to the proper repair agency for detailed estimates of damage and ultimate repairs.

A copy of the investigating police agency report should be obtained and made a part of the accident file. This report should provide all factual information determined by the investigating police officer, as well as list any citations or summonses given. In some states, this report will not reveal an opinion of the investigating officer; but this is not too important because such opinions are of little value: they are not admissible as evidence in court. If the case goes to court and the investigating officer is summoned, he can testify only to the factual information recorded in his report.

The physician who attended injured persons should be contacted to obtain detailed information about the nature and extent of injuries. If the injured have been admitted to a hospital, hospital authorities should be contacted. Whether or not the accident investigator should visit any injured persons while they are in the hospital is a moot question and each case has to be decided on its own merits in conformity with company policy.

Recording Accident Data

All accident data should be recorded and preserved in such a manner that it can be of the greatest possible value in the accident prevention program. Accident data should be transferred to permanent accident record forms essential for efficient accident control administration:

THE "ACCIDENT REGISTER"

Most fleets maintain an "Accident Register" (Form Vehicle 8) that provides a journal of ready information of *all* accidents in chronological order. As a checklist for followup, it assures that the fleet operator will have a single record of all accidents.

The "Accident Register" form provides considerable analytical information. (This form is illustrated on the next spread.)

MOTOR TRANSPORTATION

ACCIDENT REGISTER

PERIOD COVERED _____ TO _____

ACCIDENT NUMBER _____ TO _____

COMPANY _____

LOCATION _____

NATIONAL FLEET SAFETY CONTEST

KEY CODE NO. _____

DIVISION OF CONTEST _____

	ACCIDENT DATE	ACCIDENT NUMBER	DRIVER'S NAME	DRIVER'S HOME TERMINAL	VEHICLE NUMBER	ACCIDENT TYPE	SHOW NEA CITY & STATE
1							
2							
3							
4							
5							
6							
7							
8							
9							
10							
11							
12							
13							
14							
15							
16							
17							
18							
19							
20							
21							
22							
23							
24							
25							
26							
27							
28							
29							
30							
31							
32							
33							
34							
35							
36							
37							
38							
39							
40							

STOCK NO. 229.39 !

MOTOR TRANSPORTATION ACCIDENT REGISTER, National Safety Council For

THIS FORM CAN BE CONVENIENTLY FILED IN A
THREE RING BINDER. TEAR OFF THIS FLAP AND FOLD
AS INDICATED AND THE PAGE IDENTIFICATION WILL
WILL BE UNCOVERED FOR REFERENCE.

FOLD

← TEAR OFF HERE →

CIDENT LOCATION			OBJECTS, PERSONS OR VEHICLES INVOLVED	ESTIMATED COST INFORMATION						ANSI D-15						
URBAN	SUBURBAN	RURAL		COMPANY		OTHER PARTY		TOTAL	REPORTABLE	NOT REPORTABLE		REPORTS FURNISHED				
				PERSONAL INJURY	PROPERTY DAMAGE	PERSONAL INJURY	PROPERTY DAMAGE				CO. HDQTS.	INS. CO.	POLICE	I.C.C.		
																1
																2
																3
																4
																5
																6
																7
																8
																9
																10
																11
																12
																13
																14
																15
																16
																17
																18
																19
																20
																21
																22
																23
																24
																25
																26
																27
																28
																29
																30
																31
																32
																33
																34
																35
																36
																37
																38
																39
																40

Vehicle 8, unfolds to 16½ by 11 inches. Upper right corner tears off for filing ease.

In large fleets, the register may be kept at the office that has direct supervision over the driver involved and that is also responsible for initially receiving the driving report of the accident. In small fleets, records are usually kept by the person responsible for loss control. Information from accident reports should be transcribed to the register and kept up to date as follows:

1. Accident date: This is the date the accident occurred, not the date the accident was reported. File chronologically.

2. Accident number: In this column enter the number which has been assigned to the accident file. This serves as an excellent cross-reference to the file itself.

3. Driver's name: This is another excellent cross-reference to the master file in that it will identify the accident and refer back to the number of the master file.

4. Driver's home terminal: When a control register is maintained at the company's general office, this column helps to locate accidents by terminal and provides a quick résumé of the number of accidents that occur.

5. Vehicle number: The vehicle number assists the maintenance operations, and safety departments. Whenever practical, the numbering system should give an indication as to the type of vehicle.

6. Accident type: This is the first major breakdown with regard to type. This breakdown should include head-on, sideswipe, right angle, front end (your vehicle), rear end (your vehicle), overturn, other.

7. Accident location: This section will furnish location data of a general nature that can be used later for analytical purposes. These data can indicate where the preponderance of accidents are taking place and where special emphasis must be laid.

8. Objects, persons, or vehicles involved: Here, as in (7), descriptive information should be recorded that can be analyzed by categories; *e.g.,* truck and car, truck and pedestrian, truck and utility pole.

9. Estimated cost information: The importance of this area cannot be overemphasized. A company must know what accidents are costing or might be going to cost. Accurate estimates furnish the data for making realistic financial projections.

10. National Fleet Safety Contest: One of the most successful programs for measuring fleet performance is the National Fleet Safety Contest of the National Safety Council. This contest serves as a medium for collecting motor vehicle fleet accident statistics. Participation in the program is open to NSC members receiving the Motor Fleet Safety Service and who have motor fleet vehicles that operate in the U.S. and/or Canada. Member companies may enter one or more fleets in the contest at no cost. Fleets are grouped with other fleets in compatible classifications such as: common carrier, private carrier, school bus, transit and intercity buses, and passenger cars. The fleets are further divided into city, intercity, and suburban operation groups. All that is required is a simple monthly report, including your mileage, accidents, and number of vehicles. You will receive monthly bulletins showing the safety standings of the fleets in your group. This contest is a very effective accident prevention tool and a source of discussion at your safety meetings. An added attraction, of course, is the national recognition to be gained in winning top honors among the fleets in your group. An attractive NSC plaque is presented to the winner. The guides for reportability are the American Standards Association publications *American Standard Method of Recording and Measuring Motor Vehicle Fleet Accident Experience,* D15.1, and *Recording and Measuring Motor Vehicle Fleet and Passenger Accident Experience,* D15.2. When in doubt as to correct interpretation, refer the case to: Secretary, D-15 Committee on Interpretations, American National Standards Institute, Inc., 1430 Broadway, New York, New York 10018.

11. Reports furnished: Specific reports must be furnished to company headquarters, the insurance company, the police, and the I.C.C. This area furnishes a handy reference check to make sure that such reports have been made.

THE "AWARD AND ACCIDENT RECORD" CARD

The safety performance of each driver is important in his overall job performance. A special form, NSC Form Vehicle 6, "Award and Accident Record," illustrated here, lists dates of all accidents and summarizes the essential facts about each. The card also records commendations for good performance and dates of safety awards earned. The cards may be kept in a special file or included with other personnel records of the driver. (Card is shown next spread.)

Analyzing Accident Data

Although an accident, as noted previously, usually results from several contributing factors or multiple causes, it usually could have been prevented by the removal of one or more of these factors.

Accident analysis—a means of studying accident data to determine what actions will result in the greatest improvement—requires breaking down every accident into its component parts, and tallying the information so that it can be viewed objectively. Accident-causing factors must be isolated so an attempt can be made to eliminate them.

MOTOR TRANSPORTATION
AWARD AND ACCIDENT RECORD

JAN	FEB	MAR	APR	MAY	JUN	JUL	AUG	SEP	OCT	NOV	DEC
			X								

National Safety Council
Form Vehicle 6

Name ...Smith,............ Bill............ E...
         Last   *First*   *Middle*

Company ......Highway Express......

Location ...Midwest Division......

Address.....123.... Home St.,.... Any Town....
     Number   *Street*

Badge
Number ...123....

Date
Employed...Feb. 1, 19—.... Age...29
          Month *Day* *Year*   *At Emp.*

DRIVING TESTS

Date	Score	Remarks
2/4/19—	90	Slow reaction time

SAFE DRIVER AWARD RECORD

Earned....2.... Year N. S. C. Award during period
from ..3/2/19—.... to ..3/2/19—....with
Company ...Overnight Freight, Inc.....
Certified by...F. J. O'Connell, supt.....

Award earned	Certificate Number	Date Award earned	Preventable Accidents		Non-Driving Time	
			File No	Date	From	To
3	468950	3/2/19—	1016	4/10/19—	12/1/19—	1/1/19—
4	501850	3/2/19—				
5	600100	4/2/19—				

REMARKS: 12/1/19— took
one month leave of absence.

STOCK No. 229.36

66

MOTOR TRANSPORTATION AWARD AND ACCIDENT RECORD, NSC Form Vehicle 6. (See p. 69 for list of factors.)

ACCIDENT RECORD

Accident File No.	Date of Accident	Co. Veh Number	Type of Company Vehicle	Type of Accident	Location	Preventable or Not-Preventable	Violation
1016	4/10/19—	84	Semi-trailer	Sideswipe	I-94 4½ miles east Ypsilanti	Prev.	Improper passing

REVERSE SIDE OF AWARD AND ACCIDENT RECORD. Card is 5⅛ by 8 inches. (Typical entries have been made.)

PURPOSE OF ACCIDENT ANALYSIS

Accident investigation reports have little use if they are merely placed in files and forgotten. They must be properly evaluated. Accident analysis—by evaluating the causes—pinpoints bad situations and suggests a remedy. Should it indicate that defective equipment is a contributing factor, it would reveal that the maintenance program has shortcomings. Should it show that a large number of accidents occur at intersections, then the safetyman could conclude that drivers need additional education and training.

Accident analysis can reveal significant causes. If defective brakes, for example, are a contributing factor, then the mechanic who is responsible for inspecting and maintaining brakes should be called to account. If a large number of drivers are shown to be accident repeaters, then the person who is responsible for driver selection may not be using adequate selection techniques, or may not have an effective training program, or both. Analysis may point out discrepancies between a problem and any action taken to remedy the problem. It may further indicate ways of taking the necessary corrective action.

Should a truck operator receive inside information that robbers planned to highjack a valuable cargo, he certainly would take the necessary corrective action to prevent it. Similarly, accident analysis provides fleet operators with "inside information" of what accident experience is likely to be. Because it relates the times, places, conditions, causes, and other factors that most often contribute to accidents, it indicates which action should be taken to prevent the accident or to reduce the accident frequency.

HOW OFTEN SHOULD AN ANALYSIS BE MADE?

An analysis should be made as often as the number of accidents indicates a trend or reveals a need for any change in accident prevention activities. This would indicate that the intervals between accident analysis reports would depend upon the size of the fleet operation. A ten-vehicle operation that has very few accidents may not warrant an accident analysis summary more than once a year (or possibly every two years), unless accidents increase. In a much larger fleet, a summary may be warranted once a month.

MECHANICS OF ACCIDENT ANALYSIS

Analysis is the process of taking a thing apart. In the analysis of a group of accidents, the separate factors in each accident are isolated and counted. This is largely a mechanical process, once the analysis system has been designed. In order to establish this system, the safety director must decide (1) what accident facts to analyze, and (2) what subcategories to use for each factor to show either its presence or absence or its relative effect.

SELECTING FACTORS TO BE STUDIED

Because an accident can be highly complex, it is very difficult to record for study all the factors that may have brought it about. Therefore, there must be some guidelines to follow in selecting factors:

1. Availability of the information. What information is available and how easily can it be obtained? Because analysis is usually confined to those items on the "Driver's Accident Report," all the items that are to be analyzed should be filled in.

2. Suspected importance of the factor. There are many factors surrounding an accident that may or may not be associated with its causes; to study them all would complicate the analysis and make it too costly. For example, operator's height, weight, and hair color are quite unlikely to be associated with accident causes and, even if they were, probably nothing could be done about them. The safety director should limit his analysis to those factors which are related in such a way that they are subject to some control if found to be accident-producing factors. (Suggested factors are listed a little further on—in paragraph 4.)

3. Mechanical limitations of the system. Because sorting is mechanical (either done by hand or by machine), the amount of data that can be placed on any card is limited. This, in turn, limits the number of factors that can be studied, but should not, however, preclude the safety director's making various special studies occasionally of unusual factors that he may suspect as being related to accident causes. Such studies will be set up independently of the regular analysis system.

4. Selecting the factors. The following are some of the accident factors usually selected for accident analysis:

Name of driver	Vehicle number
Time of day	Object struck
Accident location	Age of driver
Type of accident	Direction traveling
Vehicle type	Vehicle doing hitting
Weather condition	Responsibility for accident
Light condition	Any failure of company driver
Road condition	Other vehicle or object
Hours worked since first re- porting	Pedestrian
	Length of service of driver
Traffic violation	Cost of accident

CONSTRUCTING THE CLASSIFICATION

Once you have decided what factors to analyze, construct a classification by categorizing each factor and designating the relative values for each. For example, to study the pedestrian factor requires only two categories: "Pedestrian" and "No Pedestrian." More detailed information about pedestrians can be obtained by constructing a classification composed of the categories: "Male (age)" and "Female (age)."

Because the value of a classification depends entirely on how useful it is to the safety director, the following considerations should help in constructing them:

1. The categories should be *mutually exclusive*—that is, a certain weather condition should be classifiable into only one category. Categories must also be *collectively exhaustive*—that is, there should be an appropriate category for every type of weather condition. A system of categories is known as a *classification*. A classification whose categories are not mutually exclusive and collectively exhaustive is defective and can introduce many errors into the analysis.

2. The classification should be sufficiently detailed to provide as much specific information as needed. If categories are too general, they become worthless. For example, a classification by time of day into "A.M." and "P.M." categories is too general to be meaningful. A better classification would be into categories made up of 24 one-hour time brackets, 12 two-hour brackets, or 6 four-hour brackets.

3. However, a classification should not be too detailed. This is the other extreme. Because the analysis seeks to arrive at a useful generalization about the fleet's accident experience, it is searching for a trend or a constellation of factors. This will not show up if the classification is excessively detailed.

One classification useful in guiding the training program is classification by type of accident. When well constructed, such a classification provides a certain amount of built-in analysis, and a fairly ready-made answer to the questions: "What are we doing wrong?" and "What must we do to correct it?"

The simplest and most widely used classification by type of accident is composed of the following categories:

Head-on	Rear end (Your vehicle)
Sideswipe	Backing
Right angle	Overturn
Front end (Your vehicle)	Other
	Noncollision

70

Using Accident Data

After painstakingly gathering the facts about all fleet accidents and carefully analyzing them, the safetyman now knows the "what," "when," "where," "who"—and to a large extent, the "how" and "why"—of his accident experience. He is now prepared to put these facts to work for the prevention of future accidents.

Every accident, even if not severe, must be treated as a matter of real importance. Management cannot afford to shrug off or dismiss any accident as being "a necessary part of doing business," "bad luck that could happen to anybody," or "regrettable, but just one of those things." *Any display of indifference on the part of the management or the supervisory force will lead the driver to feel that safety is not important and this will inevitably breed slack safety performance.*

Although this attitude must be forcefully impressed upon the driver who had the accident, management, however, cannot go to an extreme and fire a driver simply because he may have needlessly cost the company a great deal of money. He will only have to be replaced, and his replacement will have to be trained. This replacement may prove to be just as poor a driver, or even worse than the one discharged.

How management handles a driver who has had a motor vehicle accident can be a turning point that will determine whether the driver learns anything from it and is helped to improve his performance, or whether the incident, by being allowed to drop, will actually confirm a bad driving practice.

The use of accident data in the prevention of accidents will be discussed under the headings: (1) using accident data in dealing with individual drivers and repeaters, (2) using accident data in selecting and training drivers, and (3) using accident data in reporting to management.

THE POST-ACCIDENT INTERVIEW

Every driver who has an accident should be interviewed as soon as possible after the accident by his immediate supervisor or his terminal manager. The safety director can advise, but supervision must run the interview, otherwise authority is diluted.

The objectives of the post-accident interview are to:

1. Impress upon the driver the importance of safety.

2. Determine whether the accident in question was preventable or nonpreventable in accordance with company standards of safe driving practice.

71

3. Permit the driver to learn from this accident how to prevent similar accidents in the future.

The supervisor should prepare himself for this interview by studying the entire past safety record of the driver, by examining all his

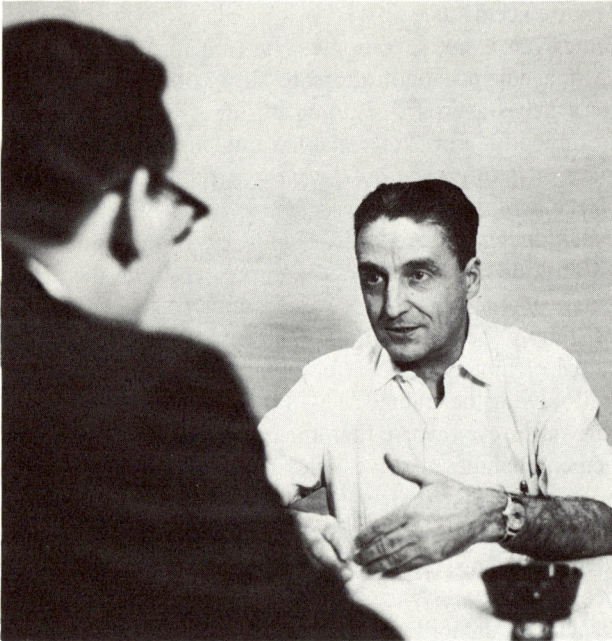

GOOD PREPARATION BY THE SUPERVISOR helps the driver to "think through" his accident. Let him do the talking. Let him explain how he could have prevented it.

accidents to determine whether there is any pattern common to them.

For example, the driver's record may show that he had three years' driving experience with tractors and semi-trailers before the date of his employment, and, in the 29 months since coming to the company, he has driven the same type of equipment. The card shows further that he has had one other accident while driving for the company, 11 months prior to the date of the present accident, and also that he was once arrested for failing to stop at a stop sign.

The current accident occurred at dusk, four-hours driving time away from the terminal. The truck was sideswiped as the driver was pulling away from the curb after a temporary stop. According to the accident report, the driver was attempting to maneuver into the center lane in order to make a left turn at an intersection and had signaled, but not soon enough to warn the car behind.

In the previous accident which occurred shortly after sundown, after about four hours driving, the company vehicle was struck from the rear while turning out to pass another vehicle which had slowed down abruptly. The accident report showed that, although a quick turn out was necessary to avoid striking the vehicle ahead, the company driver had been following too close at a speed too fast for the conditions of visibility, and that he had not allowed himself sufficient time to signal the vehicle following.

Noting the factors common to the two accidents—that they both occurred at twilight after a period of steady driving, that both involved failure to watch out for vehicles behind when entering a different traffic lane, and that both involved improper signaling—the supervisor will plan his interview to emphasize these points.

In the preparation phase, the supervisor should also note all nonpreventable accidents the driver has had. He should draw up an informal tabulation showing the frequency the driver has had accidents —preventable or nonpreventable—in comparison with the group average of the fleet. He may also tabulate the cost of the accidents the driver has had and project these costs over the years remaining before the driver's retirement. The purpose of this information is to make the driver aware of his rating as a safe driver in relation to other drivers in the fleet and the fact that the accidents he is having reflect on his driving ability as well as cost the company money. The safetyman can be of real service here.

The supervisor should also study all material available on the current accident and arrive at a tentative decision as to whether the accident was preventable or nonpreventable.

The post-accident interview should be conducted in a place where the supervisor and driver can have complete privacy and as much time as needed should be allotted. While it is important that the interview should be conducted with an air of objectivity, it must also be in a spirit of friendly helpfulness.

Even though the severity of the accident may be minor, the driver should be impressed that the important thing is to discover whether any faulty driving habits caused the accident. It should be pointed out that even though the severity of the present accident may be minor, the faulty driving habit that caused it could cause a much more severe accident in the future if allowed to persist.

After impressing the driver with the importance of safe driving, comparing his rating with that of other drivers, and projecting cost of accidents that could be expected in the future, the supervisor should then turn to a discussion of the present accident. The supervisor himself already has studied all available information about the accident and the driver in order to be thoroughly familiar with the details. The purpose of the interview is to "think through together" the details of the accident: what was—or was not—done, what might—or might not— have been done, what should—or should not—have been done. In this part of the interview, the driver does most of the talking and the supervisor guides the discussion by means of a question or observation now and then.

After the accident has been thoroughly discussed, the supervisor should ask the driver whether he thinks he could have prevented it or not by displaying a higher degree of defensive driving. If the driver says "No," the supervisor should then say, *"Does this mean that if you are permitted to continue to drive, and that every time this situation occurs, you will be involved in an accident?"* To answer this key question, the driver is forced to view the accident more objectively in terms of its *preventability.** This is therefore an important question.

At the conclusion of the interview, the supervisor should sum up the accident details, announce that he has arrived at his own decision as to its preventability, spell out what that decision is and why, and tell the driver what he can do to prevent a recurrence. If he has made a sound decision and conducted the interview properly, the driver will agree with and accept this decision with good grace. The driver will leave the interview feeling that he has been given a fair hearing, that he has been given a reasonable decision, that he has learned something about safe driving, and that he has a heightened respect for safe driving.

In the event the driver does not agree with the supervisor's decision as to preventability, some companies provide for a review of the accident and a decision by an accident review committee. In the event the driver is still not satisfied (or perhaps the company itself is not sure how the accident should be classified), the accident facts can be submitted to the National Safety Council for decision.

The decision should be made by the immediate supervisor wher-

* *This concept is defined in Chapter 7 under "Defensive Driving."*

ever possible, or at least by some authorized person at the location where the driver works. Decisions made at a distant headquarters tend to lack force. The decision should be made as soon after the accident as possible. Time tends to forgive an accident. Drivers will learn more from the interview and accept a preventable decision with better grace when the accident is still fresh in their minds.

It should also be pointed out that sound decisions on preventability can be made by a supervisor regardless of his driving experience. The old saying that "You don't have to be a hen to know that an egg is rotten" applies here. Supervisors may not have had as much road experience as some of the veteran drivers, but they should at least have made a careful study of the concept of accident preventability and, through the experience of having reviewed and discussed numerous accidents with different drivers, have acquired an authoritative grasp of the essentials.

DEALING WITH ACCIDENT REPEATERS

One of the most important functions of an accident record system is to quickly spot accident repeaters in order to bring them to the attention of management and the safety department for remedial training. Fleets seem to differ in their definition of an accident repeater, but usually it means having a second accident within a period of six months, nine months, or a year. This time period depends upon whether the driver drives in city or inter-city operations, with the city drivers permitted a shorter time period between accidents due to the greater accident hazard of city operations.

Drivers having their second accident are given the post-accident interview in accordance with the regular procedure. In addition, they may receive additional attention:

1. They are sent a warning letter, with a copy to the union if the driver is represented by one.
2. A driver trainer or supervisor is assigned to ride with the driver to report on his driving habits.
3. Special safety meetings or training courses are scheduled periodically for all accident repeaters. New approaches to learning, new films, and techniques can be used to keep the meetings from being "old hat" and being more of a penalty than a learning experience.

There are a number of other corrective procedures that are sometimes used. These include special physical examinations and special counseling. When in spite of such efforts, a driver continues to have accidents, the company has no recourse but to reassign the man to a nondriving job or to discharge him. Accurate records are important if the discharge is taken to arbitration.

Other Benefits

AWARDS AND INCENTIVES

Accurate accident records serve a very positive function as the basis for fleet contests, driver awards, and incentive systems. The operation of award and incentive plans is discussed in Chapter 8 under "Encourage High Performance."

THE DRIVER TRAINING PROGRAM

The training program for new drivers as they join the company is designed to train them how to drive safely. Accident records may indicate that the fleet drivers were not given enough instruction in some specific area, for example, how to avoid backing accidents. As a result, the training program should be altered to correct this deficiency. The training program should constantly be reevaluated to cope with the type of accident problems encountered.

DRIVER SELECTION

The safety performance of the drivers hired should be checked. If some drivers do poorly and leave the company or have to be discharged this information should be reviewed to improve ability to select better drivers.

SAFETY MEETINGS

If regular safety meetings are a part of the safety program, the content of such meetings should be based on accident data. Accident prevention effort should always be aimed at the biggest and most remunerative target. If accident records indicate that a certain location, weather condition, or type of accident accounts for most accidents, safety meetings should be geared to showing drivers how to avoid these. Appendix C gives details.

REPORTS TO MANAGEMENT

Management interest and support of the safety effort will be high only if all management (middle management and supervisors as well as top management) are kept informed as to the progress of safety achieve-

MOTOR VEHICLE DRIVING SKILL and traffic accident prevention are improved by training. Programs should be constantly evaluated so that they cope with the type of accident problems encountered.

ment within the company.

One of the most important measurements of accident experience is the accident rate. The rate for motor vehicle accidents is based on the number of reportable accidents per million vehicle miles driven. The American National Standards Institute D15.1 and D15.2, *Method of Recording and Measuring Motor Vehicle Fleet and Passenger Accident Experience,** should be used to compute rates.

Management will also be interested in employee injury rates. These should be computed in accordance with the *Method of Recording and Measuring Work Injury Experience,* ANSI Standard Z16.1.*

Management should also contact the Occupational Safety and Health Administration (OSHA) regional office for its area for informa-

---

* *Available from American National Standards Institute, Inc., 1430 Broadway, New York, N.Y. 10018. (Some discussion is given in the next chapter under "Counting Injuries and Figuring Rates.")*

tion on reporting and recording of occupational injuries and illnesses.

Reports should be made to management monthly and summaries made annually. These should show the actual number of accidents and the accident rate for the separate terminals, divisions, or company locations, as well as company-wide totals.

So that management can have some basis for comparison, figures for the previous calendar year to date should be shown. The information should be prefaced by a brief written summary that points out the most noteworthy facts in the report.

Other information that might be included in monthly and annual reports to management is:

Accident rate by type of equipment and type of accident
High-accident locations
Accidents by seniority groups
Miles operated per accident
Accident costs

5

Organizing fleet accident data— employee

The objective of an occupational accident reporting and investigation program is to eliminate from everyday work all unsafe acts and unsafe conditions which could cause personal injury, property damage, or fire. If these are removed, then employee injury accidents can be controlled. In spite of safe conditions, however, accidental injuries may still occur. And when they do, efforts should be made to learn as much about them as possible in order to prevent repetition. This is up to the employee's immediate supervisor, or, as is usually the case in serious accidents, to an accident investigation committee.

From time immemorial, various reasons have been given as to why some persons get hurt and others don't. Some reasons have been valid, such as "lack of experience" or "lack of attention." Many of them blame "fate": "he was just careless" or, "he was just plain stupid."

Only a valid reason points the way to proper corrective or preventive action. Also, there is little reason to seek out the basic cause or causes of a personal injury if there is not first a *determination* to set up practical measures for the prevention of a similar accidental injury.

The most important responsibility of an accident investigation committee is to gather all the facts, then to evaluate them to determine the cause or causes of the accident, and finally to propose ways and means for preventing or at least reducing the number of such accidents in the future.

Each will be discussed in turn.

Evaluation Standards

In 1920, the U.S. Bureau of Labor Statistics published Bulletin No. 276, *Standardization of Industrial Accident Statistics*. In 1937, the American Standards Association (ASA) published and distributed for trial use its *American Recommended Practice for Compiling Industrial Accident Causes*. In 1939, the representatives of thirty-four industry associations, insurance companies, governmental groups, including the National Safety Council and the American Standards Association, started to revise the trial 1937 code, inspired by the clear thinking of W. H. (Bill) Heinrich. The revised code as it appeared in 1941 has thus been generally known as the Heinrich Cause Code. It was the national standard on "Accident Causes" for twenty years (as ASA Standard Z16.2), and has been instrumental in bringing about a wide acceptance of the safety philosophy that "Accidents Are Caused." It recognized six major accident factors classified as:

1. The agency
2. The agency part
3. The accident type
4. The unsafe mechanical or physical condition
5. The unsafe act
6. The unsafe personal factor

The first five factors were usually determined without controversy. The sixth invited speculation as to bodily defects or improper attitude.

In 1962, the Z16.2 Standard was offered in a new format. No longer known as a cause of accident code, it is titled, *Method of Recording Basic Facts Relating to Nature and Occurrence of Work Injuries*. It has been subdivided into the following categories:

1. Nature of injury
2. Part of body affected
3. Source of injury
4. Accident type
5. Hazardous conditions
6. Agency of accident
7. Unsafe act

Now called American National Standard Z16.2, it provides accident investigation committees with a check list of the answers they should seek as to determine how and why the accident happened.

Causes of Accidents

Because safety and accident investigation committees cannot be expected to memorize all of the provisions of the revised Z16.2 Standard, the accompanying "Guide for Determining the Hazardous Conditions and/or Unsafe Acts Related to an Employee Injury" is for reference.

80

Guide for Determining the Hazardous Conditions
And/or Unsafe Acts Related to an Employee Injury

*(Based on American National Standard
Z16.2, as revised in 1962)*

HAZARDOUS CONDITIONS

Defective, Inferior or Unsuitable Tools, Machinery, Equipment, or Materials

Broken	Loose	Improperly designed
Cracked	Slippery	Improperly assembled
Corroded	Dull	Improperly constructed
Decayed	Rough	Improperly compounded
Frayed	Sharp-edged	Improperly maintained
Worn	Defective insulation	Improperly lubricated

Dress or Apparel Hazards

Improperly clothed; inadequate clothing; loose clothing; loose jewelry

No shoes; shoes defective or unsuitable

No goggles, face shields, eye shields, or safety glasses; unsuitable eye protection

No respirators; respirators unsuitable or defective

No gloves; gloves unsuitable or defective

No head protection; safety hats or caps unsuitable or defective

No body protection; aprons, jackets, etc. unsuitable or defective

Environmental Hazards *(Not elsewhere classified)*

Congested working space; inadequate aisle space, inadequate clearance

Improper illumination; general illumination inadequate; insufficient light at point-of-operation; poor lighting due to glare, shadows, dirty fixtures, etc.

Improper ventilation; lack of a ventilating system; ventilating system of wrong type, insufficient capacity, improperly installed; poorly maintained

Hazardous Methods or Conditions

Improper assignment of personnel; inadequate help for heavy lifting, etc.

Use of inherently hazardous methods or procedures

Use of inherently hazardous (not defective) materials or equipment

81

Placement Hazards

Unsafely piled materials (overloaded; unbalanced; not crosstied)
Inadequately secured against undesired motion (not unstable piling)

Inadequately Guarded

Unguarded mechanical or physical hazards
Inadequately guarded; poorly guarded power transmission equipment; poorly guarded at point-of-operation
Uninsulated or ungrounded (electrical)
Unshielded or inadequately shielded (radiation)
Unlabeled or inadequately labeled materials

Hazards of Outside Work Environments (*Not public hazards*)

Defective premises of others; defective materials or equipment of others
Natural hazards; wild animals; poisonous plants or insects; exposure to the elements; hazards of irregular or unstable terrain

Public Hazards (*Encountered away from employer's premises*)

UNSAFE ACTS

Cleaning, Oiling, Adjusting or Repairing Equipment That Is Moving, Electrically Energized, or Pressurized

Failure to Use Available Personal Protective Equipment

Goggles	Gloves	Aprons
Safety glasses	Hats	Shoes
Hoods	Caps	Lifelines

Failure to Wear Safe Personal Attire

Loose clothing	Neckties	Loose hair
Long sleeves	Jewelry	High heels

Failure to Secure or Warn

Failure to place warning signs, signals, tags, etc.
Starting or stopping vehicles or equipment without giving adequate warning
Releasing or moving loads, etc., without giving adequate warning
Failure to lock, block or secure vehicles, switches, valves, or other equipment

Improper Use of Equipment

Using material or equipment in a manner for which it was not intended

Overloading

Improper Use of Hands or Other Body Parts

Using hands instead of hand tools to feed, clean, adjust, repair, etc.

Gripping objects insecurely. Inattention to footing or surroundings

Making Safety Devices Inoperative

Disconnecting, blocking, plugging, tying, or misadjusting safety devices

Operating or Working at Unsafe Speeds

Feeding or supplying too rapidly. Throwing material instead of carrying or passing. Jumping from elevations (vehicles, elevators, platforms, etc.)

Running

Taking Unsafe Position or Posture

Unnecessary exposure to suspended or swinging loads

Unnecessary exposure to moving materials or equipment

Entering tanks, bins or other enclosed spaces without proper supervisory clearance

Riding in unsafe position: on platforms, forks of lift trucks, etc.

Unsafe Placing, Mixing, Combining, etc.

Creating a tripping, slipping or bumping hazard

Pouring water into acid

Using Tools or Equipment That Are Known To Be Unsafe

Driving Errors (*By a vehicle operator on public roadways*)

Horseplay (*Distracting, teasing, abusing, practical joking, showing off*)

Not in Revised Code (*Failure to follow instructions or a proper job procedure*)

To determine the basic cause or causes of an industrial accident, it is recommended that the accident investigation committee, after hearing all the known facts surrounding the accident, come to a conclusion as to whether it was due primarily to a "mechanical cause," a "personal cause," or a combination of both. Personal causes are of three principal types:

1. **Bodily defects** such as defective eyesight, defective hearing, muscular weakness, organic weakness. A safety committee will probably phrase their findings in terms of "Probable. . . ."
2. **Lack of knowledge or skill** such as being unpracticed or unskilled, or being unaware of the safe practice. These result in some "unsafe act."
3. **Temporary lack of safety mindedness at the time of the injury** due, possibly, to distraction, confusion, mental worry, fatigue, inattention, etc., and resulting in some "unsafe act."

Once an organization reaches the point in its accident prevention work that it readily accepts the understanding that accidents are caused, then it will more readily ferret out the individual causes with ever increasing skill, and it will buckle down to the task of preventing future accidents.

Occupational Accident Reporting and Record System

Records of occupational accidents are essential to efficient and successful safety work just as records of production, costs, sales, and profits and losses are essential to efficient and successful operation of any business.

The basis for such records is contained in two American Standards, previously discussed: Z16.1, *The American Standard Method of Recording and Measuring Work Injury Experience,* and Z16.2, *The American Standard Method of Recording Basic Facts Relating to the Nature and Occurrence of Work Injuries.*

When kept in accordance with the standard method, work accident records provide a safety director and management with an objective evaluation of their safety program, they identify high accident-rate fleets, terminals, or departments, and they give the safety director information he needs to work hardest on the accident causes that contribute most to high rates.

More specifically, standardized work accident records are used to:

1. **Create interest in safety** among supervisors by furnishing them with information about the accident experience of their particular company units, whether a division, terminal, department, or other subdivision.
2. **Determine the principal accident sources** so that efforts may be made to reduce them.

FIRST-AID REPORT (4 by 6-inch card) is prepared by the first-aid attendant at the time of treatment. A report should be prepared for each case, whether minor or serious. Report serves as a record, and permits quick tabulation of such data as department, type of work, and the pertinent facts of the accident.

3. Provide supervisors and safety committees with information about the most frequent unsafe practices and unsafe conditions so that these persons can utilize their time and efforts to the greatest advantage.

4. Judge the effectiveness of the safety program by showing whether the accident experience is getting better or worse and by allowing comparison with the experience of organizations doing similar work.

The medical and first-aid program is intimately tied in with the system of accident records and reports.

Medical Treatment and First Aid

Since employees may be injured at any time, smoothly operating first-aid and medical procedures should be established to ensure prompt, adequate treatment.

Every fleet should have a qualified physician to provide essential emergency medical care for all employees. Arrangements can be for full-time, part-time, on-call, or consulting services. Drivers away from home should know what to do in the event of accident or illness.

In addition to providing emergency medical care, the physician can also conduct preplacement physical examinations, periodic physical examinations, and, sometimes, exit examinations for those employees who quit or are discharged. This is covered more completely in the *Accident Prevention Manual for Industrial Operations,* published by the National Safety Council.

In many fleets or in outlying fleet operations, it is neither practical nor justifiable for minor injuries to have full-time qualified professional medical personnel. In such cases, the best arrangement is to provide a suitable first-aid kit or a station administered by a trained first-aid attendant who follows procedures and treatments outlined by the company's medical advisor. A doctor should be on call or available for referral to take care of emergencies.

A first-aid program should include the following:

1. Properly trained and designated first aiders on every shift and at every company location.

2. A first-aid unit and supplies, or first-aid kit.

3. A first-aid manual.

4. Posted instructions for calling a physician and notifying the hospital that the patient is en route.

5. Posted instructions for transporting ill or injured employees and instructions for calling an ambulance or rescue squad.

6. An adequate first-aid record system.

First-Aid Report

The first piece of paper in the work accident reporting and record system is the first-aid report, illustrated on page 93.

The general safety rules will usually spell out that all employees must report to the first-aid station for treatment immediately upon being injured, regardless of the extent of the injury. The report is prepared by the person authorized to give first aid. If an injury is so minor that the employee treats himself, he can note this on his time card.

Copies of this report should be sent to the safety department, the injured employee's supervisor, and any other departments as determined by management.

Supervisor Accident Report

The second basic type of injury report is the "Supervisor Accident Report." Much more detailed, this form describes the accident that resulted in the injury. The form need not be completed, however, for

SUPERVISOR'S ACCIDENT REPORT

(To be completed immediately after accident, even when there is no injury)

Company name and address _____

1. Name and address of injured_____ SSN_____ 2. Age_____

_____ 3. Sex_____

4. Years of service_____ 5. Time on present job_____ 6. Title/occupation_____

7. Department_____ 8. Date of accident_____ 9. Time_____

10. Accident category (check) ☐ Motor Vehicle; ☐ Property Damage; ☐ Fire; ☐ Other_____

11. Severity of Injury (check) ☐ Non-disabling; ☐ Disabling; ☐ Medical Treatment; ☐ Fatality

12. Amount of damage $_____ 13. Location_____

14. Estimated number of days away from job (including weekends and holidays) _____

15. Nature of injury?_____

16. Part of body affected?_____

17. Degree of disability?_____
(Temporary total; permanent partial; permanent total)

18. Causative agent most directly related to accident? (Object, substance, material, machinery, equipment, conditions)

_____

_____

_____

Was weather a factor?_____

19. Unsafe mechanical/physical/environmental condition at time of accident? (Be specific)

_____

_____

_____

20. Unsafe act by injured and/or others contributing to the accident. (Be specific, must be answered)

_____

_____

_____

21. Unsafe personal factors (improper attitude; lack of knowledge or skill, poor reaction)

_____

_____

_____

(over)

SUPERVISOR'S ACCIDENT REPORT. The front side provides a record of contributing circumstances to an accident. It is the basis for specific remedial action. Form is 8½ by 11 in. in size. Users should be trained to fill it out properly.

87

22. Personal protective equipment required? (Protective glasses, safety shoes, safety hat, safety belt)_____

Was injured using required equipment?_____

23. What can be done to prevent a recurrence of this type of accident?
(Modification of machine; mechanical guards; correct environment; training)

_____

_____

24. Detailed narrative description (How did accident occur; why; objects, equipment, tools used, circumstance, assigned duties.

Be specific)_____

_____

_____

_____

(Use additional sheets, as required)

25. Witnesses to accident_____

_____

Date prepared_____   Signature of Foreman/Supervisor_____

Department_____

SUPERINTENDENT'S APPRAISAL AND RECOMMENDATION

a. In your opinion what action on the part of injured or others contributed to this accident?_____

_____

_____

b. Your recommendation_____

_____

_____

Date_____   Signature of Superintendent_____

FOR SAFETY OFFICE USE ONLY

Temporary Total ☐	Permanent Partial ☐	Death or Permanent Total ☐
Started losing time_____	Part of Body_____	
Returned to work_____	Per cent loss or loss of use_____	
Time charge_____	Time charge_____	Time charge: 6,000 days

Compensation $_____ Medical $_____ Other $_____ Total $_____

Name of hospital_____ Name of physician_____

Form IS—1A—25M—117201   Printed in U.S.A.   Stock No. 129.21

Reverse side of report. Central portion is filled in by higher level of management. Bottom portion of form is filled in by the safety department (as the facts become available) and contains data for computing injury rates and costs.

every injury requiring first aid, but it is completed (1) if the injury was severe enough to require a doctor's attention or (2) it required three or more treatments at a first-aid center. The reason the supervisor's report is not required for all injuries is that this would result in undue time being spent by the supervisor on paper work. Therefore, some minimum standard of severity needs to be established.

Employee Injury Record

To maintain a record of the injury experience of each employee, information about all injuries, first-aid cases, and disabling injuries is entered in a log or folder. A special form, "Injury Record of Employee" (illustrated), can be used.

INJURY RECORD OF EMPLOYEE_____

_____(Write Name)_____(Number)

Occupation_____Department_____Date Employed_____

Case Number	Date of Injury	Type (Fatal, Perm., Temporary, Non-disabling)	Days Charged	Compensation and other costs	Nature of Injury and Part of Body	Source of Injury (object or exposure, etc.)	Accident Type (event: struck by, fell, etc.)

Stock No. 129.23   IS3 Rev.

(Reverse side may be used for remarks)

INJURY RECORD OF EMPLOYEE, a 4 by 6 inch card for recording injuries.

Because supervisors cannot be expected to remember the experience of individual employees over a period of time, a periodic study of the injury record forms may reveal that some employees are having far more accidents than others. This may be a signal for individual corrective action such as counseling, retraining, or reassignment to a less hazardous job.

The form illustrated on the next eight pages shows the detail in which one company keeps these records.

89

Form EAI-1

90

GREYHOUND LINES, INC.
Greyhound Tower
Phoenix, Arizona 85077

REPORT NUMBER _____
1-5

EMPLOYEE INJURY AND ILLNESS REPORT FORM

THIS IS A

6, 1 ☐ First report

2 ☐ Revised report (complete *items and any items changed
from First report)

* **LOCATION NUMBER** _____
7-12
(Stamp assigned location number here)

INJURED OR ILL EMPLOYEE

* **Name** _____

* **Home Address** _____
(Street)

_____   _____   _____
(City)   (State)   (Zip)

* **Social Security Number** _____

1. **Age** 13-14

2. **Sex:** 15, 1 ☐ Male   2 ☐ Female

3. **Check the pay classification of injured or ill employee as shown on
employee's P-3 or P-4 form.**
16-17, 01 ☐ Mechanic

INSTRUCTIONS FOR COMPLETING THIS FORM

Carefully read these instructions *before* you begin filling out the
form below.

A. Your assigned LOCATION NUMBER must be stamped by you in
the space provided.

B. Print all handwritten information.

C. Be sure to fill in employee's social security number.

D. Carefully review the instructions included in each question before
answering. Each question can have only ONE answer or box
checked.

E. If you check "Other" be certain to print explanation in the space
provided.

Note: For occupational illness, questions 5 and 6 refer to date of
initial diagnosis or first day of absence, if absence occurred
before diagnosis. Skip question 7.

* 5. **Date injury occurred or illness diagnosed:**

_____ / _____ / _____

Month   Day   Year
19-20   21-22   23-24

Example: May 12, 1972, write 5/12/72

6. **Day injury or illness occurred or illness diagnosed:**

02 ☐ Apprentice mechanic (helper)

03 ☐ Combo man

04 ☐ Utilityman or hostler

05 ☐ Cleaner-washer

06 ☐ Storekeeper-partsman

07 ☐ Baggage clerk

08 ☐ Package express clerk

09 ☐ Porter-platform worker

10 ☐ Building maintenance or engineer

11 ☐ Janitor

12 ☐ Redcap

13 ☐ Attendant-Matron

14 ☐ Starter

15 ☐ Clerical employee

16 ☐ Office-Management

17 ☐ Sales Supervisor

18 ☐ Transportation Supervisor

19 ☐ Maintenance Supervisor (including working foreman)

20 ☐ Driver

21 ☐ Safety Superintendent

22 ☐ Other _____ (specify)

4. This report involves: (see definitions at end of form)

18, 1 ☐ Occupational injury

2 ☐ Occupational illness

25, 1 ☐ Sunday

2 ☐ Monday

3 ☐ Tuesday

4 ☐ Wednesday

5 ☐ Thursday

6 ☐ Friday

7 ☐ Saturday

✻ 7. Time (check closest time to injury occurrence)

AM	PM		AM	PM	
26-27, 01	13	1:00	07	19	7:00
02	14	2:00	08	20	8:00
03	15	3:00	09	21	9:00
04	16	4:00	10	22	10:00
05	17	5:00	11	23	11:00
06	18	6:00	12	24	12:00
			Noon	Night	

8. In or near what type of facility did the injury or exposure to illness occur?

28, 1 ☐ Garage

2 ☐ Terminal

3 ☐ Reclamation plant

4 ☐ General offices (Phoenix, Cleveland, San Francisco, Calgary)

5 ☐ Enroute-on-the-road (away from a company facility)

6 ☐ Other _____ (specify)

9. If injury or exposure to illness occurred away from company premises at an identifiable address, give that address. If it occurred on a public highway or any other place which cannot be identified by number and street, provide place references locating the place as accurately as possible.

_____

10. If injury or illness occurred in Garage or Reclamation plant, check specific area.

29-30, 01 ☐ Service lane area—in-pit
02 ☐ Service lane area—floor level
03 ☐ Service repair area—in-pit
04 ☐ Service repair area—floor level
05 ☐ Major repair area
06 ☐ Body shop area
07 ☐ Battery room or area
08 ☐ Tire room
09 ☐ Cleaning tank or steam room area
10 ☐ Small unit shop area
11 ☐ Dynamometer room
12 ☐ A/C department
13 ☐ Welding shop area
14 ☐ Loading dock area—Garage or Rec. plant
15 ☐ Part or stores room, or area
16 ☐ Strip room or area
17 ☐ Paint room or area
18 ☐ Wash room area
19 ☐ Bus parking lot area—garage or ready-line area

12. Task or activity the employee was engaged in when the injury or exposure to illness occurred (choose the ONE response that shows the GENERAL TYPE of work activity which the employee was doing regardless of the specific piece of work he was doing).

33-34, 01 ☐ Bus inspection work—service lane area
02 ☐ Interior bus cleaning—service lane area
03 ☐ Exterior bus cleaning—service lane area
04 ☐ Repair work outside the bus—service repair area
05 ☐ Repair work inside the bus—service repair area
06 ☐ Electrical work
07 ☐ Welding
08 ☐ Tire servicing or change
09 ☐ Tire chains—installing or removing
10 ☐ Unit parts rebuilding
11 ☐ Loading—unloading trucks
12 ☐ Materials and stock handling
13 ☐ Loading—unloading or handling baggage or GPX
14 ☐ Driving
15 ☐ Housekeeping (cleaning garage or terminal)
16 ☐ Building and grounds repair work (painting, construction, etc.)
17 ☐ Office clerical work
18 ☐ Horseplay
19 ☐ Not performing any task, e.g. waiting for or walking to an assignment
20 ☐ Other_____
(specify)

20 Engine tear-down area
21 Engine assembly line area
22 Transmission shop area
23 Electrical shop area
24 Water test section area
25 Machine shop area
26 Maintenance Superintendent's Office
27 Other area in Garage or Reclamation plant _____ (specify)

11. If injury or illness occurred in Terminal facility, check specific area.

31-32, 01 Terminal service area
02 Baggage room
03 GPX room
04 Loading platform area—terminal
05 Bus parking lot area—terminal
06 Auto parking lot area—terminal
07 Waiting room area
08 Rest room
09 Ticket office
10 Telephone information room
11 Lost baggage storage
12 Operations—dispatch office
13 Terminal Manager's office
14 Transportation Superintendent's office
15 Regional Manager's office
16 Other Terminal facility _____ (specify)

13. Position of the employee's body or his movement at the time of injury (choose the ONE response that BEST FITS the position or body movement; if this is an illness case, skip this question).

35-36, 01 Lifting object, no twisting or turning
02 Lowering object, no twisting or turning
03 Lifting object while twisting or turning
04 Lowering object while twisting or turning
05 Twisting or turning (body movement only—no object or material involved)
06 Pulling or pushing materials or objects
07 Boarding bus or alighting
08 Walking other than on stairway
09 Running other than on stairway
10 Walking or running up a stairway
11 Walking or running down a stairway
12 Standing (no object involved)
13 Standing (working with tool or material)
14 Standing (holding object or material)
15 Squatting, sitting or kneeling (no object involved)
16 Squatting, sitting or kneeling (working with tool or material)
17 Squatting, sitting or kneeling (holding object or material)
18 Climbing
19 Jumping
20 Lying down
21 Other _____ (specify)

94

14. How did injury or illness occur? (choose the ONE response that MOST CLOSELY DESCRIBES what happened)

37-38, 01 ☐ Caught part of body in something
02 ☐ Caught part of body between something
03 ☐ Caught part of body under something
04 ☐ Struck against object or by object or material
05 ☐ Struck by falling object or material
06 ☐ Struck by flying object or material
07 ☐ Contact with sharp object (knives, sharp tools, etc.)
08 ☐ Foreign object or material struck employee or lodged in him (such as dust, metal particles, etc.)
09 ☐ Fall, same level (such as flat floor surface)
10 ☐ Fall, different level (such as raised platform or stairs)
11 ☐ Fall, unknown whether same or different level
12 ☐ Contact with electric current
13 ☐ Contact with fire or hot object
14 ☐ Contact with hot substance including steam
15 ☐ Contact with corrosive or toxic liquid
16 ☐ Contact with other harmful liquid (diesel fuel, paint, etc.)
17 ☐ Overexertion (strain or exhaustion)
18 ☐ Inhaling gas or vapor
19 ☐ Exposure to or physical reaction from materials used on job
20 ☐ Other_____
(specify)

16. Part of body injured or affected (if more than one part of body involved, check the ONE body part MOST SEVERELY injured or affected).

41-42, 01 ☐ Head, all parts except eyes
02 ☐ Eyes
03 ☐ Neck
04 ☐ Shoulder
05 ☐ Arm including elbow
06 ☐ Hand or wrist
07 ☐ Finger or thumb
08 ☐ Chest
09 ☐ Trunk, except back or chest
10 ☐ Back, upper and lower areas
11 ☐ Leg including hip and knee
12 ☐ Foot or ankle
13 ☐ Toe
14 ☐ General (includes internal disorder or condition affecting entire body)
15 ☐ Other_____
(specify)

17. Nature of injury or illness (if more than one, CHECK THE MOST SEVERE)

A. Nature of Injury

43-44, 01 ☐ Cut, puncture, bruise or scrape
02 ☐ Sprain, strain or dislocation
03 ☐ Fracture

15. **Hazardous condition around the work area (check the ONE condition you believe CONTRIBUTED MOST to the injury or illness)**

39-40, 01 ☐ Floors slippery from oil, wax, liquids, etc.

02 ☐ Foreign objects lying on floor

03 ☐ Floor uneven

04 ☐ Holes in floor

05 ☐ Loose tile edges on floor

06 ☐ Curled or wrinkled carpeting on floor

07 ☐ Improperly stored tools or materials around work area

08 ☐ Unguarded machine or improper use of guard

09 ☐ Available personal protective equipment not used

10 ☐ Personal attire not safe (loose clothes, long hair around machinery)

11 ☐ Inadequate or blocked aisle space

12 ☐ Improper lighting on stairs

13 ☐ Improper lighting in work area

14 ☐ Improperly stacked, piled or stored materials

15 ☐ Improper bracing or blocking

16 ☐ Unsafe act on part of another employee

17 ☐ Improper venting

18 ☐ Exposure to excessive noise in general work area

19 ☐ Exposure to excessive heat in general work area

20 ☐ Exposure to excessive cold in general work area

21 ☐ No hazardous condition

22 ☐ Other_____
            (specify)

---

04 ☐ Heat burn or scald

05 ☐ Chemical burn

06 ☐ Electric shock

07 ☐ Foreign body in eye or other body opening, or imbedded in skin

08 ☐ Hernia

09 ☐ Crushing

10 ☐ Amputaion

11 ☐ Infection—aggravation of minor injury

12 ☐ Other injury_____
            (specify)

B. *Nature of Illness*

43-44, 13 ☐ Occupational skin disease or disorder

14 ☐ Dust disease of the lungs

15 ☐ Respiratory conditions due to toxic agents

16 ☐ Poisoning (internal effects of toxic materials)

17 ☐ Disorder due to physical agents (heat stroke, frost bite, effects of welding flash, etc.)

18 ☐ Disorder due to repeated motion, vibration or pressure, e.g. hearing loss, bursitis

19 ☐ Other illness_____
            (specify)

18. **Did injury occur inside a bus? (if illness, skip this question)**

45, 1 ☐ Yes

2 ☐ No

95

Note: For questions 27 and 28 see definitions at end of form

27. Injury or illness was

53, 1 ☐ First aid case

2 ☐ Nonfatal case without lost workdays

3 ☐ Lost workday case

4 ☐ Fatal

28. Number of lost workdays _____ 54-56

29. Employee was

57, 1 ☐ Returned to his own job

2 ☐ Permanently reassigned to another job because of disability

3 ☐ Terminated because of disability

4 ☐ Other _____
(specify)

30. Describe how the accident or exposure to illness happened including what the person was doing, what specific objects or substances were involved, and the action or movement which led to the injury or illness.

EXAMPLE: While walking down stairs, tripped on screwdriver on stairway and fell striking head on railing.

_____

_____

_____

_____

Report
Prepared by _____

_____ _____
(name)

_____ _____
(title)   (date)

---

19. Was a machine, tool, or material involved in the injury or illness? (check the ONE object that DIRECTLY INFLICTED the injury or illness)

46-47, 01 ☐ Stationary shop machinery

02 ☐ Portable power tools

03 ☐ Hand tools

04 ☐ Baggage or express packages

05 ☐ GPX carts, hand trucks or power lift trucks

06 ☐ Frame work of storage racks

07 ☐ Projecting materials from storage racks

08 ☐ Projecting objects from buses, buildings, or machinery

09 ☐ Battery or battery acid

10 ☐ Conveyor machinery

11 ☐ Office furniture and equipment

12 ☐ Motor vehicle (collision or other accident)

13 ☐ Driver's seat

14 ☐ Rubbish can

15 ☐ Water hose

16 ☐ Air hose

17 ☐ Cleaning tools and materials

18 ☐ No object involved (if checked, skip questions 20, 21, and 22)

19 ☐ Object unknown (if checked, skip questions 20, 21 and 22)

20 ☐ Other _____
(specify)

20. Item checked in 19 above was:

48, 1 ☐ Defective

2 ☐ Not defective

3 ☐ Other _____
(specify)

21. Item checked in 19 above was:

96

Properly used

2 ☐ Properly used

3 ☐ Other_____

(specify)

22. Item checked in 19 above was:

50, 1 ☐ Improper machine, tool, or material for the job

2 ☐ Proper machine, tool, or material for the job

3 ☐ Other_____

(specify)

23. Was injury or illness treated by a physician?

51, 1 ☐ Yes

2 ☐ No

24. If treated:

Name and address of physician.

_____

_____

25. If hospitalized:

Name and address of hospital.

_____

_____

26. Employee:

52, 1 ☐ Returned to work on same shift in which injury or illness occurred with no subsequent lost time

2 ☐ Returned to work on same shift, but did not report to work on a subsequent shift

3 ☐ Did not complete shift in which injury or illness occurred, but returned to work on next scheduled shift

4 ☐ Did not complete shift in which injury or illness occurred, and did not report on one or more subsequent shifts

DEFINITIONS

OCCUPATIONAL INJURY is any injury such as a cut, fracture, sprain, amputation, etc., which results from a work accident or from exposure in the work environment.

OCCUPATIONAL ILLNESS of an employee is any abnormal condition or disorder, other than one resulting from an occupational injury, caused by exposure to environmental factors associated with his employment. It includes acute and chronic illnesses or disease which may be caused by inhalation, absorption, ingestion, or direct contact.

FIRST AID CASES are those cases which involve one-time treatment and subsequent observation of minor scratches, cuts, burns, splinters, and so forth, which do not ordinarily require medical care, even though such treatment is provided by a physician or registered professional personnel.

NONFATAL CASES WITHOUT LOST WORKDAYS are those cases of occupational injury or illness which did not involve fatalities or lost workdays but did result in:

1) transfer to another job or termination of employment, or

2) medical treatment, other than first aid, or

3) diagnosis of occupational illness, or

4) loss of conciousness, or

5) restriction of work or motion.

LOST WORKDAYS are those days which the employee would have worked but could not because of occupational injury or illness. The number of lost workdays should not include the day of injury. The number of days includes all days (consecutive or not) on which, because of injury or illness:

1) the employee would have worked but could not, or

2) the employee was assigned to a temporary job, or

3) the employee worked at a permanent job less than full time, or

4) the employee worked at a permanently assigned job but could not perform all duties normally assigned to it.

See also original OSHA No. 101 and Recordkeeping Requirements under the Williams-Steiger Occupational Safety & Health Act of 1970 for more details.

97

Counting Injuries and Figuring Rates

The fleet manager and the fleet safety director need some method for measuring how well the employee safety program is doing and whether it is succeeding in cutting down accidents.

Safety performance is relative. Only when a fleet compares its injury experience with its own previous experience or with that of similar fleets, can it obtain a meaningful evaluation of its achievement.

A useful yardstick for this is the American Standard method for determining injury frequency rate. This is the number of disabling injuries per million employee hours worked, computed according to the following formula:

$$\text{Frequency Rate} = \frac{\text{Number of disabling injuries} \times 1{,}000{,}000}{\text{Employee-hours of exposure}}$$

For example, if the total employee hours of exposure in a given year are 2,000,000 and there are 25 disabling injuries during that period, the frequency rate is 12.5 disabling injuries per million man-hours worked.

While the accident rate can be a valuable yardstick, it is generally not too reliable a measurement of safety success in exposures of less than one million man hours: it would take a fleet of 500 employees approximately one year to compile this exposure. Most transportation fleets are much smaller than that. Even so, the rates should be computed monthly and annually. Cumulative rates will provide meaningful information and trend indications for comparative purposes.

Using Accident Information Effectively

Three statistics should be brought to management's attention: (1) The injury frequency rate of the company and then of some particular work group, (2) the date of the last lost-time injury, and (3) the manhours worked since the last lost-time injury.

The four-page employee injury and illness report form used by Greyhound Lines, Inc., reproduced on the preceding pages, is designed for computer analysis of the data.

At year's end, it is recommended that each company furnish the National Safety Council with a summary of its accidental injury experience. (The Council will furnish the reporting forms.) More and more companies are showing such facts in their annual report to stockholders, particularly when outstanding safety records have been achieved. Once a good record is established, it seems to breed a still better one.

6
Driver selection

People differ in their ability to act and to drive safely. Because we know little about *why* this is true or how to rate a job applicant's future on-the-job safety performance with any degree of exactness, this situation challenges the fleet personnel officer. Of all occupations, few involve a greater need for safety than that of the motor vehicle operator. A properly selected, trained, and motivated driver can usually avoid accidents that inflict property damage or injure persons.

General Abilities and Aptitudes

Before discussing the personal traits to look for in a job applicant, let's check the general abilities and aptitudes required. The next chart illustrates a job evaluation work sheet. Look closely at items 6, 7, 8, and 12.

RESPONSIBILITY FOR VEHICLE (ITEM 6). It is possible for the professional driver to damage or demolish his vehicle in an accident. The cost can range from $2,000 for a compact passenger car to $30,000 or more for a city bus or line-haul trailer-tractor combination.

RESPONSIBILITY FOR SAFETY OF CARGO OR PASSENGERS (ITEM 7). It is possible to inflict damage to costly cargo, especially human cargo.

RESPONSIBILITY FOR SAFETY OF PEDESTRIANS AND OTHER MOTOR-ISTS (ITEM 8). Every vehicle operator has the potential to injure pedestrians and collide with other motorists.

PERSONAL HAZARDS (ITEM 12). It is certainly possible for any

EVALUATION OF DRIVING JOB

Inter-City Truck, Semi-Trailer	Taxicab
Inter-City Truck, Straight	School Bus
Inter-City Bus	Passenger Car
City Truck, Semi-Trailer	Utility Truck
City Truck, Straight	Route Delivery Vehicle
City Bus	Other _____

		High		*Average*		*Not Important*
	JOB FACTOR	1	2	3	4	5
1	Education					
2	Experience					
3	Technical Training					
4	Physical Demand					
5	Mental Visual Demand					
6	Responsibility for Vehicle					
7	Responsibility for Safety of Cargo or Passengers					
8	Responsibility for Safety of Pedestrians and other Motorists					
9	Contacts with Customers					
10	Responsibility for Company Funds					
11	Driving and Working Conditions					
12	Personal Hazards					
13	Supervision Received					

100

ABILITY TO AVOID ACCIDENTS—One of the top requirements of any driver.

professional driver to suffer injury to himself in a traffic accident.

The potential of any driving job is such that one of its paramount requirements is the ability to avoid accidents.

ACCIDENT REPEATERS

Any discussion of individual differences related to the ability to avoid accidents must first deal with the problem of accident repeaters. It appears that some persons have repeated accidents while others can work or drive for years without having any accident at all. It has also been learned that everyone is potentially an accident repeater and can become a temporary accident repeater under certain conditions of stress.

The supervisor must select drivers with the best potential for driving safely, he must train them in the techniques of safe driving, and he must provide the kind of supervision that will maintain safe driving performance at a very high level. Thus the relationship between management and drivers must be different than ordinarily found between management and employees, supervisor and supervised. The

101

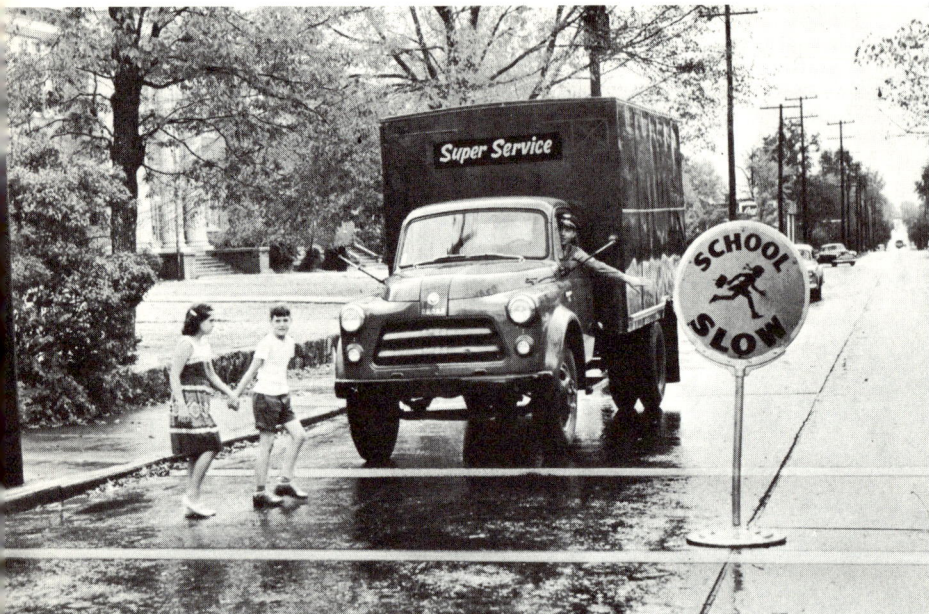

COURTESY AND CONSIDERATION—Not only helps avoid accidents, but helps advertise your company or fleet as being one of the best.

relationship is more akin to that which exists between the players on a big league baseball team and the coaches and managers: club managers not only must select good players, they must work closely with each individual player to keep him in good physical and psychological condition. Thus management must field a group of carefully selected and highly trained safe drivers. The safety program and the supervisory program must keep the drivers conditioned to turn in a high level of safe driving performance.

Selecting Safety-Conscious Drivers. Can the safe driving potential of an applicant be predicted at the employment office? The answer is a qualified "Yes." It is possible to screen out many of the poor risks, and a selection program that succeeds only in doing this has already made a substantial contribution. However, predicting safe driving ability is less exact.

Once the obviously bad risks have been screened out, selection should be confined to hiring the whole man without becoming obsessively preoccupied with attempts to further measure his potential ability to drive safely. Safe driving ability is conditioned by so many placement

102

factors that matching the total man to the total job holds out the best promise for success.

PROFILE OF THE GOOD DRIVER

What, then, is a good driver? An analysis reveals that the good driver must possess the following abilities:

1. **Drive well**
   a. Avoid accidents
   b. Follow traffic regulations
   c. Care for the vehicle
   d. Avoid schedule delays
   e. Avoid irritating the public
2. **Perform the nondriving parts of the job**
3. **Find satisfaction in the job**
4. **Get along with others**
5. **Adapt himself to meet existing conditions.**

Driving experience. Previous experience in driving as a professional driver or as a private motorist is the most critical indicator of potential ability to drive safely. It has been fairly well established that a man who has had frequent motor vehicle accidents in the past will continue to have frequent accidents in the future. This is one of the oldest and most reliable predictive factors, and means that one of the most important facts to be ascertained about the applicant is how many motor vehicle accidents he has had and how many times he has been cited for traffic violations. Since the applicant will ordinarily try to minimize or conceal a record of past accidents and traffic violations, his word alone is insufficient evidence. Previous employers and police records should be consulted.

The fact that an applicant has had past accidents should not be considered as a disqualification for employment. Each instance should be discussed with the applicant in an effort to determine his attitude toward the preventability of such accidents and the importance he attaches to observance of traffic rules and regulations.

The amount of previous driving experience to require of the applicant will depend much upon the scope of the company driver training program and the personnel philosophy of the fleet.

Ordinarily, previous experience in driving ought to be viewed as an asset in a new employee, particularly if it is experience driving the same kind of vehicle the applicant will drive on the job. Fleets which lease equipment from owner-drivers seldom have training programs. In such cases, the management of such operations should carefully examine the applicant's past driving experience, accident record, and demonstrated ability to drive safely.

Skill. The degree of driving skill possessed by the applicant can sometimes be determined from an examination of his past driving experience. When this cannot be done satisfactorily, the only way to judge skill is through a work-sample test; that is, put the applicant behind the wheel of a vehicle and observe his driving ability over a prescribed course.

Fleet safety administrators support two types of driving tests: one involving that kind of test—referred to as "driving range test"—which determines whether or not the driver is aware of the physical limitations of the vehicle; his ability to make starts, stops, turns; and various other maneuvers. The other type requires the applicant to drive through traffic wherein he is subjected to various kinds of traffic patterns. In both cases, an attempt should be made to standardize the testing procedure as much as possible.

It must be borne in mind, however, that this test is an attempt to make a determination as to how skillfully the applicant can handle equipment. Based upon available studies, it has no correlation to the accident experience that might be anticipated of the applicant.

The weight that is placed on the applicant's performance on these skill tests should depend on the extent of subsequent driver training. If no driver training is offered, the applicant's performance during the test may prove to be qualifying or disqualifying. If the training program is comprehensive, even a driver who shows below-average skill can gain the necessary skill for his job during the training program.

Ability to avoid accidents is the paramount criterion for judging driving performance. No matter how well qualified a driver may be in his other job requirements, repeated accidents can soon make him a bad investment. Even a "star salesman" can become a liability if he has too many accidents. Ability to avoid accidents is largely a result of the driver's natural ability, strengthened with training and conditioned by good supervision.

Ability to follow traffic regulations. Strict observance of traffic rules and regulations is important to good driving. No company can afford to keep drivers who repeatedly violate traffic rules and regulations. Even though company policy may require the driver to pay any fines himself,

104

his behavior as a law violator makes him a public relations liability. There is also a close correlation between repeated traffic violations and repeated accidents.

Ability to care for the vehicle. Drivers differ in their ability to conserve a vehicle. Fleets that assign the same vehicle to the same driver every day have found that some drivers get more miles between overhauls than do others. The smooth operator also consumes less fuel. When fleet operating costs are figured to the decimal point per mile of operation, ability to drive smoothly shows up as a substantial factor in fleet economics and a relevant measure of driving ability.

Ability to meet schedules. The fleet motor vehicle represents a capital investment whose purpose is to produce transportation service and resulting revenue. There is a time and distance dimension involved in such a service. The fleet dispatcher knows what he can reasonably expect in terms of production output per vehicle per day. The driver who dawdles at stops, is unduly slow in negotiating traffic, and who wastes time in other ways is not meeting his production schedule and is not getting maximum return on the company's investment. In city bus service, for example, failure to stay on schedule or to run ahead of schedule creates difficulties and "headaches" for other bus operators on the line and is a direct factor in producing accidents. It is obvious that schedules must be carefully drawn up with safety and traffic conditions in mind. After this is done, however, it is reasonable to consider ability to meet schedules as a factor in rating driving skill.

Avoid irritating the public. Most fleet vehicles are painted in distinctive colors and carry the company name. (See Appendix E.) Because of this, they are traveling billboards whose advertising value to the company, if duplicated in conventional advertising media, would require the expenditure of huge sums. But this advertising value can become a negative factor if the vehicle is operated in an unsafe manner. Speeding through residential areas, racing the engine at traffic stops to hurry pedestrians out of the way, unnecessary use of the horn, bulldozing through traffic and many other such discourteous actions on the part of the fleet driver can irritate, frighten, disturb, and otherwise alienate the public. Ability to drive a vehicle with courtesy and consideration for pedestrians and for other motorists is important.

Nondriving parts of the job. In many professional driving occupations—that involve such things as meter reading, appliance servicing, food delivering, and route selling—the nondriving part of the job is usually more time-consuming. The man must be able to do his nondriving job well, because if he feels insecure or nervous about it, it will be reflected in unsafe driving. This situation is covered in detail in Chapter 15, "The Sales Fleet."

Ability to find satisfaction in the job. If a man is not satisfied with his job, his dissatisfaction will result in poor performance and sooner or later he will quit (if he is not discharged first).

The cost of recruiting, selecting, and hiring a man is conservatively estimated at $500. To properly orient and indoctrinate him in the organization will cost approximately another $500. This adds up to a total cost of $1,000 for filling a job vacancy. If the man does not prove satisfactory and quits or is discharged after a short time, this thousand dollar investment is lost. Added to this is the inevitable confusion and disruption created when it becomes necessary to terminate a driver's employment.

Selection is, therefore, a two-way street. Not only must the man be suited to the job, but his job must also be one that he finds suitable for his personal needs.

When considering an applicant for the driving job, both the minimum and maximum levels of his ability should be considered. An applicant with too high a level of ability for a given job can be just as frustrated by his work as one whose level of ability is too low. Be sure the higher educated applicant is really seeking a driving job.

The factor of an applicant's demands for personal status should be considered. Usually, there is an implicit level of status attached to any given job. Thought should be given to whether the driving job offers the applicant the degree of status that will satisfy him. If there are any indications that he would probably not be satisfied with the job, he is not a good employment risk.

Ability to get along with others. Hiring a new employee is an all-or-nothing proposition. One cannot hire merely skills and aptitudes; one hires the whole person, including whatever positive or negative personality traits he may have. Personality is considered here in terms of the candidate's likeableness and his ability to get along with others. One misfit can upset an entire employee group by spreading malicious gossip, creating cliques, turning one employee against another, and indulging in other mischief of this kind. Inability to get along harmoniously with other people can seriously detract from a worker's value as an employee even though he may rate high in all other job requirements.

It is, therefore, relevant to ask, "How well will he fit in with the other employees he will have to work with? Will he feel superior, or will

106

he accept his fellow workers as equals? Will they accept him? How well will he get along with customers and other members of the public he will meet as a representative of the company?"

PERSONAL TRAITS RELATED TO GOOD DRIVING

So far we have discussed in a general way the requirements of the driving job in terms of broad general abilities and aptitudes. We have answered the question "What kind of a person do we want and what

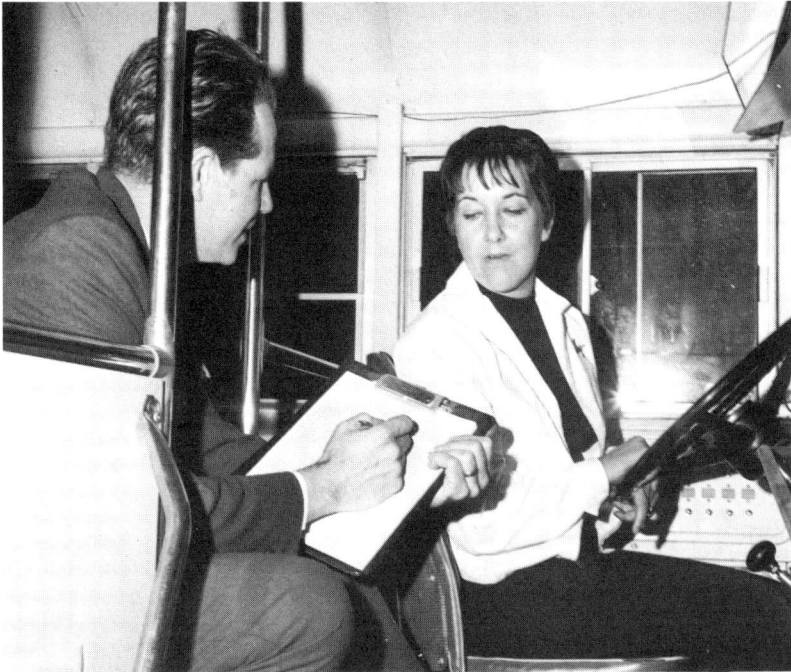

WOMEN, TOO, MAKE GOOD DRIVERS. Skillful selection, training, and supervision makes the big difference. Only by riding with a driver can a supervisor observe driving habits and responses to different traffic situations.

must he be able to do?" But how do we know when we have such a person? How does one go about measuring a man at the employment office? There are certain facts about the individual job applicant that should be determined during the selection procedure. What these facts

107

are, how they can be obtained, and their degree of relevance to the driving job are now described:

Age. Drivers under the age of 25 have an abnormally high accident rate. This is probably due to their inexperience and immaturity, and it makes them poor risks from the standpoint of safe driving.

After 25, however, age does not seem to affect safe driving ability until age 65, after which the accident rate climbs.

For many years, the age range for new drivers in many motor transportation fleets has been between 25 and 35. The upper limit of 35 is probably an arbitrary one and could, with equal justification, be placed at 55 without effect on the learning ability or accident potential of the applicant. No purpose is served by arbitrarily limiting the group from which drivers can be recruited.

The age of automation will displace many workers and these will have to be retrained in other skills. Some of these may very well make good employees in the motor transport industry.

Studies have shown that older workers are as efficient as younger ones, are safer workers, are less prone to job-hop, have lower rates of tardiness and absenteeism, and often make more acceptable employees than younger ones. Still, health considerations are a valid reason for rejecting older drivers.

Sex. Driving is not an exclusively male occupation. Women have been employed successfully as city bus operators, school bus operators, taxi-cab drivers, and even truck drivers. No basis exists for discriminating against women in motor vehicle-driving jobs on the basis of comparative accident rates between the two sexes. Women represent a good source of employee recruitment for certain driving jobs.

Physical traits. Short men may have difficulty in manipulating the controls of certain motor vehicles. Extremely tall or obese persons may have difficulty in fitting into the cab. Minimum height and maximum weight limitations, based on the physical characteristics of the driving compartment of the vehicle to be operated, should therefore be set.

Intelligence. A number of good "paper-and-pencil tests" exist for measuring intelligence. There appears to be no correlation, unfortunately, between what the tests measure and satisfactory performance as a driver—except at the extremely low or high ends.

It is known that highly intelligent drivers are likely to have accidents—not because they can't learn to drive, but because their minds are so active they can't "stay tuned" to the routine business of driving a vehicle. Personal mental distraction can be more dangerous than external physical distraction. (There's a good example of this in Chapter 16, "The Utility Fleet.")

Persons with extremely low mental capacities have less reasoning ability; they may, therefore, be difficult to supervise and could make poor witnesses in accident cases.

Education. The amount of formal education of the applicant is usually not detrimental to his safe driving abilities. It may, however, have a bearing on the nondriving part of his job, or his ability to adjust to his job. This is especially true if he has difficulty in reading or writing. A person who cannot read well has a hard time understanding the many written communications upon which management depends—memos, rule books, bulletins, training booklets, and safety materials.

In the present labor market, a high school education (or equivalent) is sufficient, especially in line-haul work.

Completion of a high school driver education course is of value to a professional driver. Some employers surmise that only those who are predisposed to drive safely ever take such a course. If this be so, then just the fact that a person took such a course is a favorable indicator of his attitude toward safe driving. Another reasonable inference is that the applicant learned correct driving habits and attitudes when he first started to drive and, because of this, these made a lasting impression.

If the applicant has been trained by previous employers, find out how extensive it was. Ask specific questions about course content in order to find out how much the applicant remembers. This also shows his degree of interest in the fine points of safe driving.

Marital status. One does not just hire part of a man. One hires his whole personality. Because his family (especially his wife) can influence his on-the-job performance, a man's marital status can be critical to satisfactory job achievement.

Some firms will not hire single men. They believe that married men are more settled and dependable because they must earn a steady income to support their dependents. The single man, under this assumption, is more independent and less likely to be concerned if he loses his job because of substandard performance. This may mean that he is not as strongly motivated to make good as is the married man.

On the other hand, a married man with domestic troubles can be an accident repeater during periods of severe emotional stress. The working conditions of many driving jobs—such as extended absences from home—can strain a driver's home life. Unless the applicant's wife understands and accepts the working conditions of her husband's job, she may not adapt to them and thus become dissatisfied. If this happens, she may cause him to have accidents or change his job.

Employment in intercity bus and truck fleets often involves being out of town for several days at a time, or working nights and weekends. For this reason, such fleets are careful to ascertain the wife's attitude toward such working conditions before finally hiring the applicant.

Some personnel officers call at the driver's home to discuss the proposed job with the applicant and his wife to make sure that the wife understands and will accede to the conditions under which her husband will have to work if he is hired.

Social adjustment. Another important factor in predicting a man's ability to drive safely is the overall success he has had in adjusting to the responsibilities of adult life. A man often drives as he lives. If he has a record of motor vehicle accidents, of arrests for traffic violations, arrests for other crimes or misdemeanors, a succession of jobs, moved his place of residence frequently, a poor record of paying his bills, and a record of divorces, separations, or other marital discords, evidently he has not been able to make a satisfactory adjustment to authority, social norms, and the responsibilities of adult life.

In appraising this vital area of the applicant's background, the total picture or pattern of his life should be taken into consideration. It should be remembered that one robin does not make a summer. No one's life runs smoothly all of the time and the stresses of modern living take their toll in various ways.

The profile of the good driver, the accident-free driver, is that of a man who has been successful in conforming to expected patterns of behavior, is conservative in his outlook and views, and who has achieved a high degree of stability in his living habits.

The Selection Procedure

As stated previously, the hiring of a new driver is an important decision. Because it must be done carefully and thoroughly, the fleet manager should be willing to allocate as much time and manpower to this activity as is required. Normally it should take a week to ten days and sometimes two weeks between the time the applicant applies for a job and the time he is actually hired.

The selection procedure is designed to uncover facts and opinions about the applicant on which an inference can be made as to his suitability for employment. This data will come from a number of sources: what the applicant says about himself, what others who have known him in the past think about him, and what objective tests and medical examinations reveal about him. Since the gathering of such information involves an expenditure of time and money, the procedure should be organized into a successive hurdle sequence designed to discover as quickly as possible those applicants who do not meet the job requirements and who, therefore, can be eliminated from consideration without further processing.

While each fleet must find its own best sequence based on the number of techniques used in the selection procedure and the volume of hiring, the following steps are suggested:

STEP 1—RECRUITING

It should be remembered that applicants can only be selected from the group that applies for jobs. If only poorly qualified applicants apply for work, the most elaborate selection procedure, though selecting the best of that group, will still yield a relatively poor employee. The selection procedure must therefore begin by attracting an adequate number of well-qualified persons to apply for employment.

An excellent source of applicants is friends and acquaintances of present employees. Many companies have established a policy which prohibits the employment of relatives of present employees. Objections raised on this issue, however, do not prevail in the employment of friends and acquaintances of present employees. If it is known to employees that their friends will receive due consideration, they will tend to refer them to the company for employment. They will try to send better-qualified ones because this is a reflection on themselves.

Establish contacts with other fleet supervisors. This can be another dependable source of applicants.

The State Employment Service of the U.S. Department of Labor provides services which a personnel administrator can use. If he places specific orders for personnel and provides specific job requirements, the Employment Service will screen applicants and refer those persons who possess the desired qualifications. Some fleet supervisors report this to be a poor source of driver personnel, unfortunately.

It is also considered a good practice to establish a working relationship with private employment agencies in cities where hiring is done. Unlike the State Employment Service, which is a tax-supported agency, there is a fee involved with private agencies. The fee, for services rendered, is the sole support of the private agency; experience, however, has shown that reputable service is well worth the fee involved.

PRELIMINARY APPLICATION FORM

XYZ COMPANY

We are pleased to have you apply for the _____ position. A list of the minimum qualifications for this job is given below. Please read it carefully. Check the blank space to the right of each qualification if you believe you meet it.

1. Must have high school education or equivalent. _____
2. Must have _____ vision with (without) correction. _____
3. Must be in excellent physical condition. (No organic disease or heart trouble, high blood pressure, etc. No missing extremities, including toes and fingers.) _____
4. Must be between _____ and _____ (feet-inches) tall, in stocking feet.
5. Must be of good moral character. _____
6. Must have good credit rating. _____
7. Have no court record (or record as juvenile delinquent). _____
8. Must not be a habitual traffic law violator. _____
9. Must not be a habitual user of alcohol or drugs. _____
10. Must have no serious domestic problems. _____
11. Must have (or be qualified to obtain) a chauffeur's license. _____

Now read the "release" statement that follows. This certifies your statements and gives us permission to refer to your previous employers and others who may be familiar with your background. Please read this statement carefully and then sign your name in the space provided.

RELEASE

I hereby certify the above information is correct, and is given of my own free will and accord. I also certify that I have not knowingly withheld any information which might reflect upon my fitness as a candidate for the position for which I am applying. I understand that giving false information, or withholding pertinent information can disqualify me for this position. I also understand that if I am employed because I gave false information, this will serve as just cause for my removal from the job at any time that it might be revealed that the false information was given.

I understand that the XYZ Company, or an agency it may designate, will investigate my background and experience by contacting my references, former employers, and others who may be able to verify my qualifications or provide additional background.

This is my express permission for such an investigation to be made. For the consideration shown me in accepting my application, I hereby release the XYZ Company, any agency it may designate, and persons the XYZ Company or it agency may contact in the course of this investigation from any liability that may result from the conduct of such investigation and from the result of the investigation itself.

_____
(Signature)

Date: _____.
Witness: _____.

[Additional space can be given for listing job history and references.]

PRELIMINARY APPLICATION FORM is designed to eliminate applicants who obviously could not qualify. Applicants who cannot meet minimum fleet qualifications should be thanked for applying, then dismissed. First page of a typical form is shown at left; second page, above. Be sure to check applicable regulations as to what minimum vision must be with and without correction (line 2).

Trade schools, vocational schools, discharge centers of the armed services, and other similar places provide excellent sources of recruitment.

STEP 2—PRELIMINARY APPLICATION

Use a preliminary application form (such as shown in the accompanying example) to eliminate those who obviously can't qualify. Every fleet should set minimum qualifications. Applicants who do not meet them can be thanked for applying, and then tactfully dismissed.

Part 391 of the Bureau of Motor Carrier Safety Regulations establishes mandatory qualifications. Part 391 gives the carrier the right to set additional qualifications, based on his experience or general industry experience.

Applicants who meet these minimum standards should now be given a formal application.

STEP 3—APPLICATION FORM

The employee application form should be highly individualized, carefully drawn up, and frequently revised to reflect only those facts that the hiring officer deems pertinent to the driving job in his particular company. There is no need to have such forms printed; they can be typewritten and duplicated. In fact, a typed form is probably preferable to a printed form because a hiring officer is tempted to use a printed form as long as the supply lasts and this may be many years after it has become outdated.

Since it is a form that just one company will use for hiring its drivers, it should reflect the need of the company. The hiring officer should know the kinds of information he can elicit in writing from the job applicant that will be relevant to his potential ability to satisfactorily perform the given job.

With employee application forms there is the temptation to use a form designed for someone else or, if constructing one's own, to clutter it with all sorts of questions which are irrelevant to the purpose of the form. The danger of using a form constructed for someone else is that it may not give the hiring officer the information he wants and often contains some questions or blanks asking for information that he does not need and cannot use. Using someone else's employee application form is a little like using someone else's prescription for eye glasses—it may work, but why take the chance.

In constructing one's own form, there is a danger of cribbing from other job application forms and ending up with a form that will elicit

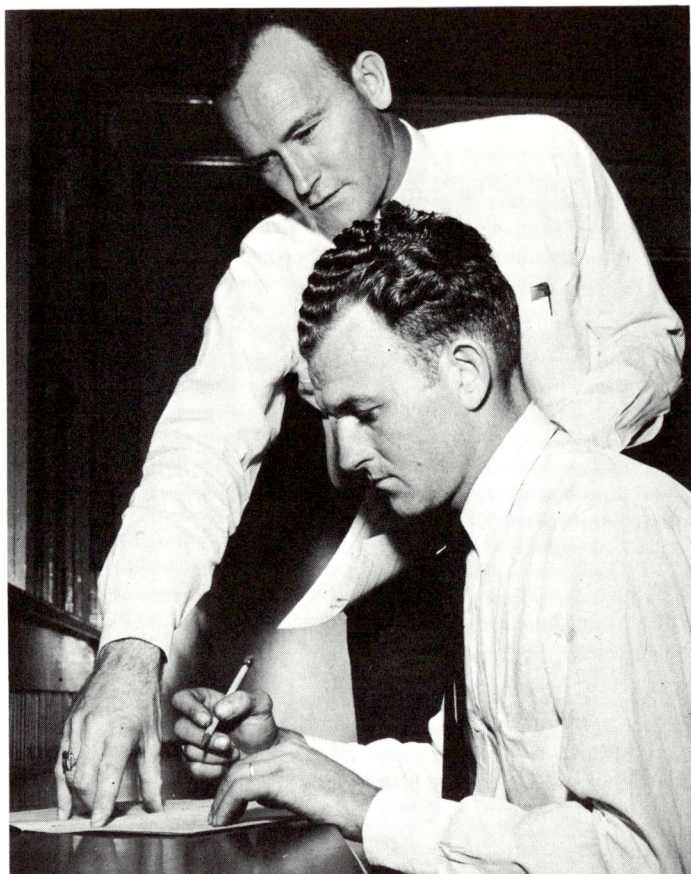

APPLICATION FORM SHOULD REFLECT COMPANY NEEDS.
Make sure each question is justified, not just one that "sounds good."

such a wide variety of information as to distract the hiring officer from his main objective—to appraise the applicant's qualifications in terms of company job demands. For example, such questions as: "How many brothers and sisters did you have?" or "Were you an only child?" or "In what order were you born in your family?" may be significant to a trained psychiatrist grappling with an emotional problem of the applicant; such questions do not give information the average hiring officer can use in determining the applicant's suitability for a driving job.

No questions or blanks should be permitted on the form unless they are justified. The hiring officer must apply this test to each item:

a. Why do I need this information?
b. Am I likely to get a correct and honest answer from the applicant?
c. From the information likely to be given, what will I be able to infer as to the applicant's potential ability to satisfactorily perform the job for which he is being considered?

If the hiring officer is reluctant or timid about constructing his own employee application form, it may be because he does not fully realize his responsibility in the selection procedure. On the other hand, if he has studied the needs of the job and informed himself on the human qualifications he is looking for in job applicants, he should not be satisfied with any form other than one he has constructed himself.

There may be certain background information about the applicant that will be useful to the personnel department only should the applicant survive the selection process and end up on the payroll. These details can be left off the application form, if desired. Later, if the man is hired, he can provide this information to the personnel office on a special form designed for this purpose.

Completed application forms should be carefully studied by the hiring officer to determine applicants who appear most promising. He should then decide which ones to reject and which to call in for the next step in the selection procedure. Those who are rejected deserve to be notified promptly. Any applicable provisions of the Fair Employment Practices Act should be complied with.

STEP 4—PSYCHOLOGICAL TESTING

Should the fleet hiring officer utilize psychological tests in the selection procedure? The answer to this depends on a number of factors. Certainly, he can do without psychological tests. But properly used and interpreted, these tests can make a valuable contribution to the efficiency of the selection procedure.

It is very important to understand what tests can and cannot do. Tests can never replace the other employment techniques, such as the application form, interview, reference checks, and investigations. Tests cannot isolate the accident repeater. They can only supplement

115

information developed in the other parts of the selection procedure.

Granted that psychological tests can prove helpful in selecting better drivers, the important question is "What tests should be used?" Just as the services of an architect are needed in planning and building an efficient and well-proportioned house, the assistance of a qualified personnel psychologist should be secured in setting up any psychological testing program. It should be remembered that tests are devices for obtaining samples of behavior under controlled conditions. To the extent that the sampled behavior is related to subsequent behavior on the job, predictions of probable success or failure can be made. To find tests that are related to successful driving for a particular fleet involves a kind of "fitting" process or experimental process that only a trained psychologist is capable of conducting.

Once a battery of tests has been selected, tested, and proved in a given situation, the routine administration and scoring of such tests can be entrusted to a personnel clerk of average intelligence. Interpretation, however, is another specialized function.

In the selection sequence, tests should be administered prior to the employment interview so that the interviewer has before him the test scores achieved by the applicant.

STEP 5—THE EMPLOYMENT INTERVIEW

The employment interview between applicant and hiring officer is normally the most decisive step in the selection procedure. While not the final step, it is the one at which a provisional decision is made as to whether the applicant, barring any disqualifying information developed subsequently, should be hired or not.

Prior to the interview, the hiring officer will have looked over the information on the employment application form and will have noted and considered any test scores achieved by the applicant in the testing program. He will try to form a mental image of the applicant's total qualifications in terms of the job demands. He will conjecture what the applicant's strong and weak points might be and what lines of questioning to pursue in the interview to verify or probe into the applicant's background.

The setting for the interview should provide complete privacy. No other person should be in the room but the interviewer and the applicant. The room should be quiet. It should be arranged beforehand that the interview proceed to conclusion without distraction. The interviewer's manner should be friendly and informal.

116

It should be remembered that an interview is a conversation with a purpose. The interview should develop the following information about the applicant:

a. Verify or expand on information shown on the application blank.
b. Enable the interviewer to form a judgment about the applicant's personality, appearance, attitude toward employment, and attitude toward safe driving.
c. Give the applicant an idea of what the job involves and what working for the company would be like.

It is well for the interviewer to keep in mind that the employment interview has many weaknesses as an objective device for measuring the potential capabilities of an applicant. Studies have shown that interviewers are frequently influenced by their prejudices and biases for or against an applicant. Equally competent interviewers frequently disagree in their appraisal of the same applicant. The interview often results in inaccurate information about the applicant.

In spite of its weaknesses, the interview remains the primary employee selection tool. All other selection procedures are designed merely to develop information on which the interviewer can make a final judgment as to the suitability of the applicant for the job. In the final analysis, this has to be a personal judgment. No computer or objective-scoring mechanism has yet been developed to perform this task.

The interviewer should, therefore, approach his task with humility. He should strive to remain completely objective in his appraisal of the applicant's abilities, and should keep his mind focused on the requirements of the job. He is not a politician handing out patronage jobs to his friends. He is more like a purchasing agent bent on finding quality raw material for the enterprise.

The interview is a complex social encounter. The technique itself has produced extensive literature. The conscientious personnel officer will avail himself of all the literature he can find on the subject, study it, and strive to put it into practice. For successful interviewing is a difficult art and proficiency can be attained only through conscious study and practice.

After interviews have been completed, the hiring officer makes a further judgment of candidates. Those who have been rejected as a result of the interview should be notified. For those who have survived the interview, the next step in the selection procedure should be undertaken, that of checking references.

117

STEP 6—CHECKING REFERENCES

Thus far in the selection procedure, the hiring officer has pretty much relied on what the applicant has said about himself and what objective tests have revealed. Most of what the applicant has said about himself can be taken at face value; but it is only human that he would exaggerate his good points and minimize or conceal anything in his background that would reflect unfavorably on his chances of getting a job.

It is, therefore, very important to consult other persons who have known the applicant in the past and who can provide details about his professional abilities and general character.

The most important source of this information is previous employers. These can provide information as to length of employment, type of work performed, number of accidents, and general character. The applicant should be asked to provide names and addresses of his past three employers or of his previous employer if he was employed for a period of ten years or more. (Some fleet supervisors say five years.)

There are three methods of checking with past employers; the telephone check, the form letter, and the personal visit.

• The telephone check is usually conducted by a personnel clerk using a printed form which serves as a checklist to make sure all pertinent information is requested and also as a form on which to record the information. The advantage of this method of checking references is that it is fast. The disadvantage is that previous employers may be reluctant to relay unfavorable information over the telephone, although he'll probably give information verbally that he would not put in writing. To double-check a caller, some companies will ask for a phone number and only call back after checking it. (An example of an "Employment Inquiry" checklist is shown on the next page.)

• Checking references by correspondence is perhaps the most frequently used method—usually a printed form and a stamped return envelope is used. The advantage of this method is that it is a routine clerical operation that results in a written report from the previous employer. The disadvantage is that the previous employer may be reluctant to make any signed report about a former employee, especially if it contains derogatory information. Another disadvantage is that letters are slow. (An example of the form letter reference check is at the right.)

• A personal visit to the previous employer to discuss the past work history of the applicant is perhaps the most reliable method. Previous employers will discuss an applicant much more frankly in a personal

118

EMPLOYMENT INQUIRY
XYZ COMPANY

Name of Applicant: _____.

Previous Employer: _____.

Former Supervisor: _____. Telephone: _____.

Mr. _____ has applied for employment with our firm. May we please confidentially verify some of the information he has given us?

1. When did he work for your company? From _____ to _____.

2. What type of work did he do? _____.

3. Did he have any lost-time injuries while on the job? ☐ Yes ☐ No. How many? _____.

4. Was he involved in any traffic accidents? ☐ Yes ☐ No. How many? _____ Were any considered preventable? _____.

5. Was he able to get along well with supervisors? _____.

6. Was he considered to be trustworthy? _____. Honest? _____. Punctual? _____. Steady? _____.

7. Did he have any garnishments? _____ Or troubles with creditors? _____. Explain please: _____.

8. Why did he leave your company? _____.

9. Is he eligible for rehire? ☐ Yes ☐ No. If not, why not? _____
_____.

10. COMMENT: _____
_____.

Date of Inquiry _____. By _____.

EMPLOYMENT INQUIRY FORM gives easy-to-use and easy-to-file checklist.

REQUEST FOR EMPLOYMENT INFORMATION
XYZ COMPANY

TO: ⌐   ⌐

RE: _____

S.S. No. _____

States he (she) was employed by you from:

_____ , 19 ____ TO _____ , 19 ____

Working in the capacity of: _____

Has applied for the position of: _____

                                └

The above-mentioned person has made application with us for employment and has authorized the release of any information you may have in regard to his past employment record and character. You will greatly assist us in estimating the applicant's qualifications for work if you will furnish the information requested below. Action of this case is pending. Therefore, we solicit your cooperation in completing and returning this questionnaire at your earliest convenience. A duplicate copy of this request is enclosed for your files. Also a self-addressed return envelope is enclosed for your convenience in returning this information. We will be happy to return this courtesy at any time.

Very truly yours,
XYZ Company
by:

RELEASE: Having made application for employment with XYZ Company, and desiring them to be informed as to my previous record and character, I hereby authorize them to investigate my past record and to ascertain any and all information which may concern my record and character, whether same is of record or not, and release my present and past employers, references, and all persons whatsoever from any damage because of furnishing said information.

Signature _____

Date _____

Witness: _____

1. How long have you known the applicant _____

2. Is applicant related to you? YES ( ) NO ( ) If yes, how? _____

3. Between what dates employed by you. _____

4. What was applicant's position or job? _____

5. Why did applicant leave your service? _____

6. If Company Policy permitted, would you re-hire? YES ( ) NO ( ) If not, please explain: _____

120

7. Has applicant been known to drink intoxicating beverages to excess? YES ( ) NO ( )

8. Did applicant have any personal trouble which interfered with his work? YES ( ) NO ( )

9. Is applicant considered to be:

Courteous?_____YES ( ) NO ( )   Financially responsible?_____YES ( ) NO ( )   Nervous?_____YES ( ) NO ( )

Of good habits?_____YES ( ) NO ( )   Honest?_____YES ( ) NO ( )   Entitled to full confidence and trust?_____YES ( ) NO ( )

10. Did applicant operate a motor vehicle while in your employ? YES ( ) NO ( ) If yes, what types? _____

11. Was applicant involved in any accidents while in your employ? YES ( ) NO ( ) How many? _____ Give dates: _____

(Attach accident reports if available.)

12. Please check the most applicable rating:

QUALIFICATIONS	EXCELLENT	GOOD	FAIR	POOR
Quality of Work				
Quantity of Work				
Dependability				
Cooperation With Others				
General Ability				
Character				
Initiative				
General Desirability				

NEED SUPERVISION?

Seldom............( )
Occasionally.......( )
Frequently........( )
Constantly........( )

AVERAGE MONTHLY ABSENCE

Less than 1 day......( )
2 to 4 days..........( )
Over 4 days..........( )

13. Would you recommend that we employ this person for this position? YES ( ) NO ( )

REMARKS: _____

DATE: _____   SIGNATURE: _____

TITLE: _____

ONE COPY TO BE RETAINED BY COMPANY FURNISHING THE ABOVE INFORMATION.

121

interview than they would by other methods. The disadvantages are that it is costly and time consuming, and is almost impossible when hiring a large number of drivers.

Professional agencies exist which will conduct personnel investigations for a fee. Such investigations usually include checking with the police department, credit agencies, and neighbors and acquaintances of the person investigated.

Check the applicant's State Department of Motor Vehicle Registration. Also request your Secretary of State's office to check the applicant's record at the National Driver Register Service. (This is a national service available only through state offices.)

To guard against any legal liability resulting from personnel investigation activities, all applicants should first sign a release which contains the statement:

"I hereby release the _____ company or any agency it may designate, or any persons the _____ company or agency may contact in the course of its investigation, from any liability which may result from the conduct of such investigation or from the result of the investigation."

If as a result of all these investigations, no disqualifications have turned up, the applicant should be called in for a physical exam.

STEP 7—PHYSICAL EXAMINATION

Motor carrier safety regulations for bus and truck operators (a) require a physical examination for all new drivers and (b) provide that motor carriers must have on file a certificate showing each new driver to be physically qualified. These regulations also require that the driver carry on his person evidence of such physical fitness.

All applicants for driver positions should be examined by a qualified physician as a part of the employment procedure.

The Bureau of Motor Carrier Safety has set minimum requirements which could well be adopted by fleet operators as a part of their minimum standards:

a. Mental and physical condition.
1. No loss of foot, leg, hand, or arm.
2. No mental, nervous, organic, or functional disease, likely to interfere with safe driving.
3. No loss of fingers, impairment of use of foot, leg, fingers, hand or arm, or other structural defect or limitation, likely to interfere with safe driving.

CHECKING EYESIGHT is an important part of the physical examination.

b. Eyesight. Visual acuity of at least 20/40 (Snellen) in each eye either without lenses or by correction with lenses, form field of vision in the horizontal meridian shall not be less than a total of 140 degrees; ability to distinguish colors red, green, and amber; drivers requiring correction by lenses shall wear properly prescribed lenses at all times when driving.

c. Hearing. Hearing shall be adequate in the better ear, for conversational tones, without a hearing aid.

d. Liquor, narcotics, and drugs. Shall not be addicted to the use of narcotics or habit-forming drugs, or the excessive use of alcoholic beverages or liquors.

123

As previously mentioned, these are minimum standards and most fleet operators establish physical requirements which are much more selective than the ones set out above.

A physician selected to conduct the physical examination should be familiar with the requirements of the job for which the applicant is being considered. In larger cities, some physicians specialize in industrial practice and, therefore, are conversant with the DOT regulations and requirements, as well as the attitude of state agencies who administer workmen's compensation laws. Such physicians can render valuable assistance to motor carriers in establishing standards, conducting examinations, handling workmen's compensation cases, and maintaining the physical well-being of all drivers.

An example of this is given by the American Medical Association's Committee on Medical Aspects of Automobile Injuries and Deaths. This Committee has published *Medical Guide for Physicians in Determining Fitness to Drive a Motor Vehicle,* a brochure which covers all aspects of the physician's role in ascertaining physical, mental, emotional, or physiological impairments as they relate to safe driving.

The next step is to conduct the acceptance interview.

STEP 8—ACCEPTANCE INTERVIEW

If the applicant passes the physical examination, he should be called in and told that he is either hired or being placed on a waiting list. This acceptance interview should reinforce the applicant's enthusiasm for the job. It is important that he be made to feel that, although company employment standards are rigorous, he has attributes the company sincerely wants. He should be welcomed to the company as a valued new employee. He should be given further orientation about the company and told what training he will receive, and when and where to report. His wages and working conditions should be finalized at this time.

Legal and Social Restrictions

The motor transportation fleet is a constructive social and economic force in the community in which it operates not only because of the transportation service it renders, but also because of the jobs it provides. Placing a man on the payroll, therefore, has social and economic significance not only to the man hired, but to the fleet and to the community.

In this context, the employer today is no longer as free as he once was to hire whomever he pleases. Laws in many areas now forbid

124

discriminating against job applicants on the basis of race, color, creed, or sex. Several states now prohibit discrimination against an applicant on the basis of age and this restriction may soon spread to more states. There is also mounting organized moral pressure on the employer to hire the handicapped. Society often takes the view that if the employer wishes to avail himself of the local labor market, he must do so without caprice but with due regard for every able man's right to fair consideration for a job.

These are not unreasonable restrictions. They should certainly not —in any way—force the employer to hire the unqualified. It is no favor to an applicant to hire him for a position for which he is not qualified and in which he will be a source of accidents and unproductive work. The hiring officer has a moral obligation to the applicant, to the company, and to the community to perform his job well. He alone knows the demands of the job and the qualifications required of the applicant. His decision should always represent a choice that is beneficial to the applicant and to the fleet. Such a decision will automatically benefit the community.

7

Driver training

The most important ingredient of efficient and profitable transportation service is safe-driving skill. A $20,000 diesel tractor is a frozen asset until a driver gets behind the wheel, starts the engine, and puts the vehicle to work.

The degree of skill with which this vehicle is maintained, operated, and managed will determine how much and what quality service it will provide, how long the vehicle will last, and the number of traffic accidents in which it will be involved. Management must, then, set high standards and take great pains to see that drivers possess a high degree of safe-driving skill.

The selection program described in the previous chapter should provide men capable of meeting management's standard. A good training program will bring men's skills to this level, so that good supervision (discussed in subsequent chapters) can further improve it.

HOW MUCH TRAINING IS NECESSARY?

To what extent is training related to safe driving? Is not the operation of a motor vehicle a fairly common skill? No, it isn't. Safety experts have long known that safe driving ability is far from being a simple skill. It requires the ability to make traffic decisions quickly. Although good driving is as vital to our well-being as is good English, it is plagued—like English—by a take-it-for-granted attitude on the part of most drivers. This is why driving skill should be acquired through planned training instead of being picked up haphazardly.

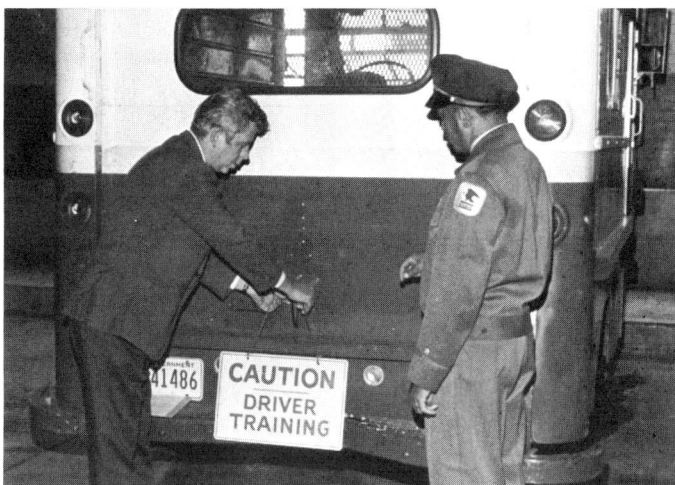

The professional driver's skill has an added economic dimension. Regardless of his former training, a driver must meet his company's standard of safe driving. Previous training quality cannot be taken for granted. The only sure way to assure a high degree of driving skill is to train each new man. Training will provide the driver with the knowledge needed to do the job, the skill necessary to do it properly, and an appreciation for the importance of the job and the necessity of doing it safely.

BENEFITS OF TRAINING

Although training costs money, time, and effort, management can expect to obtain the following benefits from it:

1. Reduced number or complete elimination of accidents. The trained driver will be a safer driver because he will know how to be safe and what situations to avoid.

2. Reduced maintenance costs. The driver who knows the mechanical limitations of his vehicle and develops a philosophy of vehicle conservation will develop smooth operating habits, will take better care of his vehicle, and will cooperate more fully with the maintenance department.

3. Reduced absenteeism and labor turnover. Training develops an understanding of both job and fleet problems which helps the driver gain job satisfaction.

4. Reduced supervisory burden. Training establishes a standard of

127

performance and a basis for effective corrective action by supervision when needed. The trained driver usually requires less supervision because he understands these standards clearly and knows how to meet them without continued reminders from his supervisor.

5. Improved public relations. The driver represents the company in frequent daily contacts with customers and other users of the highway. His good training is obvious and reflects credit not only on the driver but also his company.

Development of a Training Program

Because there are many different approaches to training, the detailed development of the fleet training program is highly individualized. Factors to be considered include the philosophy of fleet management, personalities involved in driver training, the function of the fleet, the time allotted to training, and labor union relations.

Developing a training program is much like writing a speech. Each person must write his own, but can use material from many sources. The program must cover the subject thoroughly and interestingly. Since it will be presented over and over as new drivers are hired, it must be constantly revised in terms of audience reaction, in terms of trainee success on the job, and in terms of the changing needs of the fleet.

The following ideas should help build a good driver-training program.

WHEN TO TEACH

Training should be thought of as a process of personal development that begins when the driver is hired and continues until he retires. The most effective time for extensive, systematic training is right after the driver has been hired and before he is assigned to a vehicle.

The amount of time devoted to initial training will depend on the selection program, the type of man that is hired, his background, and the amount of usable training and experience he brings to the job.

HOW LONG TO TEACH

To indicate the training time that may be necessary in various areas of driver training, note the following:

- High school driver education authorities recommend that teenagers, who presumably have never operated a motor vehicle before, be given 90 hours of instruction—six or eight hours in actual driving, the rest in the classroom.
- The professional Truck Driver Training School at North Carolina State

College gives a four-week, full-time training course involving both classroom and behind-the-wheel training. Graduates are employed as truck drivers for common carrier truck fleets.

• The National Safety Council's Defensive Driving Course, used by many firms to polish their drivers' abilities, requires four 2-hour sessions.

• A large intercity bus company gives new operators 14 days of classroom training, followed by five days on-the-road training.

• The new-driver training program for a large progressive taxicab fleet lasts two days—all classroom instruction.

The only practical gauge for determining initial training time is that it should be adequate to bring the knowledge and skill of the new driver up to that necessary to perform his job properly. It is false economy to skimp on a training program.

Refresher training is often needed. This usually consists of one or two days of classroom instruction in which initial training material is reviewed or new material (designed to familiarize drivers with new equipment or new operating problems) is presented. Refresher training is often given annually or as needed.

A special type of refresher training is presented by a large city bus company 90 days after a new operator has finished his initial training. The theory is that during the initial training, trainees accept material pretty much without question because many of them have had no actual experience driving a bus. After 90 days on the job, however, they have faced many situations not fully covered before and now have many questions. This refresher course lasts one day and is devoted mainly to discussion periods.

Remedial training is yet another kind provided for all drivers who have had a certain number of accidents. Best results occur when course content is related to the type of accidents the repeaters have been having and the discussion technique is used. One technique is to describe an accident that one member of the class has had and have the other members discuss how it could have been prevented in this way, all learn a lesson from it. Remedial training has been successful in improving the performance of accident repeaters and is well worth the effort.

Education should be continuous and should go on day after day to provide the driver with a continuous exposure to safety information and ideas. This type of education utilizes safety posters, dash cards, bulletin boards, safety booklets, and driver letters, in addition to classwork.

SPECIAL TRAINING ROOMS can be located in buildings . . .

WHERE TO TEACH

The most effective training is done in a *specially designed training room* —something every fleet should have. If a separate room is not feasible, then a place should be found that can be adapted. The training room should be sound-proof, well lighted, and ventilated. It should be equipped with tables and comfortable chairs, because if trainees are not comfortable, the environment will not be conducive to learning and a good deal of training effort will be wasted.

The training room should be equipped with a blackboard, a magnetic board for showing traffic situations and model vehicles (these can be 2- by 6-inch slightly pointed ¼-in. boards, with two concealed magnets in them), and other aids to training. (A magnetic blackboard can serve both purposes. See photograph on page 151.)

Care taken in the layout, design, decoration, and equipment of the training room will pay off in terms of better-trained drivers. Also, the room can be used for training other employees, for committee meetings, and for management conferences. In fact, the training room can be a very important communications center for the entire organization.

130

. . . or in truck trailers or buses, such as this air conditioned unit.

Behind-the-wheel training is also important. Only by riding with the driver can the supervisor observe his driving habits and his responses to different traffic situations. The usual pattern is for the trainee to drive the vehicle over a prescribed course while the supervisor rides as observer. The supervisor refrains from pointing out errors until the completion of the test drive, at which time he discusses any driving errors observed and points out the correct method.

A special type of behind-the-wheel training is known as "commentary driving." Here the supervisor also rides with the driver, but the driver talks about what he sees in the traffic situation ahead and how he plans to adjust to it.

Such commentary could go something like this: "The speed limit sign says 20 miles per hour. I'm well under that speed. There is an unregulated intersection ahead. A blue station wagon is pulling into the intersection. I think it is going to stop. Now I see it isn't, so I'm reducing my speed. He is now clear of the intersection and I can resume speed. My turn is up ahead. I can see no vehicles following in my rear view mirror, but I am putting on my right turn signal anyway. I

131

BEHIND-THE-WHEEL TRAINING and . . .

am edging over to the curb lane, slowing down to make the turn. . . ."

Commentary driving allows the supervisor to gauge how much a driver notices in any traffic situation; it also teaches the driver how to use his eyes more effectively and take note of all the elements that enter into any driving situation.

Another place for driver training is on a closed test course in a vacant parking lot or driving range. Driving problems requiring close clearances and careful maneuvering are practiced. Because trainees are shown how to maneuver their vehicles between barrels, flags, wooden horses, and pavement marks, these sessions are sometimes referred to as skill drills. (See Appendix H.) Drivers should be permitted to practice on the test course until they become proficient.

Skill drills are also used as a basis for driving "roadeos" in which drivers match their skills.

The safety supervisor's office is another setting for training. It is especially effective when the safetyman and a driver discuss an accident in an attempt to determine whether it was preventable or not. This is an

132

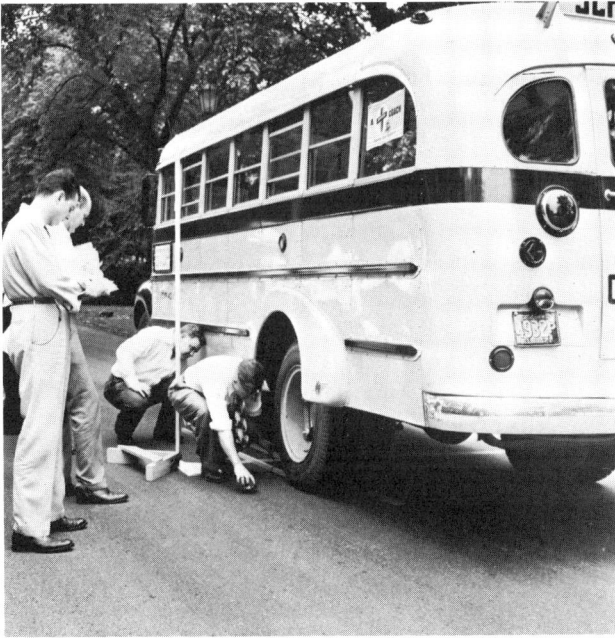

. . . skill drills are effective.

excellent training situation and should be regarded as such rather than as a disciplinary action.

Appendix C gives details of training meetings.

TRAINING IS CONTINUOUS

While there are special times and places for training, it can be effectively carried on at any time and in almost any place. The good trainer or supervisor will know when and where to take advantage of training opportunities as they arise.

What To Teach

The most important part of a training program is its subject matter. Because training is useful only when it fills a need the subject matter should cover what the driver needs to know to do his job well. Before assembling any training material, the instructor should first list the things he wants the trainee to learn and decide on their relative importance:

1. Vital subject matter—absolutely essential to success on the job;

2. Important subject matter—provides basic understanding of the job;

3. Helpful material—related to the job and gives a broader base of understanding on which to build performance; and

4. Incidental material—"nice to know" but not necessary to job performance.

It is not always easy to decide into which of these categories any piece of training material may fall. In making his final selection, each driver trainer should use his own judgment.

The amount of time devoted to each area will again be a matter of individual determination. The trainer will have to assemble the individual facts and details of subject matter from the abundant literature on the subject available to him.

Here is a guide to subject areas that should be covered. Much of this is covered in NSC's "Driver Improvement Program."

THE MOTOR VEHICLE ACCIDENT PROBLEM

Describe the national traffic accident problem: number of fatal accidents, and the number of property damage accidents and their cost. Show both direct and indirect cost of traffic accidents in the company. Show how rates are determined, and how company rates compare with those of other fleets and in the industry.

Describe cost of accidents to the driver himself: possible disablement or death, and loss of earnings should he be hospitalized or disabled for an extended period.

Describe how safe driving performance contributes to community safety: by reducing number of accidents, and setting a good example to other drivers. Show how it contributes to the health of the company: reducing costs, improving efficiency of service to customers, creating a favorable impression on the general public. Describe safe driving ability in terms of employee welfare: how it ensures job security and continuity of earning power.

Stress that the company has high standards of performance in everything it does, including safe driving. State that the company expects not just average safe driving performance but award-winning safety performance because it knows that this is possible. Read and discuss the company's written safety policy (see Chapter 2).

Be sure that the material provides the driver with a strong basic motivation to develop and maintain safe driving skill.

TRAFFIC REGULATIONS

Cover state and municipal traffic laws and ordinances. If the fleet operates in interstate commerce, Bureau of Motor Carrier Safety regulations that affect drivers should be taught.

Review traffic signs and correct use of hand and automatic signals.

Stress that the company—as well as the law—expects all drivers to observe all traffic rules. Explain the company's attitude should a driver be arrested or cited for a traffic violation.

This training unit should not only impart knowledge of traffic rules and regulations, but also develop understanding and respect for them.

CAUSES OF TRAFFIC ACCIDENTS

Develop the principal idea that motor vehicle accidents are not the result of chance, but are caused by factors, most of which can either be controlled or compensated for by the driver himself. These factors are the physical, mental, and emotional condition of the driver, the mechanical condition of his vehicle, and the acts of pedestrians and drivers of other motor vehicles. Discuss such other accident factors as road surface conditions, weather conditions, and light conditions.

Stress that the trainee is expected to be alert to all these accident-producing factors, to recognize how they can contribute to accidents, and to take the proper precautions in regard to each so as to avoid an accident. This lesson should build in the trainee a strong conviction that motor vehicle accidents are preventable and that, as a driver, he can do the most to prevent them.

PERSONAL TRAITS AFFECTING DRIVING

To build a renewed respect for the importance of good health habits to safe driving, describe how the physical, mental, and emotional well-being of a driver affects safe driving. Tell what the driver should do.

A number of psycho-physical testing devices are available to demonstrate how a trainee measures up in each trait so that, if need be, he can acquire compensating habits. For example, if the trainee has very narrow peripheral vision, he can compensate for it by forming the habit of moving his head from side to side to observe traffic conditions.

The trainee should be impressed with the importance of keeping himself in good physical condition, avoiding extreme fatigue, avoiding the use of drugs or medications that might adversely affect his driving ability, and keeping his mind free of worries and unnecessary distractions.

DEFENSIVE DRIVING

An entire unit of instruction should be devoted to one of the most important safe-driving concepts—that of defensive driving.

135

Defensive driving, essentially, requires both the desire and the ability of a driver to control the accident-producing situations he meets in order to avoid an accident. To practice defensive driving, a driver must acquire a proper attitude and refine certain components of his driving.

The defensive driving attitude is one that accepts the highest degree of responsibility for being on top of accident-producing situations and avoiding accidents, rather than passively surrendering to an adverse situation. It is a positive attitude; namely, that the driver can prevent accidents by taking the initiative.

But attitude alone is not enough. The defensive driver must implement it by his alertness, foresight, knowledge, judgment, and skill. All of these qualities lend themselves to development in the training program and can be further improved by experience.

Preventable concept. Closely allied to defensive driving are the terms "preventable" and "nonpreventable" used in describing an accident. These two terms measure the defensive driving skill exercised by the driver in a given accident. If he did everything he *reasonably* could have done to prevent the accident and it still happened, then the accident is graded "nonpreventable." If he failed to do so, then the accident is graded "preventable." The trainee must know the ground rules under which he will be judged, and how he can appeal an adverse decision.

For additional details, see the discussion in Chapter 4 under "The Post-Accident Interview." "Reportable accidents" are discussed in Chapter 17 under "National Fleet Safety Contest."

These two ideas (defensive driving and accident preventability) dovetail and thus make possible a third idea of equal importance to the safety program; a workable and enforceable standard of safe-driving performance: *the standard of safe driving performance is driving without a preventable accident.* This standard must be thoroughly understood by top management, by supervisors, and by drivers, if there is to be effective safety supervision.

These three ideas are sometimes difficult for drivers to comprehend at first. But they are so essential to the development of professional safe driving attitudes and skills, that time should be allotted to explain them clearly. Once the rules are understood, drivers will acquire a new respect for safe-driving ability, will be more receptive to safety information and help, and will develop a personal concern for their own safe-driving records.

TWO-VEHICLE COLLISION PREVENTION

Another unit of training should be devoted to demonstrating how two vehicles can collide from each of six positions, and what defensive measures apply in each situation.

Modern traffic offers problems of such variety and complexity that unless these situations are grouped, the training program could easily become an exhaustive list of impossible-to-remember "do's" and "don'ts."

Fortunately there are several ways to unify these problems to make the subject more manageable. One of these is the six-positions of the most frequent type of traffic accident—collision between two motor vehicles.

From the standpoint of *our* vehicle, there are only six positions that the *other* vehicle can take relative to ours from which both vehicles can collide: (1) it can be ahead of us, (2) behind us, (3) approaching us from an angle, (4) approaching from the opposite direction, (5) passing us, or (6) being the vehicle that we pass.

USING THE EYES IN DRIVING

Systematic seeing habits can detect accident-producing situations before they become critical. Make sure the driver: (1) aims high in steering, (2) gets the big picture, (3) keeps his eyes moving, (4) leaves himself an out, and (5) makes sure others see him. The system also incorporates various driving strategies to dispose of hazards before they become accident-producing situations. This is known as the Smith System.

BACKING ACCIDENT PREVENTION

Because another high frequency accident is due to backing, this subject belongs in the driver training program. Even though the severity of this type of accident is usually minor, the cumulative cost mounts up. Sometimes, a backing accident can have serious results.

Points to be taught in avoiding backing accidents are—(1) get out before moving and size up the situation, (2) back from the driver's side, (3) back slowly, (4) check both sides as you back, and (5) use a reliable person to guide you.

Drivers should also be taught that backing should be avoided whenever possible, that backing around corners or out of driveways or alleys is especially dangerous, and that—if there is a choice—backing out of traffic is safer than backing into traffic.

BRAKE DETONATOR DEVICE SHOWS STOPPING DIS-
TANCE. When vehicle is moving, instructor in cab with driver
pulls string (that runs over truck hood to the detonator mounted
on the bumper). This fires the first charge that marks pavement
with chalk and alerts driver to stop. When vehicle's brakes take
hold, second charge is automatically detonated. Distance between marks is the driver's "reaction distance." After vehicle
stops, instructor and driver dismount and measure the distances.
Distance of stopped vehicle from second chalk mark is "braking distance." Test proves dramatically that drivers cannot
"stop on a dime."

STOPPING DISTANCE DEMONSTRATION

The brake detonator is a device which will vividly show drivers the
distance it takes to stop their vehicle. Because most drivers firmly
believe it is a mark of driving skill to be able to stop their vehicle on a
dime, this misconception is hard to dispose of without convincing
proof. The brake detonator demonstrates this fact dramatically and
forcefully.

The device, equipped with two firing chambers for firing chalk

138

marks onto the pavement, is attached to the vehicle's front bumper. The first charge is fired by the instructor at his discretion when the vehicle has attained a predetermined speed. This makes a mark on the pavement and also signals the driver to apply his brakes and stop his vehicle in the shortest possible distance. The moment the brakes take hold, the second charge is fired and makes a second mark on the pavement. When finally the vehicle is stopped, the driver and his instructor get out and mark the point on the pavement that is even with the front bumper.

There are now three marks on the pavement: the first, the point where the instructor fired the first charge and signaled the driver to stop; the second, the point at which the vehicle's brakes began to take hold. The distance between these two marks—*the reaction distance*—is how far the vehicle traveled while the driver was responding to the signal and getting his foot on the brakes. The third mark is that made when the vehicle stopped.

The distance between the second and third marks—known as *the braking distance*—tells how far it took the brakes to stop the vehicle. The two measurements represent total stopping distance required in every stop a driver makes from that speed. Tests can be run at different speeds.

Sometimes all drivers can be tested. When time will not permit this, volunteers are selected while the rest of the training class observes. Even to observers, this demonstration of stopping distance convinces them that they cannot "stop on a dime."

This demonstration teaches drivers that they must follow a vehicle at a safe distance, be alert for sudden stops, and start braking as soon as they anticipate that they might have to stop.

THE DRIVER AND HIS VEHICLE

The driver should know the mechanical principles of the gasoline or diesel engine, the power transmission train, the braking system, the electrical system, and other components of his vehicle. Even drivers with many years of experience can profit from a review of these subjects. When new vehicles are added to the fleet, differences and new equipment should be reviewed with drivers. They should be familiar with the new vehicle's characteristics before they take it on a run.

Of course the driver is not expected to be a trained mechanic, but he should know enough about his vehicle to recognize and describe mechanical defects when they arise and to know how to avoid abusing his vehicle. He should be able to know when trouble is serious enough to warrant assistance.

This training unit should include practice drills in the step-by-step procedure to be followed in making a pretrip inspection and how inspections should be made en route. (See Chapter 13.)

BASIC DRIVING MANEUVERS

The basic driving maneuvers are starting the engine, shifting gears, starting and stopping the vehicle, backing, turning, and parking. The correct method must be mastered if driving is to be smooth, safe, and efficient. If the vehicle has several speeds forward, training should also cover double clutching when gearing up or down.

The instructor should demonstrate to each trainee the correct method of performing each of these tasks and then have the trainee do it himself. The instructor should correct any errors, make suggestions, and then allow the trainee to practice until he can perform it correctly and with ease.

The trainee must understand that he becomes skillful only when he can perform these maneuvers the right way *every* time.

DRIVING IN TRAFFIC

Allot time for the trainee to test drive the type of vehicle to which he will be assigned over a preselected course. The best time is near the end of the training program, after the trainee has had the benefit of classroom instruction and has been checked out on the basic driving maneuvers.

The test drive should be conducted under the supervision of a driver trainer and the route selected should include a variety of traffic situations: controlled and uncontrolled intersections, residential and congested areas, narrow streets and freeways, railroad crossings, and dock areas.

The same route should be used for each test drive so that the instructor can become familiar with the situations that cause the trainee the most trouble and best test his skill. This will also enable the instructor to better help the trainee and be more consistent in grading him.

The test drive builds the trainee's confidence in his ability to handle the vehicle properly and safely, and it lets the instructor observe the trainee under actual road conditions so that he can decide whether the trainee is sufficiently trained.

If the trainee passes the test, he may be assigned to a regular run, with or without an instructor. In bus operations, the new driver is often placed on a regular run with an experienced operator riding with him for several days as a final check on his competence, and to make sure he knows the routes.

Should the trainee fail the test, a decision must be made: provide additional training or practice, assign him to a nondriving job, or terminate his employment.

'BE PREPARED' IS GOOD ADVICE, providing driver can get free of the accident itself. Drivers should be trained in what to do to protect passengers and bystanders, freight and adjoining property. They should know how to summon help. Fortunately, all accidents are not as serious as this one. But an unskilled driver can compound the seriousness.

PROCEDURE IN CASE OF ACCIDENT

Although training is designed to keep drivers out of accidents, nevertheless they should be carefully taught the correct procedure to follow if they are involved in an accident with a company vehicle. The main considerations in such an event are: protect others at the scene of the accident, care for the injured, secure all pertinent details so that an accurate and complete accident report can be written, and return the vehicle to service as soon as possible.

Usually the fleet has developed a written procedure for drivers to follow when involved in an accident. Such procedures are the product

141

of long experience and should be used as the basis for instruction. When such a written procedure is not available, one should be developed. Since considerations of liability are involved, the procedure should be written in collaboration with the claims department and the legal department (or their equivalents), and the insurance company.

Include practice in completing the company accident report form by giving case histories of actual accidents with the information presented just as it might be in such a situation. The trainee uses this to complete an accident report form.

Trainees should be taught to make out a report for every accident, no matter how minor it may seem. Because one purpose of the accident report is to learn more about accident prevention, much can be learned from even a minor accident.

The cause of good accident reporting discipline, so essential to the success of any safety program is aided greatly if this subject is taught thoroughly and well. Details are given in Chapter 4 and 5.

Handling passengers. Drivers of passenger-carrying vehicles should be taught how to prevent passenger accidents. This will include how to position the vehicle for safe boarding and alighting of passengers, how to drive smoothly and slow down gradually in order to avoid on-board falls, and how to look for and remove tripping and slipping hazards aboard the vehicle.

If passengers are hurt, summon medical service if possible. At least notify police of injury so they can better help.

Handling freight. Any applicable regulations to loading or transporting cargo should be taught. Items should not be placed so that a sudden stop would send them flying toward the driver.

Drivers should be taught what to do if an accident scatters cargo about. It is important to:

- Minimize damage to other vehicles (by broken glass, spilled liquids, scattered boxes in the road).

- Notify police of a specially dangerous cargo. People in the area and other motorists must be warned if necessary. (The Manufacturing Chemists' Association Inc., 1825 Connecticut Ave. NW., Washington, D.C. 20009, is especially concerned about preventing highway accidents involving tank trucks carrying hazardous chemicals. They issue *Chem-Cards* for a number of substances. Each card briefly states the hazards of a chemical and makes broad recommendations for action in case of fire, leak, or human exposure.)

- How to prevent (or minimize) additional damage to cargo or theft.

Because each driver will be in daily contact with the safety program, he should develop an understanding and cooperative attitude toward it. Time devoted to explaining it will pay dividends.

Trainees should know why the safety program is necessary, its main elements, what safe driver awards and/or bonuses are offered under it and the rules for earning these, and what fleet contests the company has entered and the rules governing these.

TRAINING METHODS AND TRAINING AIDS help your program to be effective. They can be geared to individual fleet needs.

How To Teach

Teaching is more than telling or exposing the trainee to information: the trainee must exert mental effort. The process is like playing ball. The instructor makes the pitch, but the learner must make the catch. The responsibility for the success of the exchange, however, is always the instructor's. It is up to the teacher to motivate the trainee to learn. This he can do by making his presentation clear, interesting, memorable, and of personal value to the trainee.

The new trainee has a natural motivation to learn because he is embarking on an important venture—a new job. If he has been selected

143

WHAT TO DO	WHAT TO SAY

14

Card C-5

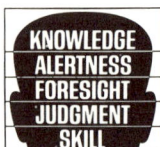

**SKILL AS AN
ELEMENT IN
DEFENSIVE
DRIVING**

Card C-6

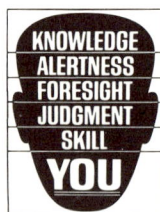

Last, but not least, we come to skill.

By skill, we mean the ability to manipulate the controls of a vehicle to successfully perform basic traffic maneuvers such as making turns, passing, reversing gears and parking. There is a right way to do each of these.

Skill is developed through learning how to do them the right way, and then DOING THEM THE RIGHT WAY EVERY TIME.

All these elements make YOU a defensive driver. If you can use them at all times when behind the wheel, it will indicate that you are using your head.

LESSON PLANS have directions on left—script on right of page. Here is the lesson plan for the flannel board presentation shown in the photograph above, from the NSC motion picture "A New Way To Drive." Actor Tony Mockus portrays the safety director of a trucking company that uses NSC's "Defensive Driving Course" to train its drivers.

144

wisely, he will be the kind of person who will be anxious to learn to do his job well. In spite of this, the trainee may have certain barriers to learning, which the instructor must anticipate: the trainee may feel that he already knows the subject, he may feel that the instructor is exaggerating the importance of the subject matter, or he may find that the material is too difficult to understand.

The good instructor is sensitive to these attitudes and develops ways to overcome them. He understands that his job is to present the material but also inspire the trainee to learn. If the trainee doesn't learn, the instructor hasn't taught.

The instructor must be a salesman, have an attractive personality, and be full of energy and enthusiasm for his subject. He has something to sell, but until the trainee buys, there is no sale.

Just as every good leader is also a teacher, so every instructor is a leader. As a leader, he should exemplify the qualities he seeks to impart to the trainee. By his manner, he must demonstrate that he has pride in himself, pride in his job, and pride in his company. He will be neat in appearance. He will be fair and firm in his relationship, but still friendly.

TEACHING METHODS

Having decided what material to present, the instructor must then organize it into lessons.

Lessons have dimensions in time and space. A good *time* dimension is 50 minutes, with a 10-minute break between sessions to allow the class to relax. The *space* dimension refers to the amount of material to be covered in a given session, and should always be based on the amount of material the trainees can comprehend. Four or five main points are about all an average trainee can learn in one lesson. To attempt to crowd more material into it will usually result in less learning rather than more.

The **lecture method** (in which the instructor stands before the class and tells about and explains the material) is the most commonly used teaching method because it can cover a great deal of material in a short time. The danger is that the lecture can become monotonous and boring.

To guard against this, the instructor must strive to make his lecture interesting by keeping to a few basic points, selecting good examples or anecdotes, utilizing visual aids, asking rhetorical questions, changing the pitch and speed of his delivery, making clear transitions from one main

145

point to the next, and summarizing the material at the end of the lecture.

Demonstration is another teaching method, usually used in conjunction with other methods. Here a physical object is displayed to the class to show how it works, why it works, or how to work it.

Discussion is a third effective teaching method. This allows the class to participate by answering questions, relating their own experiences, or thinking through a problem under the guidance of the instructor. Although this is a slower method of covering a subject, it arouses good interest in the trainees, provides a more vivid learning experience, and fosters a spirit of unity in the group.

Allow trainees to practice what they learn. The instructor first *explains* how the job is to be done—for example hooking up a tractor to a trailer—he then *demonstrates how* it is done. He then allows the trainee to try it himself, correcting the trainee's performance. Then he has him do it again. After the trainee has shown that he can perform the task properly, he is given additional time to practice the task until the right way becomes more firmly imbedded in his mind.

Examination is actually another teaching method. It may be oral, written, or of the performance type, but whichever type, it permits the trainee to show what he has learned and gives him a sense of accomplishment. It is a form of repetition or review which intensifies the learning process, and should be used throughout the training program. Even a question put to a trainee during a lecture is a form of examination. By use of the examination technique, the instructor is able to gauge whether the trainee has learned. The trainee is permitted to demonstrate what he has learned, and often finds out what material he still needs to learn. Examination results can be kept confidential or posted. Choose whichever seems more effective.

Reading should not be overlooked because it plays an important part in both shortening and enriching the training program. Reading is usually done after course hours and on the trainee's own time. To make sure the trainee has read and understood the material, reading assignments should be followed up by classroom discussion or written examination, or both.

TRAINING AIDS

Because it is not always possible to express ideas vividly or quickly enough by the spoken word alone, visual aids should be used to supplement the lecture. In a discussion of accident costs, for example,

146

DUAL-PURPOSE CHALK/MAGNETIC BOARD (of thin sheet steel coated with flat green paint) is available in portable or wall-mounted types. Here, a driver trainer uses balsa wood "cars" (with magnet under each felt square) to recreate an accident situation. (For more details of how to make and use audio-visual aids, see last section of this chapter, page 155.)

writing the figures on the blackboard will aid the trainee in appreciating the dollar amounts involved. Graphs or bar charts can be used to show quantitative relationships. Although key words or points in a lesson written on the blackboard help in remembering the ideas presented, diagrams can save precious minutes of explanation.

The instructor has available to him a wide range of visual aids. He should learn how to use each effectively. He must always remember that training aids are aids only. They should never be used just because they are available, but rather because they contribute to the instructor's objective in training.

Chalk board. Perhaps one of the first and still most widely used visual aids is the chalk board. This can be used to show key words, phrases, or points in the lecture. It can be used for making diagrams, graphs, and sketches that will help the trainee understand what is being discussed. Whether writing is placed on the chalk board before class, or written there as the instructor comes to the point in his lecture, make sure it is large enough for all to see clearly. The instructor should stand at the side of the chalk board and face the class as much as possible

147

(such as shown in the photograph on page 147). The instructor can use colored chalk to add further interest to the presentation.

Flip chart. The flip chart has somewhat the same uses as the blackboard. However it contains a number of successive pages and will accommodate a great deal more prepared material than can a single blackboard. If the chart will be used over and over again, the instructor can afford to make each page as attractive and informative as possible. Words can be carefully lettered, diagrams drawn to scale, sketches painstakingly drawn, and colored inks used to add interest and readability to the chart. Each successive page should help to develop the lesson.

Sometimes blank flip charts are used, the instructor writing on the page with a colored crayon or marking pen. This can be dramatic but since the page cannot be erased, it must be discarded after each lesson. This is an asset, however, in a discussion. Old pages serve as a record.

Flannel board. The flannel board combines some of the features of the blackboard and the flip chart. It is usually about the size of a medium-size blackboard. The material to be placed on the flannel board can be used over and over again so the instructor can afford to construct the material with care. Objects to be placed on the flannel board include strips of cardboard on which key words, points, or phrases are printed or carefully lettered. A variety of other objects can be used: photographs, clips from a magazine, shapes, sample forms.

The flannel board allows the instructor to put complicated material on the board and take it off as needed. He can add material to the board as his lecture progresses, in order to develop his lesson as he would build a pyramid, by adding building blocks as he goes along.

Magnetic board. Every driver training room should have a magnetic board showing a standard traffic layout with magnetized model vehicles that will stick to the board wherever they are placed.

The magnetic board can be used to explain the correct driving maneuvers, to reconstruct accidents for class discussion, or for reenactment of an accident when counseling with the driver involved when determining its preventability. A magnetic board can be combined with a chalk board or flannel board.

Accident demonstration board. Miniature automobiles and demonstration boards can also be used for portraying accidents. An excellent board that can be used in a vertical position may be constructed at little cost by thumbtacking different colored pieces of felt on a background of wallboard to indicate curb lines, view obstructions, signal lights,

ACCIDENT DEMONSTRATION BOARD. Model trucks, cars, and buses enhance the effectiveness of instruction, and prompt discussion of traffic hazards and regulations, and thus improve safe driving performance on the job.

buildings, etc. Miniature vehicles (obtained at 10-cent stores) are fitted with pins for moving about on the board. Several types of vertical demonstration boards are currently on the market that use a simple adhesive process to hold materials to the board. They allow diagrams to be shifted and illustrations to be moved about easily.

Demonstrations. Talks given in conjunction with demonstrations using actual equipment (or a model) are effective in holding the interest of employees. An actual setup or model of the vehicle's braking system, showing master cylinder, brake lines, brake cylinders, shoes, and drums, can help the student to learn how the brakes operate. Other subjects particularly adaptable to demonstrations are ignition, cooling system, headlights, tires, electrical equipment, and carburization. Persons giving these demonstrations should be experts in their fields.

Abused equipment. Actual tires can be displayed as an example of what results from climbing curbs when making turns or the amount of rubber than can be worn off a tire in an unnecessarily fast stop. Worn

149

DRIVER TESTING EQUIPMENT can be brought to the drivers. Here is a setup that is housed in a bus. General driving public, as well as fleet drivers, can be tested. Often a cooperative arrangement is worked out with a civic group.

mechanical parts can also be displayed to show the results of careless operation.

Driver testing equipment. Although no definite relationship has been established between psychological and physiological test results in accident proneness, drivers do like to compete for honors in demonstrating their ability to operate such equipment and tests may be conducted as part of the safety meeting program. Several insurance companies and automobile clubs have testing equipment available and are glad to cooperate in giving tests. The educational value of these tests lies in explaining the compensation and correction necessary for offsetting the deficiencies indicated by the tests. Therefore, they should be given with extreme care by trained examiners.

Slides. The slide projector opens another rich source of visual material that can aid in teaching. The instructor can take color slides of vehicles, traffic situations, accidents, damaged equipment, unsafe practices, and many other scenes, and then show them to the class.

Some take pictures (slides or movies) of bad driving practices when the offending driver is unaware he is being photographed. Later, the proper practices are staged and photographed for presentation with the former. Films of this character have an excellent effect on the

150

drivers. The cost of photographic equipment is not great and reasonably good pictures can be produced with a little practice. When homemade slides (or movies) are used, the safety department should prepare a short talk discussing the practices shown and emphasizing the correct methods. Accident photos can be used too.

The slide projector can also be used like a giant flip chart. Pages of a flip chart, company report forms, graphs, and many other subjects can be photographed for projection before the class.

Many filmstrips are also available for training. They are useful in clarifying technical discussions and, because they combine a visual and spoken message, make a lasting impression on the employee.

Movies. The driver training movie can make an important and dramatic contribution to the training program. Even though the film may make only a limited number of points, it focuses attention on the problem and promotes discussion or further instruction.

SCHOOL BUS SIMULATOR uses photographed highway scenes. Video-taped views are of actual routes that drivers will follow upon completion of simulator training.

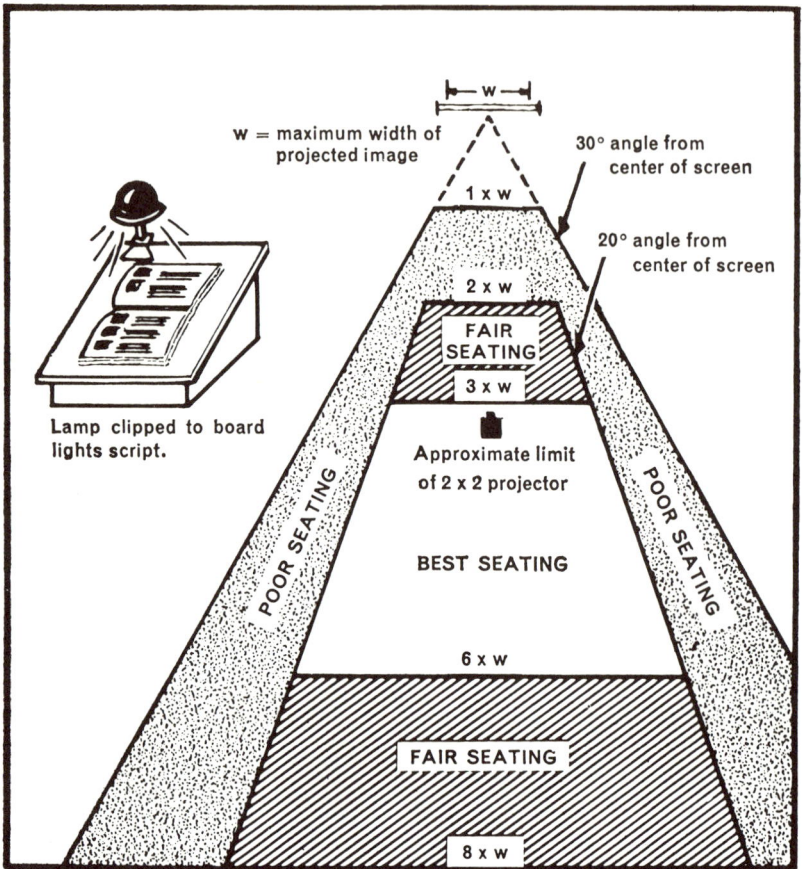

w = maximum width of projected image

30° angle from center of screen

20° angle from center of screen

1 x w

2 x w

FAIR SEATING

3 x w

Lamp clipped to board lights script.

Approximate limit of 2 x 2 projector

POOR SEATING

POOR SEATING

BEST SEATING

6 x w

FAIR SEATING

8 x w

BEST VIEWING AREA FOR PROJECTED VISUALS is within 20 degrees of the projection axis for a beaded screen, within 30 degrees for a matte screen, and within 33 degrees for a lenticular screen. Screen should be placed so that speaker, if any, will not interfere with someone's view of visual. Shown at upper left, shaded reading light permits reading script without distracting audience.

A fairly extensive library of driver training films is available. There are films on what to do in case of an accident, how to follow the vehicle ahead safely, how to determine the preventability of an accident, and many other subjects.

Since the driver training film usually runs from 10 to 20 minutes, it cannot carry a very heavy training load by itself. To make a film-based training session effective, the instructor should first describe the film, tell why it is being shown, and then direct the attention of the trainees to certain points in the film before it is shown. Following the screening, the main points are reviewed and discussed and the material applied to particular problems. Following this, a written quiz can be given to further reinforce the lesson. The quiz can be discussed at the end of class, or at the beginning of the next class.

Don't pass up a good film because it may not deal with the specific operations of the fleet. It may be true that drivers prefer films dealing with their specific vehicles, but the instructor can point out that while the film deals with passenger cars, there are many valid lessons in it for truck drivers. The good instructor can take an appropriate passenger car film and make it the basis for an effective lesson for truck drivers or take a truck driving film and use it to good advantage in teaching passenger car drivers.

Tape recorders. Tape recorders can add variety, interest, and emphasis to a training program: trainees can listen to the actual commentary of a driver during a trip, trainees can play back counseling interviews in which the preventability of an accident was determined. The resourceful instructor will think of many other ways in which the tape recorder can be used as an effective training aid.

ADDITIONAL HELP

Remember that any training program must be designed to fit the training need—not fit the training aids available. Ask "What is the trainee expected to do as a result of this training?" and "What behavioral change is expected?" Then decide (1) the method of instruction, (2) the training aids to use, and (3) how all-inclusive to make the program.

The choice must be made to best fit the subject to the audience. Be sure to check the advantages of all types of visual aids before deciding. National Safety Council publishes a series of Industrial Data Sheets to help do just that. Refer to *Motion Pictures for Safety* (No. 556), *Nonprojected Visual Aids* (No. 564), *Photography for the Safety Professional* (No. 619), *Posters, Bulletin Boards, and Safety Displays* (No. 616), and *Projected Still Pictures* (No. 574).

A number of films and other training aids are available from the Council. Write for a catalog.

8

Driver supervision

Supervision is not only the art of getting things done through people, it is the art of getting them done well.

What Is Driver Supervision?

Most driving jobs require two duties: those that relate to driving, of course, and those that don't. Both pose different supervisory problems.

In some instances nondriving duties can be supervised by ordinary techniques used throughout industry. In other situations, the supervision of occupational safety as well as driving safety is indirect. The special techniques for supervising the driving part of the job, however, is most complex.

Drivers are capable of committing any number of errors that can be costly to the company. The driver supervisor must know (1) what these errors are, (2) how they can be spotted, and (3) how to prevent them. The supervisor must enforce a high standard of performance—one that does not condone accidents that could reasonably be prevented. This chapter is designed to tell him how.

WHO IS THE DRIVER SUPERVISOR?

The driver supervisor is responsible for the quality of driver performance. In the small fleet, this man may be the fleet manager himself; in a large common carrier fleet, several persons may share supervisory

154

responsibility, each having some authority (sometimes overlapping).

For example, the terminal manager is usually thought of as the driver's direct supervisor. But the dispatcher also shares some of the supervisory load because he both (1) assigns runs and vehicles to his drivers and (2) makes sure that these runs are completed on time and correctly.

The safety director (who is responsible for overall safety performance) should work through the supervisor at the driver's home terminal. Additional supervision may be provided by a safety road patrol— supervisors who can make on-the-spot observations of driving performance and report these back to company headquarters for followup. In some instances this road supervisor may be authorized to stop a vehicle to correct the driver.

But what about that ancient rule of supervision that a man cannot serve two masters? How, then, can a driver please so many different men who all seem to have something to say about how he is doing his job? Because these supervisory practices are created by the operating conditions of a motor transportation fleet, unity is achieved only if all supervisors see eye to eye on how the driving job should be performed.

Sales fleets present a different supervisory problem. If salesmen are scattered over a wide territory, they usually operate company vehicles from their homes. In addition, very little direct safety supervision is possible, because the salesman's direct boss is the sales manager. Others interested in his safety are the fleet manager and the fleet safety director. It must be the objective of all of them to emphasize that good driving is a part of the sales job. (More details in Chapter 15, "The Sales Fleet.")

How to Head Off Accidents

Because motor vehicle accidents represent the greatest potential for loss in terms of human life, bodily injury, and property damage, the primary responsibility of supervision is to head off accidents before they happen.

There are certain techniques that the supervisor should learn and use for spotting substandard performance that results in accidents. For example:

- Personally observe the driver's performance and check driver trainer reports, road patrol reports, arrest records, and comments from other drivers and employees.
- Review complaints from other drivers or pedestrians as a possible

barometer of driving performance. If more than one incident takes place, the supervisor who knows his job can usually spot the behavioral actions—such as belligerence or indifference—that may lead to an accident. The supervisor should try to find the reason for this change in behavior and seek to help solve the problems that may have brought about such change in the driver's characteristics. Sometimes let a driver do nondriving work if he is emotionally disturbed.

Earle S. Hannaford, former Safety Engineer, Long Lines Department, American Telephone and Telegraph Company, lists some typical symptoms of accidents-in-the-making. A good supervisor should watch for them:

1. Errors in performance of work.
2. Changes in everyday behavior and manners.
3. Changes in simple habits of a routine nature.
4. Near-accidents.

These reflect mental and emotional feelings and can fluctuate with various factors: resentments stemming from childhood, weariness, fatigue, a series of disappointments. Sometimes these feelings lead to an accident.

This does not mean that the driver supervisor must be a psychiatrist. He should be aware, nonetheless, that much substandard performance can have a psychological base in order that he can be more understanding and effective in dealing with it.

Dr. A. R. Lauer, former professor of psychology at Iowa State University and a leading authority on driving behavior, offers this advice to the driver supervisor:

"Drivers seem to improve when approached about their difficulties and these are discussed with them in a semiclinical way. Because it appears that they realize they can compensate for their weaknesses, this may be the important factor in improving their record. An objective check of a driver, followed by a careful and confidential discussion of the deficiencies noted, will result in improved driving behavior and a corresponding reduction in accidents."

Because errors fall into a number of main categories, we shall discuss the importance of each and the specific errors that a supervisor should watch for. These errors may not be of equal importance to all fleets. The driver supervisor should adapt the list to fit his operation.

ERRORS THAT LEAD TO ACCIDENTS

Driving errors that frequently lead to accidents were compiled by means

156

of a survey of more than 150 of the nation's top fleet safety directors. The driver supervisor can adapt this list to aid his own fleet operation—especially in training drivers.

1. **Before starting**
   a. Failure to first check clearances, front, rear, overhead.
   b. Failure to signal when pulling out from curb.
   c. Failure to check for break in traffic before moving.

2. **Speed control**
   a. Too fast for volume of traffic.
   b. Too fast for condition of road surface.
   c. Too fast for condition of visibility (due to weather or road).
   d. Too fast for condition of light (dusk/darkness).
   e. Too fast for neighborhood or roadside environment.
   f. Too fast for street/highway layout and traffic signals.
   g. Too slow for speed of traffic stream.

3. **Lane usage**
   a. Failure to select proper lane.
   b. Failure to drive in middle of lane.
   c. Abrupt lane change.
   d. Failure to signal intent to change lanes.
   e. Weaving.

4. **Passing**
   a. Misjudging speed and nearness of oncoming vehicle.
   b. Failure to check to rear before pulling out to pass.
   c. Overtaking and passing too slowly.
   d. Cutting in too quickly after passing.
   e. Failure to signal intention of passing.
   f. Unnecessary passing.
   g. Racing other vehicle trying to pass you.
   h. Passing in an intersection.

5. **Turning**
   a. Turning from wrong lane.
   b. Failure to let oncoming traffic clear before turning left.
   c. Failure to block area to right of vehicle on right turns.
   d. Over-running curb on right turns.
   e. Abrupt turn on slippery road surface leading to skid.
   f. Failure to signal intention to turn.

6. **Stopping**
   a. Failure to make smooth gradual stop.
   b. Failure to signal stop.
   c. Failure to stop in time.

d. Abrupt breaking on slippery road surface leading to skid.

7. Parking
    a. Parking in unsafe or illegal place.
    b. Parking with front or rear of vehicle protruding into traffic.
    c. Failure to secure unattended vehicle on hill.
    d. Failure to properly mark disabled vehicle.

8. Specific signaling errors
    a. Failure to signal.
    b. Signal too late.
    c. Wrong signal.
    d. Failure to use horn.
    e. Excessive or improper use of horn.

9. Errors in clearance judgment
    a. Following vehicle ahead too closely.
    b. Failure to check clearance to rear when backing.
    c. Failure to check right side clearance.
    d. Failure to check left side clearance.
    e. Failure to check top clearance.
    f. Failure to yield space in any traffic encroachment.

10. Errors in observation
    a. Failure to observe object or pedestrian in path of vehicle.
    b. Failure to observe traffic at rear of vehicle while moving.
    c. Failure to observe to left and right of vehicle at locations from which vehicles or pedestrians could enter path of vehicle.
    d. Inadequate observation, failure to see vehicle or pedestrian approaching.
    e. Observation too late.
    f. Failure to anticipate parked vehicles pulling out.

11. Lack of personal control
    a. Inattention—any cause.
    b. Distraction—any cause.
    c. Driving while drowsy.
    d. Reacting emotionally to driving situations.
    e. Driving under influence of alcohol or drugs.
    f. Driving while ill.

12. Lack of knowledge and awareness of equipment, load, route
    a. Failure to inspect equipment (before, during, after trip).
    b. Being unfamiliar with equipment.
    c. Being unfamiliar with load.
    d. Being unfamiliar with route.
    e. Failure to secure doors or cargo.

CHECK TRAFFIC RULE COMPLIANCE

Because fleets must use public streets and highways, they have a special obligation to always operate within the law. Violation of traffic laws cannot be condoned. Even a single law violation may reflect badly on the company; a long record of noncompliance can damage the public relations image of the entire industry and may lead to more restrictive legislation. For individual drivers, repeated violations may result in revocation of their operating rights.

Fleets usually do not pay traffic fines incurred by drivers nor do they put up bonds for them. A record of traffic violations is usually kept in the driver's personnel folder and repeated violations are the basis for disciplinary action or discharge.

Following are some of the most frequent driving errors that are also legal violations:

1. **Running errors**
   a. Speed in excess of legal limit.
   b. Speed too fast for conditions.
   c. Speed too slow for conditions.
   d. Following too closely.

2. **Passing errors**
   a. Passing at illegal place.
   b. Passing at unsafe place.
   c. Unnecessary passing.

3. **Intersection violations**
   a. Failure to yield right-of-way at unmarked intersections.
   b. Running red light.
   c. Coasting through stop sign.
   d. Failure to reduce speed for intersection.
   e. Failure to yield to oncoming traffic when making left turn.
   f. Failure to yield right-of-way to pedestrians.

4. **Improper lane usage**
   a. Failure to select proper lane.
   b. Turning from wrong lane.
   c. Sudden change of lane.
   d. Failure to signal lane change.

5. **Parking and stopping errors**
   a. Illegal stopping on street or roadway.
   b. Obstructing traffic.
   c. Double parking.
   d. Failure to secure parked vehicle on hill.

159

About 10 to 25 per cent of the annual fleet maintenance cost is due to faulty operation or abuse of the vehicle by the driver, which in turn stems from carelessness, lack of training, or inadequate supervisory control.

Not only can excessive repair bills be an index to substandard driving performance, but they are directly related to the number of accidents. A "rough" driver has a high accident potential; a "smooth" driver is usually more alert to avoid accident hazards and ready for any emergencies.

Rough operation—including fast starts, delayed braking, and sudden stops—can indicate a bad attitude toward authority and be symptomatic of an attitude that may produce an eventual accident. It may also indicate driver inexperience. *Lack of aptitude* should be spotted in the selection process because it is usually an irremediable fault; if the driver is retained, he will be an expensive driver. *Lack of training* as a cause of rough operation can be corrected.

Freedom to abuse an expensive vehicle is not a fringe benefit. The company has the right to expect its drivers to act as stewards of company property by showing respect for equipment put in their charge.

Following is a list of driving abuses that lead to undue wear of the vehicle.

1. **Engine (motor) abuse**
   a. Excessive acceleration of cold engine.
   b. Stopping engine suddenly after a long run.
   c. Operating overheated engine.
   d. Operating engine with low oil pressure.
   e. Racing engine.
   f. Failure to keep checking on instrument panel gauges.

2. **Clutching errors**
   a. Riding the clutch.
   b. Snapping the clutch.

3. **Errors in shifting gears**
   a. Starting out in wrong gear.
   b. Rapid acceleration from stops.
   c. Scraping and jerking the gears.
   d. Shifting gears into neutral and coasting down hill.
   e. Failure to double clutch if necessary when changing gears.
   f. Lugging—operating in improper gear.

4. Errors in use of brakes
    a. Failure to fully release hand brake when moving.
    b. Abrupt stops.
    c. Delayed braking.
    d. Excessive brake applications.

5. Errors in tire care
    a. Operating with flat or under-inflated tires.
    b. Driving over curbs or objects, and into potholes.
    c. Rubbing tires against curbs in parking.
    d. Letting air out of tires "for better traction."
    e. Unnecessary spinning of tires on ice or snow.

6. Tampering with equipment
    a. Overriding governors.
    b. Stopping up the fuel return line to try to get more power.
    c. Tampering with trip recorder.
    d. Abuse of cab interior.

7. Lack of maintenance responsibility
    a. Driving unit even though it needs repairs.
    b. Failure to write up defects and repairs.
    c. Failure to inspect equipment properly before each trip.

SAFETY-CONSCIOUS DISPATCHERS don't set such tight schedules that drivers have to throw precaution to the wind in order to meet them.

Set Good Schedules

The motor transportation fleet cannot conduct its business without schedules. However, a schedule is only a piece of paper until a driver and his vehicle translates that schedule into on-time transportation. Observance of schedules is therefore a prime ingredient of driving skill.

161

Failure of a driver to observe schedules can be regarded not only as poor production, but probably as a symptom of a bad underlying attitude toward the job, or a personal problem which is interfering with efficiency.

Following are driving errors which result in schedule delays:

1. **Errors in departure procedure**
   a. Reporting late for scheduled run.
   b. Excessive time spent in preparation for departure.
   c. Pulling wrong trailer.
   d. Taking wrong freight bills.
   e. Stopping at home for personal business following departure.
   f. Not getting proper rest before run, resulting in having to stop for sleep along road.

2. **Errors leading to delays en route**
   a. Accidents due to errors.
   b. Arrests due to errors.
   c. Excessive and prolonged coffee stops.
   d. Excessive time at meal stops.
   e. Excessive time at scheduled stops.
   f. Excessive time at weighing stations.
   g. Failure to follow designated route.
   h. Failure to call in for instructions.
   i. Stops at unauthorized places.

Remember Your Public Relations

When a truck is painted attractively and shows the company name, it becomes a traveling advertisement. A like amount of advertising purchased through regular advertising media would cost a great deal of money. But there is one difference—the advertising on the truck can be good or bad, favorable or unfavorable, depending on how the driver behaves toward other motorists and pedestrians. Driving with courtesy and consideration for the public is therefore an important part of the driving job. Courtesy can build public good will for the company and, as a consequence, influence its ability to compete for business.

Here are some of the discourtesies that drivers commit that tear down their company's good public image.

1. **Errors in speed control**
   a. Exceeding speed limit and passing motorists who are abiding by the law.
   b. Speeding through towns and residential areas.
   c. Driving too slow so as to back up traffic.

162

VEHICLES CAN BE TRAVELING BILLBOARDS. Be sure that public good will is built up by making sure they are driven with courtesy and consideration.

2. Errors in following
    a. Following passenger cars too closely.
    b. Tailgating by two or more trucks.
    c. Following too close at night without dimming lights.

3. Errors in passing
    a. Passing when unnecessary.
    b. Cutting in too sharply after passing.

4. Errors in lane use
    a. Crowding center line.
    b. Straddling two lanes.
    c. Drifting across lane dividers.
    d. Weaving from one lane to another.
    e. Running two or three abreast on limited-access highways.
    f. Use of wrong lane for speed or traffic flow.

5. Errors that block traffic
    a. Blocking crosswalk.

163

   b. Double parking in heavy traffic.

   c. Not pulling off road to allow builtup traffic to pass.

6. Errors in noise and smoke abatement

   a. Excessive diesel smoke.

   b. Excessive engine noise.

   c. Unnecessary use of air horns.

   d. Racing engine to hurry pedestrians across intersection.

   e. Splashing pedestrians in sloppy weather.

Encourage High Performance

It should not seem that the negative aspects of supervision have been overemphasized because the observation of performance involves finding and correcting faults. Although this is an essential part of any supervisor's job, it is by far the lesser part.

For high performance, management (through supervision) must offer the driver more than good wages and fear of being discharged or disciplined. The true test of the supervisor's skill is his ability to provide the conditions under which a driver will maintain high standards because he himself wants to. Here are some methods and techniques that a supervisor can use to motivate drivers.

SET PERFORMANCE STANDARDS DELIBERATELY HIGH

Setting job standards high is one way of securing compliance. High standards are challenging: a driver feels a keen sense of pride in his job —an esprit de corps—when he feels he is meeting them. On the other hand, when mediocre standards do not inspire respect, they are just as difficult to enforce as are high standards.

SET A GOOD EXAMPLE

The driver supervisor must himself set a good example. He should radiate pride in his company and be dedicated to it. He should never say or do anything that would indicate he is not proud of his company or loyal to its officers and objectives.

BUILD A SENSE OF PARTICIPATION

Give drivers a sense of participation in their company. Keep them informed of company plans. Let them know how they are meeting their objectives. They feel that they are their part of the company when they share in information about the company.

This sense of participation is fostered when supervisors welcome suggestions for improving company services or meeting specific prob-

PUBLIC RECOGNITION OF A JOB WELL DONE goes a long way to providing drivers with a powerful incentive for better driving performance.

lems. Drivers often have suggestions which can lead to important cost savings.

Many companies have formal systems which require suggestions to be submitted on a specially prepared form. These are numbered and carefully considered by a committee. Later, the driver is informed to what has happened to his contribution. In some cases cash awards are made.

Whether or not an award program exists, a driver should get personal recognition for any idea used. If practical (and the driver OK's it), recognition should be made publicly.

GOOD COMMUNICATIONS

Communication is vital to good human relations and scientific management because it is a two-way street: management keeps drivers informed and drivers, in turn, feel free to offer suggestions. No matter which way communications travel, the receiver must understand the

165

intent of the sender, otherwise it is not real communication.

But right now we are more concerned with *what* to communicate than *how*. The most important message that management can communicate to drivers is that they hold a unique job in the company—that their job is vital. This builds pride and satisfaction in the job and improves performance.

PROMOTE A COMPETITIVE SPIRIT

Additional job interest can be created by appealing to the competitive spirit. Safety contests between fleet divisions, or with outside fleets (such as in the National Fleet Safety Contest), generate this interest when drivers understand the rules and are kept informed of contest ratings. Company publications, special posters, contest score boards, bulletin board displays, and safety meetings all promote this. Contests are not limited to large fleets. Small fleets can also use this tool.

MOTIVATE THROUGH RECOGNITION

Individual safe driving awards are a powerful incentive to better driving performance. Because drivers generally do the same type work, and because they are usually covered by a uniform union contract (that spells out wages, work conditions, special assignments, and seniority), an individual driver finds it unusually difficult to distinguish himself. Safe driver awards provide an opportunity for a driver to distinguish himself.

The National Safety Council, as well as many insurance companies and trade associations, conducts safe driver award programs. The Council program originated in 1930 and since then has presented more than four million awards. Special National Safety Council badges and awards are available, or special badges bearing a company name and emblem can be made. Awards plans should be complete in either case —rule books, certificates, and badges are required.

Awards work best when the rules are carefully explained to drivers, when decisions on accidents are consistently fair, and when fleet management takes special pains to present the awards in a dignified manner that makes it plain that these are emblems of important, worthwhile achievement. Also see Chapter 20.

There is publicity value in awards. See Appendix B for details.

The Challenge of Driver Supervision

Our civilization's high cultural values and high standards of living depend primarily on the mass production of goods and services—which

166

MORE THAN four million safe driver awards have been earned. Emblem is made of gold and silver plate, and can be obtained in cap badge, key-tag, or lapel pin. A diamond, ruby, or sapphire can be added to denote specified years of safe driving. Shoulder patches and watches are also available with the emblem and year.

is not so much a matter of working harder as it is of *working smarter*. To organize its resources, civilization depends upon management—the skill of the millions of supervisors in business, industry, and government who are in direct charge of workers and whose skill in human relations increases production. Transportation is one of these vital resources.

Motor fleets play a big part in meeting our nation's transportation needs. Efficient fleet operation demands faultless driving: driving that is as free as possible from errors that incur unnecessary waste.

To achieve this excellence, the industry must depend upon its driver supervisors, whatever their title and wherever they serve. Driver supervision is therefore a most worthwhile occupation. It should be approached by the driver supervisor with humility and determination to succeed.

9

Alcohol
and drugs

One of the greatest threats to highway safety today is the driver who drives while under the influence of drugs or alcohol. This type of driver often fails to realize that his judgment is impaired while he is so influenced.

Alcohol and Driving

Of the more than 100,000,000 licensed drivers in the U.S., approximately 70 per cent drink and drive—at least occasionally. And recent studies indicate that the consumption of alcohol in this country is increasing. Alcoholism is now classified as one of the most rampant illnesses plaguing modern man, and contributes at least 50 per cent of all fatal motor vehicle accidents. The combination of drinking and driving has become a major threat to life and limb on the highway.

Drugs and Driving

The pace of living in our complex society has increased considerably. Many people have sought relief from the pressures and tensions of this increased pace through the use of alcohol. Still others have turned to drugs for this relief or to keep up the pace of living. Illegal use of drugs is rising. Marijauna, heroin, lysergic acid diethylamide (LSD), and other drugs are very popular among young people. Prescription drug usage is also rising. Family physicians often prescribe tranquilizers for

168

relief of tension, amphetamines to combat fatigue, and antihistamines for relief from congestion. Many drugs are also available without prescription.

Studies indicate that at any one time from 10 to 20 per cent of the population is taking prescription medication. Add to this the percentage of people using drugs illegally, and it becomes obvious that a substantial portion of our driving population is exposed to the effects of drugs.

Effects of Alcohol on Driving

Alcohol is not a stimulant as many people believe, but a depressant that affects the central nervous system. It acts like a tranquilizer and lowers the activity of the brain. It slows reflexes, impairs coordination, and reduces visual acuity. Its effects on the driver are obvious.

Driving requires skill and judgment. A driver must be alert and capable of reacting quickly to avoid accident situations. After drinking even a small quantity of alcohol, a driver's thinking and normal instinct of caution are dulled and he has difficulty in concentrating. His reactions are slower, and his coordination becomes impaired. In addition, his vision—particularly his peripheral vision—becomes affected. Add to these effects a false sense of confidence that alcohol tends to promote. The result is not only an unsafe driver but a dangerous one.

169

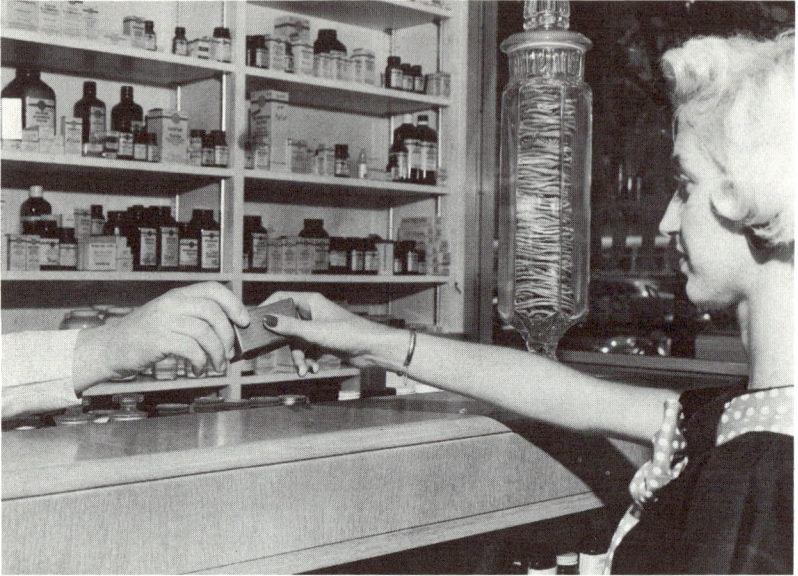

A DRUG USER does not have to be an addict or a thrill-seeker to have a drug problem. Overdosages or the combination of several drugs can make even the most respectable of persons into a "drug abuser."

Effects of Drugs on Driving

With the vast amount of different drugs in use, illegally and by prescription, it is difficult to describe drug effects in general. Different drugs produce different results and do not influence all individuals in the same manner. In addition, little scientific research has been conducted on the actual effects of drugs on driving. Therefore, the following generalized effects of certain drugs are presented as they relate to driving.

Amphetamines—Examples: Benzedrine and related compounds. These drugs may increase alertness and efficiency for a short period, but may be followed by headaches, dizziness, agitation or irritability, decreased power of concentration, and marked fatigue.

An important factor to note is that the use of amphetamines can interfere with the body's normal warning symptoms of drowsiness and fatigue. A driver can use up his body energy without realizing it until he may suddenly collapse. He is given a false sense of self-confidence, and does not realize that his driving ability and alertness are decreasing.

170

Another reported effect of amphetamines is seeing mirages or experiencing hallucinations. A driver in such a mental state may suddenly swerve into oncoming traffic or off the road to avoid an imaginary object.

Antihistamines—Examples: Benadryl, Dramamine, Pyribenzamine, Pyrilamine, and Phenergan. These drugs are used primarily for relief of nasal congestion due to colds. They may cause drowsiness, inattention, and possible confusion in the driver.

Barbiturates—Examples: phenobarbital, Mebaral, Pentothal, and Seconal. These drugs may have the same effect as alcohol, influencing the driver by sedation. Drowsiness and confusion, as well as a lack of coordination, can also result. The driver may experience tremor of the hands, lips, and the tongue. He may have difficulty in thinking and speaking clearly.

Hallucinogens—Examples: LSD, mescaline, marijuana. Little scientific research has been done on the effects of hallucinogens on driving. However, use of these results in the following: distortion of sensory perception, especially visual; disruption of thought processes, and impaired memory; alterations in perception of time and space; and feelings of unreality.

Recent research on the effects of marijuana indicates that the effects of light glare on the eyes of a user can be prolonged. Thus, a driver under the influence of marijuana can be more easily blinded by oncoming headlights than can a nonuser. The marijuana user may also experience slowed reaction time and poor driving judgment.

Narcotics—Examples: morphine, codeine, Dilaudid, Demerol, Dolophine, heroin, and opium derivatives. Narcotics may induce a pleasant sensation of emotional tranquility, but concentration, judgment, and memory are usually disturbed. Drowsiness and reduction of visual acuity may result, thus setting up the driver for an accident.

Tranquilizers—Examples: Miltown, Equanil, Librium, Compoz, Atarax, Vistaril, Serpasil, Thorazine, and Compazine. These drugs produce a mild sedative effect that may cause dizziness or drowsiness. Even this mild effect can present danger to drivers by slowing their critical reflexes and mental powers.

Interaction of Alcohol and Drugs

The *combination of alcohol and drugs* can produce a variety of effects that may severely impair the driver of a motor vehicle. Concentrations of alcohol and drugs remain in the blood stream much longer than most users realize, and the effects of this combination may arise unexpectedly.

171

Little scientific study has been conducted on the interaction of alcohol and drugs, but there is sufficient evidence to conclude that such a combination can lead to increased impairment of driver judgment and skill.

Alcohol and Drugs on-the-Job

In our society many of us have grown accustomed to the practice of having a cocktail or some other sort of alcoholic beverage with lunch. Many individuals believe that a drink or two with lunch will not affect them. There may be no actual drinking on-the-job, but the effects of alcohol do not end with the meal.

Some individuals enjoy drinking, just as others enjoy eating, and no matter how often you speak about the impairing effects of alcohol, the person who enjoys drinking will continue to do so. If you are a supervisor, it is your duty to insure that your drivers reserve their drinking for off-duty hours. Also make sure that the effects of off-duty drinking do not accompany your employees on-the-job (in the form of a "hangover"). Remember that a hangover may also impair driving.

In addition to the multitude of prescription drugs being used both on and off the job, narcotics and dangerous drugs of all types are finding their way to work. The National Industrial Conference Board of New York conducted a nationwide survey of 222 firms and found that 53 per cent reported cases of employee drug abuse.

Cost of Alcohol and Drugs

Industry loses a sizable amount of profits each year due to alcoholism and drug abuse. Lewis F. Presnall, Director of Rehabilitation Services for the Kemper Insurance Group, commented that emotional disturbances cost American business approximately ten billion dollars per year. Of that amount, four billion dollars is due to alcoholism. Drug abuse accounts for a good portion of the remaining six billion dollars.

Alcoholics vs. Addicts

With the heavy emphasis on drug addiction by the various communications media, it is possible to overlook or forget the problem of alcoholism. Currently, addicts are heavily outnumbered by alcoholics—approximately 6,000,000 alcoholics and an estimated 400,000 narcotics addicts.

Although the problem of alcoholism is still with us, a New York City Chamber of Commerce study team investigating drug abuse concluded:

"Most companies surveyed feel that drugs are a more serious busi-

172

AN ALCOHOLIC CAN BE CRAFTY. If his secret bottle is removed, he may replace it with a medicine bottle—full of booze.

ness problem than alcohol. One medical executive said that, unlike alcoholism, drug addiction is not amenable to ambulatory treatment. Whereas some companies report a 60 to 75 per cent success rate with alcoholic employees, rehabilitation of an addict is fraught with a high rate of relapse. Drug addiction also spreads to other employees and leads to theft and to drug peddling. This is not true with alcoholism."

Countermeasures

Alcoholism and the sale and use of drugs by employees may not be problems in your company at this time, but will you be prepared to cope with these problems if and when they arise?

Alcohol. As stated earlier, about 70 per cent of the more than 100,-000,000 licensed drivers in the U.S. drink and drive occasionally. The U.S. Department of Transportation, National Highway Safety Bureau, estimates that approximately 16 per cent of these drinking drivers can be classified as "heavy" or problem drinkers.

It is this small group of heavy or problem drinkers that is most tempted to drink during working hours. Even if you are fortunate enough to have no drinking on-the-job workers, remember that the problem drinker can still bring his hangover symptoms to work, and that these symptoms will interfere with his ability to drive safely both to and from work. Studies indicate that employees who are alcoholics have more than twice as many on-the-job accidents—and at least ten times as many off-the-job accidents—as non-drinkers.

Countermeasures for dealing with alcoholism begin with educating yourself and your drivers. Information on alcoholism and the effects of alcohol on driving is readily available. You may write to the following source for detailed information on alcoholism programs:

North American Association of Alcoholism Programs
1611 Devonshire Drive
Columbia, North Carolina 29204

You should try to obtain and read as much information as you can in order to be familiar with alcoholism and its effects. One good way to inform your drivers about alcoholism and the problems it can create is through the five-minute safety talk. You can also discuss drinking and driving during the next safety meeting.

The next step in an alcohol countermeasures program is the identification of problem drinkers under your supervision. Everyone is familiar with the drunk and can recognize the obvious signs of intoxication. The individual who has been drinking on-the-job will probably give himself away through his unsteady actions, or by the telltale odor on his breath. However, you should also watch for the apparently sober driver with the "continuous hangover," which may indicate a serious drinking problem.

Having identified a problem drinker under your supervision, you should examine the ways in which you might help him overcome his problem. One way is to provide the individual with counseling by trained personnel who deal with alcoholism. Check your community organizations, churches, and local American Red Cross chapter for information on programs to assist alcoholics.

Above all, as a supervisor, you must show the alcoholic that you care and have a true desire to help him overcome his problem. Simply telling the alcoholic not to drink is like telling someone who enjoys eating, not to eat. An admonition not to drink is not the solution. Alcoholism is an illness and must be handled by persons trained to deal with it. The alcoholic needs help. It is up to you to convince him to accept treatment.

Drugs. The current increase in the use of drugs is not confined to the younger segment of the population. The individual who takes an overdose of aspirin or sedatives is as much a problem as the heroin addict.

The Kemper Insurance Group has seriously considered the problem of employee drug abuse and has designed a policy to cope with it. Having had a high rate of success in dealing with alcoholism, Kemper Insurance modified and updated its safety policy to include what it terms "drug dependency." The Kemper Insurance drug abuse policy is as follows:

> In accordance with our general personnel policies, whose underlying concept is regard for the employee as an individual as well as a worker, we believe that:
> - Drug dependency is an illness and should be treated as such.
> - The majority of employees who develop a dependency on drugs can be helped to recover, and the company should offer appropriate assistance.
> - The decision to seek diagnosis and accept treatment for any suspected illness is the responsibility of the employee. However, continued refusal of an employee to seek treatment when it appears that substandard performance may be caused by an illness is not tolerated. Drug dependency should not be made an exception to this commonly accepted principle.
> - It is in the best interests of employees that, when drug dependency is present, it should be diagnosed as such and treated at the earliest possible stage.
> - *Confidential* handling of the diagnosis and treatment of drug dependency is essential.

The objective of this policy is to retain employees, who may have developed drug dependency, by helping them to arrest its further advance and before it renders them unemployable.

The Kemper Insurance Group believes that identifying employees with drug problems is much easier if a company does not take the "discover and terminate" approach. Kemper Insurance maintains that all drug dependencies cause marked changes in work behavior patterns, personal relationships, and emotional moods. Its supervisors are instructed to watch for these changes in employees. When an employee is suspected of drug usage or dependency, his supervisor will privately counsel the employee and seek the assistance of the company staff or a community agency that deals with the problem and cure of drug dependency.

The Kemper Insurance Group has established a policy for dealing with illegal drug traffic:

"Any employees found to be involved in illegal drug traffic on company premises or during working hours will be terminated and reported to proper civil authorities."

With regard to employment of rehabilitated drug users, Kemper Insurance policy holds that:

"Persons who apply for employment and who can show satisfactory evidence of recovery from drug dependencies will not be discriminated against."

Your company must first establish a written policy when planning countermeasures to deal with drug abuse. This policy must be carefully prepared, written, and made known to all employees in the same manner as your company safety policy. The Kemper Insurance Group policy for dealing with drug dependency is excellent and could be adapted to fit your company.

After establishment of a company policy on drug abuse, you should locate any community or area organizations that offer counseling and assistance to persons with drug dependencies. You should familiarize yourself with the types of drugs that can lead to drug dependencies and the effects these drugs may produce. There is a vast quantity of material available on drugs and drug abuse. The following sources can provide you with this information:

National Coordinating Council on Drug Abuse Education and Information
P.O. Box 2000, Washington, D.C. 20013

176

The National Clearing House for Drug Abuse Information
5454 Wisconsin Avenue
Chevy Chase, Md. 20015

National Loss Control Service Corporation
Long Grove, Ill. 60049

Summary

In summation, whether your problem is alcohol or drug abuse, a successful countermeasures program begins with education. Try to learn as much as you can about alcohol and drug abuse. Check to see what other companies are doing to combat these problems. Help your company issue a policy on alcoholism and drug abuse. This policy should be carefully prepared, written, and made known to all employees, just like your company safety policy.

Education of your drivers concerning the impairing effects of alcohol and drugs is a necessary part of any countermeasures program. Information on alcoholism and drug abuse can be obtained from the organizations previously listed, and will help you prepare material to present to your drivers. Discuss alcohol, drugs, and their effects with your drivers during a short safety talk, or devote a few minutes of time at your next safety meeting for that purpose.

As a supervisor, you should not strive to become a "drug detective," constantly looking for pills and drug substances or lurking in dark corners hoping to catch an addict giving himself a "fix." Instead, watch for changes in the work behavior patterns, personal relationships, and emotional moods of your drivers. Any of these changes in a driver may indicate an alcohol or drug problem.

After identifying an alcoholic or drug user under your supervision, you should counsel the individual privately. Remind the person of company policy on the subject. Remember that a person with an alcohol or drug problem needs the help of trained personnel experienced in handling such problems. Be familiar with the organizations in your community that deal with alcoholism and drug dependency so that you can refer the individual for professional help.

Above all, develop a sincere interest in and desire to help the employee with an alcohol or drug problem. Once you have developed these attitudes, you will want to help any employee solve his particular problem and again become a valuable asset to your organization.

10

Establishing the accident review committee

The two key factors in any safety incentive program are: (1) a high standard of safety performance, and (2) a method of recognizing all individuals who meet this performance standard.

Standards Must Be High

If management is satisfied with mediocre standards of performance, it will get nothing better. Setting high quality standards involves no more difficulty than setting low standards. The same amount of supervisory time and effort is involved in either case. However, when standards are set high an additional incentive is created—a challenge to each individual worker. The skilled workers have a chance to show their ability. Their example spurs the rest of the group to *improved performance*—the objective—which pays off in the profit and loss statement.

Recognition Must Be Given

Nothing discourages or annoys a skilled worker more than lack of recognition after he has met the standards of safety performance prescribed by management. Recognition is one of the chief job satisfactions of the skilled worker. It does not matter greatly what form this recognition takes—only that it be given promptly and impartially whenever it is earned.

178

Standard Safe Driving Performance

How can we define a standard of safe driving performance? *Perfect safety performance* is operation of a bus, truck, taxicab, or other commercial vehicle without having any accidents at all. Obviously such a standard is too high. Drivers may become involved in accidents over which they have no control, and for which it would be unfair to penalize them.

In most cases, however, it takes two drivers to make an accident. Usually one of the drivers has violated some traffic ordinance, whereas the other driver has violated some defensive driving principle relating to alertness or safe speed. Either driver could have prevented the accident; therefore, both are at fault.

Here then is a workable definition of standard safe driving performance: While we cannot reasonably penalize drivers for accidents they might become involved in, we can with reason penalize them for accidents that could have been prevented. Our standard of safe driving performance is therefore *the ability to drive without having preventable accidents.*

A PREVENTABLE ACCIDENT

A *preventable* accident is defined in the rules of the National Safety Council's Safe Driver Award Plan as: "any accident involving a company vehicle which results in property damage and/or personal injury, regardless of who was injured, what property was damaged, to what extent, or where it occurred, in which the driver in question failed to exercise every reasonable precaution to prevent the accident."

The key word in this definition is *"reasonable."* How this word is interpreted when applied to actual accident cases will determine how high the standard of safety performance is going to be in any particular fleet. If it is interpreted too strictly, drivers will conclude that the company expects too much of them. They will be prone to give up trying to meet the desired standard of safety performance. On the other hand, if the word "reasonable" is interpreted loosely, driving errors are likely to be overlooked and go uncorrected, and become the cause of similar accidents. As a result of this loose interpretation, the company safety record will fall far short of its possibilities.

The problem of classifying accidents as preventable or non-preventable for safe driving record purposes is one of the most important problems the safety director is called upon to solve.

179

A majority of accidents are preventable. As a result of having attended company driver training programs and safety meetings, drivers know what standard of "defensive driving" is required of them. When involved in a preventable accident they will usually be able to point out where they failed and how the accident could have been prevented. The safety director will have little difficulty in explaining to drivers why such accidents are being classified "preventable" and why the driver is being penalized in accordance with existing rules of the company incentive or safe driver award program.

Borderline Cases

A percentage of the accidents in the average fleet, however, is not so clear-cut. Their classification presents a special problem. Whether the driver did everything "reasonable" to prevent the accident depends a great deal on personal opinion. These borderline cases represent the "hot potatoes" in any accident report file. How these cases are handled can spell the difference between a superior safety record and a mediocre one.

Some safety directors feel that the deciding of borderline cases poses no particular problem at all and that the decision should be made by the safety director or the person in charge of the safety program at the particular location. They point out that since he is best informed on the subject of accident prevention and responsible for the safety program, he is the only logical person to decide whether or not an accident could have been prevented.

Borderline accident cases are the most sensitive points in the whole safety program. Whether or not the driver could have prevented the accident is a matter of conjecture, and involved drivers will resent any arbitrary decision by management that they were at fault.

Such an attitude is entirely justified and indicates that these drivers take pride in their safety records. It is a valuable asset and must not be destroyed. When drivers no longer care how their accidents are classified, the safety program will have reached a state of "bankruptcy."

The Accident Review Committee

If we expect drivers to continue to take their safety records seriously, we must provide for the classification of accidents in such a manner that drivers will feel that their rights have been scrupulously protected. Deciding such cases on the sole basis of the safety director's opinion risks undermining the safety director's proper relationship with the drivers. The decision on borderline cases should reflect the weight of informed opinion of the entire organization. For these reasons, decision by an accident review committee is preferred.

The special advantages of deciding borderline cases by the committee method can be stated as follows:

1. The importance of the individual's safety record is emphasized.

2. The help of all departments is enlisted in making the safety program successful.

3. The safety director is protected from the possibility of creating ill will among drivers who have had accidents.

4. The driver is assured that his rights are being protected.

5. For the driver involved, it takes a great deal of the "sting" out of an adverse decision.

6. The responsibility for the decision is removed from line supervision.

Who Should Serve on the Committee

Deciding whether an accident could or could not have been prevented is not a matter to be solved by popular vote.

The committee's purpose is to decide borderline cases by the weight of informed opinion. The committee should represent all departments of the organization directly involved in the safety program—safety, transportation, and maintenance—as well as driving personnel. A decision from such a group will satisfy involved drivers, and, if the individual members are carefully selected and trained, it will represent the best and most reasonable thinking of the entire organization.

For these reasons the following persons should serve on the committee:

1. One representative from the safety department to serve as chairman, who is trained in the principles of accident prevention and safety supervision. He should be familiar with company safety rules, the content of the driver training program, and the rules of the safe driver award plan or incentive plan.

2. One supervisory representative from the transportation department, familiar with operating rules pertaining to schedules, routes, speed limits, hours of work, and related subjects. He can advise when a driver claims conflict between operating rules and safe practices.

3. One representative from the maintenance department, familiar with the mechanical abilities of company equipment and with company maintenance policy. He can advise when a driver claims faulty equipment as the cause of the accident.

4. Two drivers—since drivers are thoroughly familiar with traffic conditions and the everyday hazards of the job. If given the opportunity, they often can explain authoritatively how accidents can be prevented.

It has been suggested that drivers should outnumber so-called "management" representatives on the committee. This suggestion seems to inject the view that the accident review committee is an arena for labor-management controversy. Nothing could be farther from the truth. The accident review committee is not a joint labor-management function. It is a supervisory tool and as such should be controlled by management to advance the accident prevention program. Management should never relinquish control to the point where the committee is no longer capable of producing decisions that management finds essential in sustaining a high standard of safe driving performance.

The First Committee

Members of the first accident review committee should be selected with special care, since the way they perform their functions will set a pattern for future committees. The supervisory representative and the maintenance representative should be selected for their proven interest in furthering the accident prevention program. Drivers selected should have superior safety records and command the respect and confidence of their fellow drivers.

The chairman should instruct the members of this first committee with great care. He should define a preventable accident and the meaning of defensive driving. Usually a "dry-run" is advisable; that is, the chairman selects an accident report from his file, has the committee discuss it and come to a decision, then tells them how the accident was originally classified and why. When members are thoroughly familiar with the "defensive driving" point of view toward accident prevention, they are ready to decide actual cases.

Rotating Committee Members

As far as possible, the chairman should try to share the educational benefits of serving on an accident review committee by rotating its membership. Members who have served on the committee will take this experience back to their various departments. This process alone will in time build a high degree of safety-mindedness throughout the entire organization. However, only one new member should be taken on the committee at a time. This allows the new member to absorb some of the experience of the senior members before another member is rotated.

182

Committee Procedure

Three recommended committee procedures should be adhered to:

1. The name of the driver involved in the accident should not be revealed to committee members.

2. The driver involved should not be called before the committee to discuss the accident. His accident report should represent him.

3. The decision of the committee should be arrived at by secret ballot.

PRESENTING THE FACTS

As chairman of the accident review committee, the safety representative presents the facts about each accident under review, and guides the discussion.

The chairman should refer to the accident by file number only. Introducing the driver's name would tend to bring personalities into the discussion. Members might be swayed by their prior knowledge of the man's driving habits and general conduct. The fact that the accident is being considered without reference to names enables the committee to be more objective.

The committee should not call the driver before it for questioning. The driver should have already written all he knows about the accident on his report. The facts are there. If called before the committee, he has an opportunity to argue, cloud the issue, and sway the judgment of the committee by his "salesmanship" (or lack of it). It is unfair to the driver and all other drivers.

The facts of each accident presented to members of the committee should come from the following sources:

1. Driver's report of the accident.

2. Police investigation reports.

3. Insurance company investigation reports.

4. Facts based on an investigation by company representatives.

5. Statements of witnesses.

6. Diagrams, photographs, and any other available evidence.

GUIDING THE DISCUSSION

After presenting the facts, the chairman should guide the discussion. The only question before the committee is "Could the driver have prevented this accident?"

The answer to this question depends on the kind of defensive driving philosophy that has come to be accepted in the company. This in turn

183

depends on how good a job the safety director has done in indoctrinating the entire organization in the principles of accident prevention.

But how far can any safe driver be expected to go in attempting to foresee and compensate for the driving errors of others? As stated before, the standard must be high, but it must also be reasonable. It must be the product of the safety training program initiated and maintained by the safety director. It must reflect a meeting of minds of the line organization as to what is reasonable and possible in the realm of accident prevention.

It should be remembered, however, that when a particular accident is declared non-preventable, a precedent has been set and the committee is obliged henceforth to render the same decision on similar accidents occurring under the same circumstances. A decision of non-preventable absolves the driver of all blame for the accident. There will undoubtedly be other accidents of this type and the committee should not hesitate to judge them "non-preventable." However, such a decision must be sound. If too many accidents are admitted to this classification, the safety program gradually will lose its effectiveness.

VOTING BY SECRET BALLOT

When the chairman is satisfied that the members of the committee are completely familiar with all the facts of the accident and have discussed it at sufficient length, he should pass out slips of paper and ask for a vote. Members should write "preventable" or "non-preventable" on the slips of paper and pass them back to the chairman.

The chairman counts the ballots and only casts a vote in case of a tie. Then he announces the majority decision as either "preventable" or "non-preventable." Experience has shown that when the committee is well indoctrinated, the chairman's vote will be necessary in less than three per cent of the cases.

Telling the Driver

Following the meeting, the chairman should inform each driver in writing what the committee's decision was and, if the accident was judged "preventable," what the reasons were for classifying it so. Having followed the discussion of the accident, the chairman is familiar with the majority point of view and will be able to summarize it for the driver.

A copy of the written decision should be given to the driver and another copy should be placed in his personnel file. Copies to other interested parties, such as the driver's immediate superior, union officials, and others may be provided, if desirable, depending upon company policy.

Usually, it is advisable for the safety director, or the driver's immediate supervisor, to announce the decision to the driver in a personal interview. This makes it possible to discuss corrective measures with the driver and to relate the decision to the driver's entire accident record.

Appeal Procedures

Decisions about the preventability of accidents should be made as close as possible to the bottom of the ladder of authority. As was stated before, 75 per cent of a fleet's accidents are clear-cut cases and can be decided one way or another by the safety director, the driver's immediate supervisor, or the person directly in charge of safety at the particular location. Only when there is a reasonable doubt or when the person having primary jurisdiction is unable to convince the driver that his accident was "preventable" should an accident be referred to the accident review committee.

But suppose the driver is not satisfied even with the decision of the accident review committee? In some companies, he has no recourse. Other companies, recognizing that the factor of morale is involved, provide an additional assurance of fair play. They take advantage of the National Safety Council's Accident Review Committee. Recommended practice is to allow the driver to make written appeal on any decision from the company accident review committee within 10 days after he has been informed of the decision. In his appeal, the driver is asked to state why he thinks the accident should have been judged "non-preventable."

The Council's Accident Review Committee is composed of five practicing safety directors appointed each year by the general chairmen of the Transit, Commercial Vehicle and the School Transportation Sections. In referring an accident to this committee, six copies of the accident report should be forwarded to the National Safety Council with the request that it be referred to the Accident Review Committee for a decision. *Refer to National Safety Council Safe Driver Award Rules, Section 4.*

11

Employee safety, including garage safety

We have seen in previous chapters that employee injuries in a motor vehicle fleet can occur frequently and that these injuries are costly; fortunately, they can be prevented and the cost of their prevention is less than the cost of allowing them to occur. The conditions and procedures for the control of these injuries comprise the driver and garage employee safety program—the subject of this chapter.*

What is the difference between a fleet that has an employee safety program and one that does not?

An employee safety program requires studying every job operation in the fleet in order to know the hazards connected with each, and then devising safe work procedures to control these hazards. Every employee is trained in the safety procedures connected with his job. Each supervisor checks for compliance with these safety procedures, and all those in management vigorously and continuously support the employee safety program to make it a basic part of every fleet operation.

Contrast this with the fleet that does not have an employee safety program—hazards are not studied, safety procedures are not a recognized part of operations, safety is a hit-or-miss affair depending upon the prior safety knowledge that each individual happens to bring to his job.

* *Under the Occupational Safety and Health Act (OSHAct), which became effective on April 28, 1971, most employers must render their establishments as free from potential safety hazards as possible (see Appendix J).*

How to Start a Safety Program

To start an employee safety program, the safety director must make certain that management knows the basic theories of accident prevention and how they will be put into practice. To develop both management and employee conviction that accident prevention works, these topics should be covered early in supervisor and employee training courses:

1. Accidents can happen anywhere at any time. It cannot be assumed, therefore, that any department, job, or facility is safe. Everything must be studied to eliminate hazards.

2. Accidents are not the result of chance, but are caused either by specific unsafe acts or specific unsafe conditions. Accidents can be prevented by learning what these specific acts and conditions are and then substituting safe acts and safe conditions.

3. Unless unsafe acts and unsafe conditions are corrected, an accident will eventually result. If corrective action is still not taken, accidents will repeat.

4. Everyone in the organization must assume personal responsibility for safety: top management, each department head, each supervisor, and each individual worker and driver.

It is the purpose of the safety program to disseminate information about hazards and provide the stimulus for sustained safety effort. The training program should first be presented to all supervisors. They, in turn, should help present the material to their employees.

187

Make a Safety Check First

As soon as top management knows what is to be accomplished, the safety director should see that top management sets broad policies. If the company is quite large, a top management safety committee can be formed.

After they are trained in what to look for, management or the management committee should make a system-wide safety inspection to bring all facilities up to safety standards. The composition of any committee will depend upon the size of the fleet, but should include those who have the maximum knowledge of methods, practices, and conditions of the type the committee will encounter.

More than one type committee can be formed: company-wide or inter-terminal, terminal, department, foremen, workmen, joint labor-management, inspection, and "get-it-done" committees. Enlightened management should make policies and give moral and financial support to their committees.

Every building and every yard or facility of the company should be inspected according to the housekeeping and maintenance checklists shown later in this chapter. When making inspection of separate garages or terminals, the local managers, if not already on the committee, should join it for the local inspection.

INITIAL INSPECTION

The safety director should use an initial safety inspection by a high-echelon committee to bring facilities up to date and, equally important, to train management itself. At a later date lower-echelon safety committees (listed two paragraphs earlier) should be formed and trained and assigned the responsibility for making periodic safety inspections. Following are some of the techniques to be used in this initial inspection. They apply to all properties.

1. Review and list in advance the anticipated mechanical or physical hazards.
2. Let the inspection follow the job process whenever possible. For example, when buses or trucks are to be serviced, note what equipment is being used as vehicles are being refueled, checked, and cleaned. Is any of this equipment unsafe to use?
3. Avoid disturbing or distracting those at work by not ceremoniously writing notes or memorandums in their presence. Make notes quickly or make them afterwards.

4. Don't pass up an opportunity to instruct in a safe procedure if this is necessary. Usually it is best to bring the matter to the attention of the proper supervisor, foreman, or superintendent after the inspection has been completed, unless there is an emergency which requires immediate action.

5. Be as alert as possible when making an inspection.

- **Look** for signs of poor housekeeping, poor maintenance, inadequate tools, unsuitable equipment.
- **Listen** for sounds of escaping compressed air, steam, water, oxygen, and acetylene. Listen for unusual sounds like thumps, squeaks, and squeals.
- **Feel** for equipment or machinery that is vibrating unnecessarily. Carefully check for sharp points or edges that may cut, puncture, or tear. Check for hot surfaces that may burn or radiate, causing discomfort.
- **Smell** for odors of leaking gas, spilled gasoline or diesel fuel, or other flammable gases or liquids.
- **Taste** drinking water as it comes from drinking fountains or other forms of dispensers. Taste the quality of products dispensed from coffee urns or soft drink dispensers. Is temperature proper?

On this first inspection it might also be desirable to call in trained personnel or contract for their services for appraisal and inspection of fire extinguishing equipment and of elevators and pressure vessels, if this hasn't been already done. Such inspections are usually required by a city, county, or state ordinance or code, and by insurance carriers.

Chapters 2 and 3 of the National Safety Council's *Accident Prevention Manual for Industrial Operations,* 6th ed., discuss safety organization and inspection methods. Chapter 14 of the same book lists private organizations and government agencies of both U.S. and Canada that offer help. It would be a good idea to consult this book for the nondriving safety aspects of fleet safety management.

FREIGHT AND PASSENGER TERMINALS

In freight terminals, specifically, check for condition of the docks, floors, lighting, freight-handling equipment (such as forklift trucks, dollies, pallets, conveyors, hand trucks), weighing scales, storage racks, bins. A checklist accompanies this section.

In passenger terminals, check condition of baggage-checking facilities, ticket counters, waiting room and office furniture and equipment. Usually, such inspections are made in conjunction with the inspection of public-passenger facilities in waiting rooms, rest rooms, and boarding and alighting areas. It is far better to seek and detect probable injury-causing conditions than to find them the cause of an accident.

A checklist is given on these pages. More details are given in the section "Establish Safe Practices," pages 193 to 212.

FOLLOWUP

Following this inspection, the committee should summarize all unsafe conditions observed and make recommendations for their correction. Management should then issue the orders necessary for the correction of these conditions. The safety director should follow up on each recommendation to make sure it is carried out within a reasonable time.

Mechanical and Physical Hazards To Look for When Making a Safety Inspection

QUALITY OF SHOP, STATION (TERMINAL), OR GARAGE HOUSEKEEPING

1. Are yards and outdoor premises clean?
2. Are roadway markings, lane numbers, markings for parking areas kept freshly and neatly painted or outlined?
3. Are buildings kept attractively painted?
4. Are windows clean? Are missing, broken, or cracked window panes renewed?
5. Are skylights clean? Are missing, broken, or cracked panes renewed?
6. Are building entrances unobstructed?
7. Are indoor traffic lanes kept freshly painted?
8. Are floors kept clean of oil, grease, water, dirt, or trash?
9. Are aisles kept clear?
10. Are stairs kept clear?
11. Are fire escapes unobstructed?
12. Is loose material left around building columns or walls or under benches?
    Soft drink bottles?
    Discarded lunch boxes?
    Short pieces of pipe?
    Defective automotive parts?
    Timbers or wooden blocks no longer needed?

13. Are approved containers or waste or trash cans or bins provided?
14. Are they emptied regularly?
15. Are automotive maintenance or overhaul pits satisfactorily clean?
16. Is the area under automotive hoists kept clean?
17. Are lighting fixtures dirty?
18. Are work benches and tool carts kept satisfactorily clean?
19. Are tools kept in a designated place when not in use?
20. Is portable equipment kept in a designated place when not in use?
21. Is material stored or piled neatly and safely?
22. Is fire-fighting equipment kept in a well-known, well-marked place?
23. Is fire-fighting equipment kept free of obstructions?
24. Are old brooms, mops and other gear disposed of when no longer usable?
25. Are bulletin boards kept "up-to-date" by being stripped periodically of out-of-date notices, letters, greeting cards, and the like?
26. Are locker rooms, change rooms, rest rooms, wash rooms kept neat and clean?
27. Are there any protruding nails, bolts, wire, splinters, glass, or other sharp objects?
28. Are warning or caution signs in good condition?
29. Are hose and portable electric cords allowed to become a tripping hazard when they could be kept overhead?
30. Is sawdust allowed to accumulate on the floor?
31. Are office areas kept neat and free of samples, experimental material, defective parts, catalogs, and discarded clothing?
32. Are desks and shop work benches neatly maintained?
33. Are clock faces kept clean?
34. Is the area around soft drink dispensers and candy bar dispensers kept neat and orderly?

QUALITY OF SHOP, STATION (TERMINAL), OR GARAGE MAINTENANCE

1. Are floors and stairways in good condition:
2. Are handrails provided on stairways, and kept in good condition?
3. Are aisle and work area markings provided, and well maintained?
4. Are machine tools kept well painted?

191

5. Are moving machinery parts well guarded?
6. Is materials handling equipment kept in good repair:
   Cranes?
   Hoists?
   Conveyors?
   Forklift power trucks? Pallets?
   Hand trucks?
   Wheel barrows?
   Carts?
   Dollies?
7. Are ropes, chains, cables, and slings in good condition?
8. Are elevators and manlifts well guarded and in good repair?
9. Are platforms and scaffolds in good condition?
10. Are ladders in safe condition; equipped with safety shoes?
11. Are pressure vessels regularly inspected?
12. Is compressed air equipment and piping in good condition?
13. Is gasoline and diesel oil dispensing equipment in good condition?
14. Is lubricating and transmission oil dispensing equipment O.K.?
15. Is ventilating equipment in good condition?
16. Is heating equipment in good condition?
17. Is general overhead lighting system adequate? Well maintained?
18. Is pit, storeroom, and other special lighting adequate? Well maintained?
19. Is fire-fighting equipment adequate? Well maintained?
    Fire extinguishers? (CO_2, dry powder?)
    Fire hose?
    Overhead and "beneath vehicle" sprinklers?
20. Is a safe storage provided for flammable liquids? Well maintained?
21. Are doors and windows kept in easy operating condition?
22. Are sufficient work benches provided? Well maintained?
23. Are vices, grinders, and welding equipment in good condition?
24. Are portable electric tools safely grounded? Checked periodically?
25. Are tool rooms provided and are they properly supervised?
26. Is first-aid equipment kept in an accessible place? Checked periodically?
27. Are washroom and locker room facilities adequate? Well maintained?
28. Are storage tanks provided? Well maintained?
29. Are tire storage facilities provided? Well maintained?
30. Are waste disposal drums or bins provided? Well maintained?

31. Is adequate personal protective equipment provided and well maintained?

Safety hats or caps?

Goggles, safety glasses, eye shields, face shields?

Respirators?

Gloves?

32. Do roofs leak?

Establish Safe Practices

There are certain fundamental safe practices that should be followed by everyone. These should be formulated, published, and disseminated to all employees in the form of logical and enforceable safety rules. A rule that is not logical or that cannot be enforced may seriously impair the effectiveness of other rules. Once definite safety rules have been selected and made known to employees, the company safety policy should state explicitly that they must be observed.

General safety rules should cover the following subjects after first stressing the need for safety rules for operating and maintaining a safe fleet.

1. Employee responsibility for conducting himself in a safe manner at all times, for reporting to his supervisor all unsafe practices and unsafe conditions observed, for asking the supervisor for specific instructions about unusual hazards not covered in the rule book, and for observing all signs and notices.

2. First aid. Discussion of available first-aid facilities, essential telephone numbers (such as those for a doctor and for an ambulance), and the injury-reporting system. The subjects of infection, artificial respiration, heat sickness, and all other first-aid information pertinent to terminal, garage, or highway can be given through courses.

3. Fire fighting. Location and description of emergency fire-fighting equipment in the plant, how to reach the local fire department, the specific procedure to be followed in case of fire or other emergency, an explanation of the emergency alarm system, and information on fire prevention.

4. Electrical equipment. Hazards associated with certain types of electrical apparatus and the appropriate precautions to be taken during maintenance and repair of defective equipment. How to deal with electrical fires.

5. Work clothing. Detailed item-by-item descriptions of what is safe and unsafe work clothing, and that wearing of rings, for example, is discouraged.

6. Personal protective equipment. Eye protection, foot protection, respiratory equipment, hand protection, head protection, and so on, tell whether specific items are recommended or required and the circumstances under which required equipment must be used.

7. Good housekeeping. Personal cleanliness. Hygienic use of toilet, shower, washroom, locker room, and lunchroom facilities; safe methods of piling material; and other aspects of good housekeeping.

The company rule book should be given to all employees and its contents discussed at one or more safety meetings. It should also be given to new employees, and its material should be incorporated in the company's training program.

A general safety rule book, unfortunately, cannot cover everything. Instruction in specific job-safety practices is, therefore, the responsibility of the immediate supervisor. Performance is the responsibility of the employee.

To determine the specific job hazards, use the systematic procedure known as a job safety analysis (JSA). Not only should the safety director learn this technique, but all safety supervisors should also. The reader will find details in Appendix D.

Some of the more important job hazards found in fleets are as follows:

1. HAZARDS TO EYESIGHT

Probably the most tragic injury short of death is total loss of eyesight. This need not occur if eye protection is required by safety rules, and consistently used. This safety habit can be acquired.

Employees who must wear prescription eye glasses should be encouraged to wear prescription safety glasses because these will generally withstand an impact from eight to twelve times greater than ordinary glasses can without cracking or shattering.

Because glasses will not afford sufficient eye protection for every job duty, other type protection is available. Here is a suggested list of the type of eye protective equipment that should be worn for specific job duties:

Wear safety goggles or eye shields when:
    Grinding
    Using impact wrenches and air drills
    Chipping, scraping, or scaling paint, rust, carbon, or other
        materials

194

Using punches or chisels
Cutting rivets
Cutting or breaking glass
Chipping or breaking concrete
Using paint remover
Servicing air conditioning equipment with refrigerants
Soldering
Cleaning dust or dirt from motors, generators, compartments
Removing hard putty from sashes
Using metal-cutting lathe, shaper, drill press, or power hack saw
Steam cleaning
Washing vehicles or parts with soaps or solvents
Working under vehicles

Wear face shield when:
Working around battery acid
Pouring Babbitt or other molten metals
Buffing with wire brush wheels
Doctoring brake linings
Grinding body filler
Using cyanide furnace

Wear safety goggles with light green lenses when:
Metallizing

Wear hood with clear lenses when:
Sandblasting out in the open
Pouring acid from carboys

Wear hood with dark lenses of proper shade when:
Cutting or welding metal
Doing electric welding or assisting an electric welder

2. HEALTH HAZARDS

The primary health hazards to garage men are spray-painting equipment, carbon monoxide poisoning, inhalation of metal fumes when metallizing, and inhalation of asbestos dust arising from the use of "brake doctors."

Spray-painting hazards can be overcome through the design and adequate maintenance of ventilating systems. Ventilating systems will remove most of the exhaust fumes and gases produced by gasoline or diesel engines operated within buildings (see Appendix I). Solvent vapors can be controlled through the use of properly designed equipment. Respirators can prevent employees from breathing harmful asbestos and other dusts, fumes, or mists. Refer to NSC's *Accident Prevention Manual* and *Fundamentals of Industrial Hygiene.*

3. HAZARDS OF LIFTING AUTOS, TRUCKS, AND BUSES

Three major hazards are associated with hoisting or raising automotive equipment: (a) having a vehicle fall off a hoist or a ramp because it had not been properly positioned, (b) having a hoist drop suddenly due to a loss of pressure, or binding and dropping suddenly due to a stuck or jammed piston inside of a hydraulic cylinder, (c) striking one's head against some part of the hoist or the vehicle on the hoist. Grease pits can have similar danger.

The first hazard can be safeguarded against by installing only hoists specifically designed to handle all automotive equipment used. Avoid using makeshift setups.

Competent periodic inspection of all hoisting equipment and a high quality maintenance program will minimize hoist failure.

To avoid the third hazard, men should wear a "bump-type" safety cap, which won't limit their ability to work in close quarters. Along with the wearing of suitable head protection is the necessity of using safety goggles, eye shields, or face shields to prevent eye injuries from dislodged dirt or other foreign matter. Vapor-proof lights should be used around these areas.

4. BURN HAZARDS FROM CHEMICALS, HOT WATER, OR STEAM

Oil-soaked, grease-covered, and dirt-covered parts have to be cleaned from time to time to permit accurate, expeditious maintenance or overhaul of automotive equipment. Special steam-cleaning equipment with paper nozzles is used for the purpose. The big hazard of using steam arises out of its accidental misdirection or having a steam hose burst or come loose while under pressure. National Safety Council Industrial Data Sheet No. 238, *Cleaning with Hot Water and Steam,* gives details.

Boilers and other pressure vessels must be constructed according to the *Boiler and Pressure Vessel Code* of the American Society of Mechanical Engineers,* be properly installed and fitted with all required safety devices, and be inspected regularly and conscientiously as required by the insurance underwriter. Burns arising out of accidental contact with hot surfaces can be avoided by using suitable insulation, barricades, railings, or enclosures. Check local codes also.

* *American Society of Mechanical Engineers, 345 East 47th St., New York City 10017*

196

When a heated caustic solution is used for cleaning, it presents a chemical burn hazard. This may be safeguarded against by wearing suitable safety goggles, eyeshields or face shields, gloves, and aprons. Acid burns from handling, servicing, or charging of storage batteries can be prevented by using proper personal protective equipment such as hoods and rubber gloves and aprons.

5. HAZARDS OF REMOVING OR REPLACING VERY HEAVY UNIT PARTS

When handling engines, transmissions, clutches, front and rear axles, dual tires and rims and brake drums, air conditioning equipment, and all other heavy automotive parts, use jacks, dollies, hoists, or cranes. When rope or steel cable slings or forklift trucks are used to handle these heavy loads, all equipment should be handled by properly trained and supervised personnel. There should be a high safety factor in the equipment used to handle the heavy weights involved. Equipment should be properly maintained.

Certain hazards are likely to be overlooked when using powered material-handling equipment. Be careful when raising, lowering, and tilting the hoisting ram and guides of forklift trucks. Also, as the ram ascends or descends, it can pinch off fingers unless pinch points are well guarded.

Monorail hoists and traveling cranes must have their interlocks checked periodically to make sure the stop dogs will readily drop to prevent running off the rail. Hoist load blocks and hooks should have a sheave guard to prevent fingers, hands, or arms being caught between the sheave and the wire rope. When jacks or table hoists are used to raise or lower metal parts, metal-to-metal contacts may slip and permit movement of whatever is being raised or lowered. Use a piece of cloth or properly fitted wood blocks to separate metal from metal.

6. HAZARDS OF MOUNTING HEAVY-DUTY TIRES AND RIMS

The obvious hazard in mounting tires and rims is that of blowing off the lock ring as high-pressure, heavy-duty tires are being inflated. Blowoffs can occur with such violence that they can kill a man instantly. To safeguard against this, use a metal cage to contain the lock ring should it accidentally blow off during inflation. For complete details on how to combat this hazard, see NSC Industrial Data Sheet No. 411, *Mounting Heavy-Duty Tires and Rims.*

Another hazard involved in handling heavy truck and bus tires comes from mishandling impact wrenches used to loosen or tighten wheel lug nuts.

Still another hazard that frequently causes skinned knuckles and hands is the close clearance between tires and fenders. Therefore, keep hands low when pulling tires and rims. One ever-present hazard is that of being struck by a falling heavy-duty tire, or by dual-mounted tires. They must be moved carefully and must be left in a very secure position if laid aside.

7. HAZARDS OF MACHINE TOOLS

Two principal hazards when using metal working tools are:

a. power transmission equipment such as pulleys, sheaves, belts, gears, and clutches, and

b. point-of-operation hazards.

Both hazards can be safeguarded against by the use of well designed and well maintained guards or barricades. (*The Accident Prevention Manual for Industrial Operations* contains many ideas about guarding.)

8. HAZARDS OF WELDING EQUIPMENT

Welding equipment can produce accidental burns (due to contact with the heat source or with hot metal), and eye injuries (due to exposure to ultraviolet light or popping slag). Fumes or vapors from certain metals like zinc can also produce ill effects. All of these hazards can be effectively guarded against by wearing proper protective equipment (hoods, jackets, leggings, spats, gloves, goggles, and respirators) and by having adequate ventilation.

Be sure all employees are protected from the harmful rays of electric arc welding equipment. Welder's helpers must be required to wear tinted safety goggles. Screens and barricades should be erected around welding operations to trap all harmful light rays. Welding booths should be ventilated adequately to protect those working inside. (More welding hazards in Section 10, following.)

Also, wear clear lens flash goggles under the helmet to prevent hot slag from popping into eyes when hood is temporarily raised. (See Section 1 in this chapter and Chapter 31 of *Accident Prevention Manual for Industrial Operations* for more details.)

9. HAZARDS OF POWERED HAND TOOLS

The use of portable electric drills can result in eye injuries or electric shock. Not only can hot chips or turnings cause burns, but the drill can

WELDER USES AIR LINE RESPIRATOR for protection against fumes.

puncture hands, arms, or legs. Therefore it must be handled with care.

To avoid accidental electric shock, an auxiliary grounding wire should be connected to the frame of the drill. This is usually done through a three-wire portable electric cord.

In general, it is preferable to have compressed air supply lines and electric extension cords be ceiling-suspended, if possible, on automatic takeup reels in order to eliminate tripping hazards.

10. HAZARDS DUE TO EXPLOSIVE VAPORS

Both acetylene gas and petroleum vapors are highly explosive in critical air/gas ratios. But unless acetylene welding equipment has developed a leak, there should be no explosion hazard.

Petroleum vapors can be hazardous when an attempt is made to weld an "empty" oil drum or gasoline tank that is not thoroughly vapor-free. Prohibit use of gasoline for cleaning automotive parts, because, aside from the defatting effect on skin and the ever-present possibility of spilling it on clothing, there is always the possibility that, during the

ROOF-SUSPENDED SERVICES AT FUEL POINT reduce hazards from flammable vapors and from tripping over hoses. Note plastic sky shield.

winter months, an explosive mixture will accumulate in confined areas and be detonated. In place of gasoline, use kerosene or a safety solvent for cleaning. Use them as sparingly as possible and with adequate ventilation. There are many safety codes regarding this subject. See the *Accident Prevention Manual for Industrial Operations,* for technical data.

11. HAZARD OF BEING RUN OVER

Personnel must always watch the movement of vehicles inside garages, shops, and terminals as well as outside. Drivers must permit buildup of proper air pressure for the safe operation of power brakes, otherwise there is always the possibility that a vehicle that is being moved may not only crash into the vehicle ahead, but also trap and crush someone between the two vehicles.

One particularly hazardous operation is washing the rear of motor vehicles, because the person doing this job will have his back turned to the next vehicle moving up the line. He must train himself to always be alert for the movement of vehicles behind him. The penalty for failing to do so may be crushed legs or thighs.

Legs can also be crushed when working under a vehicle while on a "creeper." If the mechanic's legs and feet stick out, they can be run over by another vehicle, particularly one that is being backed up without a watcher assisting the driver.

12. OTHER HAZARDS TO SHOP, STATION, AND GARAGE PERSONNEL

Major sources of injury are jumping across open inspection pits, falling off ladders, hurting backs while trying to move supplies and equipment, and using hand tools improperly. Prevention of all work injuries requires proper selection and training of employees, careful supervision of their work habits, review of all injury causes, and the creation of safety-mindedness in all employees, such as discussed in the previous chapter.

13. HAZARDS IN TERMINALS

Many of the hazards described in the previous section also apply to freight terminals and docks. In addition there is the ever-present hazard of being crushed between a truck and a loading dock, of being crushed between two vehicles, of being hurt by falling merchandise or equipment, of being run over by forklift trucks, or being hurt on conveyors.

Appropriate use of "highway yellow" paint* in and around freight terminals can minimize the possibility of drivers and freight terminal employees bumping objects or falling off places. For example, a yellow or white line painted six inches from the edge of a loading dock can deter persons from accidentally walking off the elevated area or driving freight-handling equipment off.

Trailer Movement. To reduce injuries to employees assigned to move freight in or out of truck trailers, the National Safety Council fully

---

* *Color cards showing "highway yellow" may be obtained from the U.S. Bureau of Public Roads.*

endorses and encourages the use of wheel chocks. Chocks provide an extra margin of safety against possible defects or deficiencies in the braking system of a trailer, which could interfere with the safe loading operation.

Trucks or trailers may be edged away from the dock as a result of the movement of heavy freight in and out of the trailer or truck body or even from an accidental bump by a lift truck. Many dockmen have been seriously injured in falls between the vehicle and dock. In some cases, lift truck operators have actually fallen under the forklift. Wheel chocks, placed firmly ahead of the rear wheels, are the best safeguard against trailer movement.

If sliding trailer tandems are left in a forward position, a heavy load, especially on a lift truck, may lift the front end of the trailer and force it away from the loading platform. This will, of course, affect the stability of the freight already in the trailer, the load on the lift truck, and the lift truck itself, which can result in an avalanche of freight, seriously injuring the dock worker. If sliding tandems are forward, the back of the trailer should also be supported by stands or the tractor should be hooked up to prevent seesawing as weight is moved in and out of the trailer.

Whenever heavy nose loading of a trailer is expected, a tractor should be hooked up or the nose supported by stands. Too much weight ahead of the landing gear of unsupported trailers can cause it to nose-dive and result in severe injury to workmen inside.

Bridge plates. Bridge plates (or dockboards) used in loading operations pose a tripping hazard and affect the stability of freight and equipment moved across them. In addition, the edges of these plates become sharpened on concrete floors and can cause serious injuries if not kept flush with the surface of the dock and trailer. Loose plates may be driven away from the dock by the wheels of a lift truck or be knocked aside by cars, thus exposing workers to danger in the unbridged threshold. Workers should not assume that the plate is secure just because it is properly positioned. They should make certain it is properly anchored.

Bridge plates should be kept clear of water, grease, ice, and other material that could create a slipping surface and result in injury to a dockworker. Also, the bridge plates should be wide enough and able to support any load that crosses them. Power truck operators should be instructed to drive over them slowly.

Handholds, or other effective means, shall be provided on portable bridge plates to permit safe handling.

Powered dockboards shall meet the requirements of Commercial

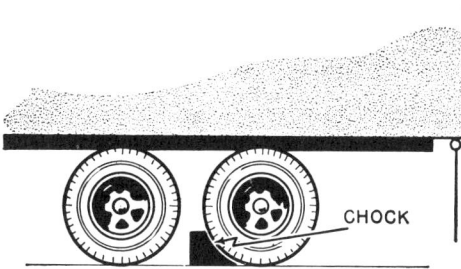

A DISASTROUS ACCIDENT may take place if a trailer is not blocked properly at loading dock. Diagram at left shows preferred placing of chocks under rear trailer wheels.

CHOCK

Standard CS 202–56 (1956), "Industrial Lifts and Hinged Loading Ramps," published by the U.S. Department of Commerce.

Interior trailer. Inadequate lighting in a truck-trailer will hide jagged edges, splintered crates, and various other hazards on the floor or walls. Many dockmen have tripped over unseen material in a dark trailer or cut their hands on rusty nails left in the floor where blocking timbers had been. If the front bulkhead of an empty trailer cannot be seen, or if a workman has difficulty in reading labels on the freight he is unloading, more light is required. When rigging additional lighting, it should be set up to minimize the possibility of bulb breakage or other damage to the lighting fixtures. Wires should be placed where they will not be run over. Also, all dockmen should know where to obtain replacement bulbs and how to rig the portable lighting equipment, when needed.

203

The interior surfaces of a truck-trailer are not always smooth and uniform. Loose, dangling roof supports, jagged punctures in the sheet metal sides, holes in the floor, damaged posts, and holes in plywood sides have caused many bruises, cuts, and broken bones. Such defects may be found even in the newest trailers. Dockmen must survey the trailer body before unloading or loading in order to spot hazards before they cause injury. When defects are discovered, immediate action should be taken by the workman to minimize the danger to himself until a permanent repair can be made. Dockmen should be instructed to report all defects in the trailer they have been assigned to work.

Some freight to be unloaded from a truck-trailer can give off particles of matter, harmful mists, or vapors. After trailers have been sealed for a period of time, a high concentration of contaminants may build up within them. The effects on the human system cannot always be predicted and can be a serious health hazard. Dock workers should be instructed to check the working atmosphere before entering any trailer. If a worker believes the air is contaminated, he should notify his supervisor. Company policy should be established on protective equipment to be maintained at each terminal and conditions under which contaminated trailers may or may not be loaded or unloaded.

Area threats. The immediate surroundings and the path of travel over which materials are to be moved are of considerable importance if injury and lost time are to be avoided. Keep your working docks swept clean. A neat, clean, orderly dock usually allows an efficient operation to be performed. Tripping and slipping hazards must be avoided. Steel bands, splintered boards, and other trash can accumulate around the dock area and should be picked up. This should be done on a routine basis, depending on the operation. Grease and other liquids must be cleaned off the floor immediately. There should be a specific place to put all material handling equipment. When the equipment is used, workmen should be held responsible for its return.

Illumination is also important to the moving of freight. Be certain that necessary lighting is available. Minimum recommended illumination on loading docks is 20 footcandles; inside truck bodies, minimum illumination is 10 footcandles, according to the Illuminating Engineering Society.

Good housekeeping is a habit-forming practice and a very important part of an effective fleet safety program.

Scattered debris. Freight and equipment are sometimes carelessly left lying in and around the working area by the previous shift. Unchecked freight, tools, wrappings, bottles, and loose dunnage are all traps for the wheels of a hand truck and for unwary feet. These traps often become more than just a nuisance to be stepped over or avoided. They have been the cause of almost every imaginable kind of personal injury from simple bruises and abrasions, through cuts and broken bones, to concussions. The first duty of any dockman, before beginning any actual work, is to make his work area safe. This means that all dunnage and tools not in use should be replaced in their respective storage racks; all trash should be deposited in the receptacles provided; and that all unchecked freight left scattered about should be checked and removed. Unloaders (strippers) should know that an "empty trailer" should be *completely* empty. Stripping is not completed until the floor of the trailer is swept clean of all trash, nails left in the floor have been removed, and the bridge plate has been pulled and stored.

Elevated areas. Appropriate use of "highway yellow" paint* in and around freight terminals can minimize the possibility of drivers and freight terminal employees bumping into objects or falling off high places. For example, a yellow or white line painted six inches from the edge of a loading dock can prevent someone from accidentally walking, or driving off the elevated area.

Cargo shifting. Safe loading of motor vehicles and protection against shifting or falling cargo can do much to prevent highway and industrial accidents. Because trailers are designed for uniform load distribution, the cargo should be distributed equally between the rear tires and the fifth wheel which transfers its load to the truck-tractor. In addition, weight of the freight should be distributed equally on each side of the trailer. A heavy load at one side will overload the springs and tires at that side. The cargo should be placed so that weight is equal on the rear tires and thus eliminate possible twisting of frame and overloading of axle housing and wheel bearings. Heavy containers, equipment, or machinery large enough to occupy the width of the trailer floor should be loaded with the center of weight over the center line of the trailer. Freight should be secured in a manner which will prevent its shifting.

Top-heavy articles, such as machinery and other equipment, should be blocked and braced to prevent tipping and damaging other freight or affecting operation safety. Such articles will generally require bracing near the top in addition to floor blocking. Blocks and bracing should be used to eliminate slack space. All cargo should be secured so that it will

See footnote on page 201.

Proper Load Distribution

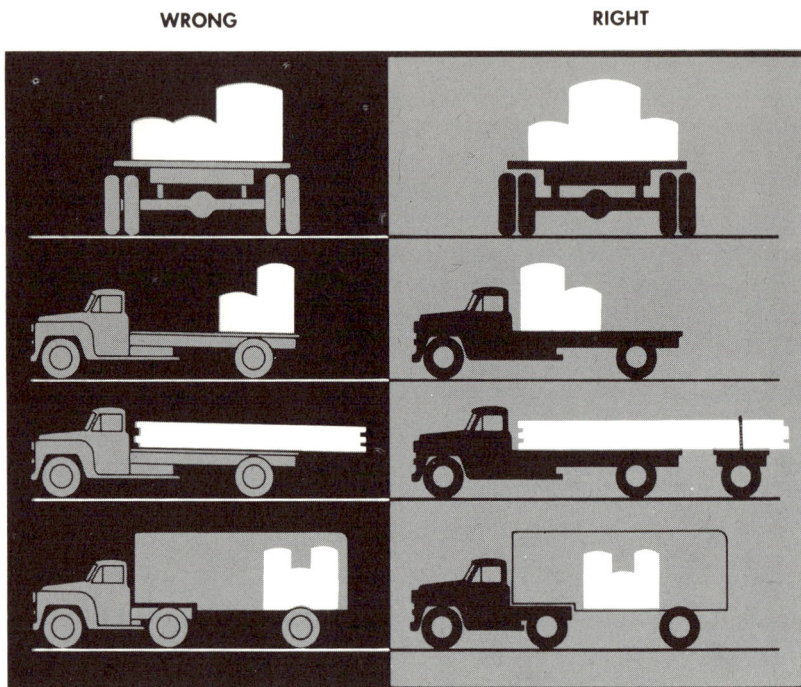

Improper load distribution shortens tire life.

It overloads the tires on one axle when the load is not distributed evenly between the axles.

The tires on one side of the truck or trailer are overloaded when that side is required to carry more than the opposite side.

This may affect starting, making driving wheels slip on light side, and cause tires to wear faster.

Remember, too, that although the gross load may not be too great, one axle or one side of the truck, or one wheel, may be overloaded due to improper distribution of the load.

Analyze . . . Equalize . . . Distribute

Analyze each truck or tractor trailer unit according to tire size—the axle carrying capacity of the tires—and distribute the load accordingly.

Equalize the loads on each axle according to the carrying capacity of the tires.

On semi-trailer units, distribute load so each axle and the fifth wheel carries its share according to carrying capacities of tires.

206

not come in contact with doors to preclude the load from shifting or rolling while in transit. Properly seasoned and undamaged lumber, free of dry rot and knots, should be used for blocking and bracing freight in the trailers. Bracing and blocking material and construction should be capable of withstanding loadings representative of the forces that may act upon them during emergency application of the brakes. The Federal Highway Administration's Bureau of Motor Carrier Safety regulations for the safe loading of motor vehicles and protection against shifting or falling cargo should be observed.

Baggage, freight, or express on buses should be stowed and secured in a manner which will assure protection of occupants against injury resulting from the falling or displacement of the articles being transported. The articles should not interfere with the driver's freedom of movement and proper operation of the bus. In addition, baggage or freight should not obstruct any occupant's access to any of the exits.

Materials handling. More workmen in the motor transportation industry are injured by improper handling of shipping materials than from any other single source. Strains, sprains, and other injuries frequently cause long layoffs from work, and can be costly to both the worker and the company. The need for knowledge of materials handling, therefore, is obvious.

The handling and stowing of objects and materials is not always as easy as it appears. It is, therefore, wise to stop and reason out every intended operation. The fleet supervisor should instruct his men to carefully inspect each load for its weight, slivers, nails, sharp edges, and weak bottoms.

If the load is too big to handle alone, the worker should be instructed to get help or, if available, use equipment designed specifically to handle the load. When handling rough or sharp-edged objects, protective gloves should be worn. Also, cartons should be gripped away from seams so that the hands do not come in contact with sharp staples. Hands should be kept off steel and wire banding. Since, material can fall out of opened or weak-bottomed cartons, workers should be encouraged to wear safety shoes. Recommended hand protection and safety shoes are a must on most jobs involving handling materials. Some require wearing goggles and/or safety hats.

Lifting is a part of almost everyone's job, but too often it's done in the wrong manner. Injuries caused by improper lifting can be very easily prevented if workers follow a few simple rules covering proper body position and lifting practices. When lifting heavy objects, keep the back

Proper Way To Lift

Lifting is so much a part of everyday jobs that most of us don't think about it. But it is often done wrong, with bad results: pulled muscles, disk lesions, or painful hernia.

Here are six steps to safe lifting.

1. Keep feet parted—one alongside, one behind the object.
2. Keep back straight, nearly vertical.
3. Tuck your chin in.
4. Grip the object with the whole hand.
5. Tuck elbows and arms in.
6. Keep body weight directly over feet.

FEET should be parted, with one foot alongside the object being lifted and one behind. Feet comfortably spread give greater stability; the rear foot is in position for the upward thrust of the lift.

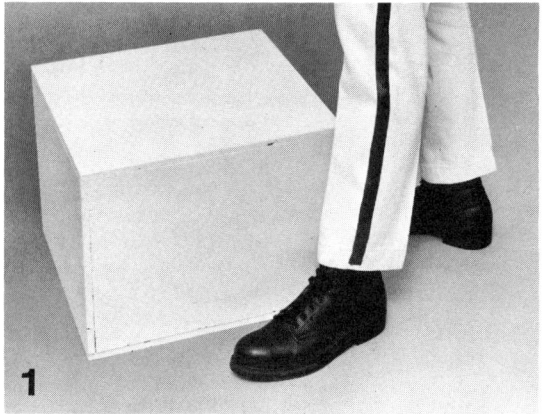

BACK. Use the sit-down position and keep the back straight —but remember that "straight" does not mean "vertical." A straight back keeps the spine, back muscles, and organs of the body in correct alignment. It minimizes the compression of the guts that can cause hernia.

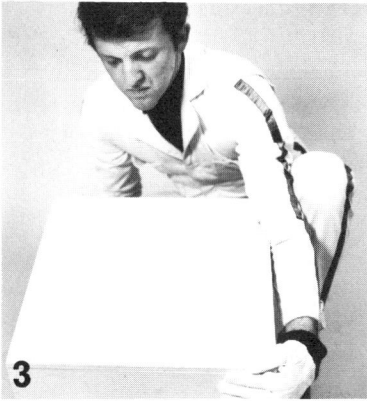

ARMS AND ELBOWS. The load should be drawn close, and the arms and elbows should be tucked into the side of the body. When the arms are held away from the body, they lose much of their strength and power. Keeping the arms tucked in also helps keep body weight centered.

PALM. The palmer grip is one of the most important elements of correct lifting. The fingers and the hand are extended around the object you're going to lift. Use the full palm; fingers alone have very little power. Glove has been removed to show finger positions better.

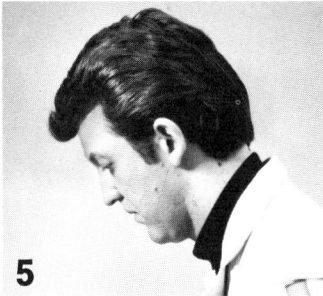

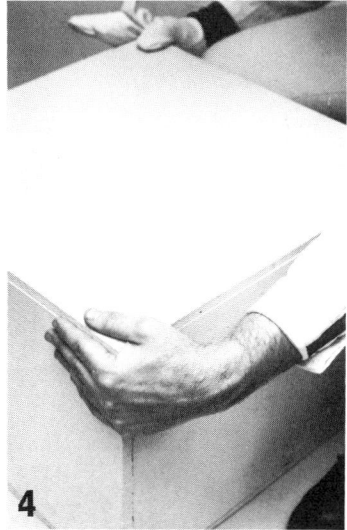

CHIN. Tuck in the chin so your neck and head continue the straight back line and keep your spine straight and firm.

BODY WEIGHT. Position body so its weight is centered over the feet. This provides a more powerful line of thrust and ensures better balance. Start the lift with a thrust of the rear foot.

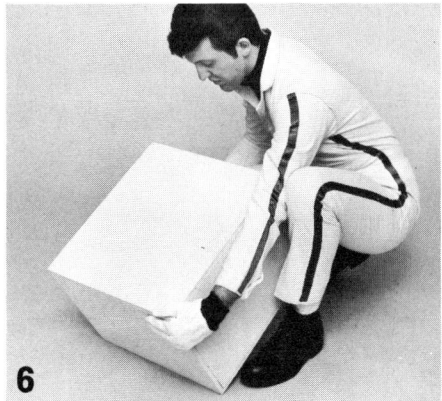

209

straight, and arms and elbows tucked into the side with the weight of the body centered over the feet. Lift with the legs. Twisting during a lift is a common cause of back injury. By simply turning the forward foot out and pointing it in the direction you intend to move, the greatest danger of twisting will be avoided.

Grip cartons away from seams, so that the hand does not come in contact with sharp carton staples. Grip them from underneath and lift with the legs. Keep hands off steel and wire banding. Change your direction of travel by repositioning the feet, not by twisting at the waist.

Move drums with a barrel truck whenever possible. Drums should be rolled on edge only when necessary, because of the precarious balance such a maneuver requires. Avoid pinch points near the top of the drum, and keep feet clear of the bottom seam. Since drums often contain hazardous materials, take great care to avoid puncturing the drum or spilling its contents. Clean up any such spills as soon as possible and before they are allowed to spread.

In handling sacks (paper and cloth), avoid cuts from wire staples at the bound end. Lift by gripping underneath the sack, and using the legs as jacks. If a large number of sacks are to be moved, two men should work together—one at each end of the sack. Do not throw sacks carelessly; keep the dust level down. If sacks are damp or warm, the possibility of chemical action should be considered.

In handling bundles, watch out for short, sharp ends of steel strapping used to bind the bundles. Keep fingers out from between the individual lengths in a bundle. Use dock equipment to move them whenever possible; bundles are often coated with protective grease at the factory which makes them hard to grip. When raising lighter bundles to load as top freight (for example, plastic tubing), try to keep both ends level; otherwise, an individual length is likely to slide back at the man on the lower end, hitting his face, chest or leg.

HAND TRUCKS

When handling freight with hand trucks, instruct the worker to place the "blade" of the hand truck completely under the load, then pull it back slowly until the weight is entirely balanced over the axle. Always push, never pull, hand trucks. The freight should be loaded on the hand truck only as high as the top crossbar so that visibility is kept clear. When pulling freight back to the siderails of the hand truck, never grip the steel strapping, wire binding, or twine of the freight. Reach across the top of the load and grip the far edge.

210

If using barrel trucks, handle the freight in the same safe manner as the hand trucks. It is, however, especially critical that the weight of the drum be centered exactly over the axle of the barrel truck. Liquid sloshing in the drum might destroy this balance, so move cautiously—especially on turns.

Freight should be loaded on four-wheel carts so that the workman can see over the top. Carts should be pushed so that the leading edge of the cart cannot run up against the dockman's heel, and should be pulled only when moving downgrade, as when coming out of a trailer down an inclined dockplate. But the dockman must face the cart and brace against it for control. Two men may be required to control heavily loaded carts.

Most "J" (Johnson) bar injuries occur when the handle is driven up with great force into a worker's face or jaw. The body should be kept in a position where it will not be struck if the grip is lost.

POWERED INDUSTRIAL TRUCKS

As in the use of any machine, certain safety rules and regulations must be observed and carefully followed to prevent serious injury. The supervisor and the lift truck operator should be familiar with the safety rules and regulations of the American National Standard *Safety Standard for Powered Industrial Trucks,* ANSI B56.1–1969*, and also with different types of lift trucks, as specified in American National Standard, *Type Designations, Areas of Use, Maintenance and Operation of Powered Industrial Trucks,* ANSI B56.2–1971 (also NFPA bulletin 505).** These standards are now part of OSHA requirements 29 *Code of Federal Regulations,* §1910.178.

14. JOB HAZARDS OF TRUCK AND BUS OPERATORS

Bus and truck operators must not only avoid traffic accidents but also those that arise out of dealing with the general public. Defensive driving practices (described in Chapter 7) can generally prevent motor vehicle collisions; considerate, friendly handling of the public can usually prevent

---

* *American National Standards Institute, Inc., 1430 Broadway, New York, N.Y. 10018*

** *National Fire Protection Association International, 60 Batterymarch Street, Boston, Massachusetts 02110*

strained relations (discussed in Chapter 8).

Operators are injured frequently when they fall while boarding or alighting from a vehicle, within their vehicle, or when they fall at terminals and rest stops. The possibility of hand, wrist, arm, shoulder, or back injuries arises when a vehicle's front wheel strikes an object or drops suddenly into a depression causing the steering wheel to jerk or spin. Injuries to operators frequently arise from adjusting the operator's seat, opening or closing doors, operating gear shift levers, or handling windows and ventilators and changing route and destination signs (if there be any).

If operators must handle merchandise, they must take care to avoid sprains, strains, or muscular overexertion, and to avoid receiving foot injuries due to falling or shifting objects. It is often felt that if an operator cannot handle himself safely, how can he be counted on to handle passengers, merchandise, or freight safely.

In order to focus attention on driver safety records, accident statistics must be maintained, reviewed, and discussed, and recommendations made as to how these injuries can be avoided. If this can be done in open safety meetings, group discussion will focus attention on injury-causing conditions or practices. If they cannot be handled this way, then the supervisor can discuss them with individual drivers. The only good that can result from an accident is its educational value.

We cannot attain safe operation without working for it. The motivation and desire for a real safety program must originate with top management, which was discussed earlier in this chapter and in Chapter 2.

Maintain Interest in Accident Prevention

Even though all facilities have been brought up to high safety standards, all jobs have been subjected to a hazard analysis, safe work procedures have been devised and are enforced, and an accident reporting and analysis system has been set up, one important task remains—to stimulate employee interest in accident prevention. Employees should want to work safely at all times. Here are ways to do this:

1. MANAGEMENT INTEREST AND EXAMPLE

Management's sincere interest in accident prevention is one of the strongest incentives for good safety performance. This holds true for all levels of management—each must reflect an interest in company safety objectives and set a good example of compliance with safety rules,

212

because a person will believe in safety only to the same degree he thinks his boss believes in it.

Supervisors should often talk personally to each of their subordinates about safety. Managers should seek every opportunity to be identified with the safety program, such as by attending safety meetings and rallies and signing safety bulletins and announcements.

2. SAFETY MEETINGS AND RALLIES

Periodic safety meetings and rallies keep interest high. Safety meetings should be small and should be conducted by the immediate supervisor. Meetings should be confined to a definite subject and deal with specific problems. For example, a safety meeting for drivers and mechanics might be devoted to discuss the safe way of getting in and out of various vehicles. Meetings can also be held to explain a new safety procedure, announce a new contest or campaign, review a specific accident, or discuss the overall safety performance of the group.

Large rallies attended by all employees, including members of management, are helpful in celebrating safety achievements such as winning an award or working a specified number of man hours without a disabling injury.

3. AWARDS FOR WORK SAFETY

Employees like to be recognized individually for safe work performance. A good method of doing this is to establish a "Safe Driver Award" or "Safe Worker Award" program (see Chapter 8). Although this program is available from the National Safety Council, companies may create their own. Awards are usually presented for working a calendar year without a disabling injury. If the worker has a disabling injury he does not receive an award for the year. Usually awards are cumulative, thus a worker can earn a 1-year, 2-year, 3-year (or higher) award for working that number of years without a preventable accident or a disabling injury. (For publicity value, see Appendix B.)

4. SAFETY CONTESTS

Various contests can be held: working the highest number of man-hours without a disabling injury, or achieving the lowest frequency rate within a specified period of time. Contests can be between units within the same fleet or between fleets in different areas.

Contests should be well promoted for maximum interest. Workers should understand the method of scoring and be kept informed of the standing of the various contestants—either individuals or units.

There should be no contest penalties for reporting very minor injuries, otherwise these may not be reported and infected wounds may result.

5. POSTERS

A good poster program can do much to maintain interest in safety—even the best drivers need reminding. Aside from the actual message of the poster, the mere fact that there are well maintained poster boards with fresh posters tells employees that management has a continued interest in safety. In addition, this helps give a terminal, dock, or driver room the look of a safety-minded company.

Special bulletin boards can also aid various safety subjects. Actual photographs of broken safety glasses which saved an eye, photographs of unsafe practices and award presentations, safety announcements, and awards can all be exhibited.

A special bulletin board showing number of days worked since the last lost-time injury can also promote interest so long as it is faithfully kept up to date.

Planning and administering a good poster program requires careful consideration of (1) kinds of poster boards used, (2) number and placement of poster locations, (3) selection of posters, and (4) regularity and frequency of change.

Poster boards. Mounting may be as simple as thumb-tacking to a wall, or as "complicated" as placing in an illuminated, glass-enclosed bulletin board. The latter is more desirable because it is not only more dignified and attractive but it also protects the posters from tampering.

Black-enameled metal poster frames, available through the National Safety Council at a nominal cost, are large enough to permit cardboard backing and a glass (or plastic) shield. They come in 8½ by 11½-inch ("A"-size) and 17 by 23-inch ("B"-size) sizes, and are especially useful when display boards are not feasible or when a single poster must be spotted at a strategic point.

Number and placement of poster locations. Like ads, posters also must be seen to be effective. This means bringing posters to employees, not employees to posters. Knowing the pedestrian traffic patterns helps in planning poster locations. So will answering these questions:

    a. Where will most employees see a poster most frequently?
    b. Will all employees see it during their normal work day?
    c. How many locations will be required to make sure that all employ-

214

ees are exposed to a poster program?

d. Where are the most effective locations for posters discussing specific work hazards? (Safe driving posters should be seen mostly by drivers; posters devoted to proper lifting techniques should be seen especially by dock and maintenance workers.)

At these optimum locations, place posters at eye level—about 53 inches (centered) from floor. Make sure poster has sufficient light and is free from obstructions so that employees can focus their attention on it. Avoid placing posters at stairways, doorways, or other places where a person may have an accident if his attention were diverted from seeing a potential hazard.

Selecting posters. Posters may be obtained from the National Safety Council by two methods:

a. Request a monthly supply of preselected posters be sent you. Council safety engineers will select posters that apply to your special type of operation—intercity bus, truck terminal, intracity truck, or what have you.

b. Select posters from N.S.C.'s *Annual Directory of Safety Posters* or from the new poster listings that appear in each issue of *National Safety News* and *Traffic Safety* magazines.

Automatic mailings assure a constant supply of carefully selected posters that touch the principal sources of accidents, and are balanced in their appeal. They range from humorous cartoons to those pointing to personal consequence of unsafe acts. An "automatic service" poster set is comprised of two "A"-size and two "B"-size posters. (This amounts to 48 posters per year.) Multiple or fractional sets can be ordered depending on the number of drivers and other employees covered.

Personal selection of posters allows choice based on actual accident experience or for special safety campaigns. Both methods can be combined. (Some sales fleet posters are shown on page 246.)

Regularity and frequency of change. Posters are most effective when used singly and changed about once per week. It would be better to use four posters per month—once each week—than to put all four up at one location and leave them there a month. Changing posters weekly gives a sense of movement to a poster program.

Administration of a poster program requires the personal attention of a capable employee. The safety director should check to make sure that poster sites are kept in good condition and that posters are changed according to a prearranged schedule.

6. FIRST-AID TRAINING

Many companies give all employees first-aid training because they find employees work more safely when they become qualified first aiders.

7. SAFETY SUGGESTION SYSTEMS

Whether formal or informal, suggestion systems are excellent methods of motivating for safety because they give all employees a chance for meaningful participation in the company safety program. In a formal safety suggestion system, a written suggestion is submitted rather than a verbal (informal) one. Usually a conveniently located box is provided so written suggestions may be deposited. Place a small writing surface adjacent to the suggestion box, along with a pencil or ballpoint pen and a supply of printed forms.

To be effective, a safety suggestion system must have a person in authority pass judgment on those suggestions which relate to the department or section he supervises. Quite often a suggestion is of such broad scope it will have to be reviewed and decided upon by top management.

One problem that always arises with a formal safety suggestion system is that often foremen and supervisors feel that any suggestion is a reflection on their supervisory ability, their planning ability, or their ability to observe. However, where safety suggestion systems have been encouraged, the result has been a better safety record. Both foremen and supervisors see that "putting everybody on the team" means fewer occupational injuries and fewer problems, and as a result—better all-around efficiency.

12

Off-the-job safety

What is off-the-job safety? An off-the-job (OTJ) safety program tries to make available to the employee when he is off his job the same life-saving and happy-living safeguards that he has when he is on his job. It is not a paternalistic "do-gooder" activity that intrudes on personal privacy, but rather a program that integrates some on-the-job safety concepts into off-duty activities, and supports them with practical off-duty safety materials and services.

OTJ safety programs tie in closely with on-the-job safety programs because most off-the-job accidents are due to the same basic causes as on-the-job accidents.

Drivers are specialists and should use the same accident-preventing techniques *off* their job as well as *on*. Actually, a person cannot act one way on his job and another off it—he can get injured just as easily.

Costs of Off-the-Job Accidents

Sometimes fleet owners don't realize how much off-the-job accidents cost. If they consider paid absences, wage loss during subsequent disability assignment, company medical checkup costs, and cost of supervision (and often legal costs), they will probably arrive at a surprisingly high figure. They will usually find that savings alone will partially underwrite the added cost of an off-the-job safety program.

217

A MAN'S ATTITUDE while on the job will be essentially the same while off the job. Accordingly, it can contribute to accidents *on* and *off* the job.

As an average, an off-the-job accident usually costs a fleet about one-fourth that of an on-the-job accident. But, also on an average, off-the-job accidents occur 6 to 12 times more frequently than do on-the-job accidents. Thus, total off-the-job accident costs can run from 50 to 300 per cent greater than on-the-job accident costs. Therefore a fleet cannot afford to delay starting an off-the-job safety program.

What Can an OTJ Safety Program Do?

Here are proven results of actual off-the-job safety programs:

1. Improved on-the-job performance.
2. Sharp reduction in off-the-job injuries.
3. Cost studies show financial soundness of program.
4. Participation in the program improves overall employee relations, and improves fleet's public image.
5 Often the new approach involved offsets "safety program fatigue."

218

Before starting an OTJ safety program, one fleet averaged 0.55 lost-time injuries per million working hours. One year after starting the program, this frequency rate was reduced to 0.33.

Another fleet had an *on*-the-job lost-time frequency rate of 0.58 until starting an OTJ program. At the end of the first year, the *on*-the-job rate had dropped to 0.37. At the end of three years, it was 0.29.

What are reasons for these drops? The answer is quite simple. A man's attitude while on the job will be essentially the same as while off the job. If he is allowed to develop careless or dangerous habits while on the job, he will carry these habits with him while off the job. The reverse is also true. If he is allowed to develop bad habits off the job, he will bring these same bad habits to his job.

How to Start an OTJ Program

As has been pointed out in earlier chapters, the first step is to sell top management on the idea that a safety program is good business—in the case of an OTJ program, this will be somewhat harder than with an on-the-job program because management often cannot at first see the tie-in.

Continuing support of top management is vital to the success of any safety program: the safety man must have it. Use this approach:

1. Decide whether a face-to-face contact or a written proposal will have the better result. Face-to-face contact has the advantages of producing immediate discussion and permitting amplification any points that might be questioned. It is also best if the safetyman responsible for the project makes the presentation. If this is not possible, then he should be in on it at least.

2. Make your presentation effective. Here is a suggested outline that has been found effective.

    a. Define off-the-job safety.

    b. Give cost advantages. Use figures given in this chapter or from other authoritative sources if actual fleet estimates are not possible. Use actual fleet figures for on-the-job accident costs, and estimate off-the-job costs by using the ratios given previously in this chapter. (Local fleets who have started an off-the-job program may give you their findings.)

    c. Discuss how and why an off-the-job safety program often improves on-the-job safety records.

    d. Explain how an off-the-job safety program can be integrated with present on-the-job safety activities without involving heavy money or time expenditures.

e. Describe how your off-the-job safety program will work in your fleet. (Gear your program to your own fleet needs, and hold to a fair budget.) Be sure to tell (1) how accidents will be reported; (2) how much time and money the program will take; and (3) how program will be introduced (list specific activities and costs).

f. Tell plans for measuring program effectiveness.

An off-the-job safety program can easily be integrated with an on-the-job program—much of it does not require an increased expenditure, but rather wider, more realistic thinking. A little added discussion and broader emphasis will add off-the-job effectiveness to on-the-job safety activities. Properly handled, this will provide a more consistent on-the-job safety program, because people live as whole people and should think safety all the time, not just while at work.

TWO BASIC PROGRAM APPROACHES: VOLUNTARY OR REQUIRED REPORTING

In any OTJ safety program, accidents should be analyzed to find the most frequent causes of injury. This requires an effective accident-reporting procedure: the nature and primary causes must be obtained. How is this best done? By having uniform reports made through a predetermined channel. Reports should include:

1. Name of employee involved in the accident.

2. Date and time of day the accident took place.

3. Brief description (such as "Painting 2nd-story window frame when ladder slipped").

4. Nature of injury (such as "Broken right forearm, sprained back").

5. Number of calendar days that employee was disabled. This can be an estimate. (When disability extends into more than one quarter of the year, days in each quarter should be counted, but the accident should be counted only in the quarter in which it happened.)

A fleet has an absence and sickness reporting system which is used to operate the payroll. The off-the-job accident reporting system can be added to this system.

Should submitting reports be voluntary or required? The system can be based upon voluntary employee cooperation or first-line supervisors can be made responsible for initiating the reports.

The voluntary approach is better than no system at all, and although it cannot give the complete picture, it gives leads and provides sufficient data to develop an effective prevention program. A sincerely conducted voluntary reporting program increases interest and cooperation.

When a required reporting system is used, sufficient information will be available in about six months to plan an effective program to combat the specific off-the-job accidents of fleet employees.

Prior to finding specific accident information, concentrate on the major off-the-job accidents: slips, trips, falls, and automobile accidents.

HOW TO INTRODUCE THE PROGRAM TO EMPLOYEES

The prestige that the program has with employees will be greatly influenced by the way it is introduced. A special announcement—one appropriate to the size and nature of the fleet—should be made by one of top management, preferably by the president. If employees can get together, this can be made at a meeting. In scattered fleets, this can be made at local-level meetings. Posters and on-the-job announcements can be used. A letter sent home helps get family cooperation.

Reporting can be encouraged if employees know that the main reason for it is to develop a program that will help them be safe.

Take care not to let any paternalistic overtones creep in (by mistake or otherwise). Stress that cooperation, in the long run, is really voluntary, and that off-the-job safety mostly benefits the employees themselves and their families. The company's interest, then, is *to help* when needed—*not to command*. A company can only get as much off-the-job safety as its people want, and therefore a company must make employees aware of the dangers, create the desire to avoid accidents, and convert this desire into action.

The real challenge in starting and following through an off-the-job safety program is changing employee attitudes and obtaining individual cooperation. This can be encouraged by always emphasizing what the program means both to them personally and to their families: that security and happiness gained through safe living mean everything.

CONDUCTING THE PROGRAM

The safetyman must spark-plug the off-the-job safety program if it is to keep going. The program must consistently push forward, because if it falters or if it is inconsistent, employees will not cooperate fully.

Interest-stimulating activities and program materials should be directed to the specific off-the-job accidents employees are having. A portion of an on-the-job safety meeting can plug off-the-job safety, and provide a chance for discussion. Personal contact helps here.

221

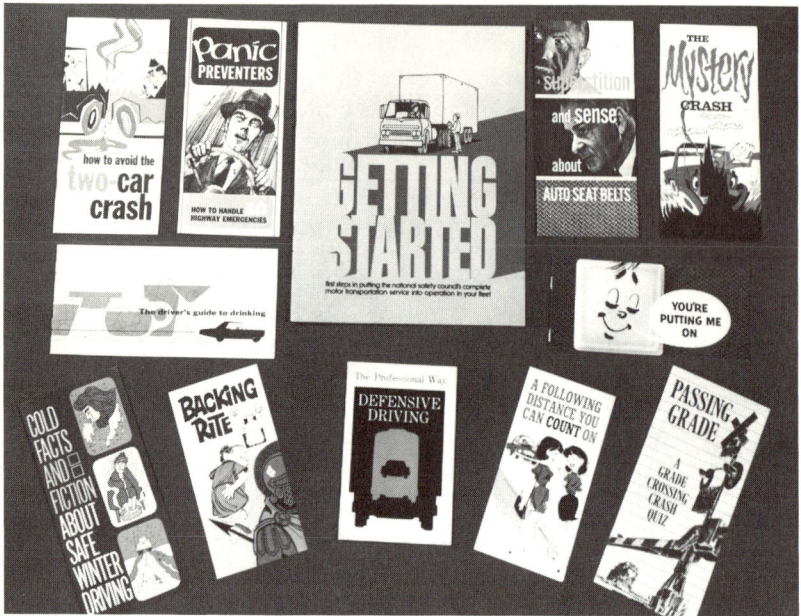

OFF-THE-JOB PROGRAM MATERIALS available from National Safety Council.

The safety department may enhance its off-the-job program by periodic mailing of home safety and defensive driving literature to the employee's residence. Thus, the employee's family will be included in the program and will tend to reinforce its effectiveness.

SELECTING AND PREPARING PROGRAM MATERIALS

No off-the-job safety program should rely entirely on either purchased or locally made program materials. Persons like to feel that they are part of both an overall movement as well as a local one. The change of pace between the two helps the program.

One rule of thumb is to give about twice as much emphasis to specific fleet problems as to general industry and country-wide problems. This ratio can vary depending upon the scope of the company program, the intensity of activities, and the budget. Seasonal and check-list materials can also be introduced effectively.

Always keep in mind the objective: emphasize continuous cooperation, individual participation, and personal responsibility in preventing accidents.

Sources of materials? The National Safety Council, insurance

222

associations, fire protection organizations, governmental agencies, service organizations, trade associations, professional societies, and state labor offices and health services. An exhaustive listing is given in Chapter 14, "Sources of Help," in the *Accident Prevention Manual for Industrial Operations,* 6th ed., published by the National Safety Council.

Measuring Program Effectiveness

How can we find how well our off-the-job safety program is doing? Not only do we want to know if our work is justified, but we must also find out how we can improve our effectiveness.

Our best information source is a good accident reporting system, well thought out and soundly administered. (You will find ideas in Chapters 2 and 4.) Accident data should be summarized quarterly in order to spot seasonal variations. The "Off-The-Job Accident Quarterly Summary" form published by the National Safety Council, categorizes injuries into three types: transportation, home, and public. In this way, basic causes can be more easily spotted.

The form can also be used to report fleet experience to the National Safety Council. The Council gathers these figures and makes industry-wide summaries available. In this way, the Council can also relate its publications and activities to industry needs.

KEEP REPORTS TO A PRACTICAL MINIMUM

Be sure that reports describe, insofar as possible, the causes of an accident as well as the actual physical injury, such as fractured tibia. Subgroupings under the main headings (transportation, home, and public) will fall naturally once individual injuries are classified.

Reports should be brief, but should supply the five points of information listed earlier in the section "Two Basic Approaches." Because followup is limited, off-the-job reports will be shorter than on-the-job accident reports. This is the nature of these reports and should not cause concern.

Fleets should start an off-the-job safety program, not only for humanitarian reasons, but to increase the effectiveness of their on-the-job safety program. Through newspapers, magazines, television, and advertising, people are being conditioned to thinking of safety as a way of life—both off and on their job. Industry has taken the lead in promoting this. Fleets should too.

13

Vehicle safety program

Although vehicles must first be chosen to handle the fleet's work, they should be standardized insofar as possible.

- Mechanics who work on the same make vehicle develop expert knowledge and can save valuable time.
- Parts room stocks are more easily controlled when there is no need to stock parts for a variety of makes and models.
- Drivers on operations where equipment is interchanged frequently can become accustomed to the similar driving characteristics.
- Finally, a distributor or manufacturer who knows that his equipment is an "exclusive" with the fleet management has an added incentive to cooperate with the fleet maintenance department in order to protect his favored position. He knows he has a lot to gain—or lose—on subsequent orders.

When standardizing, management must consider both the fleet operation and the vehicle's adaptability to it. They must weigh carefully the driver's "living room" and, in the case where frequent pickups or deliveries are made, the ease with which the driver can enter and leave the vehicle.

The cab-over-engine truck designed by one manufacturer for a nationwide soft drink company is the result of this kind of thinking: the driver can get in and get out easily, and he can reach and handle his cargo while standing on the ground. There is twofold value to this: (1) the driver is pleased with the convenience and the cab comfort, (2) management benefits from faster deliveries. Drivers do not resent

A GOOD-LOOKING VEHICLE can be easily seen—this adds both to safety and to good business. A driver of a good-looking vehicle is proud of it, and usually drives accordingly. Good appearance is good business.

"speed-up" facilities if these also give greater comfort and convenience.

There is another important consideration: the "power factor." It is far better to overpower than to underpower the job.

- An extra margin of power will add measurably to the vehicle's service life and will reduce maintenance costs and road failures.
- A higher powered vehicle is more maneuverable than an under-powered one, and has a lower accident rate.*
- Finally, drivers are less apt to become exasperated and abuse an ade-quately powered vehicle.

* THE FEDERAL ROLE IN HIGHWAY SAFETY. *U.S. Department of Commerce, 1959.*

Vehicle Appearance

Many fleets have discovered the advertising and public relations value of their "rolling billboards." Bright, attractive color design can convert a

225

fleet into an effective salesman for the company. Unattractive, dirty, sloppily driven vehicles also create an impression—a bad one.

And it is perfectly natural for the driver of an attractive well-maintained vehicle to be proud of his rig—and to drive it accordingly. If management is lax in equipment appearance, drivers will also be indifferent. They can hardly be expected to "baby" equipment that they are not particularly proud to drive, or that they think the owner does not care about.

From the safety standpoint, a brightly colored and highly visible vehicle is less likely to be the target of a highway collision than is a drab, dirty one (see Appendix E for details). Additionally, it is easier to enforce good housekeeping rules when the "house" itself is attractive.

From every standpoint—advertising, driver incentive, and safety—good appearance is good business.

Components and Their Maintenance

Built-in vehicle components directly related to safety are brakes, tires, lighting, front and rear bumpers, the steering mechanism, and power. Only slightly less important from a safety standpoint are power-train linkage, shock absorbers, the horn, and the electrical wiring system. Let's discuss each.

BRAKES

No matter how well the vehicle components are designed and chosen, the most important factor in avoiding accidents is the driver's ability to stop. If the brakes fail, the vehicle can't stop. In addition, maladjusted brakes will seriously affect steering characteristics, especially during a hard, emergency stop. It is, therefore, essential to give top priority to meticulous brake maintenance.

"Do you think you can make another round?" is an old refrain usually asked after a driver has reported "minor" brake troubles to a dispatcher or shop foreman at an "inconvenient" time. An affirmative answer to that question can lead to serious, even fatal, consequences.

There is one axiom that should be permanently posted on every fleet bulletin board: *Do Not Operate Any Vehicle With Faulty Brakes!*

GOOD TIRE MAINTENANCE

Blowouts on highways frequently cause serious wrecks because the driver loses control. Underinflated inner duals can cause costly and dangerous fires. Improper balance, toe-in, toe-out, and caster and

226

camber misalignment not only can cause costly tire wear, but can affect driver steering control adversely and can run up fleet maintenance costs. It is cheaper to make an adjustment than to repair preventable damage after it has occurred. A driver should always check his tires at coffee or refueling stops.

LIGHTING STANDARDS

Lighting standards are established by state and federal law (the latter applies to vehicles operating in interstate commerce). These are minimum standards, however, and there is no law against exceeding these requirements, particularly for truck clearance and marker lights. Ample displays of redlighting and reflector material on the rear of big rigs aid their visibility and should help prevent rear-end collisions. Four or five red lights strung across the rear top of a truck or trailer will remain highly visible even in inclement weather when lights positioned lower could be obscured by mud, moisture, road film, or snow. A good display of amber running lights to outline a vehicle's broadsides and front also increases safety at intersections.

Drivers should wipe headlamps, taillights, and stop and direction indicators at every nighttime coffee stop; the frequency depends on the weather. Clean headlights increase the driver's visibility and help reduce fatigue due to eyestrain. When a driver's seeing range is reduced, he can overdrive his lights and not even suspect it. Clean stop and direction indicators are important both day and night.

VEHICLE STEERING MECHANISM

A routine inspection, made when the vehicle is being lubricated, can frequently prevent a serious highway steering failure. Any indication of excessive wear should be thoroughly checked.

SPEED GOVERNORS ON COMMERCIAL VEHICLES

Some highly respected fleets are strongly in favor of mechanically governing a vehicle's speed; while others, equally respected, maintain that it is management's duty to govern the man and then trust *him* to govern the vehicle. By relying on devices to record speeds, duration of stops, and other data, this latter group believe that they should let the driver have plenty of power available for emergencies because to govern him mechanically might pose a potential hazard.

Probably the best compromise is to provide an rpm governor that is set between 70 and 95 per cent of the maximum engine rpm—high enough to provide almost all the power built into the engine but also set just low enough to prevent overspeeding of the engine with resulting high wear.

"Tach" charts, which are admissible evidence in the courts of many states, can be a good driver's best friend and can effectively refute the testimony of a hostile witness who declares that he was driving at a dangerous or illegal speed, or caused damage at some time or place other than where he was. Bad drivers, lazy drivers, and habitual speed violators call such devices "stool pigeons." It all depends on the individual driver's attitude towards his own professionalism.

POWER-TRAIN LINKAGE

Power-train linkage inspection is important, too. An instance comes to mind where the rear end of a truck literally pole-vaulted when the front end of a drive shaft became disengaged and dropped to the ground on an off-highway oil field operation. This caused the truck to flip over and severely injure the driver. Later analysis revealed that maintenance personnel could have located the defect by proper inspection when the vehicle was being lubricated.

Inspection should also include shock absorbers. Any malfunction should be corrected immediately.

ELECTRICAL WIRING

Finally, electrical wiring should be inspected frequently for undue wear which might cause short circuits or lighting failures.

Safety Equipment

In most states and under the provisions of the Bureau of Motor Carrier Safety, standard safety equipment is specified. Vehicles must carry a fire extinguisher (usually a 5-pound dry chemical unit—petroleum trucks carry a 15-pound unit), flags, reflectors, flares, pot torches or portable electric flasher warning devices for marking disabled vehicles parked on or near a highway. In addition, fusees (for instant emergency use) are required. Some states permit use of automatic flasher lights on the vehicle itself.

FIRST-AID KITS

Many fleets include first-aid kits as emergency equipment. (Kits are usually required on buses.) Either bulk or unit kits can be used. The

228

TYPICAL SAFETY EQUIPMENT is shown in the cargo space of this emergency road-patrol car for a truck fleet. First-aid, fire-extinguishing, hazard-marking, photographic, tire-changing, and other emergency equipment is carried.

contents of both should be checked periodically.*

Not only could these kits help a driver but, if the driver is trained in first aid, he can also help the public. The public relations value of this should be considered as well as the humanitarian value.

One large brewery fleet, for instance, provides (at company expense) Red Cross Advanced First-Aid training to every driver. Posted at the rear of each truck is a Red Cross Mobile First-Aid Unit plate. Over the years, aid rendered by drivers to injured motorists has earned much valuable public good will for the company, its drivers, and its product. (See photograph on page 307 for a Canadian example.)

SAFETY BELTS

Installation of safety belts in fleet automobiles and for the driver of other vehicles is standard safety equipment in most operations. Many trucking

---

* See *Industrial Data Sheet No. 202*, UNIT FIRST-AID KITS. *National Safety Council.*

229

companies have been successful in installing safety belts on their over-the-road vehicles. They also report good results in safety belt use.

FIRE EXTINGUISHER

Most fleets have abandoned the use of carbon tetrachloride type hand fire extinguishers. A number of cases of poisoning and lung injury have resulted from the use of carbon tetrachloride as a fire-extinguishing fluid in confined spaces. These cases are, of course, not completely attributable to the extinguisher. Rather, they are the result of several factors—for example, products of the fire and decomposition of the carbon tetrachloride.*

Carbon dioxide (CO_2) and dry or multipurpose chemicals using nitrogen or air as propellents are effective on vehicle fires, especially electrical or engine fires. Water containing a wetting agent is used for upholstery or rubber fires.

Be sure that there are no hidden embers left in upholstery and that tires are not only extinguished, but cool enough to handle with bare hands.

After choosing effective extinguishers for shops and vehicles, train all company personnel in their effective emergency use. The extinguisher supplier or the local fire department's fire prevention service can supply instruction.

There is no point in buying the best available fire-fighting tools and then depending only upon the directions on the side of a container to furnish instruction in its use—meanwhile, the fire crackles merrily! Be sure men are instructed beforehand in equipment use.

Use of the *warning devices* in the emergency kit is governed by law and it is again management's responsibility to adequately instruct all drivers in how to use them.

All equipment must be instantly available. Packed in a water-proof, dustproof wood or metal box, safety gear should be stowed within easy reach of the driver in case of emergency.

Driver Responsibility for Maintenance

The best contribution a driver can make to a good maintenance is (1) through careful pretrip and en route vehicle inspections and (2)

---

* See Industrial Data Sheet No. 331, CARBON TETRACHLORIDE. *National Safety Council.*

DRIVER'S INSPECTION REPORT

(See instructions on reverse side)

Date..

Mileage In...

Mileage Out...

Truck
Tractor No. ....

Trailer No. ....

Mechanic's **Driver's**

Use √ for Okay and X for disapproved

		Approaching Unit – Check:			Under Hood – Check:
		General Condition			Oil and Water Levels
		Existing Body Damage			Leakage
		Leaks: Water, Fuel, Oil, Grease			General Condition

In Cab: (Start engine and turn on all lights)

		Gauges – Normal readings Air pressure or vacuum; Ammeter, Oil Pressure, Fuel, Water Temperature			Heater & Defroster
					Mirrors
		Windshield Wipers			Spare Fuses
		Horn(s)			Emergency Warning Signals (Pot torches, Fusees, Reflector Flares, Flags)
		Steering (Excessive Play)			Fire Extinguisher

Outside Unit: (Engine running and lights on. Start at left front wheel and go around unit)

		Wheels, Tires, Lugs or Studs			Lights: Tail, Stop, Clearance, Side-Marker, Identification, Turn Signals, Headlights
		Brake Hoses			
		Electric Lines			Reflectors
		Hook-up and Fifth Wheel			Load and Fastening Devices
		Tow-bar, Pintle Hook, Safety Chains and Converter Gear			Springs
					Cab, Body, Doors, Windshield and Windows

Miscellaneous:

		Operation of Brakes			Cooling System
		Operation of Tractor Protection Valve			Driveline: Clutch, Transmission, Driveshaft and Universals
		Motor			Exhaust System
		Fuel System			Battery

Remarks: (Explain unsatisfactory items noted above)

_____

_____

Driver's Signature _____

Mechanic's Signature _____

DRIVER'S INSPECTION REPORT of the American Trucking Associations.

231

KEEP 'EM ROLLING LONGER

DRIVER'S DAILY REPORT

Date_____

Driver's name_____

Truck No._____

Speedometer reading_____

DRIVER'S CHECK LIST

_____Oil pressure	_____Engine noises
_____Water temperature	_____Spark control
_____Generator	_____Choke control
_____Lights & horn	_____Fuel control
_____Speedometer	_____Clutch
_____Windows & doors	_____Gear shift & transmission
_____Starter	_____Foot-brake system
_____Battery	_____Hand-brake system
_____Tires, rims, & wheels	_____Steering
_____Windshield wiper	_____Power take-off
_____Rear-vision mirrors	_____Leaks - Oil, fuel, water

DRIVER'S DAILY REPORT FORM on condition of his vehicle helps garage mechanics keep equipment safe to operate and keeps equipment operating longer.

through the making of thorough and conscientious defect reports.

Most major fleet managements believe a driver is paid to drive, and that the mechanical department is paid to repair—therefore, they discourage attempts by their drivers to make roadside repairs (tire changes excepted).

It is a driver's responsibility to make thorough inspections, however. That this is an integral part of his job is widely recognized. For example, the American Trucking Associations' annual "Roadeo" requires a vehicle inspection by the driver to be rated by official scorers.

If the driver's predeparture inspection is well organized, it can detect defects at the terminal where they can more easily be corrected than they can along the roadside after a breakdown. The driver should learn that a methodical approach to the inspection is necessary to get the job done in the quickest and easiest way.

He should also check his instrument panel gauges frequently. The oil pressure gauge needle should not fluctuate at cruising speeds and the ammeter needle should not drop below "charge" when engine is idling. Both of these are reportable defects. (Some vehicles have red warning lights to indicate these two troubles.)

232

ALTERNATE METHODS

Some fleets hold the mechanical department responsible for predeparture services which include a thorough inspection. "Yard men" or "hostlers" make all equipment checks. Whoever inspects the vehicle should follow a printed checklist which he should later sign or initial. A copy should be given the driver to assure him that an inspection has been made. The driver, in turn, includes the checklist in his trip report and also lists any defects that may have developed en route.

Some fleets go a step further. Whenever a vehicle is found defective, a red tag is affixed to the steering wheel and the vehicle impounded until repaired. The red tag is only removed by a shop foreman when he makes a report certifying that the defect has been repaired and that the vehicle is in safe operating condition. Red-tagged vehicles cannot be driven until repaired.

Whatever method of preventive maintenance and inspection is adopted, fleet safety and economy reflects program thoroughness.

Vehicle Assignment

Assignment practices vary widely among fleets across the nation. Bus operators seldom drive the same vehicle on successive assignments. Many truck fleets and most passenger car fleets assign vehicles to individual drivers while others maintain pools from which vehicles are drawn as required. Specialized vehicles and driver-owned leased vehicles usually are a one-man vehicle operation. There are some general rules to follow, though, when assigning, routing, and scheduling vehicles.

DEVELOP RESPONSIBILITY

The ideal arrangement is to assign a vehicle to an individual driver. Comparative individual performance records of safety, vehicle abuse, efficiency, and economy of operation increase the degree of personal driver responsibility and result in lower operating costs. Often a regular driver who has been off will complain bitterly that whoever drove "his" vehicle during his absence has abused it or left it sloppy. This attitude, which is particularly typical among oldtimers, is a healthy one because it shows that the individual feels a real sense of pride and responsibility for the appearance and operating efficiency of his vehicle. In the long run it will usually be found that such drivers compile the best safety records and have the lowest operating costs. Their vehicles usually have that "spit-and-polish" appearance—both inside and out—which fleet owners find pays off in public relations value.

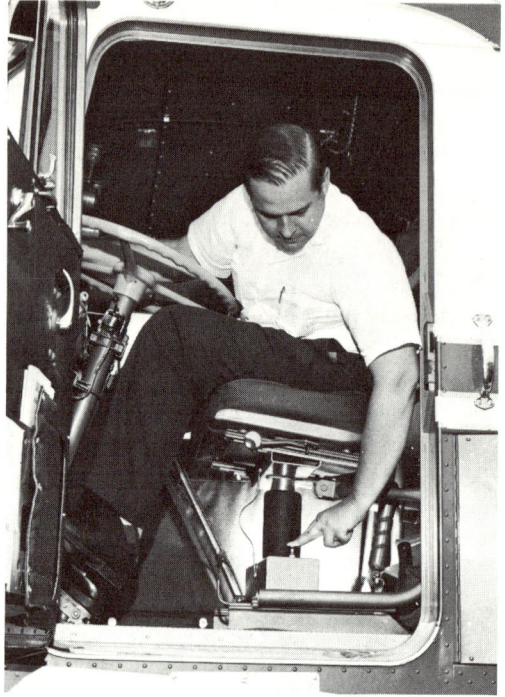

EACH DRIVER ADJUSTS TO HIS VEHICLE.
If responsible for it, the driver keeps it adjusted
to his likes—he keeps it clean and working well.

SELECT DRIVER TYPE TO FIT THE VEHICLE

Bus operators, when hiring a new man, try to find one who can work under the pressure of passengers. Such a driver may be a bit of an extrovert; he gets satisfaction from working before a "live audience." The best bus operators are also careful of their personal appearance and maintain a "captain of the ship" attitude in dealing with passengers. They take pride in their ability to make smooth starts and stops. Their adherence to schedules, and their competent, safe handling of both passengers and vehicle give them a personal feeling of accomplishment.

 Truck operators, on the other hand, know their drivers are usually a bit introverted—satisfied to drive mile after mile alone, busy with the task of moving cargo safely and on schedule. Truck drivers usually take pride in being safe and in operating efficiently. If asked why they like trucking, they will sum up their philosophy by remarking, "My cargo can't talk back or bother me with foolish questions."

234

SAFE ROUTING AND SCHEDULING POLICIES

Routing policies may differ widely, depending upon the fleet operations.

Route deliverymen follow well defined routes. So do driver salesmen who have assigned customer territories. Bus and interstate truck routes are usually prescribed by law, ordinance, or management.

Usually, only specialized contract carriers, utility and service fleets, or passenger car sales fleets offer much driver choice in route selection.

Scheduling often presents a problem in fleet operations, because of the conflict of interest between safety and sales or operating departments.

One of the most frequent complaints of safety men is that the sales department, goaded by competition, often "promises the impossible." A specific instance of poor scheduling came to light a few years ago when a state highway patrol chief visited the president of a bus line to point out that his published time tables indicated that drivers had to exceed posted speed limits in order to maintain on-time arrivals at connecting points. A red-faced traffic manager admitted that he had not considered speed limits when he set schedules. He had made a slide-rule estimate of the average speed between points because he wanted to compete with other forms of passenger transportation. Actually what had happened was that the safety director appealed to the police chief after months of vain attempts to adjust the schedules to the legal speeds.

Another common scheduling fault lies in lack of consideration given to the time of day. The same elapsed time is often allowed for travel between two metropolitan areas, whether it be during peak-traffic hours or during light traffic. Bus drivers frequently claim that they have to "beat their brains out" to maintain on-time schedules during rush hours, but have to kill time during other hours of modest loads to avoid running ahead of schedule.

Stops on long runs offer additional scheduling problems. No matter what time allowance is made, variables such as the type of load or special freight or baggage handling conditions affect departure times. A driver shouldn't be expected to arrive on time at the next principal terminal if he leaves late at the preceding terminal. You just don't make up time in traffic without jeopardizing safety.

A frequent reason for excessive speed is emergency deliveries. A good customer will call and declare that he needs certain material at a given time because of an "emergency." The sales department will

235

promise unrealistic delivery and then dump the problem on the operating department. The driver should not (under any circumstances) be dispatched with instructions to meet what may be an impossible schedule "at all costs."

OVERLOADING

Management policy concerning deliberate overloading places a driver in a delicate position. Regardless of the economy of payload vs. fines, overloading increases maintenance and reduces vehicle life when safe limits are continually exceeded. When a vehicle is called upon to do more than it was designed to do, that vehicle becomes a highway hazard. A vehicle that is underpowered for the load might, under certain conditions, jeopardize both the driver's safety and company's profits. If brakes are required to stop loads that are in excess of what the brakes were designed to control, it can lead to early or unexpected brake failure.

Company Policy

If a fleet is to conduct an economically sound operation—one in which safety pays—it must adopt policies reflecting that concept and then declare that there will be *no deviations* from it due to "unforeseen emergencies," the pressure of competition, or any other consideration. In the long run, operating efficiency, safe and sure arrivals, and good insurance experience will far outweigh any temporary advantage that might accrue from attempting to meet an irresponsible competitor on his own ground or from promising the impossible.

If fleet management is to be governed by immediate expediency and on-the-spur-of-the-moment policy changes, it will be advertised by chewed-up equipment, high turnover of unhappy driving personnel, and bankrupting operating costs.

A vehicle is the basic operating tool of a fleet. The profit and loss statement of any transportation company will reflect the care with which that vehicle is selected, maintained, and—most important—driven.

14

Supervising
a scattered
fleet

Working with widely separated units of a fleet poses special problems. In some respects it is similar to administering a safety program for a collection of small fleets, each with separate local management and problems of its own. If a fleet safety program is to be directed effectively from a central location, each fleet unit must be required to operate on a common basis—observing standardized procedures, and using standard forms, awards, and other program elements established by headquarters.

In all probability, it will take work to keep safety programming uniform throughout the company. Difficulties often arise because of a breakdown in communications between headquarters and local fleet management. These troubles probably will be worse in organizations in which transportation is incidental to the basic function. A bakery, utility, insurance company, department store, newspaper, or other enterprise that uses motor vehicles may find it difficult to create an interest in safe driving. For example, if an insurance salesman operates a company-owned automobile to visit his customers, what happens when he comes in with a bent fender—and also the first premium payment on a new $100,000 life insurance policy? In all probability he is told he is a great salesman and to forget the bent fender. (Sales fleet problems are covered in Chapter 15.)

In similar situations, creating interest and enforcing standardization in the safety program may be difficult. Yet, the fact remains that companies have gone out of business because they spent more money on accidents than they made profit on sales.

Profitable operation is safe operation. All segments of an organization must be operated safely too. A good safety record is usually a by-product of good operations throughout the company.

Standardize Policy and Fix Responsibility

Standardization of the safety program at all locations of the scattered units of a fleet is the most effective approach to a good safety program. Such a uniform program will actually cost less in terms of management and safety staff time and expenses.

RESPONSIBILITY FOR SAFETY

One of the first steps to standardization is fixing the responsibility for safety: line management—from top to bottom—is fully responsible for safety results. The safety director is an advisor to management: he serves in a staff capacity.

FUNCTIONS OF A HOME OFFICE SAFETY STAFF

The function of the home office safety staff should be to help both home and field management by (1) counseling them, (2) by participating in the establishment of safety objectives, and (3) by analyzing, planning, and organizing the safety program to reach these objectives.

Time spent on the various home office safety activities will vary with conditions, but the percentages are often as shown in the accompanying table "Safetyman's Time Distribution." (Next page.)

In carrying on these activities, items that most likely will present in-company difficulty in securing understanding and uniformity are:

1. Securing the support of the management in a uniform, company-wide accident prevention program.

2. Securing uniform reporting of accidents.

3. Determining whether accidents (or accidental damage) are motor vehicle fleet accidents per the ANSI Standard D15.1—*Method of Recording and Measuring Motor Vehicle Fleet Accident Experience* and then securing acceptance of the decisions about "preventability."*

4. Establishing a policy for supervisory counseling of employees who violate safe practices or disciplining those who are repeatedly involved in accidental occurrences.

* *As explained in Chapter 7 under "Defensive Driving."*

238

SAFETYMAN'S TIME DISTRIBUTION

Home Office Activities (40 to 95 per cent of time)	*Per Cent of Time Spent*
1. General duties of developing, establishing, and promoting the program, carrying on the necessary correspondence, supervising the reporting, record keeping, and statistics	30 to 50
2. Preparing for and participating in conferences, and consulting with officers and management people and committees—developing and guiding the acceptance of the safety program	5 to 20
3. Selecting, training, coaching, and appraising the safety staff	5 to 15
4. Reviewing safety orders, regulations, rules, etc., of regulatory agencies	0 to 5
5. Committee work for trade associations or professional societies—such as Private Truck Council, National Safety Council, American Society of Safety Engineers, National Fire Protection Association, American Trucking Associations, and National Committee for Fleet Supervisory Training	0 to 5

Field Activities (5 to 60 per cent of time)	
1. Working with company field management on explanation, promotion, and stimulation of safety program, and on inspecting equipment and operating habits	5 to 40
2. Working with official agencies regarding safety orders, rules, regulations, etc.	0 to 10
3. Working with trade associations or professional societies.	0 to 10

MANAGEMENT COMMITTEES

A good way to achieve the goals of the safety program is through the use of a management safety committee, discussed in Chapter 2.

The committee should include top officers (president and vice presidents) of the company. Local unit managers should be an integral part of the management team and should be included. The committee should review the performance of the company, and determine policies, procedures, and features of the safety program. The safety director should counsel and advise this committee.

Such a committee can establish, with authority, the methods of operation and the elements of the operating and safety program. The committee will assure that the program is practical, and that it will be

239

fully supported as it is carried out down the line as official company policy.

Always remember that it is top management's responsibility to support the safety program and to make policy decisions whether they operate through a management safety committee or not. Firms that operate without such a safety committee forego many benefits.

Make the Policy Known

One of the first things management should do is to make known and support the company policy on accident prevention.

SAFETY POLICY STATEMENT

Although small (one-location) organizations may be able to function without a formal safety policy statement, larger organizations (especially those operating from scattered locations) are at a disadvantage unless they publish their safety policies.

Basic to such a policy declaration are these statements: (1) that the company intends to comply with all safety laws and ordinances, (2) that the safety of its employees, the public, and its operations are paramount, (3) that safety will take precedence over expediency, or short cuts in the operations of the company, and (4) every attempt will be made to reduce the possibility of accident occurrence.

The policy declaration should be signed by the president.

The policy should be given wide publicity throughout the company and should set the pace of operations for both field management and employees. Such a policy makes it easier to enforce safe practices and conditions. It makes it easier for supervisors to comply with company policy. It also makes it easier for employees to follow safety instruction. Finally, it makes it easier to obtain good preventive maintenance of equipment or selection of proper equipment when purchased.

COMPANY PUBLICATIONS

As a company starts operating in more and more locations, the need for printed procedures, rules, and manuals grows. Field management will be helped by having up-to-date publications that outline company policies and practices covering employee selection, training, and supervision. Methods of investigating and reporting accidental occurrences and detailed outlines (covering such important subjects as counseling, retraining, and discipline) are a must.

A local manager must operate his unit profitably. All the codes,

240

standards, and instructions issued by the main office should be designed to help him make a profit. Manuals must clearly show overall policy and standard methods of procedure, but should not be so needlessly detailed as to reduce the unit manager to a chief clerk.

Make the Policy Understood

The benefits will be reflected in improved performance as new employees are more carefully selected, more effectively trained, adequately appraised as to their job performance, and given more effective supervision. Accidents that do occur will be more thoroughly investigated to get the facts, in order that all can learn how to prevent future accidents.

The safety director should check to see that procedures are complied with, but it's up to management to enforce them.

THE SAFETY AUDIT

One of the things a safety director should do both at headquarters and at any other company location is to sample or audit local programs, practices, and procedures, to (1) check understanding of and compliance with the established and published company policies and practices, and (2) to make sure safety inspections are adequate. By checking actual field practice, the safety director will be in a position to help field management to do a better job. Often, while looking for weak points, the safety director can help supervisors to improve their understanding of company policies and practices.

The safety director should develop a check sheet for evaluating the accident prevention program and for checking conditions or practices during field visits.

Document Program Effectiveness

HOME OFFICE RECORDS

The home office should keep the official company accident statistical records. However the various locations of the company should keep local counterpart records of accidental occurrences. In many cases this will be required by law or regulations such as required by the Bureau of Motor Carrier Safety and Workmen's Compensation laws. Central records are desirable, whether required or not, for these reasons:

241

1. To check company accident trends,
2. To determine those departments or areas that need attention,
3. To discover what types and basic accident causes are most prevalent,
4. To determine those employees who have earned safe driver awards,
5. To learn what safety program features are needed, and
6. To calculate how much accidents cost the company.

Even though local statistics will indicate the local accident story, the whole picture will only be available through central records.

Home office records are necessary because employees transfer from one location to another or from one department to another. Without central records it would be extremely difficult to keep track of changes and records.

STATISTICAL REPORTS

Home office central accident records can be used to compile and issue monthly, quarterly, and annual reports. Such reports are necessary to keep the various branch managers informed of their relative safety performance. Such comparison helps local accident control by building interest in accident prevention. They will build a spirit of competition between the various units of the company. Special reports, summaries, and analyses of accident experience by type of accidents, basic causes, and other factors should be prepared for top management. These were discussed in detail in Chapters 4 and 5.

In general, the areas that should be covered in periodic reports are:

1. Injuries to employees at work,
2. Injuries to employees "off-the-job,"
3. Injuries to the public (the people who come on company property in their contact with the company and are involved in accidents in which a company vehicle is involved),
4. Product liability situation,
5. Motor vehicle accidents,
6. Fires,
7. Loss and damage to cargo or persons,
8. Other details.

The cost of each of these during the reporting interval should be included in the report.

As mentioned in these earlier chapters, statistics on motor vehicle accidents should be based on the *Method of Recording and Measuring Motor Vehicle Fleet Accident Experience,* ANSI Standard D15.1, and *Method of Recording and Measuring Motor Vehicle Fleet and Passenger Accident Experience,* D15.2.

The reports covering motor vehicle accidents should be broken down by operation units and should include at least the following:

1. Number of fleet accidents,
2. Mileage operated by all vehicles (breakdown by types if more than one),
3. Frequency rates for each category, and
4. Number and per cent of fleet accidents judged "preventable."

Statistics on employee injuries should be compiled in accordance with the *Method of Recording and Measuring Work Injury Experience,* ANSI Standard Z16.1, discussed in detail in Chapter 11.

Special studies of motor vehicle accidents should be made to guide the direction of the accident prevention program. Items that should be carefully analyzed are:

1. Types of accidents,
2. Basic causes,
3. Geographical location (spot maps are useful),
4. Types of vehicles involved (owned by or operated for company),
5. Hour of day and day of week of occurrences, and
6. Other factors deemed significant by repeated occurrence.

"Drivers involved" should determine repeaters. Other significant factors about those who are having the most frequent accidents should be cataloged.

UNIFORMITY OF REPORTING

Uniform accident reporting is essential to conduct a safety program for a scattered fleet. Establishing uniformity may be a time-consuming and difficult undertaking, but it must be done. Any difficulty will probably be due to the program's not being fully understood or accepted by various company units. There may be a tendency on the part of field management to "coverup" in order to look good or avoid embarrassment. Sometimes a branch manager will try to protect an employee, rather than to report all facts and conditions.

Whatever the reason, lack of uniformity in reporting accidents hampers the accident prevention program and leads to a vital breakdown in morale and effective supervision.

There are, fortunately, national standards. These should be followed. American National Standards Institute D-15 (already referred to) defines and classifies motor vehicle fleet accidents; the National Safety Council, through its "Safe Driver Award" rules, has established an acceptable and workable method to determine the preventability of accidents. When all units in a company understand and practice the provisions of these two standards, uniformity of accident statistics will result.

Both the ANSI and the NSC provide interpretation committee service to decide questionable or borderline cases. Individual cases can be submitted to these agencies for a decision.

Most companies have established written procedures governing how and by whom accidents will be classified as to reportability and preventability. These procedures vary from company to company but most require that the first decision be made at the local office. When necessary a local committee, usually composed of the employee's supervisor, the supervisor of the garage or maintenance unit, and two fellow employees can review borderline cases or protected decisions. The local decision is then submitted to the home office for a final review. Any decision based on inadequate or biased information should be returned to the local manager for correction if the decision is contrary to company policy.

HEADQUARTERS FOLLOWUP

Periodically, headquarters safety staff should personally check the terminals of scattered fleet units. What is the tipoff that a visit is needed? When there is evidence of poor accident reporting and investigation.

Often, poor safety performance goes hand in hand with poor local management. When operational headquarters people find this out, they will usually try to find what caused the local breakdown. The safetyman can get in on this audit.

Accidents are frequently one of the "early warning signs" that indicate a local management is going down. Other evidences are: unusual overages or shortages, unusually high damage claims, and expensive road failures, increased theft, and declining morale.

Characteristics of the Scattered Fleet

Although the units of a scattered fleet resemble, in many respects, the operation of a small fleet, they differ in that each local unit benefits from (1) the specialized headquarters staff, and (2) well established company guidelines. Thus, the accident record of local units should be

244

better than the average of a number of small, separate fleets.

The headquarters safety staff can best aid the units of their scattered fleets by (1) preplanning schedules for training consultation, driver meetings, and introduction of new systems and equipment; (2) systematizing procedures; and (3) preparing standard forms.

When headquarters staff visits the units, they should use their time wisely. Visits should be planned well in advance. Forms and instructions should be sent ahead in sufficient time to allow local supervision to prepare themselves and to review any instructions and new information.

There must be a smooth-functioning line of contact between headquarters of the local units. A definite program of visits and followups should be worked out; deviations from this can undermine an otherwise well-planned accident control program.

When headquarters staff (especially safetymen) visit local units, they must use the highest degree of diplomacy and tact. The safetyman must remember that he *advises* management. His is a staff function—he must not assume any line authority. He should report defects and unsafe practices to line management who, in turn, has the responsibility to correct these situations.

TYPICAL SALES FLEET POSTERS published by the National Safety Council.
These were distributed in collaboration with American Bakers Association.

246

15

The sales fleet

Salesmen think they are a special breed: forceful, independent, energetic, and, of necessity, self-assured. Although great for bolstering the ego, this self-image can present special problems in safety programming, and often can run counter to the needs of safe driving.

Because the overriding criterion used in assessing work performance is ability to meet sales quotas, a salesman is unlikely to worry too much about the other aspects of job performance, unless these aspects are directly related to meeting a sales quota.

Yet the traveling salesman who drives a car needs defensive driving skills as much as any other professional driver. Regardless of what he sells, a salesman has only so much selling time. Anything that cuts into his selling time cuts into his sales. Vehicular accidents can not only put a salesman in the hospital for days, weeks, or months, but also result in lost sales opportunities and lost income.

Because of the direct tie-in between sales and income, the salesman has more to fear from lost time due to accidents than perhaps any other individual.

His company, too, has much to lose. In addition to the direct expense of the accident, there is the loss of a sales territory not being worked and sales followups not being made. If a salesman is injured, a substitute may not know the prospects and may not be as good a sales representative as the injured one.

Sales management has an obligation to protect the sales force from motor vehicle accidents. Through a safe-driving program, a company can improve driving performance and help to protect salesmen from being involved in motor vehicle accidents.

Management Interest

The safety program of the sales fleet must, as always, start with top management—management that realizes their sales organization on wheels is both a selling force and a transportation organization, and, as such, has the same accident problem as any other fleet. Management must demand safe driving. This Manual repeats this again and again.

Management interest must be vocal, visible, and continuous. From top management through division managers and subordinate supervisors, there should be no sales meeting so crucial as to fail to mention the salesman's safety on the road. Letters, bulletins, or publications can be utilized to emphasize management interest in safety during the periods between face-to-face sales management meetings.

SELL SAFETY

Most sales organizations should be endowed with the talents necessary to carry on a successful safety program. A safety program is largely a matter of selling a group of employees on a set of attitudes, a body of knowledge and a set of skills. Because selling safety is much like selling anything else, the same techniques should be applied to selling safety to the salesmen. A good salesman is intelligent and highly adaptable, too. If he can adapt to the demands of a customer, he can certainly adapt to the requirements of safe driving.

SAFETY ORGANIZATION

Ideally, a qualified safety technician should be responsible for planning and carrying out the details of the sales fleet safety program. The sales fleet safety program should follow the basic principles set forth in this Manual.

Hire Safe Drivers and Help Them Stay Safe

Most salesmen are hired for their sales ability—naturally. But if the new man is going to be given an automobile, then his background as a safe driver should also be checked before he is hired. It should be borne in mind that the salesman who continually abuses or wrecks company vehicles is no asset to the sales organization—either financially or "public-relations-wise." It is possible to have a super salesman whose "cost ledger for accidents" makes him a financial liability. The selection

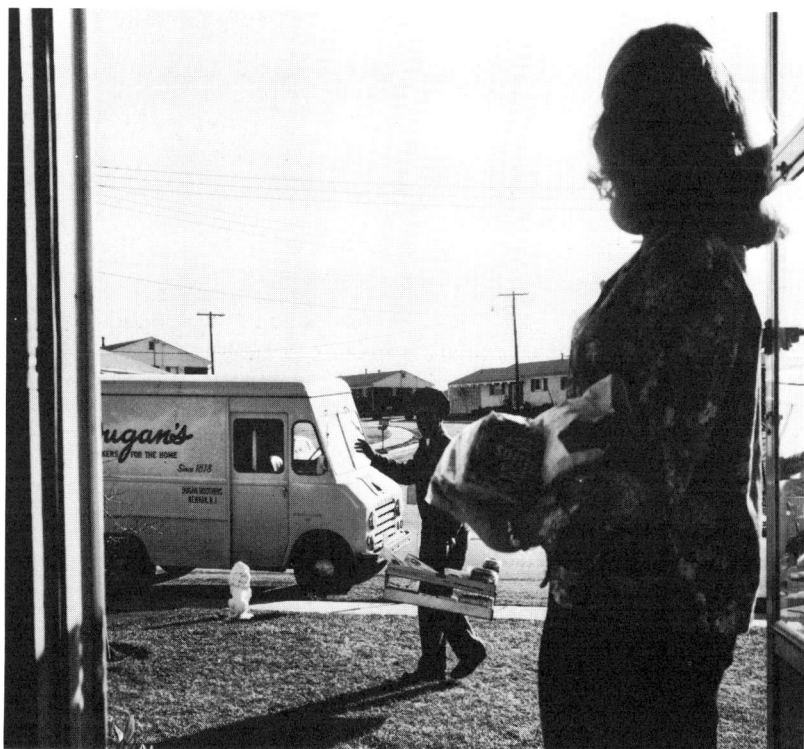

COURTESY—whether in selling or driving—characterizes a good man.

program should be designed to eliminate such accident-repeater salesmen from new recruits. (Review the ideas given in Chapter 6.)

DRIVER TRAINING

Salesmen who must drive should be given driver training. This training should cover:

1. Defensive driving,
2. How the preventability of accidents will be determined,
3. How safe driving records will be determined,
4. What part the salesman will play in the company safety program, and
5. The company's safe-driving policy.

In addition to covering the basic principles of defensive driving, the man should be told:

1. How procurement of fuel and maintenance service will be handled,

249

2. Any restrictions on private use of the car (if a company car), and
3. How accidents should be reported.

Classroom training should be utilized, if possible. In many cases, the district sales manager may have to personally teach the new employee. Printed material, such as company rule books and safe driving literature, should be explained in the training program. Investigate the benefits of NSC's "Driver Improvement Program."

ACCIDENT RECORDS

Companies usually provide salesmen with presentations, directives, and product literature. It is customary to require a variety of regular weekly reports concerning all aspects of the sales activity. He should be told that he must also report *all* motor vehicle accidents.

Failure to report an accident should be treated as a serious violation of company rules and penalties assessed. Not only is such reporting necessary to provide remedial training, it is imperative to claims settlement (fixing of liability).

DRIVING SUPERVISION

Driver supervision—the process of checking driver performance, detecting and correcting substandard performance, and motivating good performance—is discussed in detail in Chapter 8.

Because most salesmen are seldom under direct observation, a sales supervisor must rely upon other means to detect poor safety performance.

These will include:

1. The accident report.
2. Vehicle maintenance records (excessive repair bills can indicate substandard driving performance.)
3. Traffic citations and letters of complaint when persons write in about observed acts of reckless driving on the part of the salesman. Take remedial action if investigation proves the complaints valid.

MEASURE PERFORMANCE

Sales management should check the performance of the fleet by keeping records of the fleet accident rate.

Accident trends should be studied for irregularities. Because month-to-month comparison can be misleading, longer periods should be used when possible.

Sales fleets should participate in the National Fleet Safety Contest.

By participating in this contest the sales fleet manager can compare the record of his fleet with that of a number of similar fleets.

The average sales organization will be familiar with many types of contests, awards, campaigns, and other devices for creating and maintaining interest. These can be as effective in the field of safe driving as they are in the sales field. These are discussed in Chapters 11 and 12.

Safe-driving performance must be considered an integral part of the salesman's job. If treated properly, the subject of safe driving can be made interesting, profitable, and desirable to salesmen.

16

The utility fleet

During the past decade, gas utility fleets that report to the National Fleet Safety Contest substantially reduced their accident frequency rate. This drop reflected a stepped-up tempo of training at all levels—training directed to eliminating the worst accident situations first.

Training has been coupled to accident analysis in order to direct efforts where they can be most effective, as shown in the accompanying analysis. Here 1,300 motor vehicle accidents that occurred to 20 gas

ANALYSIS OF 1,300 MOTOR VEHICLE ACCIDENTS
Data from 20 gas utility fleets

Most Common Type of Motor Vehicle Accident	Number	Per Cent
Involved front end of company vehicle	454	33
Involved rear end of company vehicle	428	31
Sideswipe	276	20
Other	222	16
Movement of Company Vehicle		
Going straight ahead	669	48.5
Parking	195	14.1
Stopped in Traffic	186	12.5
Backing	147	10.6
Turning	107	7.8
Other	76	5.5

252

UTILITY EMPLOYEES, hired because of their technical abilities, must understand that driving is not secondary to their main job, but that it is a full-time job when they are in the driver's seat.

utility companies were classified by type. Although gas utilities provided the data, the ratios no doubt parallel the experience of electric, water, and communications utilities.

Many utilities have achieved excellent motor vehicle fleet safety records and have reduced lost time, maintenance, and insurance costs— besides improving public relations. Public relations will improve when a utility fleet is operated safely and courteously on the streets and highways of the communities it serves.

Hiring Policies

Many utility fleets now realize that they must hire safe-driving employees for linemen, servicemen, engineers, and other specialty workers. A utility—even more than a factory-centered company—depends on the efficiency with which it can assemble men, materials, machines, and equipment and move them without mishap to where they are needed.

Mobility requires that technicians *know how to drive their vehicles*

ACCIDENT CASE HISTORY—Boom extended over roadway when vehicle tipped over. Two employees in the baskets, both belted in, sustained nondisabling injuries—bruised right hip and thigh, and stiff shoulder and neck. Photo report shows stability was lost when weld that joined piston of leveling jack to the jack foot plate (small photograph) broke. Examination showed a defective weld.

254

as well as *know how to operate their equipment*—thus making *both* driving and technical skills part of their jobs.

Some utilities, unfortunately, still accept a prospective employee's drivers license as evidence of his ability to drive safely. These same utilities would not dream of hiring an electrician, welder, or other tradesmen merely on his say-so or on his showing an up-to-date union card.

Utilities should carefully investigate the vehicle accident record of each man before placing him on a job. They should show the same concern that a new employee is qualified to drive as they show for his technical ability.

Accident Record System

Utilities seem to be worse off than other industries when it comes to vulnerability to public liability. Juries often regard a utility as having superior ability to pay damages, and very often they decide in favor of the opposing side, seemingly regardless of the merits of the case.

For this reason, utility drivers must report every accident no matter how minor the damage whenever there is contact between a utility vehicle and another person, vehicle, or other property. This must be done regardless of who was at fault.

Having a complete report of all accidents not only protects the driver involved but also enables the utility to better defend itself if the incident results in a law suit. But this is not the only purpose for which reports of accidents should be obtained. Facts gleaned from these reports should be used as the basis for corrective action, for preventing the occurrence of similar accidents in the future.

In following up each accident, actual costs should be calculated. These should be compiled and summarized in periodic reports to management. It is a necessary procedure if management's continued interest and support of the accident prevention program is to be secured. Once a proportion of indirect costs to direct costs has been established, it can be used to estimate total costs.

Case Histories

Followup by fleet safetymen—to company management and district supervision and to drivers—has been found to increase the effectiveness of utility programs. Safety reminders to drivers include dashboard stickers, posters, pamphlets enclosed with payroll checks, and movies that show special driving problems and their solutions.

THREE-POINT SAFETY PROGRAM

A medium-size utility (347 drivers) found this program helped reduce vehicle accidents over a period of several years.

> • Safety meetings are held regularly—thirty minutes every Monday morning for drivers; one hour every three months for supervisors.
> • Annual safety campaigns were launched. These were tied in with National Safety Council themes—for example, "Zero In On Safety." All the Time" was the 1961 and 1962 theme.
> • Recognition is given for good performance. The National Safety Council "Safe Driver Award" is presented annually to eligible drivers. Safety suppers for all groups that have no preventable accidents are held every six months.

The "Safe Driver Award" program was found to be a definite factor in maintaining a good safety record. Older drivers are proud of their good records; new men soon acquire the same attitude. The basic fairness of the Award program appeals to drivers—they respect the awards and take pride in them.

'INFORM, SUPERVISE, AND FOLLOW THROUGH'

"Inform, supervise, and follow through" is the success formula of one 84-driver utility. The company is small, management is close to employees, contact is sincere and person to person.

Safe-driving instruction is geared to seasonal hazards—immediate and potential hazards are pointed out. Management is genuinely interested in promoting safe driving—a vehicle is promptly maintained once an unsafe condition has been reported. This stimulates employee cooperation.

When an accident does occur, the driver must file a comprehensive accident report. He must gather all information, check police headquarters for their report, and reviews the details of the accident with the company superintendent.

TRAINS AND SUPERVISES

A utility with 2,500 drivers found that driver training has been one of the main factors in reducing its accident frequency to 7.21 reportable accidents per million miles. (Company vehicles travel about 28 million miles a year.)

Another large utility that also provides driver training finds that it gets a good reception from drivers. A spokesman says, "We have taken the attitude that a training program will not be a cure-all, nor will it prevent all of our avoidable accidents. But we do feel that a program of this nature—which we prefer to call an 'improvement program'—will mentally challenge our people to strive to improve their poor seeing habits, which probably cause their being involved in an accident."

The company also gives credit to hard-working field supervisors who stress vehicular safety.

Self-Discipline Important

Because utility employees are hired because of their technical ability, each driver must learn to discipline himself to the task of safe driving. The two disadvantages that a technical employee has are (1) he believes driving to be secondary to his main job, and (2) he is trying to solve his technical problems between jobs, while he is driving. He must discipline himself to drive safely and to keep his mind on his driving.

SUPERVISORS MUST WORK AT IT TOO

When an employee is driving, it is impossible for a supervisor to guide every move. Supervisors, therefore, must develop self-discipline in their drivers.

Let's go over a six-step procedure for developing this self-discipline:

1. Decide the items for which self-discipline is needed—in this case, safe-driving procedures.
2. Set up a planned work procedure for the employee.
3. Train the employee in the planned behavior—be firm, but understanding. Tell "why" as well as show "how." Shape everything so that the employee builds self-confidence.
4. Keep letting the employee work on this himself until he is able to operate on his own with the desired degree of self-control. As his self-control increases, commend him and show more confidence in him.
5. Periodically follow him up, but gradually decrease the frequency of the checks. Reinstate limited supervisory control on a temporary basis only when necessary, and then relinquish it as soon as possible.
6. Let employee try his self-control. Increase the length of time between periodic checks until regular supervisory contacts and checks are sufficient.

The procedure for developing self-discipline actually summarizes how we go about carrying out any on-the-job training. Thus what might appear to be a complicated procedure turns out to be nothing more than adapting everyday supervisory methods to developing safe behavior.

AN ILLUSTRATIVE CASE—
HOW TO CHANGE SAFETY BEHAVIOR

The six-step procedure just discussed is brought into sharp focus by this case history.

The employee concerned. A well trained, competent electronic technician used a car to travel his assigned area. His job was to diagnose and correct troubles in unmanned radar stations. This man was highly regarded by his superiors, even considered one of their best men. He had five years' experience with his company, was 28 years old, and had completed his military service.

Description of accident cases. This employee had two motor vehicle accidents approximately one year apart.

In the first, he and a fellow employee, both assigned to temporary patrol duty, were driving from station to station because there had been serious sabotage in which a station had been blown up. Three stations, spaced about thirty miles apart, were covered by the patrol. Both men had been instructed to alternate in driving on an hourly basis. It was pointed out that the second man had been assigned solely for safety reasons.

At the time of the accident, they were driving an 8:00 P.M. to 4:00 A.M. tour. Shortly after midnight, the employee in question went to sleep while driving, and the car ran off the road. The accident severely injured both him and the alternate driver. It later developed that the alternate driver was asleep in the back seat at the time—not beside the driver where he could check on the situation and the driver. Both employees were hospitalized with serious injuries; the driver was unable to return to the job for over two months.

After the investigation, both employees were informed that another work error of any type could result in their discharge.

Approximately one year later, the employee who was the driver in the first accident had a second motor vehicle accident and was suspended pending the investigation and a decision.

Accident diagram is on the next page.

In this accident, the employee was driving on a one-way street in the left-hand lane. A slow-moving truck was in the right-hand lane. As the employee approached the truck, he saw a boy on a bicycle cross from the left to the right and disappear from view ahead of the truck. The employee blew his horn and started to pass the truck because he intended to make a right turn into the street at the end of the block in

258

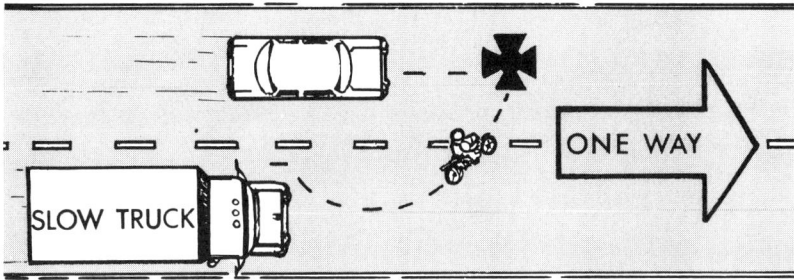

which they were traveling. When the employee's car came even with the front of the truck, the boy on the bicycle, who had decided to recross the street from the right to the left, suddenly reappeared in the car's path and was struck.

Results of investigation. Although the superintendent and department head felt there was no alternative to discharging the employee, they were completely puzzled by the two accidents, particularly the second one. The technician was a fine employee, one who had had no personal injury accidents in his five years employment. The employee's supervisor who believed in him completely, maintained that there must be some obscure emotional reason.

The investigation revealed:

1. The employee should have followed the slow-moving truck, instead of speeding up to cut around it and make a right turn at the end of the block.

2. The employee maintained that, during his driving, he had been thinking out a plan to correct the trouble at the station and get on to the next one. This was consistent with his fine record as a craftsman.

3. In his youth, the employee had been an enthusiastic automobile racer, which had included drag racing.

4. His present hobbies were flying his own airplane plus motor boat racing.

5. When he saw the boy disappear ahead of the truck, he instinctively speeded up to pass the truck and make the right turn. This was done without thinking, apparently as a result of his years of racing driving.

6. Ordinary motor vehicle driving was viewed as a sort of humdrum procedure from an emotional standpoint.

7. In the driving test given following the accident, he rated about the same as he did in previous driving checks and in the driver training course required by his company (70 on the scale of 100 placed him as satisfactory but below the expert range). During the driving test, he talked constantly and turned his head while conversing.

It was decided, as a result of these findings, to try rehabilitating the employee by changing his behavior through a planned course of action. The employee sincerely wanted to change and was surprised and pleased that he was not to be discharged.

Behavior change plan as carried out by the supervisor:

1. The employee was to continue on his driving assignment.

2. It was made clear that driving was to be his only job while in the driver's seat, and if he found his mind wandering to trouble-shooting or anything else, he was to find a safe place to pull off the road, stop, think out his problem, and then proceed with his driving.

3. Prior to starting his assignment, the employee and his supervisor were to sit down and, insofar as possible, plan in advance the work at each trouble location he was assigned.

4. Each of his poor driving habits was discussed, and the nature of the corrective procedures was stressed. He was drilled in the correct procedures.

5. For the first week, the supervisor rode with him on his maintenance trips.

6. The second week, the supervisor rode with him every other day. Following that, the supervisory checks were less frequent, but were unscheduled.

7. The behavior-change training was conducted on a planned basis for a full six-month period, with spot-check training and followup conducted during the second six months. Changes in behavior are only accomplished by learning the new response-pattern and unlearning the old one. The so-called "neural traces" or habitual stimulus-response patterns in the brain are not formed or reformed with only a few performances of the correct pattern.

8. The employee was informed that in the event of another motor vehicle accident, a completely fair evaluation would be made, and if the responsibility were his, he would be discharged. He would not be held accountable for things beyond his control.

Results of the behavior-change training were many. During the year, the employee had no motor vehicle accidents and was observed to be applying himself faithfully to the training procedure when he was not aware he was under observation. The supervisor fulfilled his responsibilities in every detail.

The driving check and test at the end of the year showed a dramatic change which placed the employee in the expert driver range. The driver instructor observed: "Employee held his conversation to a minimum, did not turn his head, and took no part in discussions between passengers. He devoted all energies to driving." This was markedly different from the test given following the accident. He gave concrete evidence of behavior change.

In unsolicited comments made to others and passed on to the supervisor, the employee stated that the training had changed his flying habits and his speed-boating habits completely. He felt he was now driving safely, and moreover, he was really enjoying it. Up to the present time, approximately two years after the second accident, the employee has not had any accidents, motor vehicle or other types, on or off the job.

Although this case involves motor vehicle accidents, the procedures for changing unsafe to safe behavior apply to all behavior changes.

17

The police fleet

Approximately 90 per cent of reported police accidents occurred when the police vehicle was either parked or engaged in normal patrol, according to a survey conducted by the Highway Safety Division of the International Association of Chiefs of Police.

When a large Midwest police agency analyzed their motor vehicle accidents for a twelve-month period, they discovered that approximately 78 per cent occurred during routine patrol duty, and only 22 per cent occurred during emergency or pursuit driving. Although they were not sure how much they could reduce emergency or pursuit driving accidents, the agency found they could do something about the 78 per cent category—those accidents sustained during routine patrol duty. By reducing accident frequency by just 25 per cent, the agency saved enough to purchase 12 new patrol cars a year.

How many other police departments would welcome the opportunity to squeeze a few new motor vehicles out of their budgets—especially when it is quite unlikely that a budget will be increased in the immediate future? Many fleets find no better way to secure needed new equipment than from the dollars saved by reducing unnecessary and preventable accidents through a fleet safety program.

Individual police fleets have shown remarkable progress in the reduction of accidents in recent years. For example, among the municipal police fleets we find reductions such as 85 per cent in Riverside, Calif., during a three-year period; 37 per cent in Burbank, Calif., for three years; 47 per cent by the Chicago Park District Police

SPECIAL OPERATIONS, SPECIAL VEHICLES. Efficient and safe operation must rest on a well-thought out and administered accident prevention program.

for a three-year period; 30 per cent in Phoenix, Ariz.; 30 per cent in Springfield, Ohio; 25 per cent in Saginaw, Mich.; and 20 per cent in Dallas, Tex.

Similarly, in the state police category there were reported reductions of as high as 86 per cent in California, 66 per cent in Nebraska, 40 per cent in Florida, 30 per cent in Kentucky, 24 per cent in Texas, and 12 per cent in North Carolina.

Even greater than the financial motive for stressing safe police vehicle operation stands another reason: the public expects police to be the shining example of accident prevention. The spectacle of a badly-damaged police vehicle, especially if the police is at fault, destroys much good achieved through patient traffic law enforcement. Public reaction is swift and often severe when a police vehicle causes serious injury or death. Like clergymen who are expected to avoid sin, police drivers are expected to avoid accidents.

Requirements for an effective police accident prevention program —both for normal and emergency operation—are similar to other fleet safety programs. Special considerations are described in this chapter.

263

Patrol Operations

Most police vehicle collisions occur during normal patrol operations—not during pursuit. The sudden erratic movement of another vehicle at a time when the police officer is concentrating on observing something else while cruising can bring about collisions in much the same way as accidents occur to John or Jane Doe.

Can such accidents be stopped? Yes. When attention is focused on them and police supervision will no longer tolerate the often high handed attitude of the patrol officers that they are "above suspicion." The sad commentary is that too many police fleets fail to use the assistance available to them.

Unfortunately, there are several special psychological factors working against a police fleet operation.

First—every squad car driver knows that if he receives an emergency call, he must go to a given address in the shortest possible time. In doing so, he can ignore many traffic rules and regulations to get there as quickly as possible.

This attitude, however, is apt to carry over to routine patrol driving. If the police driver cheats a little on the yellow lights, turns left where left turns are not permitted, exceeds the speed limit, fails to observe stop signs, or abuses the privilege of a Mars light—who is going to give him a ticket or even call him down?—unless he is observed by a superior. So there is an understandable tendency among police car drivers to become lax in observing traffic rules and regulations, which are actually meant for the safety of all. Police must obey them at all times except emergency pursuit.

A second handicap is that police vehicles are usually well marked and are highly visible. In consequence, other vehicle drivers give them a wide berth. Few motorists ever have the temerity to dispute the right-of-way of a squad car. Over a period of time, squad car drivers get used to having their way in little day-to-day traffic encounters. They've become less wary of traffic hazards—not as defensive-driving minded—as they should be to keep out of accidents.

A third handicap often results from the action of police administrators. They do not insist emphatically enough that departmental vehicles be driven safely. If a police officer bangs up a squad car in an accident, his chief will undoubtedly bawl him out. But, too often, the chief betrays the feeling that having a little accident now and then is an inescapable part of the job.

For these reasons, then, we cannot assume that police drivers are "automatically" safe drivers merely because they *know* all the traffic rules and regulations.

Each person's responsibility for safety can be made part of general department policy. The New York City Police Department has done just this in their policy statement on their safety program—each level of responsibility is spelled out. The following recommendations concerning first-line supervisors were made by Lt. V. K. Hipskind, Departmental Safety Officer, Dallas Police Department.

The first-line supervisor should:

1. "Think safety" at all times.
2. Be cognizant of safe practices and procedures.
3. Give a good "safety example."
4. Exact proper performance of duty from his subordinates.
5. Continually educate his subordinates in safety meaures.
6. Correct unsafe practices immediately upon observing them.
7. Investigate injuries to and accidents involving his subordinates, and recommend measures to prevent future similar accidents.
8. Carry out preventive safety through inspection of equipment.

Regardless of whether a driver operates a squad car—or a truck, bus, or taxicab—he must learn how to protect himself against all kinds of adverse driving. The general techniques of fleet safety apply to these normal fleet operations.

Emergency Operations

Police officers are often called upon to operate vehicles in a manner which involves imminent risk of danger to themselves as well as others. The public and the courts give police every encouragement to discharge their duties fully and fearlessly. Adequate specialized training, however, is vital.

WHAT THE LAW SAYS

Officers and department officials are concerned about liability occurring while in pursuit of law violators. One court decision reads:

"It would be an affront to the intelligence of the legislature to hold that, in enacting a statute designed to suppress 'speeding,' it intended to restrict peace officers in the prescribed speed limits when in pursuit of violators of the statute. . . . An officer so engaged is performing a public duty. He cannot successfully perform it unless he is accorded privileges not possessed by private citizens. He would be seriously hampered if statutory provisions limiting the speed of motor vehicles applied to him while in pursuit of a fleeing criminal.

"We do not hold that an officer, when in pursuit of a lawbreaker, is under no obligation to exercise a reasonable degree of care to avoid injury to others who may be on the public roads and streets. What we do hold is that, while so engaged, he is not to be deemed negligent merely because he fails to observe the requirements of the Motor Vehicle Act. His conduct is to be examined and tested by another standard. He is required to observe the care which a reasonable prudent man would exercise in the discharge of official duties of a like nature under like circumstances."

Thus the driver of an emergency vehicle is bound to take reasonable precautions against causing injury or damage, and cannot proceed in reckless disregard for possible consequences. But at the same time his conduct is to be judged in the light of what he must do then and there in the performance of his duties and responsibilities toward the protection of life and property.

INSTRUCTION IN EMERGENCY DRIVING

It takes much training to make the important decisions of emergency driving. Emergency operation demands a high degree of skill, knowledge of the physical laws governing motor vehicle operation and the rules of the road, knowledge of the streets where the driving is done, good judgment and good eyesight, and lots of experience.

Since emergency driving cannot be avoided, specialized training should be given in efficient operation and in taking every reasonable precaution against causing injury or damage to an innocent bystander. The minimum subjects that should be covered in this training are:

1. Right-of-way problems,
2. Approaching side streets and rural highway intersections,
3. Approaching a traffic signal which is against the emergency vehicle,
4. Wrong side of the road operation,
5. Passing techniques,
6. U-turns and other turns,
7. Curves, hills, and hidden dangers, and
8. Emergency braking and acceleration.

The International Association of Chiefs of Police states that an officer engaged in high-speed pursuits must apply sound judgment and follow such accepted safety precautions as:

1. Estimate speed of vehicle being overtaken and the distance of the oncoming traffic in order to determine the margin of safety before attempting to pass the vehicle.

2. Never pass on hills or curves.

3. Return to your traffic lane as soon as the passed vehicle is clearly seen in the rear-view mirror.

4. Check the rear and the side traffic lanes before pulling into traffic.

5. Keep both hands on the wheel at all times.

6. Slow down before entering a curve. Then accelerate as the curve permits. Never cut corners.

7. Signal intentions well before stopping or slowing down by flashing your brake lights or by using a hand signal.

8. Stop gradually. Don't wait until the last second.

Police drivers must understand that it is no light decision to exceed safe speed limits, abridge right-of-way, or take other risks to apprehend a fugitive. Too often, unfortunately, a chase abuses the privilege of emergency right-of-way.

Before pursuing a fugitive, the driver must weigh the end result against the risk involved. The apprehension of a dangerous criminal, detrimental to public safety and an immediate menace, would naturally call for extreme urgency. However, a minor traffic violator or a person charged with a misdemeanor would be a poor cause to risk lives of patrolmen and other motorists by hazardous pursuit.

Basic data on emergency driving is provided in the book *Police Pursuit Driving,* by Edward W. Jones of the North Carolina Highway Patrol, Raleigh, N.C. (available from International Association of Chiefs of Police, 1319 18th St., Washington, D.C. 20036), and in the booklet *Pursuit Driving,* published by the U.S. Treasury Department (available through the U.S. Government Printing Office, Washington, D.C. 20402).

Special Problems

As with all fleets, efficient and safe operation must rest on a well thought-out and administered accident prevention program, based on policies consistent through all levels of command: the budget must be adequate, the supervision and enforcement must be consistent, fixing of responsibility must be objective, and vehicle and equipment selection must be intelligent. General rules have been given in earlier chapters.

Special police problems in training and motivation, personnel selection, records and forms, accident review, and vehicle selection are also important.

POLICE DRIVING SCHOOL combines three days of classwork and behind-the-wheel instruction. Track (pictured) provides for instruction in precise stopping techniques, straight backups, and maneuvering in complex patterns. Instruction is given in curbing a violator, high speed chase, setting up roadblocks, and handling the occupant of a violator's car.

TRAINING

Training must be used to provide the know-how, develop the skills, and shape the attitudes required for an effective prevention program. Training benefits wane rapidly, however, unless fortified regularly by supervision of driver compliance and competence. Discussion of vehicle safety requirements through regularly scheduled rollcall sessions and field training is recommended.

Often after a training course ends, department personnel have the feeling that emphasis on improving driving habits was shifted to some other area. Always keep the objective clear and in sight.

Regularly scheduled short training sessions are more valuable than long sessions at infrequent periods with nothing in between, particularly once basic driving skill and knowledge have been taught. Since required knowledge is related to training service provided, regular use of short training sessions as a form of motivation must not be overlooked.

The police chief's continuing concern for an accident-free fleet is

268

reflected by his use of regularly planned and conducted discussions of the department's fleet safety record, of lessons learned in a recent accident, and of individual driver performance. Personalized ("coffee-cup") field training helps drive points home and develops comprehension.

A police agency is under constant pressure to upgrade its level of performance in many activities. For example, marksmanship practice to develop the highest firearm skills is common in every police outfit. The importance of having the highest driver competence and skill possible during routine and emergency driving merits such priority and respected consideration. Participation in the police fleet safety program will provide both suggested techniques and guides to improved driver and fleet operation. Other motivational techniques are given in Chapter 8, "Driver Supervision."

Special features that can be brought out in police training are:

• **Psychological factors**—If an officer is exposed to an unpleasant or shocking experience (such as a particularly obnoxious traffic violator, or investigation of a heinous crime), the experience often occupies his mind for some time. He must be aware that the mental prominence of the particular incident may impair his driving ability by dividing his attention.

• **Physical condition**—Fatigue poses the greatest physical threat because it lowers visual efficiency and increases reaction time. This potential danger may appear anytime an officer reports for duty without being well rested. If drowsiness sets in, the officer can obtain temporary relief by (1) opening car windows to circulate fresh air, (2) talking out loud, and (3) making frequent stops to conduct security checks or inspect trouble spots. Use of caffeine ("stay awake") pills is not recommended because they cause undue strain on the nervous system and disturb the reflexes.

• **Driving is a full-time job**—Driving requires full attention all the time. Partners should not talk so much that the driver's attention is diverted from the roadway. If an off-roadway situation needs checking, the vehicle should be stopped.

National Fleet Safety Contest. Every police department should have a safety program for those who drive. Participating in the National Fleet Safety Contest should be a part of that program. Even though participation in the contest cannot solve all fleet problems, it will, however, furnish a reference point for such a program, and stimulate interest in it.

It is basic to compare the accident frequency of a fleet. This

IN-DEPTH TRAFFIC ADMINISTRATION AND ENFORCEMENT program is provided at the Northwestern Traffic Institute, Evanston, Illinois.

accident frequency rate should be computed in terms of reportable accidents per 1,000,000 vehicle miles. And in order to get a rate that is significant, a reportable fleet accident must be defined. (Also see discussion in Chapter 7, page 136, under "Defensive Driving.")

Contest rules give a definition that has been standardized throughout the motor transportation industry. The rules define a reportable accident as follows: ". . . Any accident in which the contestant's vehicle is involved, unless properly parked, where such accident results in death, personal injury, or property damage. An accident is reportable regardless of who was hurt, what property was damaged or to what extent, where it occurred, or who was responsible." This definition includes everything from a fatal accident on down to a scratched fender. Interpretations of the rule by the International Association of Chiefs of Police include pursuit accidents as well as patrol. An exception to the rule is damage to a patrol vehicle used as an emergency road block.

By comparing rates with other fleets, a police fleet can tell whether it is doing better or worse than average. And, if entered in the contest, each fleet will receive a monthly contest bulletin showing the accidents

270

rates of all contestants. Identification of individual fleets is by code. If a fleet wishes to exchange information with other contestants, code numbers can be exchanged if mutually agreeable.

Participation in the contest tells the general public that police officers, individually and collectively, are pointing the way toward safer driving habits and accident reduction. Fleet participation shows citizens that their police department is providing the type of leadership in traffic safety that they want others to follow.

Participation in the safety program builds morale. To prevent accidental injuries is in the best tradition of law enforcement agencies.

PERSONNEL SELECTION

The high physical and mental standards required of police recruits may lead to the assumption that all police personnel have the qualities required for good driving. Such an assumption bears careful examination. For example, most police recruits are under the age of 25. Although these recruits are usually at the peak of their physical capacities, they sometimes lack the maturity and responsibility required for safe vehicle operation. This is shown by the high accident rate of this age group: the motor-vehicle accident death rate is higher for the 15 to 24 year old age bracket than for any other group, except the over-75 year olds. In fact, most commercial fleets avoid hiring a man as a driver if he is under the age of 26.

The practice of recruiting young men for police work is not questioned, as long as there are realistic and workable controls. Where possible, men in this group may be assigned to the stop-and-go type of driving involved in city assignments. While this could involve more frequent minor accidents, it would avoid the severity of high-speed accidents. Assignments likely to result in high-speed chase or emergency operation might be restricted to the more experienced and mature drivers.

Training the younger men cannot be over stressed. The experience of the Texas Highway Patrol will illustrate what can be accomplished. Patrolmen in the 21- to 25-year bracket, they found, had *fewer accidents in proportion to their numbers*. This was attributed to the fact that driver training, an advantage that older officers had missed, was given major emphasis during the recruit training program.

Physical requirements for recruits seem well established in most departments. A similar awareness of mental standards required for continued safe operation of police vehicles must also be developed.

271

- Requirements for commercial truck drivers established by the Bureau of Motor Carrier Safety were discussed in Chapter 6, "Driver Selection." The physician can assess the man against the standards. Lacking such a measure, a physical examination will have limited value. Police must indicate to the physician what factors are deemed essential to police driving.
- Performance as a driver of police vehicles should be constantly reviewed with specific attention to the known conditions and requirements for safe operation during each major type of driving. An examination by a physician every two years (the Bureau of Motor Carrier Safety standard) is recommended.

RECORDS AND FORMS

Keeping score is basic to a well-managed accident prevention program. Police, like most people, try to do what is held out to them as important to do.

Each accident, therefore, should be charged to the driver, to his section or division, and to the station or district where supervisory or command accountability exists. Records can indicate which men seldom err and those who make frequent driving errors. Factual data from records and opinions expressed by those who review the accidents provides the guide to corrective action: individual coaching, a reprimand, praise, reward, or discipline. When a police fleet cannot tell whether its accident experience is getting better or worse, the accident prevention activity has hit "rock bottom."

Burdened with other records, nevertheless, police organizations must organize a system and utilize record data to guide police fleet accident prevention activity. The data helps indicate when, where, and how accidents occur.

ACCIDENT REVIEW

Fleets participating in National Safety Council's Motor Fleet Safety Service use an accident review committee as standard procedure.

Basically, use of the procedure assures that "a lesson" in each accident will be learned by the driver and the organization. Those lessons are taught by the inquiry and decision of the accident review committee.

A prime purpose in the review of accidents is to determine their preventability or non-preventability as far as drivers are concerned. Since reward or discipline is decided, it is essential that a standard guide

272

be applied when reviewing an accident.

The review procedure emphasizes for each driver that accidents are not a whim of fate. He learns that "filling out a report" does not close the matter, that he cannot be excused because other drivers violated the law, or when the other drivers admit the blame and pay the bill. Hundreds of drivers and fleet supervisors have found that use of the review technique will reduce the occurrence of accidents.

VEHICLE AND EQUIPMENT SELECTION

Opportunity to influence the selection of equipment, maintenance procedures, and equipment should be provided when planning a fleet safety program, because decisions in these matters influence safe operation.

Knowledge of vehicle characteristics with regard to cornering, suspension, braking effectiveness, can be significant in successful high speed use of the police vehicle. Accident control requires a knowledge of accident causes related to the vehicle and a voice in determining the procedures and policies concerning the vehicle, its selection, its equipment, its ownership, and its inspection and maintenance. Safe operation of police motor vehicles is the result of many activities. Unless it is made clear to all that the chief requires accident-free performance, some of the necessary steps *will* be overlooked.

Accident experience should influence decisions when a choice exists as to selection and use of vehicles and equipment. Recommendations for seat belts, roll bars, protective helmets, door fasteners, tire types, and other items of equipment illustrate the range of technical advice that should be sought.

Vehicle upkeep is as important as proper vehicle selection. Some jurisdictions require supervisors to inspect each police vehicle before it is turned over to a new shift watch. Final responsibility, however, must rest with each vehicle operator.

Here are vehicle checks recommended by the International Association of Chiefs of Police:

1. Check all lights, including tail lights and turn signals.
2. Check the horn, siren, and emergency lights.
3. Check gas, oil, and water.
4. Check brakes by seeing if there is "enough pedal."
5. Check proper inflation of tires. Slow leakers should be replaced.
6. Clean windshield, windows, and mirror.
7. If windshield wipers streak, replace them.

8. Check condition of the spare tire.

9. Check departmental equipment, such as flares, first-aid kit, tire-changing tools.

Conditions, such as a defective muffler, steering mechanism irregularities, or other mechanical defects, can only be discovered when the vehicle is in operation. Any such conditions should be immediately noted and rectified.

Seat belts must be worn in order to reduce chances of injury if an accident happens.

Administration

The chief and supervisors must build and maintain the kind of organization in which the concepts of driver selection, training, and motivation can be effectively applied. The concepts are simple. Application, however, requires thoughtful compliance with policy and with value-proved procedures.

If an accident occurred every time there was a slip-up, few slip-ups would happen. Best safety records occur when errors would be disastrous. In such cases, errors are just not permitted. In many situations repeated errors occur without serious consequence until some combination produces the moment of awesome loss. The safe way must be done thousands of times for the sake of the one moment that matters.

Voluntary compliance to standards of performance, and safety procedures are achieved only when the chief's desire is known and accepted. The chief must firmly establish his position by committing his drivers and vehicles to high standards.

18

The ambulance fleet

The ambulance fleet operator has but one service to provide: the emergency transportation of people. This service must be performed safely and efficiently.

The ambulance driver, in turn, must be one of the best professional drivers:

1. He must do more than the average driver to prevent accidents,

2. He must anticipate what other motorists are going to do in order to avoid an accident, even if the other fellow is wrong,

3. He must drive in such a way that he will not cause further discomfort, illness, or injury to his passengers.

To give safe and efficient service, the fleet needs good operating policies and requires good driver selection and training techniques. Each will be discussed in turn.

Fleet Operating Policies

DISPATCHING PROCEDURES

Because people become excited when they are confronted with an unexpected illness or injury, they don't think clearly. They often give sketchy information when they call an ambulance. Therefore, the person who handles incoming calls must be trained to get the necessary facts quickly and accurately. He must find out if there are any unusual

EMERGENCY INFORMATION CHECKLIST
AND DISPATCH FORM

1. Date _____ Time _____ a.m.
   p.m.

2. Name _____
   (of person calling)

   Telephone No. _____

3. From _____
   (address where patient is)

   _____

   _____

   To _____
   (destination of patient)

   _____

   _____

4. Type of Emergency
   ☐ Vehicle Collision
   ☐ Illness
   ☐ Other: _____

5. Description of Emergency
   ☐ Bodily Injury   ☐ Bleeding
   ☐ Heart Attack   ☐ Stroke
   ☐ Drowning   ☐ Convulsion
   ☐ Poisoning   ☐ Heat Stroke
   ☐ Other: _____

6. Type of Driving
   ☐ Routine call—Observe all traffic regulations
   ☐ Unusual call—Avoid unnecessary delays but waive traffic
      regulations *only* when necessary and then
      only with great caution

7. Driver: _____

   Attendant: _____

8. Remarks: _____

9. Dispatcher: _____ Dispatch a.m.
   Time: _____ p.m.

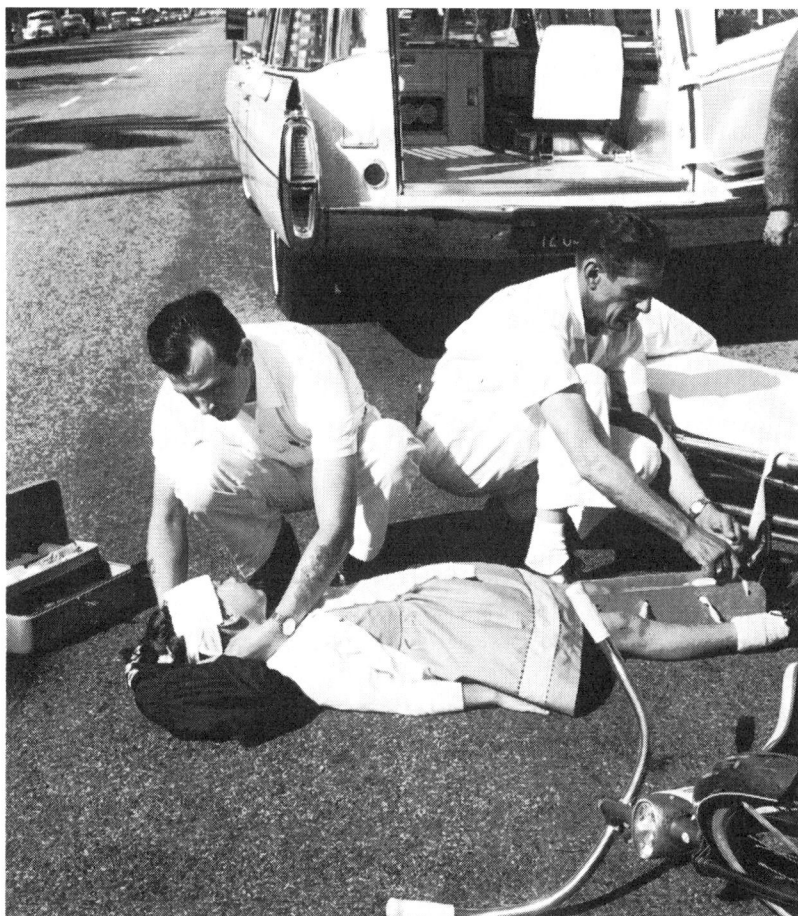

MINUTES COUNT IN EMERGENCIES. Get the information accurately and dispatch unit promptly. Advance planning pays off in quality service.

conditions that need special attention. A checklist and dispatch form (illustrated at right) helps the dispatcher gather necessary facts.

An effective dispatching procedure is as follows:

1. Dispatcher receives call and records time.

2. He records information on dispatch form.

3. If an ambulance cannot be dispatched immediately and the situation calls for immediate action, dispatcher should accept call and notify another company to handle it. Dispatcher should have telephone numbers of alternate facilities.

4. Give caller an estimated time of arrival.

5. Give information to driver (use dispatch form):
    a. Type of emergency to expect,
    b. Location.

6. Tell driver if emergency traffic regulations should be observed. (See section "Emergency Driving Skills," on page 284.)

7. Record time ambulance was dispatched.

8. Make sure that medical care is available to patient at hospital or other destination.

9. Notify police if an emergency run is to be in their jurisdiction so they can look out for it.

A dispatcher must know where drivers and units are at all times so he can assign them effectively. Here is a procedure designed to give this necessary control:

1. Ambulance driver radios or calls in when he arrives at destination to pick up a patient.

2. He should report unusual delays or unusual circumstances. The dispatcher can offer assistance if needed.

3. Driver again radios or calls in when he is at final destination to see if he should drive to another call or return to the garage.

4. The time of each call is recorded.

If complete control of your drivers is desired, require them to radio in for permission to use the siren, exceed speed limits, or waive certain operating precautions. Some ambulance operators install a Tachograph, a mechanical device that records vehicle speeds and nonmoving intervals in relation to time of day. By checking this record with the known route taken by the driver, excessive speeds can be spotted. The driver should be cautioned not to abuse emergency running times.

EMERGENCY RUNNING TIMES

It is not the purpose of emergency equipment—flashing lights and sirens —to aid a driver in exceeding speed limits, but rather to keep the ambulance moving at a safe and constant speed. The need for excessive speed, emergency right-of-way, use of sirens and flashing lights has been challenged by many physicians and ambulance fleet operators.

A one-year study in New York City showed a one-third reduction in accidents when ambulance drivers obeyed traffic regulations and did not use sirens. (This reduction was made in spite of twice as many calls during the test year as during the previous year.) Another portion of this study showed that many ambulance accidents were caused by

278

drivers who relied too heavily on a siren to give them the right-of-way. Use of emergency equipment lulls drivers into a false sense of security. Often other drivers do not heed these warnings.

A study of 2,500 Flint, Mich., city ambulance runs showed haste in transporting the injured was unnecessary in 98.2 per cent of the cases. In the other cases, expeditious handling was considered necessary, but a speeding ambulance could have increased the severity of the injuries.

These studies pointed out that—except in rare cases—speed is not necessary and that traffic regulations and controls should be followed when going to or from an emergency. Prompt response to a call and prompt first-aid treatment at the scene usually eliminates the need for excessive speed.

ROUTE PLANNING

To save time, plan the routes ahead of time. Planned routing will give the best and most direct routes to various sections of a city and will reduce the possibility of a driver's being delayed by slow traffic or congested routes during certain periods of the day. Alternate routes should be planned. A routing plan should include:

1. Dividing the area served into sections.

2. Conducting test runs over selected routes at various times of the day and night to pinpoint congested roads and determine alternate routes.

3. Rechecking routes at regular intervals to see if new construction, heavier traffic, or reduced speed areas require reroutings. Runs should be made in a passenger car. If made in an ambulance, never use emergency lights or siren.

4. Maintaining an up-to-date area map.

5. Having drivers include in their trip report any information that will help keep the routings up-to-date.

If the fleet and the city is large enough, drivers can be assigned to specific areas of the city. In smaller fleets or in smaller cities, drivers should be acquainted with the entire street system.

When arriving at the emergency scene, the driver should park his ambulance close enough to facilitate handling of the patient and, at the same time, minimize interference with traffic.

Typical emergency equipment carried on an ambulance is shown on the following spread.

AMBULANCE EQUIPMENT. Equipment carried by this West Coast ambulance service has been spread out for this photograph.

1	7-level cot	20	Bed pan
2	Safety hats	21	Stethescope
3	Folding stretchers	22	Bandage scissors
4	Blankets	23	Airway for rescue breathing
5	Stretcher hanger	24	Cardboard splints
6	Fracture stretcher	25	Crowbar
7	Male and female urinal	26	Flashlight
8	Antiseptic (in bottles)	27	First-aid bag
9	Self-adhesive bandages	28	Auto jack (scissors type)
10	Gauze pads	29	Rescue breather
11	3-way radio	30	Electric lantern
12	Hack saw	31	Oxygen tank (large)
13	Adhesive tape	32	Oxygen masks
14	Roller bandages	33	Emesis basin
15	Fire extinguisher	34	Resuscitator head
16	Elastic bandages	35	Restraints
17	Fusees	36	Oxygen tanks (small)
18	Hemostats	37	Pressure regulator
19	Ammonia inhalants		

Also carried, but not pictured: O.B. kit, poison kit, burn kit, sterile burn sheet, balloon splints, chemical ice packs, and sandbags.

EMERGENCY EQUIPMENT

Each ambulance should carry adequate equipment for dressing wounds, splinting fractures, controlling hemorrhage, and resuscitation (see photograph and description on preceding spread). This includes:

Oxygen	Dressings
Mask	Adhesive tape
Splints	Mouth-to-mouth airways
Bandages and shears	Tongue depressors
Tourniquets	Other first-aid equipment

Rescue equipment often proves helpful, especially to gain entry into a smashed vehicle. When this equipment is carried, it should be stored where it won't contact sterile equipment. Especially useful are:

Pry bars	Dry chemical, multi-purpose extinguisher
Tow cable (about 50 ft)	Warning devices

Driver Selection and Training

Personal supervision is difficult once a driver is dispatched. Driver control begins with driver selection and is reinforced by proper training.

DRIVER SELECTION

Qualities to look for in a prospective driver to help predict whether or not he will be a good driver:

1. Can the applicant operate a vehicle effectively?
2. Are his physical qualifications acceptable?
3. Does he have a proper driving attitude?
4. Can he recognize and anticipate possible accident-producing situations?
5. Is he emotionally stable? Does he have good character traits?

Four elements of preselection screening are directly related to driving. Be sure to check these thoroughly.

1. **Driving experience.**
   a. Check type of vehicle and length of time.
   b. Check type of operator's license.
   c. Check type of driving that applicant did previously.
2. **Past driving record.**
   a. Check both professional and personal history of traffic violation citations.

282

b. Check accident history. Check number, nature, and cause. Try to determine if these were preventable or not.

3. Previous driver instruction.

 a. Classroom: how much and by whom?

 b. Behind-the-wheel: how much, by whom, and on what type vehicle?

4. Physical fitness.

 a. Is a physical exam required before hiring? Is a periodic exam required once he is hired?

 b. Does applicant meet minimum standards prescribed by the American Medical Association.* If he does not, can effective corrective measures be taken to bring him up to standard?

In addition to checking these elements, go over his past employment record, his personal references, and his credit references for clues.

Three types of tests can be given to help determine an applicant's behind-the-wheel attitudes and abilities. These are used in conjunction with previous factors that were listed.

 1. Traffic and driving knowledge tests.

 2. Driving skill tests.

 3. Attitude tests. (Some authorities still question the value of these tests in predicting individual performance.)

DRIVER INSTRUCTION

Because ambulance driving is a specialized skill, each new driver should be given specialized driving instruction, both in the classroom and behind the wheel.

Classroom instruction should include:

1. Orientation:

 a. Describe the driver-training program and its content.

 b. Describe the traffic problem and its relation to accidents.

 c. Describe the nature of ambulance driving and its specialized problems.

 d. Describe the fleet safety program.

 e. Discuss areas covered by the fleet. Cover the routes and describe the hazards to be expected.

 f. Tell how to use and fill out necessary forms.

---

* See MEDICAL GUIDE FOR PHYSICIANS IN DETERMINING FITNESS TO DRIVE A MOTOR VEHICLE, *by Committee on Medical Aspects of Automobile Injuries and Deaths, American Medical Association, Chicago* 60610.

2. Physical laws and their effect on driving:
    a. Kinetics (study of vehicle motion and stopping).
    b. Centrifugal force (study of turning).
    c. Friction (study of braking and skidding).
    d. Gravity (study of weight, climbing hills).

Physical laws affect braking and stopping distance. Kinetic energy of a moving vehicle, friction, and gravity all come into play when bringing a vehicle to a stop. Friction and gravity tend to hold the vehicle to a given course, but they can be overcome by the speed and steering of the vehicle. Bad weather and slippery road conditions affect stopping distances and vehicle maneuverability. The relation between visibility and operating speed is also important.

3. Laws and ordinances; safe driving rules:
    a. Local and state traffic regulations.
    b. Specific regulations for emergency driving.
    c. Obligations the ambulance driver assumes because of these special conditions.

4. **First-aid training** (Red Cross Advanced, or U.S. Bureau of Mines) for both driver and attendant.*

Behind-the-wheel training should include:

1. Training in basic driving skills. (See previous chapters.)
2. Training in specialized emergency driving skills.

EMERGENCY DRIVING SKILLS

The general rules of emergency driving were given in Chapter 17, "The Police Fleet," in the section "Instruction in Emergency Driving." Now we will discuss emergency driving as it specifically applies to driving an ambulance.

* Three good books on the subject are:

• FIRST AID—A BUREAU OF MINES INSTRUCTION MANUAL. *Superintendent of Documents, U.S. Government Printing Office, Washington, D.C.*

• FIRST AID TEXTBOOK. *Prepared by the American National Red Cross, Washington, D.C., for the instruction of first-aid classes, Doubleday and Company, Inc., Garden City, N.Y.*

• FUNDAMENTALS OF FIRST AID FOR AMBULANCE ATTENDANTS. *Committee on Trauma, North Carolina Chapter, American College of Surgeons.*

BOTH PROFESSIONAL AND VOLUNTEER SERVICES need training.

To start, the trainee can ride as a third man on actual ambulance calls to see the reaction of the public as the ambulance goes through traffic both under emergency and nonemergency conditions.

To get the patient's point of view, the trainee can ride on the emergency stretcher or cot while a skilled driver goes through traffic under nonemergency conditions. He should feel how all the physical laws of motion affect the patient's comfort. How braking and stopping relate to the care and treatment of a patient. How sharp cornering and abrupt changes in speed should be avoided in order to keep the patient comfortable.

The trainee should practice driving in bad weather and over slippery surfaces in order to learn how to cope with them.

He must learn to adjust his speed to the roadside environment: buildings, commercial areas, and recreational areas. He must experience driving in various traffic conditions and over various types of roads.

The trainee must learn that his performance is affected by his physical and mental health. Both the trainee and his supervisor must be taught to recognize temporary changes and make necessary adjustments. An angry or upset driver cannot respond quickly and is usually

285

quite nervous. A driver in this condition should be taken off the driving roster until he returns to normal. This may inconvenience the fleet at the time, but it could save expense and trouble in the long run.

Vehicle and Equipment Maintenance

Both the ambulance and its equipment must be ready when dispatched. A well-defined maintenance policy will ensure that the vehicle is in top mechanical condition at all times.

Routine check of brakes, steering, exhaust system, windshield wipers, radio, emergency and driving lights, and audible warning devices should be made each day.

Tires should be checked carefully:

1. Check proper inflation each time the ambulance is gassed. If pressure continues to be lost, check for hidden defects.
2. Check for abnormal wear, cracks, and scuffs every 500 to 1,000 miles.
3. Rotate tires every 1,000 miles for maximum tire life.
4. Check tires for possible replacement every 8,000 to 15,000 miles. Replace tires when tread depth has worn to 1/16th of an inch.

Windows should be kept clean and free of all obstructions. Lights must be kept clean and properly adjusted. Safety belts should be visually checked for signs of wear or weakness. Emergency equipment must be looked over to make sure it is all there and in usable condition.

In parts of the country where winter brings ice and snow, special duty or snow tires can be mounted, or else chains can be used. Snow tires should receive the same maintenance as regular tires, and tire chains—when used—should be checked daily for wear and proper installation.

INSPECTION BY DRIVERS

Drivers should check their vehicle and its equipment at the start of each shift; include: gas and oil, tires, two-way radio, windows, heaters, and warning devices. Report any deficiencies to the dispatcher. A typical vehicle and equipment checklist is illustrated on the next page.

Next, drivers should adjust the driving seat to provide good posture, comfort, and maximum driving efficiency. All driving mirrors should be adjusted to suit the driver, as should the safety belt.

All this should be complete by the time the driver is ready for a call.

286

VEHICLE AND EQUIPMENT CHECKLIST

VEHICLE	OK	Needs Adjusting		OK	Needs Adjusting
1. Gas	☐	☐	9. Turn signals ..	☐	☐
2. Oil	☐	☐	10. Emergency		
3. Water	☐	☐	lights	☐	☐
4. Battery	☐	☐	11. Wipers	☐	☐
5. Brakes	☐	☐	12. Horn	☐	☐
6. Tires	☐	☐	13. Siren	☐	☐
7. Head lights	☐	☐	14. Windows	☐	☐
8. Stop lights	☐	☐	15. 2-Way radio ..	☐	☐
			16. Heaters	☐	☐

Remarks: _____

_____

EQUIPMENT	OK	Short	Re-placed		OK	Short	Re-placed
1. Pillows ...	☐	☐	☐	9. Mouth-to-mouth			
2. Blankets and				Airways ..	☐	☐	☐
Sheets	☐	☐	☐	10. Tongue			
3. Oxygen ...	☐	☐	☐	Depressors	☐	☐	☐
4. Mask	☐	☐	☐	11. Tourniquets	☐	☐	☐
5. Splints ...	☐	☐	☐	12. Other first-aid			
6. Bandages and				equipment	☐	☐	☐
Shears ...	☐	☐	☐	13. Fire-extinguishing			
7. Dressings .	☐	☐	☐	equipment	☐	☐	☐
8. Adhesive				14. Warning			
Tape	☐	☐	☐	devices ..	☐	☐	☐

Remarks: _____

_____

Driver: _____ Date: _____

PORTABLE OXYGEN EQUIPMENT (in aluminum cases at right) allows resuscitation to be administered at the accident site. Some ambulances also carry equipment that can be strapped to the rescuer's back. This keeps his hands free for ladder, pole, or excavation rescue and therapy.

Quick Reminders

Seven rules of thumb recommended by the Pennsylvania Department of Health* can serve as reminders to ambulance drivers and might be used for posting and repeated emphasis. Basically, they are:

1. Use warning lights and siren *only* on bona fide emergency trips. They should not be used on practice runs or other nonessential trips.

2. When warning lights and siren are in use, don't assume other motorists and pedestrians will give you the right-of-way. As you drive, check other traffic to make sure other drivers are responding to your signals correctly.

3. If it is necessary to go through a red light, approach the corner

---

* *Richard A. Brose,* AMBULANCE ATTENDANT TRAINING PILOT PROJECT REPORT. *Pennsylvania Department of Health.*

288

cautiously and slowly. The siren and light must be functioning well in advance of the crossing. Do not proceed through until you are sure all other traffic is stopped.

4. The use of siren and warning light should be used with discrimination.

5. Do not exceed the speed limits posted or dictated by weather and traffic conditions except under extreme conditions.

6. In unfavorable weather conditions such as ice, snow, or rain, always reduce speeds. Use snow tires or reinforced tire chains when necessary.

7. Don't endanger your own life and the lives of your patients. Many instances of D.O.A. have been caused by *poor* ambulance service and unnecessary chance-taking.

SPECIFIC TYPES OF EMERGENCIES

For a number of specific types of emergencies requiring immediate care by the ambulance attendant before moving the patient, the same Pennsylvania Department of Health's publication cites three basic rules:

- Do not panic,
- Reassure patient with a confident manner,
- *No siren or fast ride* in most all cases.

The specific types of trauma to which these rules refer are:

1. Uncontrolled hemorrhage,

2. Respiratory failure or blockage (in which resuscitation is not totally effective),

3. Petroleum-base poisonings,

4. Cardiac failure due to fibrillation (in which closed-chest heart compression is used en route but cannot stop the fibrillation),

5. Acute burns (2nd and 3rd degree over large part of body),

6. Full-term maternity cases involving complications of normal delivery.

19

The school bus fleet

This chapter discusses some of the unique facets of the school bus and its operation. The school bus is a motor vehicle similar in many respects to other types of mass transportation on the streets and highways. However, the school bus and its operation and maintenance does involve some special features. For an extensive treatment of special school bus fleet administrative and operational problems, see the NSC publication *School Transportation—A Guide For Supervisors.*

School Bus Design and Construction

Pupil transportation programs had a very humble beginning. Initially, horse-drawn wagons with makeshift canvas covers to protect pupils from the weather were commonly used and sleighs frequently were used during the winter season in snowy areas.

As we entered the age of the motor vehicle, box-shaped, homemade wooden bodies were built onto automotive chassis to accommodate the pupil passengers. Though crude at first, these were refined and improved as automotive technology progressed. Today most school buses are almost as sophisticated and "luxurious" as commercial buses.

Though the development of the school bus has in many respects kept abreast of applicable technological advances, the school bus still retains one of its unique construction features—a conventional motor vehicle chassis but with a *uniquely designed body.*

The automotive industry has become so versatile in meeting the diversified transportation needs of our society that there are literally hundreds of options available in the construction of bus chassis and bodies,

290

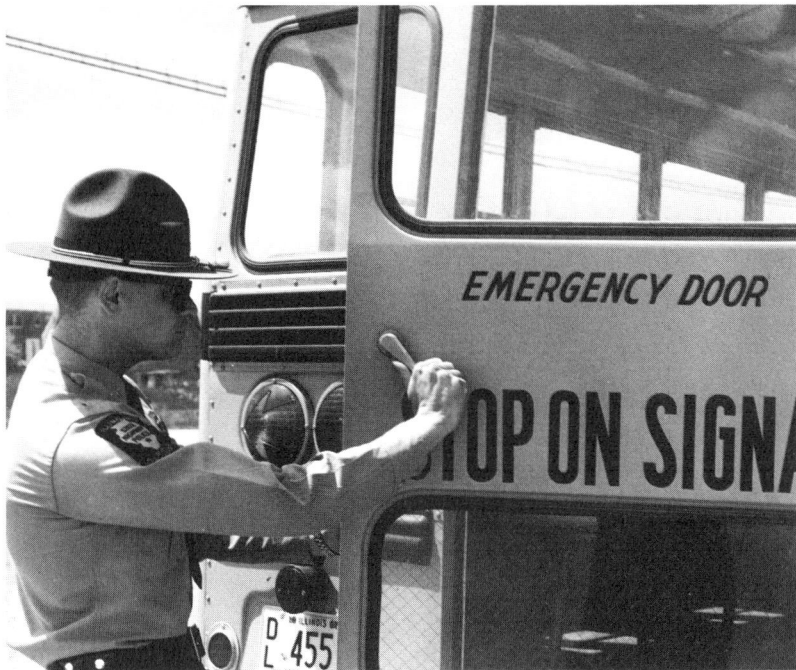

MANY STATES make both regular and unannounced inspections of both bus condition and safety equipment. State departments of public safety are vitally interested in safe operation of school buses.

offering both advantages and disadvantages to the fleet operation and the pupils transported. There is a decided advantage for the fleet operation in that the bus configuration best suited for each operational and environmental need can be put together, making possible a vehicle with safety, strength, and handling characteristics desirable for each blend of route and operational conditions. The disadvantage is that inexperienced and excessively cost conscious fleetmen might mismatch the components and design a vehicle that cannot provide the safety and efficiency to which pupils are entitled.

It is, therefore, important that today's school bus fleet directors and administrators have the background and experience necessary to write specifications for bus purchases. These specifications should guarantee the pupil the safety of adequate, properly matched components—such as axles, springs, brakes, tires—for the bus chassis. Every school bus chassis should be equipped with an emergency braking system that meets or

291

exceeds the requirements on page 14 of the 1970 edition of National Minimum Standards for School Buses. Bus body specifications must be carefully written to provide the safety features of proper rear vision and convex mirrors, non-skid, durable entrance step and aisle tread, defrosters, energy-absorbent padding, and other features. The latest proven safety innovations should be included in every new specification written.

In today's school bus specifications, it is extremely important to include well padded seats, readily accessible stanchions, and guard rails. Padding is also available for retrofitting buses that were purchased without it. Today's pupils are entitled to this safety protection, for without it they are unduly exposed to facial injuries that may result from the sudden lurching or stopping of the bus because of traffic congestion or road problems.

Specifications should be studied and written in detail. Operation, efficiency, and pupil safety depend heavily upon this facet of transportation administration. For this reason, administrators in direct charge of the transportation program must have the background, experience, and training to qualify them for the job. Otherwise they could be grossly negligent in maintaining fleet efficiency and pupil safety.

Vehicle Specification and Purchase

Because the school bus is a special vehicle, constructed for a specific purpose, those responsible for specifications and purchase must be intimately familiar with every detail of its design and construction, and all of the safety options available.

Among those considerations particularly important when specifications are being written are:

1. The terrain, environment, and special conditions under which the vehicle will operate. For example, very special buses and bus equipment are required in transporting handicapped children.
2. Proper chassis and component sizing to be certain that each subsystem is of sufficient strength and durability to function with utmost safety, efficiency, and economy. For instance, axles, springs, tires, steering, and frames.
3. Brakes should have a completely independent back-up system capable of controlling the vehicles under all circumstances, and responsive to driver's control.
4. A realistic seating arrangement. The 13 inch "rumproom" is inadequate for today's junior high school pupils. The 3-2 seating arrangement which provides 15 inch rumproom is much more realistic.

292

5. Padding for hard seat back rails, stanchions, and other force-amplifying structures are imperative to reduce facial injuries to pupils. (NHTSA* Standards will soon make this mandatory.) Padded seats are available. Padding for retrofitting seat rails and stanchions is also available. Research, testing, and experience have indicated this need, and school bus fleets can no longer afford to be without this protection.
6. Defrosting equipment that will keep windshields and windows clear.
7. Heaters that will provide reasonable comfort for driver and pupils.
8. Mirrors—including the convex type—that will afford the driver a good view of his pupil passengers. Also, the exterior and traffic view needed for protection of his pupils and movement in traffic.

Maintaining the Fleet

Fleet or vehicle maintenance is treated in detail in another section of this manual. Proper maintenance is extremely critical in school buses:

1. The lives and well-being of pupil passengers depend upon it, plus the normal traffic safety reasons for proper vehicle maintenance.
2. Poor maintenance is a waste of funds. School systems traditionally seem beset with financial problems and can ill afford such waste.
3. Neglected vehicles and equipment will tend to destroy public confidence in the school system that operates them.
4. Special brakes with automatic emergency braking features, and other special school bus safety equipment, cannot provide the intended pupil protection unless the equipment is adequately maintained.

Maintenance, to be adequate, must keep the vehicle and its systems operating at the level of safety, efficiency, and economy designed into them. Maintenance cannot be adequate or effective without proper facilities, equipment and trained personnel.

The Service the School Bus Provides

Basically, pupil transportation was originated for the express purpose of getting pupils from home to school—and home again. However, this simple mission has evolved into a much more complex operation in today's traffic.

Initially, traffic volumes were low; streets and roads were rough and often unpaved; busing vehicles were crude and lacked many of the safety features of today's bus; and drivers often maintained their own vehicles and received no training, relying almost wholly upon whatever experience

---

* *National Highway Traffic Safety Administration of the D.O.T.*

THE SCHOOL ADMINISTRATION should provide the care needed for pupil safety. Special activities trips should be under the supervision of a competent person other than the bus driver.

and expertise they brought to the job.

Advancing technology brought better roads, faster vehicles, and shrinking traveling times. Educational facilities and experiences once out of reach for pupils began to be included in the teaching programs.

These made greater demands on and increased responsibilities to school bus fleeting. Fortunately with increased technology came better buses and bus safety equipment. The increasing complexity of vehicles, traffic environments, and pupil handling gave a sense of urgency to driver training programs.

Leaders in industry have developed safety programs to meet these new needs. Every school transportation administrator must keep abreast of new developments and be able to implement them.

School buses now carry more pupils greater distances to and from school, and at higher speeds. Educational programs often require transportation to other school buildings or facilities that afford pupils worthwhile educational experiences. Inter-scholastic events and tours often call upon school buses for pupil transportation to activities many miles outside the school district.

In the light of these developments, hazards to pupils have multiplied significantly. Every reasonably accessible technological advantage should be used in bus design and purchase specifications for pupil protection. Sophisticated procedures in driver selection, training, supervision, and safety programs are available and, in all fairness to all concerned, should be used in the transportation program of every school district.

Special Passengers and Their Care

Every pupil passenger is special and cannot be thought of in terms of a carton, box, crate, or shipment of freight. Every pupil is very special to his or her parents. A failure to recognize this basic fact can trigger all kinds of problems for bus drivers, supervisors, and administrators.

Accordingly, pupil handling and safety is strongly coupled to school and community relations. The hazards of stopping repeatedly to take on and discharge pupils in the traffic stream cannot be overlooked from a standpoint of responsibility. Special care should be taken to provide the safest possible location for bus stops, to allow the pupil to get on and off the bus safely.

Pupils come in all sizes, conditions, and from many environments, bringing special care and safety problems. Some are too immature to cope safely with exposure to traffic. Others are mentally handicapped and their ability to make prompt, accurate decisions is limited. Some are physically handicapped and require specially-equipped buses.

It is the responsibility of the school administration, through its transportation program, to provide the care essential to pupil safety. Parents share this responsibility.

Special Passenger Training

Being required to ride a bus to school often places the very young pupil in a hostile environment. Having been sheltered from hazards heretofore, the very young are poorly equipped to cope with the unfamiliar dangers of the traffic environment. In a recent study of the reactions of people in traffic, Professor Stina Sandels, of Sweden, concluded that children under 10 years of age do not have the maturity to cope with the hazards encountered in traffic.

Other studies have shown that two-thirds of our pupil passenger fa-

BUS ROUTES AND PUPIL PICKUP POINTS should be chosen so that they interfere the least with normal traffic flow. Even in low-traffic locations, pupil-passengers should wait until traffic-control signal stops traffic or until bus driver checks traffic conditions and signals pupils to cross the street.

296

talities occur outside the school bus, and that approximately 75 per cent of these are pupils under 10 years of age (see NSC Fleet Safety Memo No. 66). From these facts we must draw the obvious conclusion that pupil passengers on school buses, especially those under 10 years of age, are not receiving the help they need from adults to cope with the hostilities they encounter in the traffic environment.

It is imperative that these pupils receive safety training. It is not enough that the parent, teacher, or bus driver cautions the pupils to be careful while in a traffic environment. Safety must be made a part of their school curriculums.

The very young pupils have been conditioned to expect others to watch out for them and avoid injuring them. When they play, adults walk around them. When they are in the street—cars stop for them. How can they be conditioned to be careful when people and vehicles have always taken extreme pains to avoid hitting them?

They must be trained to be alert, to know that someone may forget to watch out for them, or may not see them in time. They need to be trained to know what to do in traffic and why; how to be certain they are seen; how to avoid injury by motorists who are too preoccupied to watch out for them.

Their safety training must condition them to rely on themselves and not on the bus driver to remind them to practice the safety teaching they receive.

Safety program material and guidelines are available at a nominal cost from libraries, book stores, and other sources. Your school system can readily adapt these to fill the void. The time for implementation is now.

School Bus Routing Problems

Many considerations must be met in planning school bus routes. Pupil transportation is a special service whose effectiveness must be measured in terms of service provided in relation to environmental and other factors—weather, road, vehicle, maintenance, driver and pupil characteristics, conduct, performance—that affect safety, dependability, and cost.

Bus routing is not merely a matter of getting pupils to and from school. High priority must be given to efficient use of buses at minimal risk to pupil passengers. School board policies and procedures should ensure the priority.

Not many vehicles have the right that the school bus has to intermittently disrupt the normal flow of traffic. Extreme care should be ex-

DRIVERS SHOULD BE TRAINED to park so that they do not have to back up their buses. If they must back up, they should first check carefully behind their bus.

ercised by the driver not to abuse this privilege. It was granted for pupil safety, but its abuse is both unfair to other motorists and detrimental to the safety of pupil passengers.

It is not uncommon for school buses to be hit in the rear end by other vehicles when stopped in traffic at pupil pick-up points and railroad grade crossings. Every effort must be made to minimize this hazard by:

1. Planning bus routes to avoid crossing railroad tracks. Use of overpasses and underpasses would preclude such stops. When this is not possible, bus routes should include grade crossings that have automatic signals and good visibility, even at the expense of adding a few miles to the routes. When school buses and trains collide, pupils are always the losers.

298

2. Avoiding personal privilege abuses in scheduling school bus stops not in keeping with board policies and best safety practices, that is, near curves, over the brow of hills, too close together, and so on.

3. Where possible, using side or local streets and roadways for picking up and discharging passengers to avoid unnecessary interference with the normal flow of through traffic.

4. Making every effort to plan stops so the bus can stop at curbs, or in off roadway areas, to minimize traffic interference.

The importance of exercising constant care to avoid trapping other vehicles in panic stops, or impossible situations, should be repeatedly emphasized to drivers.

It is becoming more imperative to pick up and discharge pupils on their "home side" of the roadways to avoid the hazard of crossing busy streets and highways. Avoid, as much as possible, situations where the bus driver must direct traffic and pupils depend upon buses as "shields."

Arrange protected routes for special trips and arrange for off-street collector areas for pickups and discharges of pupils. Use only drivers experienced with the particular type of vehicle, traffic, and environmental factors likely to be encountered. Provide competent adult supervision for the pupils and allow enough time on lengthy trips for rest stops to avoid driver fatigue.

When all bus routes are carefully planned and drivers are required to follow these routes, most of the potential hazards will be avoided or minimized. (See NSC's publication *School Transportation—A Guide for Supervisors.*)

Responsibilities and Requirements for Drivers

As pointed out elsewhere in this manual, when you employ someone you do not hire just part of a person. Idiosyncrasies, relationships, and attitudes come with the individual. It is therefore extremely important to evaluate all of these and select each driver for his or her potential to improve the fleet's record and performance.

Almost all of the requirements and responsibilities, listed in this manual's chapter on driver selection, would be applicable to the school bus driver. In addition to those, the driver must have the following special qualities:

1. Relate well to pupils and influence them to act positively and favorably.

2. Relate well to teachers. Many of the driver's problems in handling pupils can be minimized if the teachers are cooperative.

299

3. Relate well to the public. The transportation program is very important in developing the public image of the school system.

4. Be capable of accepting full responsibility for safety and well-being of pupils in his custody.

5. Not be easily irritated or distracted. With pupils on one hand and traffic on the other—distractions could be disastrous.

6. Be able to reach accurate decisions promptly, as related to the safety of pupils.

Driver Training

The single most important facet of the transportation service is safe driving skill. The training program must cover the entire range of driver responsibilities and relationships, and include everything the driver must know to do his job well.

School boards and administrators must guard against entrusting the transportation of pupils to drivers with inadequate training. In addition to the training that every professional driver should have, the following special training and knowledge are needed by school bus drivers:

1. A full understanding of federal, state, and local laws, regulations, policies, and procedures that pertain to the operation of a school bus, its special equipment, and handling of its passengers.

2. Vehicle standards, components, use, and maintenance that are peculiar to the school bus.

3. Handling emergency situations that could arise in connection with vehicle accidents or disruptions—such as riots, strikes, tornadoes, earthquakes, storms, or vandalism—that pose a threat to pupil safety. This would include proper reporting of the incident.

4. Pupil control and rules for pupil behavior.

5. Protecting the pupil from injury in the process of loading, unloading, riding, or in crossing streets and highways, to and from the bus.

6. Handling, with teachers and parents, any incidents of misconduct, as necessary.

Driver Supervision

Most of us need help to perform at our maximum potential. School bus drivers are no exception, and so very much depends upon their performance. The supervisor is the cohesive force that brings together the driver, the school bus, and its maintenance in order to produce the desired results.

The right supervisor with the experience, background, training and support needed will efficiently provide for pupil safety and program success. Accordingly, it is an injustice to the pupil passengers and the school system to appoint some unqualified person to this position.

Other chapters of this manual, and NSC's publications *School Transportation—A Guide for Supervisors* and *Successful Supervision* provide excellent material on the duties, responsibilities, and challenges of supervision.

However, some aspects of supervising the school bus driver are peculiar to his unique type of operation. His cargo is the precious children entrusted to him. His supervision must help him in successfully relating to the pupils and being constantly alert to their need for safety.

Depending upon the nature and scope of the operation, driver contact with the supervisor may vary from two or more contacts daily, to as little as one contact a month. Obviously, the former is the more desirable, but the driver's needs for supervision must be fully met in both cases. The supervisor must have the ability to get things done, and done well, through his drivers, regardless of the frequency of personal contact.

Special responsibilities and qualities of the school transportation supervisor require:

1. Public speaking and public relations experience.

2. Screening applicants and determining their ability to relate to the pupil passengers.

3. Counseling drivers (and pupils, with their parents and teachers).

4. A relationship with news media and service organizations that keep the public aware of the needs and accomplishments of the transportation program, and enlists the aid of other groups as needed.

5. Writing bus specifications that offer the utmost in safety for pupil passengers in terms of capital outlay.

6. Making the driver training program effective in keeping drivers abreast of changes in applicable laws, regulations, policies and procedures, and pupil handling techniques.

7. Planning and constant evaluation of bus routes, schedules, and trips in relation to pupil safety and convenience.

8. Working with schools in instructional programs and materials to develop knowledge of rules, safety awareness, and practice in dealing with pupil passengers.

20

Be a safety salesman

Inspire Others

To good men everywhere who now ask, "But what *else* can I do to improve traffic safety?" we suggest the following—over and beyond the on-the-job practices we have discussed throughout the Manual:

1. RECOGNIZE YOU ARE BOTH A PROFESSIONAL AND A PRIVATE CITIZEN

There are people in your life who respect you and are influenced by what you say and what you do. You might not realize it, but because of your position, they copy what you do and they attach importance to what you say. You actually influence the way others behave behind the wheel of their vehicles. Because of this, you have a great responsibility to stand for traffic safety.

2. CONSCIOUSLY EXERCISE THAT ROLE

Don't make safety a hit-or-miss proposition. Don't just be safe on your job. The image you present must be of a person who is more than casually interested in better driving and who is, in fact, vitally concerned about promoting better driving both on and off your job.

3. SPEAK UP FOR SAFETY

Any chance you have to speak up for traffic safety—take. Again, just don't think about on-the-job training or talks at industry meetings. Traffic

302

SPEAK UP FOR SAFETY—Your enthusiasm is contagious.

safety is a frequent subject of private conversation. Speak up. Express positive attitudes. Correct misconceptions. Show that you regard traffic safety as a serious matter that deserves the informed support and co-operation of every citizen.

Your objective here is not to overwhelm the other person, but rather to nudge his attitudes in the right direction. Your strategy is to keep your manner conversational. The moment you start to preach, your listeners tune you out. Your influence will be less.

Speak up for traffic safety—but don't be a bore.

4. KNOW YOUR FIELD

If you are to be an effective influence, you must know the facts. One of your first tasks is to educate yourself. In addition to this Manual, a basic fact-source is the driver's handbook issued by your state driver

303

licensing bureau. The odds are that at least 40 per cent of the information in this little book is new to most people. As your interest in the field grows, you'll probably purchase and read several books on the subject. (A list is given a little later in this chapter.) Working with your local safety council and other safety groups (see point 6) will provide guidance.

5. BE A GOOD DRIVER

Your example as a driver speaks louder about your attitude toward traffic safety than anything you can say. Learn and put into practice good driving principles. Learn each basic driving maneuver; then perform it correctly every time.

6. SUPPORT OTHER TRAFFIC SAFETY EFFORTS

If high school or adult driver education courses, or Driver Improvement Training are available in your area, you will be repaid for time and money spent in helping such courses by your effective influence on other drivers. Cooperation in giving the National Safety Council's "Defensive Driving Course" can help both the public and fleet drivers.

As you become more familiar with traffic safety, you will find more and more groups and agencies that are devoted to the great cause of making motoring safer. Among these are your local safety council, the safety committees of your church and service club, high school groups, and others. Each attacks the problem from a different angle and each deserves your support. They can learn a lot from you—and you can learn a lot from them.

Encourage Training and Build Safety Attitudes

Encourage driver training. Although the program has been discussed in detail in Chapter 7, "Driver Training," let's emphasize a few points.

In planning a training program, we must consider:

- **What to teach,** and
- **Methods and materials for training.**

We must remember that a program must teach attitudes as well as facts and skills. Attitudes are caught, not taught.

- One attitude that should be fostered is: **"Accidents can be prevented."** This positive approach challenges the skill of any driver.

HIGH SCHOOL OR ADULT DRIVER EDUCATION deserves your support. Be a good safety influence to your church, social, and fraternal groups. Work with youth organizations as a safety counselor. They can learn a lot from you—and you, from them.

- Another is **"Take personal pride in driving safely."** The driver must believe that preventing accidents is one of the most important measures of professional driving skill.
- **"Respect traffic rules and regulations"** is another important basic driving attitude. A driver will better appreciate the contribution traffic agencies make to driving safety if he understands the problems of traffic enforcement, traffic engineering, driver licensing, and traffic courts.
- One of the most important attitudes to teach is **"Courtesy."** Practicing courtesy is good insurance that antisocial attitudes won't creep in to affect one's driving habits. A courteous attitude is a sound basis for better driving.

How do we influence attitude? In addition to our own example and in addition to what we teach personally, we can use these aids:

- **The 'Safe Driver' magazine.** This small, monthly pamphlet, published by the National Safety Council, is designed for quick reading

305

and for getting across practical safety information. *Safe Driver* is heavily laced with human-interest material and carefully selected factual items for improving driving habits and attitudes.

• **Driver Letters.** Published monthly by the National Safety Council, this minimal training medium—a one-page letter—covers a single subject (such as good turning technique or holiday driving hazards). Written in light style, it is designed to motivate as well as inform.

• **Posters** utilize the same technique as outdoor advertising. A variety of posters for professional drivers is available from the National Safety Council. The key to an effective program is to change them each week—not only the subject, but the size, if possible. If posters are left up too many weeks, drivers get the impression management is only giving lip service to safety.

• **Booklets** are another valuable training medium. The National Safety Council, insurance carriers, and manufacturers have them available on a wide variety of subjects.

• **Safety meetings** can be built around a training film. The same sources listed for booklets can be contacted. The National Safety Council publishes a list of safety movies each year. Ask for the *National Directory of Safety Films.*

Whatever is done, there must be a flow of sound, factual information on good driving. Something is better than nothing, of course, but the more training that is provided, the better that drivers will perform.

The safetyman is the key. He is the influential person in traffic safety. He must encourage drivers, management, and the community. His attitude and training abilities count; unless he decides to do a good job, it won't be done.

Recognize Safe Drivers

Recognition for safe driving can be as simple, and sincere, as a few words of appreciation and a pat on the back. Even if more elaborate recognitions are used, the sincerity should still remain.

More elaborate recognition includes cards or pins, especially National Safety Council "Safe Driver Awards." Often awards can show the company name. (Awards were discussed on page 166.)

It is very easy to go too far if cash or merchandise is awarded. The history of driver incentive programs is filled with examples of well-meaning management going overboard for elaborate and expensive safety bonuses. Such programs backfire—the machine breaks down when dollar signs get caught in the gears.

"Safe Driver Awards" have proved to be a more effective incentive

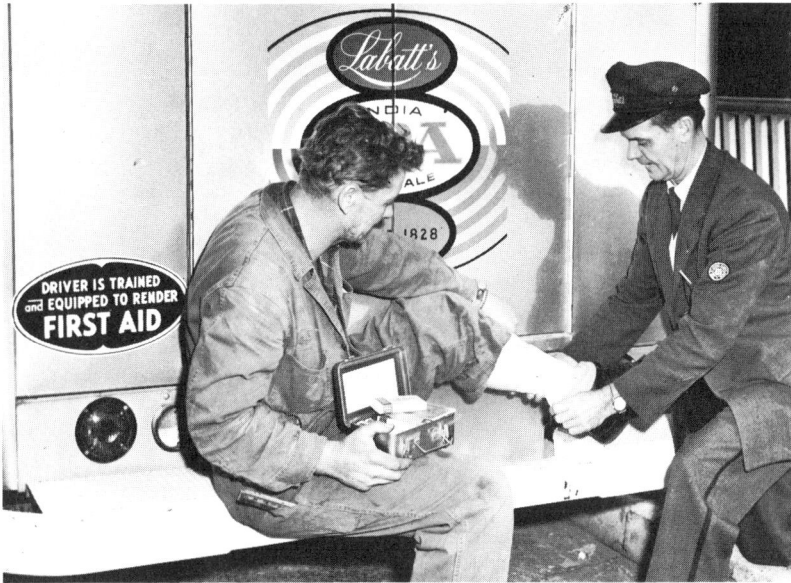

A DRIVER TRAINED IN FIRST AID not only can help the public, but sets a good example. Safety and the public interest are worth the extra investment in time and money.

than any other. They can be given at a dinner, which should not be considered as going too far. They afford a systematic manner of according recognition while still giving the driver something tangible. The fact that he wears the pin or the patch gives him recognition and helps build his image as a safe driver.

Awards can be added each year so the incentive value becomes cumulative, and exerts a stronger pull each year. Actually, "Safe Driver Awards" become a status symbol of professional skill. These awards have stood the test of more than three decades of use in all types of fleets throughout the United States and Canada. These fleets find that:

1. The award is based on well-defined achievement—operating without a preventable accident for certain periods of time. More drivers recognize this award and know what it stands for than they do any other.
2. The award is based on a substantial achievement. The requirements are reasonable, however, and take into account the possible and impossible.
3. The award is governed by rigid rules to make sure that it is given

only to those who measure up.

4. Awards are accompanied by a pocket certificate that must be signed by a company official and the president of the National Safety Council.

5. All awards are recorded at N.S.C. headquarters. If a driver transfers to another company, he takes his award status with him (providing the new company also uses the program).

6. The award is part of a packaged program. This makes sure that drivers and supervisors are continuously provided with in-service training materials on how to produce a high safe-driving standard.

7. Because so many drivers are in the program (about 360,000), the award and the supporting materials are available at a very low per capita cost.

Influence the Private Motorist

If we as professionals can be a good influence toward traffic safety among our employees, friends, and family, why can't a program be developed to help our private citizens? This question is asked over and over again.

The late Hallie L. Myers, executive director of the Indiana Traffic Safety Foundation, was a man of wide experience in working both with employee groups and private motorists. He had this to say:

> "Each year I am becoming more firmly convinced that the principal reasons for the greater success of fleet programs over public safety programs is the lack of incentives in the public safety programs. I honestly believe we could cut at least 25 per cent from our public accidents and injuries if we could find a practical award plan for the motorist. As it now stands, a driver can go 40 years without an accident or an arrest and not even his next door neighbor knows about it —yet if he has four convictions on minor traffic offenses in a three-year period, he will lose his license to drive. There is too much accent on penalty and none on incentives."

President Howard Pyle of the National Safety Council told motor transport members:

> "Perhaps in the field of public safety we can borrow some of your ideas and invent some type of program that will give the private motorist of this country a sound basis for building pride in his individual safe driving record."

Someone—somewhere, someday—will devise a workable training and incentive program for the private motorist. Whether he receives it or not, he will deserve a million dollars for his invention. For if Hallie

OPEN HOUSE FOR THE PUBLIC—New equipment or new facilities can be "shown off" to the public, especially the press. Larger operations can cooperate with social and youth groups to arrange tours. Safety—and what the fleet is doing to promote it—should be part of every tour.

Myers' prediction were to result from such a program, it would mean the saving of over 10,000 lives per year in traffic accidents, the prevention of 350,000 disabling injuries, and the saving of a billion and a half dollars each year.

Whatever the details of such a program might be, it is almost certain to contain the four elements discussed in this Manual:

1. **Set a standard of performance,**
2. **Show them how,**
3. **Keep score,**
4. **Provide recognition.**

Three of these elements are already possible. The difficulty is in the third point—a method for keeping score on individual performance. At the moment the only available method is one based on the honor system and that is hardly good enough to ensure the degree of prestige such a plan should have if it is to be effective.

A possible avenue of scorekeeping might be through insurance companies or state motor vehicle departments. However, scorekeeping is an expensive process and is probably not economically feasible with current machine data processing equipment.

In view of the potential saving in lives and property damage that one could reasonably expect from such a program one can only hope that the day of its realization is not far off.

In the meantime, the fleet operator should already be profiting from a fleet-size program. Let us all hope that he uses it to the fullest.

Be a Safety Salesman

High performance standards, consistently applied, prove very effective in reducing accidents—the goal of every successful fleet operation.

The fundamentals of a fleet safety program are again summarized:

1. Set standards—let drivers know what is expected of them.

2. Show them how they can meet these standards. Demonstrate by your own performance that they can be met.

3. Keep score—collect and use complete accident records to make sure drivers meet the standards.

4. Motivate drivers—show appreciation for those who do a good job of meeting the standards. Always be a safety salesman—both on your job and off.

Appendices

A

Case history: loss of profit due to one minor accident

No matter how many humane reasons we can come up with for having a good safety program, the question that each businessman must answer to his own satisfaction is—How much safety effort is economically feasible?

Accident costs come directly out of profit. They also result in losses—money that never gets a chance to become a profit. Yet, accident prevention programs are operating expenses. Management must be convinced that the cost of accident prevention is less than the cost of accidents it prevents. Although the time-proven answer is *yes,* the point of optimum return can only be approximated. It would differ for each fleet. One point *is* certain, though—it does not take too many mistakes to turn profit into a loss.

The tables show one company's cost data and automotive accident statistics. The figures are furnished as a contribution to the safety movement by E. J. Emond, former safety director of Armour & Company. For his safety efforts, Mr. Emond won the National Safety Council's Marcus A. Dow Memorial Award in 1953 and was named "Safety Director of the Year" by the American Trucking Associations in 1964.

The truck involved in the accident reported in Table A-1 was carrying meat, on which Armour's net profit is 1/5 of a cent per pound. If the cost and profit loss of this accident—$5,611.16—had to be made up from this profit, it would require that Armour buy, slaughter, process, merchandise, and deliver 2,805,580 pounds of product. At the time of the accident, there were 750 persons working in the Armour Denver plant. They would have to work a full week to process this much meat.

OVER THE ROCKIES, Armour refrigerated truck hauls fresh meat products.

With choice steers (about 900 pounds each) selling for about $27.00 a hundredweight, it would take almost 3,200 head to dress out this much meat. Cash outlay for the steers would require about $756,000. The labor to process them would cost about $37,500. Thus a cash outlay of nearly $800,-000 would be needed to recover the $5,611.16 loss.

Table A-2 documents the results of a three-phase safety program at Armour & Co. Table A-3 shows accident distribution by type vehicle—sales automobiles, intra-city trucks, and over-the-road trucks.

PROFIT LOSS DUE TO ONE 'MINOR' ACCIDENT

This tabulates the loss to Armour and Company due to one accident, which occurred July 20, 1949, at 2:30 A.M. near Chamber, Arizona, in Apache County, on U.S. Highway 66. Considering the rise in the cost of living index since 1949, you will be aware that this is a relatively conservative estimate.

Type of Auto Accident—Rear end collision
Property Damage only.
Weather conditions—clear
Road conditions—dry, black top
Light conditions—bright moonlight

Damage to other vehicle (covered by insurance)		$ 200.00
Damage to Armour vehicle		$2,000.00
Driver phoned Denver plant	$5.00	
Denver plant phoned driver at Chamber, Arizona	5.00	
Denver plant phoned safety engineer at Salt Lake City, Utah	5.00	
Engineer at Salt Lake City, Utah, called driver at Chamber	5.00	
Telephone bill		20.00
Denver plant sent a tractor to pick up trailer at Chamber, Arizona—		
976 miles @ 26¢ per mile	$254.00	
Salary of two men	46.75	
Meals	15.00	
Total		315.00
Towing tractor off of highway and to railroad siding and loading damaged tractor onto flat car		120.00
Cost of freight from Chamber, Ariz., to Kenworth truck factory at Seattle, Washington, and back to Denver plant at Denver, Colorado		1,000.00
Loss of revenue because tractor was out of service for three weeks. The freight rate from Denver to Phoenix, Arizona, is $1.45 per hundred weight and our average pay load is 35,000 pounds. A loss of $507.50 per week for 3 weeks.		1,522.50
We guarantee our drivers a weekly pay. **Six drivers' salaries** at $70.26 per week		427.26
Loss of depreciation of damaged tractor. We use a 6-year plan of depreciation. Cost of tractor $21,000. Depreciation per week on this unit—$67.30 for 3 wks.		201.90
Cost of Property damage and public liability insurance on idle unit		3.45
Total cost of accident not covered by insurance:		$5,611.16

TABLE A-2

ARMOUR AND COMPANY AUTOMOTIVE ACCIDENT STATISTICS

	Year	No. of Vehicles	Accidents	Accident Ratio	Insurance Total	Cost Per Vehicle	Mileage	Accident Frequency Per One Million Miles
PHASE A	1947	4,362	3,005	0.6889	$204,790	$ 48	58,637,458	51.25
	1948	5,155	3,429	.6652	296,802	58	72,124,194	47.54
	1949	5,200	3,084	.5931	399,346	77	78,628,973	39.22
	1950	5,612	3,228	.5752	371,662	66	78,972,334	40.87
	1951	6,209	3,948	.6359	386,583	62	94,847,428	41.62
	1952	6,021	3,923	.6516	458,953	76	103,947,151	37.74
PHASE B	1953	6,106	3,561	.5832	645,241	106	105,311,182	33.81
	1954	6,303	3,347	.5310	689,721	109	108,707,841	30.79
	1955	6,531	3,163	.4843	766,468	117	112,640,157	28.08
	1956	5,940	3,289	.5537	860,698	145	109,299,180	30.09
	1957	5,642	2,669	.4731	733,952	130	105,139,574	25.38
	1958	4,997	2,246	.4495	692,451	138	92,935,259	24.17
PHASE C	1959	4,369	1,899	.4347	563,266	129	83,194,143	22.83
	1960	4,351	1,890	.4344	743,594	171	82,893,697	22.80
	1961	4,550	1,682	.3696	609,352	134	86,325,850	19.48
	1962	4,445	1,586	.3565	339,943	76	103,236,017	15.36
	1963	3,899	1,280	.3283	382,359	98	109,154,891	11.73

PHASE A Used house-trailer with psycho-physical testing equipment to test drivers at local units.

PHASE B Used bus equipped with scientific testing apparatus to test drivers at local units.

PHASE C Inaugurated expanded program through the appointment of automotive safety representatives at each local unit to provide closer control of program.

TABLE A-3

ACCIDENTS BY VEHICLE TYPE

Vigorous safety promotion program initiated in 1961 has paid off in sharply reduced insurance costs and greatly reduced accident frequency rates.

SALES AUTOMOBILES

Year	Number of Vehicles	Accidents	Miles	Frequency Per Million Miles
1961	2,088	503	25,817,301	19.48
1962	2,019	432	37,858,269	11.41
1963	1,838	400	40,619,800	9.84

CITY AND SUBURBAN TRUCK OPERATION

Year	Number of Vehicles	Accidents	Miles	Frequency Per Million Miles
1961	2,250	917	42,052,505	21.80
1962	2,206	934	45,410,510	20.57
1963	1,882	713	50,590,042	14.09

OVER-THE-ROAD TRUCK OPERATION

Year	Number of Vehicles	Accidents	Miles	Frequency Per Million Miles
1961	212	262	18,456,044	15.47
1962	220	220	19,967,238	11.02
1963	179	167	17,945,049	9.30

B

Getting publicity from 'Safe Driver Awards'

Many times company publications and local newspapers, radio, and TV will carry a story based on presentation of "Safe Driver Awards" (also of "Safe Worker Awards," see Chapter 11). But to carry a story, they must first know in advance that these awards are going to be presented. The process of telling the news media, working with them to develop a story, and then having them publish it is known as "getting publicity."

The news media are alert to the public's interest in the street and highway accident problem. With over 50,000 persons killed in the U.S. each year, and more than one million persons injured in motor vehicle accidents every year, hardly a family in our nation has been left unaffected. Moreover, virtually everyone either operates or frequently rides in a motor vehicle and should therefore be interested in safe driving.

Recognition of local men (and women) with pictures of the award presentations, a personality sketch, or a story about the accident prevention program itself is certain to attract reader interest and result in goodwill for your company, as well as promote interest in better driving. The award presentation itself can build goodwill. Community knowledge that your company has many award-winning safe drivers can result in sales being directed your way.

How to Prepare for Publicity
Advance planning counts. Plan the program and set the date at least a month ahead for daily and weekly media, three months for monthly media. This permits the story to be printed about the same time the award is made. Some media, especially TV, will cover the presentation itself. Your company publication will probably do both.

MILLION MILE CLUB. Kenneth Stasch (2nd from left), Midwest Emery Freight System, Inc., receives first membership plaque from NSC President Howard Pyle, as company officials look on.

The amount of publicity will usually be in proportion to the "fuss" you make over the awards, the number of awards, and the length of time the awards are for. You can't make a big fuss over one or two awards given each month, but you can over 15 or 20 awards given once a year. High company officials can be present—high city and state officials can be invited. Some firms invite a representative of the police department, usually the traffic captain. Inviting a representative of the local safety organization is also a good idea.

What to Expect

"Names make news" may be an old adage, but each edition of a paper or magazine needs fresh names. Local papers and local editions of larger papers feature local doings and local names. Editors know this pulls readers. Local papers usually can't afford their own Washington Bureau, but they can afford stringers in the many small communities they cover They leave the Washington news to the big papers and cover local happenings in depth.

Be that as it may, you still

FLEET SAFETY AWARDS deserve publicity too. Same techniques apply.

have no assurance that every editor or radio/TV director you contact will be just wild about your story. One paper may play up your story one year, and give it mere mention the next. Another may be cold to you year after year and suddenly give you a big play. A third may promise you that they will run a big story, and at the last minute, other more important news crowds your article out.

How *not* to approach an editor: telephone him at the last minute and tell him he must send out a reporter and cameraman because you have a great story.

Instead, anticipate the questions he will ask you. Write the answers up in a "news release" (an example follows), and send it to your local papers, radio, and TV.

Editors are trained to ask these questions about all stories—who? why? what? when? where? and how? So tell them—*who* is getting the awards and *who* will be there to give them; *why* is this event important to the editor and to the readers he serves; *what* does the award mean; *when* will the event take place; *where* will it be held; and *how* can the editors get more details if they want them.

Give them the facts. Let them determine their relative importance. Of course, try to present the facts in such a way that they will interest the editor. Each editor will usually try to find some "angle," some approach to handling the story that will appeal to his readers and be different from the stories other news media carry. Work with

320

him if he wants you to.

The news release will not only contain details of the ceremonies, but also tell about the award winners themselves. Some editors may send over a photographer. Others may ask you to get photographs for them. Usually, you'll want to take your own pictures whether they take them or not.

Three to four persons in a photograph are tops, unless it is an overall group shot. Photos should have some action—even a nice smile gives some variety to the "present plaque—give handshake" routine. (See photo.)

Example

A simple method of preparing the draft can be illustrated by a hypothetical case.

John Jones, a dairyman, operates a fleet of 50 trucks delivering milk in Middletown and vicinity. Fifteen of his drivers have operated their vehicles for at least a year without a preventable accident. Jones has just received emblems and billfold cards from the National Safety Council. He lists the following facts as help in preparing a story for Middletown papers:

1. Who? Jones Dairy Co., 201 Main St., John Jones, President.

2. What? Presentation of National Safety Council Safe Driver Awards in Middletown.
First awards to be given by a dairy fleet in western Kentucky. National recognition for safe driving to 15 of 55 drivers. List the winners as follows:

4 Year	3 Year	2 Year	1 Year
——	——	——	——
——	——	——	——
——	——	——	——

3. When? Awards presented by Jones to the qualifying drivers, Thursday June 15, at 7:00 P.M. Following guests to be present (list those present, giving names, titles, companies represented, and addresses).

4. Where? Jones presented awards at a dinner meeting held at the Smith Hotel.

5. Why? Awards given in recognition of 15 drivers operating a total of 100,000 miles, four times the distance around the earth, during the past year without a preventable accident.

6. Other highlights. (Indicate other outstanding figures or facts pertaining to the fleet as a whole, or as the safe drivers as a group.)

7. Statements. (Jones prepares in advance three statements for quotation: one by himself from the talk he will give when making the presentations; one provided by the National Safety Council; one by his guest speaker, such as the Police Department Traffic Captain, Mayor, or Chamber of Commerce Secretary.)

Jones then drafts the following story (in news release format) which he gives to the news media sufficiently ahead of his Thursday evening meeting so that the editor can get it into an edition close to the award time.

The story is on the next page.

June 1, 19__

FROM: JONES DAIRY CO.
      201 MAIN ST.
      MIDDLETOWN, KY.

FOR IMMEDIATE RELEASE

             Fifteen Jones Dairy Drivers Receive
             First NSC Safety Awards in
             Western Kentucky

MIDDLETOWN, KENTUCKY . . . June 15——Four times around the
earth, 100,000 miles, driven this year without a preventable
accident!

That's the record 15 drivers for the Jones Dairy Company set
during the past year on the streets of Middletown and its
suburbs. In recognition of their accomplishments, the drivers
were presented with the first National Safety Council Safe
Driver Awards earned by a firm in this city. The presentations were made at a dinner held tonight at the Smith Hotel
which was attended by all drivers of the Jones fleet.

                  27,000 Safe Miles

Those drivers honored are: John Smith, 1608 Maple Avenue, 1st
year award; Thomas Brown, 458 E. Second Street, 2nd year
award; and Harold Johnson, 103 Fifth Avenue, 3rd year award.

Smith had the best safety record, operating his truck
27,000 safe miles during the past year.

Johnson compiled his safety record despite volunteering to
drive under almost impossible conditions during the recent
floods near Evansville, Indiana. He transported drinking
water around the clock to needy families, often with part of
his truck submerged in the flood waters.

                  Green Praises Drivers

In the winter, Jones' drivers provide a real public service
by keeping the roads open, clearing their routes with a huge,
specially built tractor—equipped snow plow.

                     (over)

Traffic Captain Henry Green, speaking briefly at the dinner, payed tribute to the winners' fine records. He said, "You have proved safe driving is a good investment. I hope your example will be followed by every driver in the city. It goes to show what caution and good sense behind the wheel can do."

Green pointed out that five persons had met death in Middletown automobile accidents since New Year's day. "Everyone of these accidents could have been avoided had the drivers shown the courtesy and care exercised by you award winners," he asserted.

Accidents Down 30 Per Cent

John Jones, President of the local dairy, cited official figures from the National Safety Council in his presentation talk, and noted that the overall company safety program had reduced the Jones' fleet accident rate more than 30 per cent in the past year. He thanked the award winners and also voiced his appreciation to the entire group of drivers and helpers for their cooperation.

The awards symbolizing national recognition for professional drivers are also the first to be won by a dairy fleet in western Kentucky.

(30)

Advertising Possibilities

Many companies—especially operators of passenger-carrying vehicles—stress safety in their advertising. Newspaper display advertising can be purchased to announce awards and to play up fleet safety records. Be sure to keep clear the distinction between advertising and publicity—advertising you pay for and you get what you pay for. Publicity is "free" (sometimes you work awfully hard to get it, though), and it is entirely up to the editor how much space you are going to get, if any. Although news media are friendly to advertisers, the editor judges news on its merits.

C

Safety meetings for commercial drivers

Safety meetings for drivers are an integral part of a balanced commercial vehicle program. Their function is to arouse and maintain interest in accident prevention, to develop attitudes sympathetic to the safety program, and most important of all, to educate and train both drivers and supervisory personnel in every factor entering into safe commercial vehicle operation.

In accomplishing these objectives group meetings improve the efficiency of all operations. They bring out a common bond of interest and instill in each individual a closer feeling of identity with the group. This fosters loyalty and a desire to be well thought of by the group, and results in a more conscientious group of employees.

Types of Safety Meetings

There are numerous ways of classifying safety meetings but for the purpose of this discussion they will be grouped as follows: (1) inspirational meetings; (2) celebrations of accomplishments in accident prevention; (3) group instruction and training.

INSPIRATIONAL MEETINGS
The major theme in meetings of this type is of a general and inspirational nature. Usually emphasis is placed on courtesy and good will, loyalty to the group or humanitarianism. A few fleets, however, are carrying on regular meetings where citizenship or Americanism is stressed with little mention of safety. The objective of these inspirational meetings is to exert a favorable safety influence by developing a greater civic and moral responsibility in the employees.

Little if any attempt is made to inject specific accident prevention instruction. Through these meetings, however, employees do become more competent.

CELEBRATION OF ACCOMPLISHMENTS IN ACCIDENT PREVENTION

These meetings are called as the occasion demands. This may be at the close of a contest or for presentation of bonuses or awards; or at any time for the express purpose of recognizing good records. The theme closely parallels that of the inspirational gathering. The talks are inspirational and there is little opportunity for definite training. When practical it is desirable to hold a celebration of this kind in conjunction with a banquet or buffet luncheon as this helps to give it the significance of an important event. How to get maximum publicity from these award meetings is discussed in Appendix B.

GROUP INSTRUCTION AND TRAINING

Drivers must understand the operating policies of the company and all the factors that enter into the safe and efficient handling of the business. They should be instructed in the elements of safe, courteous, and efficient driving and informed about accidents which have occurred and how they could have been avoided. Group instruction and training affords the most practical medium for this education and is indispensable to an effective safety program. "Driver Training" is the subject of Chapter 7.

Factors to Consider

SCHEDULING

The first step in planning the program should be to arrange a schedule of meetings extending over a designated period such as six or 12 months. This schedule should be considered as a course of safety education and each meeting planned to cover a desired objective. Safety meetings are far too

325

important to call them on short notice without (1) careful consideration of the field to be covered and (2) intelligent selection of the discussion subjects.

TYPE OF MEETING

Specialized meetings. Most meetings can be planned to be of interest to all drivers. In large fleets, however, where the operations include several distinct types of driving it may be advantageous to schedule separate meetings for different groups. For example, it may be desirable to hold separate meetings for pickup and delivery drivers or for long haul drivers. Even when this practice is followed it is advisable to hold several meetings during the year for the entire personnel and the program for these gatherings can be planned accordingly. Employees should not be required to attend meetings where the instruction and training is irrelevant to their particular work.

Small meetings. The size and nature of the fleet will determine arrangement of meeting schedules. Operations in scattered locations or over more than one shift may necessitate smaller groups. Regardless of how small the meetings may be they should be scheduled and planned in advance. Even in fleets of no more than three to five vehicles, regular meetings should be held where drivers and owner or manager get together to discuss safety. In small meetings of this kind more emphasis can be placed on round table discussion, and dinner meetings can often be held.

Short meetings. Many of the firms which do not hold regular meetings of an hour or more conduct brief meetings lasting 10 to 15 minutes, more often not exceeding 10 minutes. The general practice is to hold these meetings at least once a week and in some instances they are made a daily part of the program. Because of their brevity, in many cases they can be held during the day or at close of work.

At the end of the day, however, drivers are tired and anxious to get home and by the next morning the safety message is not fresh in their minds. For this reason the early morning meeting is far superior; the employees are receptive and receive the safety message at a time when it is apt to do the most good—just before they set out for the day's work. Some fleets have been successful in holding "safety breakfasts." There are no stragglers, and, because of the limited time before starting work, the meeting must be snappy.

It is impossible to accomplish much actual training or to enter into detailed discussion at short, snappy meetings. Their purpose is more for inspection or issuance of warnings about current, daily hazards. Usually, only one subject can be treated at each meeting. Some firms using this plan prepare special bulletins which are read to the group and then posted on the bulletin board for future reference. Such bulletins are particularly useful to caution drivers about seasonal hazards.

Full-length meetings. Extensive educational meetings require more time. It is the general opinion, however, that with the exception of dinner meetings and other special events, regular full-length meetings should not extend for more than one hour. A one-hour program each month is preferable to longer sessions every two or three months. These meetings may be scheduled during working hours, or arranged at a time which permits drivers to have their evening meal or other relaxation before going to the meeting.

In the regular full-length meeting, instructions should be given to improve driving technique. This training should be supplemented by a thorough analysis of the accident experience as well as a discussion of recent accidents. Continuous training is necessary for both new and old drivers.

Generally it is not advisable to attempt to cover more than two subjects at any one meeting, even if it is a long one.

Wives and girl friends can help. It is an excellent plan to schedule at least one meeting each year to be attended by the wives and lady friends of employees. The facts about accidents are seldom discussed at home and most wives have the notion that their husbands are superior drivers, the other fellow always being to blame. When armed with reliable information much influence can be wielded by the family in improving driver records and it is well to capitalize on this outside assistance.

MEETING TIMES

Conditions peculiar to each fleet govern the hour at which meetings may be held. In many operations it is practically impossible to hold meetings during working hours because all drivers are never present at the same time. Dinner meetings must usually be held during non-working hours.

In areas where unions are particularly active, it is advisable to confer with the steward or other officials before arranging the schedule. Some union contracts stipulate definite days on which meetings may be held. Others do not permit meetings to be conducted during leisure time of employees. Management should use every opportunity to impress union officials with the fact that safety meetings directly benefit employees by reducing the chance of injury and making jobs more secure.

Regardless of the hour at which meetings are held it is important that they be scheduled at regular intervals such as the second Tuesday of every month. A time when employees are most likely to be able to attend should be selected. In most operations, the second week of the month is a good time because summaries of the accident experience for the preceding month will have been prepared and can be discussed at the meeting.

Some fleets do not schedule full-length meetings during the summer months but substitute early morning sessions so the routine will not be disrupted. Many

327

SAFETY TRAINING TRAILER, built by employees, is air conditioned, and has built-in sound system and audio-visual equipment.

fleets have their bad accident months in November, December, January, and February, and find it to their advantage to schedule full-time meetings beginning in fall.

MEETING PLACES

The meeting place should be free from noise or other distractions. Short 10 or 15 minute meetings may be held in the garage if suitable facilities are available but longer sessions require a room with adequate heat, light, and acoustics. The room should be located as conveniently as possible to the terminal or garage where drivers come on or off duty.

Teaching rooms are described under "Where to Teach" in Chapter 7, "Driver Training."

Subjects to Cover

Although the major emphasis should be placed on instruction and training, provision should also be made for the inspirational theme. The proportion of time allocated to each phase is largely determined by the accident experience of the fleet, the interest of the employees and the tone of their morale. Some of the more important subjects which should be covered are listed below. They need not be taken up in the order given but those which are pertinent to the most serious problems of the particular operations should receive attention first.

1. Thorough explanation of operating and public relations policies of the firm.

2. Instruction in driving practices, courtesy, and safety in general.

3. Traffic rules and regulations: Explanation of the purpose and intent of the regulations; require drivers to become familiar with the legal wording. Discussion of standard signs and signals and their significance. Tie in with company policy and good will.

4. Mechanics of the vehicle, its care and maintenance. Whenever possible, demonstrations should be conducted by expert mechanics or specialists.

5. Explanation of the physical problems involved in driving such as reaction time, stopping distance, skidding, passing distance, centrifugal force, force or impact, etc.

6. Accidents: Thorough coverage including past accidents, common situations, unusual accidents, seasonal hazards, what to do in case of an accident, how to report, etc. Analysis of the major types of accidents, both from a frequency and severity standpoint with drivers participating in blackboard discussion of their causes and prevention. Touch upon costs, trends, prevalent types and accident repeaters.

7. First aid and general health: The importance of first aid; value of regular physical examinations; discussion of fatigue, illness and general health; and explanation of company policy with respect to these subjects.

8. Loading and unloading: How to lift large and small articles, proper storage of cargo, and handling of passengers, for example.

9. Necessity for and proper use of special equipment such as flares, flags, chains, standards, foglights, windshield wipers, spot lights, tarpaulins, ropes, tailgates, the fifth wheel, air brake equipment and connections, lighting equipment and connections, etc.

10. Bureau of Motor Carrier Safety, state, city or other special regulations.

11. Open forum with questions to be asked and answered.

A full discussion of "What to Teach" is given in Chapter 7, "Driver Training."

Planning the Program

Just as the meetings should be scheduled in advance, each program should be planned sufficiently ahead of time to assure its success. Variety and unique methods are needed to maintain interest and insure attendance; drivers must look forward to each meeting. Strive to make the program interesting, entertaining and educational. Do not become discouraged if the first meetings fall short of this goal. Poor reception by employees calls for a review of planning and handling technique.

TYPE OF SPEAKERS

Specialists and instructors. The selection of specialists to instruct is very important. They should be able to talk authoritatively, instill confidence, and convince listeners on the benefits of safety. Unqualified speakers or teachers cause employees to lose confidence and in-

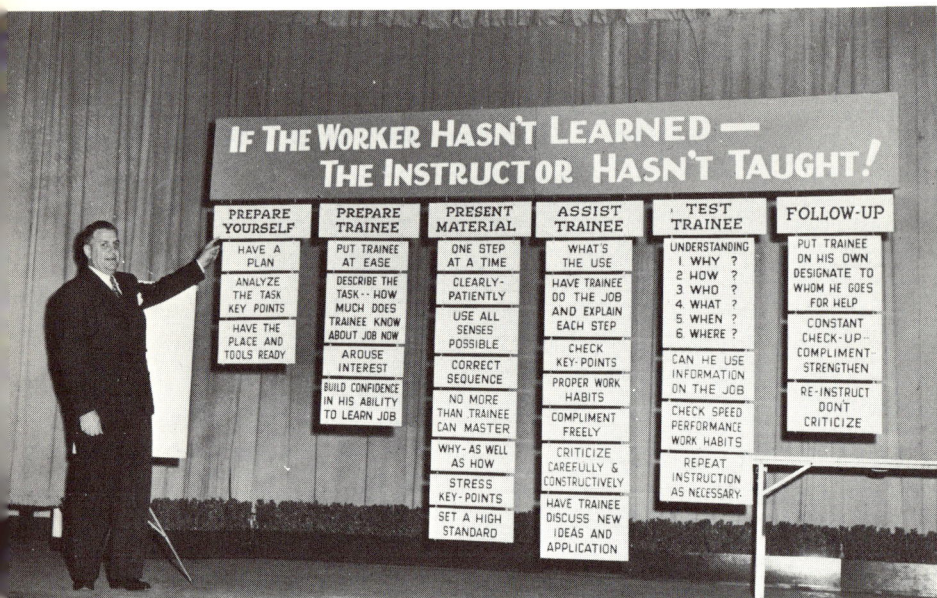

IF THE WORKER HASN'T LEARNED —
THE INSTRUCTOR HASN'T TAUGHT!

PREPARE YOURSELF	PREPARE TRAINEE	PRESENT MATERIAL	ASSIST TRAINEE	TEST TRAINEE	FOLLOW-UP
HAVE A PLAN	PUT TRAINEE AT EASE	ONE STEP AT A TIME	WHAT'S THE USE	UNDERSTANDING 1. WHY ? 2. HOW ? 3. WHO ? 4. WHAT ? 5. WHEN ? 6. WHERE ?	PUT TRAINEE ON HIS OWN DESIGNATE TO WHOM HE GOES FOR HELP
ANALYZE THE TASK KEY POINTS	DESCRIBE THE TASK -- HOW MUCH DOES TRAINEE KNOW ABOUT JOB NOW	CLEARLY- PATIENTLY	HAVE TRAINEE DO THE JOB AND EXPLAIN EACH STEP		
HAVE THE PLACE AND TOOLS READY		USE ALL SENSES POSSIBLE			CONSTANT CHECK-UP- COMPLIMENT- STRENGTHEN
	AROUSE INTEREST	CORRECT SEQUENCE	CHECK KEY-POINTS	CAN HE USE INFORMATION ON THE JOB	
	BUILD CONFIDENCE IN HIS ABILITY TO LEARN JOB	NO MORE THAN TRAINEE CAN MASTER	PROPER WORK HABITS	CHECK SPEED PERFORMANCE WORK HABITS	RE-INSTRUCT DON'T CRITICIZE
		WHY- AS WELL AS HOW	COMPLIMENT FREELY		
		STRESS KEY-POINTS	CRITICIZE CAREFULLY & CONSTRUCTIVELY	REPEAT INSTRUCTION AS NECESSARY.	
		SET A HIGH STANDARD	HAVE TRAINEE DISCUSS NEW IDEAS AND APPLICATION		

JOB INSTRUCTION METHODS have been worked out by educators who tested different methods and found which were most successful. Note instructor's graphic presentation—each section can be hung in place as he discusses it.

terest. Outside speakers add variety but should not be used for a major share of the program. Persons not familiar with the details peculiar to each fleet may make conflicting statements if required to cover too broad a subject. Procedures and methods adopted by the company should be furnished in the form of a manual to all employees engaged in a supervisory capacity. It will guide those who act as instructors in presenting recommended practices correctly and uniformly.

Company officials. In addition to the safety director of the fleet or the persons responsible for safety who should preside, at least one high official in the firm should participate in every meeting. This is of utmost importance in demonstrating the management's interest and support. If possible, this assignment should be rotated throughout the year among different executives. By scheduling subjects in advance, impromptu talks can be discouraged. Officials are generally at their best in handling inspirational addresses so it is advisable to schedule them for the latter part of the program. They are then less likely to detract from the major objectives of the meeting. A well-directed 10-minute talk is sufficient. Courtesy, company plans for the future, employees' welfare, plant deliveries, progress, and financial condition are suggested subjects.

330

Insurance company representatives. The insurance company representative can help by taking part in the meeting program. It must be remembered, however, that usually he services many other fleets and cannot be expected to know every detail of operation peculiar to each fleet. He is an expert consultant on the subject of accidents but should not be requested to give instructions on questions which vary from fleet to fleet as he may, inadvertently, make statements that conflict with company policy.

In the past, most of the fleet safety meetings have been planned and conducted by the insurance companies, not because it was their job but because fleets hesitated to accept the responsibility. Management must do its part. One of the most important objectives of a safety program is to impress emphatically on the employees that the management is determined to stop accidents. The insurance company cannot substitute for management in accomplishing this objective.

TRAINING AIDS AND QUIZZES
Training aids and quizzes are discussed in Chapter 7.

DOOR PRIZES
Many fleets introduce some sort of a door prize to stimulate attendance. The expense involved is small and the results exceptionally good. One plan is for the employees who attend to place their names in a box at the beginning of the meeting. At the close of the meeting the winning card is drawn from the box by an uninterested person. One fleet uses a $5.00 bill as a prize at every meeting. Other prizes which may be used are parts of uniforms, safety shoes, tools, goggles, pen and pencil sets, gloves, hams, chickens, etc. This plan reduces tardiness to a minimum because the cards must be deposited before the meeting begins.

PROGRAM ARRANGEMENT
The character of the program and the sequence in which the various parts should be presented depends, of course, on the type of meeting. An essential requisite of every safety meeting is stimulating interest. There must be no lag in the discussions, no lull in the proceedings, and no tiresome or aimless digressions from the subjects. Snappy meetings bring the best results. Typical program features are listed below:

Inspirational program where good records are recognized:
1. Dinner (often with music).
2. Entertainment (if desired).
3. Introduction of visitors (by chairman).
4. Address of welcome and preliminary remarks.
5. Principal address.
6. Presentation of awards (by the firm president or manager).
7. Closing remarks (by chairman).

Group instruction and training type of meeting:
1. Roll call.

2. Introduction of visitors (by chairman).

3. Preliminary remarks with emphasis on high frequency types of accidents to be discussed at this meeting (by the person responsible for safety).

4. Films or other visual aids on the subject.

5. Discussion by person responsible for safety, and open forum.

6. Summary and conclusion (by chairman).

It is seldom possible to include all the items listed in a meeting of one hour. Some can be omitted entirely or others substituted for them. For instance, a buffet lunch is easily adaptable to this type of meeting. Some firms feel that if the lunch precedes the meeting the employees are in a more receptive mood for the meeting which follows. Many others, however, are of the opinion that there is a decided value in the good fellowship and discussions which result from the mingling of the employees in the meeting room when food is served at the close of the meeting.

Conducting the Meeting

Chairman. The person responsible for the safety program, or some selected representative of management should preside.

Relevancy. The chairman must be sensitive to digressions from the essential purpose and tactfully guide the meeting along a relevant and lively course.

Criticism. Harangue or invective criticism evokes resentment rather than willing cooperation and has no place in the meeting. Individuals should not be corrected or reprimanded during group gatherings but this should be handled by private conference at other times. Of course, the correction of individual faults is covered indirectly in discussions of bad practices to the group.

Formality. The meetings should be conducted in an orderly manner with sufficient formality to lend the program dignity and respect but not overdone to the extent of making it stiff and boresome. It should be started, carried through and adjourned according to schedule. Humor should not be injected where it will detract from emphasis on serious points.

Personal touch. Collection of invitation cards at the door by an official of the firm affords an opportunity for a personal handshake or greeting and tends to stimulate attendance. Also it serves to express the management's interest and to impart prestige to the proceedings.

Attendance. A record should be made of the names of those in attendance at each meeting. One safety director sends a personal note to the homes of each absent driver to tell him that he was missed at the meeting, and expresses the hope that he will be present at the next one.

Notification of Meeting and Publicity

It is not good policy to compel employees to attend safety meet-

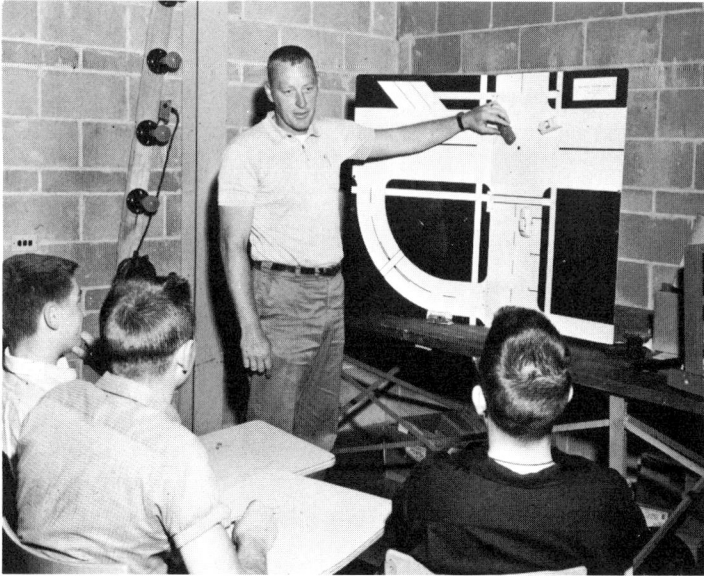

SPECIAL PROBLEMS are discussed at meetings for those involved.

ings. It should not be easy, on the other hand, for them to give excuses for not attending. Announce the meeting well in advance, giving all details such as time, place, and the nature of the program. Notices are more impressive when signed by the person in charge of safety or other official. They should be posted on all bulletin boards and published in employee publications. Some firms inform drivers of meetings by letter. Others issue invitation cards or tickets. These are collected at the meeting and often must be signed by the person attending.

Develop interest in the meeting by building it up through publicity channels. Report regularly in house organs and other publications all interesting developments in connection with each meeting. Keep employees informed of the purpose of each meeting and the subjects which will be discussed.

Importance of Details

Many meetings fail because seemingly insignificant matters are not taken care of beforehand. An ample number of chairs, for instance, should be placed in an orderly arrangement before the meeting begins. The room must be kept at a comfortable temperature and well ventilated. Provision should be made for a place to put hats and coats. Drinking water should be furnished for speakers. If films or slides are used, windows must have shades which will keep out light, and a screen of adequate size must be provided.

333

D

Job safety analysis

To uncover hazards that may have been overlooked in the layout of the plant and in the design of machinery, equipment, and processes, or may have developed after production was begun, a continuing program of activities must be carried on. One of the most important of these activities is job safety analysis.*

Definition

A job safety analysis is a procedure to make a job safe by:

1. Identifying the hazards or potential accidents associated with each step of the job.
2. Developing a solution for each hazard that will either eliminate or control the exposure.

Once the hazards are known, the proper solutions can be developed. Some solutions may be physical changes that control the hazard, such as placing a guard over exposed moving machine parts.

Others may be job procedures that eliminate or minimize the hazard, for example, safe methods of piling materials.

Some job steps may have no hazards associated with them, but other job steps may each be accompanied by one or more hazards. Some hazards are conditions; some are actions. All are potential causes of accident.

A job safety analysis can be written up in the manner shown in the illustrative example. In the left-hand column, the basic steps of the job are listed in the order in which they occur. The middle column describes the hazards or potential accidents associated with each job step. The right-hand column gives the safe procedures that should be followed to guard against the haz-

* *Bethlehem Steel Company, Bethlehem, Pa. "Job Safety Analysis."* BETHLEHEM STEEL'S SUPERVISORY SAFETY MANUAL. *Chapter 5.*

ards and to prevent potential accidents. (Turn page for illustration.)

For convenience, both the job safety analysis procedure and the written description are commonly referred to as a JSA.

The four basic steps in making a job safety analysis are:

1. Select the job to be analyzed.
2. Break the job down into successive steps.
3. Identify the hazards and potential accidents.
4. Develop ways to eliminate the hazards and prevent the potential accidents.

Let's discuss each.

Selecting the Job

A job is a sequence of separate steps or activities that together accomplish a work goal. Some jobs can be broadly defined in general terms of what is accomplished. Making paper, building a plant, mining iron ore are examples. Such

broadly defined jobs are not suitable for a JSA. Similarly, a job can be narrowly defined in terms of a single action. Pulling a switch, tightening a screw, pushing a button are examples. Such narrowly defined jobs also are not suitable for a JSA.

Jobs suitable for a JSA are those job assignments that a line supervisor may make. Operating a vehicle, washing a vehicle, piling boxes at a terminal are good subjects for job safety analyses because they are neither too broad nor are they too narrow.

Jobs, even though they fit the description just given, should not be selected at random for analysis. The most hazardous and those with the worst accident experience should be tackled first. This approach will yield the quickest possible return from a JSA program.

In selecting jobs to be ana-

335

JOB SAFETY ANALYSIS—WORK SHEET 29276 (Rev.A)

BETHLEHEM STEEL

JOB SAFETY ANALYSIS—WORK SHEET
29276 (Rev.A)

Plant	Sparrows Point
Department	42" Cold Strip Mill
Section	Continuous Pickler

Required and/or recommended personal protective equipment

Hard hat and eye protection

SEQUENCE OF BASIC JOB STEPS	POTENTIAL ACCIDENTS OR HAZARDS
Break the job down into its basic steps; e.g., what is done first, what is done next, and so on. You can do this by (1) observing the job, (2) discussing it with the operator, (3) drawing on your knowledge of the job, or (4) a combination of all three. Record the job steps in their normal order of occurrence. Describe what is done, not the details of how it is done. Usually three or four words are sufficient to describe each basic job step. For example, the job of "replacing a light bulb" may break down into basic steps as follows:	For each job step, ask yourself what accidents could happen to the man doing the job step. You can get your answers by (1) observing the job, (2) discussing it with the operator, (3) recalling past accidents, or (4) a combination of all three. Ask yourself: Can he be struck by or contacted by anything; can he strike against or come in contact with anything; can he be caught in, on, or between anything; can he fall; can he overexert, is he exposed to anything injurious such as gas, radiation, welding rays, etc.

1. Get a step-up ladder.
   2. Climb ladder.
   3. Remove light globe.
   4. Replace light bulb.
   5. Replace light globe.
   6. Descend ladder.
   7. Remove and store ladder.
	Record and number potential accidents by using the right abbreviation for the type of accident that could happen and by describing the agent or contact or exposure. For example, SB—cranehook means the man could be struck by a cranehook. Use these abbreviations:
	  1. SB—Struck by 7. CI—Caught in
	  2. CBy—Contacted by 8. FB—Fall-to-below
	  3. SA—Struck against 9. FS—Fall-same-level
	  4. CW—Contact with 10. O—Overexertion
	  5. CBe—Caught between 11. E—Exposure
	  6. CO—Caught on

1. Remove extinguisher from hanger.	1. SB -- falling extinguisher.
2. Carry extinguisher in upright position to fire.	2. FS -- tripping, slipping, etc.
3. Hold hose or horn in one hand, extinguisher in other hand.	3. CW -- dry chemical contents.

4. Use the extinguisher.	4. (a) CI -- spread of fire.
	
	    (b) CW -- clothing catching fire.
	    (c) CBy -- reflash of fire, loss of heat protection afforded by dry chemical.

5. Promptly report use of extinguisher.	----------

APPROVED:------------------------------DATE------------------

------------------------------   ------------------------------

------------------------------   ------------------------------   (CONTINUE ON REVERSE SIDE)

A JOB SAFETY ANALYSIS is only as good as details recorded on standard JSA form.

Using Dry Chemical Fire Extinguisher

All employees

RECOMMENDED SAFE JOB PROCEDURE

For each potential accident or hazard, ask yourself how should the man do the job step to avoid the potential accident, or what should he do or not do to avoid the potential accident. You can get your answers by (1) observing the job for leads, (2) discussing precautions with experienced job operators, (3) drawing on your experience, or (4) a combination of all three. Be sure to describe specifically the precautions the man must take. Don't leave out important details. Number each separate recommended precaution with the same number you gave the potential accident (center column) that the precaution seeks to avoid. Use simple do or don't statements to explain recommended precautions as if you were talking to the man.

For example: "Stand clear of lift before signaling."
Avoid such generalities as "Be careful," "Be alert," "Take caution," etc.

When, even before, you have completed this column, ask yourself if there is a different way to do the job that is safer and better all around. Consider such improvements as more efficient tools, equipment, materials, or methods. If it is a service job, also consider ways to increase the life of the job. If you have any such ideas, jot down the core of the idea, and then discuss it with higher supervision at first opportunity.

1. Grasp extinguisher securely.

2. Observe walking areas, obstacles, slippery surfaces, etc.

3. Maintain control of extinguisher, avoid exposing individuals to contents.

4. (a) Apply contents with rapid sweeping motion at nearest point of flame.
   (b) Keep proper distance. Be alert to tripping and falling hazards.
   (c) As extinguisher empties, be ready to move away. Do not turn back to fire. Watch for and renew attack when indicated.

L.S. Adams
Signature of person making Job Safety Analysis

9/28
Date

Sample shows complete JSA for typical job: "Using a dry chemical fire extinguisher."
Courtesy Bethlehem Steel Company

337

lyzed and in establishing the order of analysis, top supervision of a department should be guided by the following factors:

1. Frequency of accidents. A job that has repeatedly produced accidents is a candidate for a JSA. The greater the number of accidents associated with the job, the greater its priority claim for a JSA.

2. Production of disabling injuries. Every job that has produced disabling injuries should be given a JSA. The injuries prove that preventive action taken prior to their occurrence was not successful.

3. Severity potential. Some jobs may have no history of accidents but may have the potential for severe injury.

4. New jobs created by changes in equipment or in processes obviously have no history of accidents, but their accident potential may not be fully appreciated. A JSA of every new job should be made as soon as the job has been created. Analysis should not be delayed until accidents or near misses occur.

Breaking the Job Down

Before the search for hazards begins, the job should be broken down into basic steps. The steps should describe what is being done and should be given in the order of occurrence. Details should be omitted.

Here is an example of a step-by-step breakdown of a simple job —planting a tree:

1. Select the site.

2. Bring tools, equipment, and the tree to the site.

3. Dig the hole.

4. Prepare the hole.

5. Put the tree into the hole.

6. Backfill, tamp, and water.

7. Brace the tree.

8. Clean up and return the equipment.

There are two common errors made in breaking a job down into its basic steps. One is to make the breakdown too detailed. The result is an unnecessarily large number of job steps, many of which may not be basic. For example, the same tree planting job might be overloaded with details:

1. Pick up the shovel.

2. Position the shovel so that it points down.

3. Place the right foot on the top edge of the shovel blade.

4. Press the shovel into the ground with the right foot.

5. Tilt the shovel handle backward and down to pick up the dirt.

The other common error is to make the job breakdown too general. The result is that important basic steps are not recorded, as in this two-step breakdown of the tree planting job:

1. Dig the hole.

2. Plant the tree.

In this case, all but one of the basic steps have been omitted. Obviously, the JSA will not show the hazards associated with all the basic steps and will be worthless.

Key points in breaking a job down into successive basic steps:

338

1. **Select the right man** to observe.
2. **Brief him** on the purpose.
3. **Observe the job** for breakdown by basic steps.
4. **Record each step** in the breakdown.
5. **Check the breakdown** with the man who is observed.

If the observer has an opportunity to choose one of several men doing a job, he will have to determine which man best meets the requirements. The man selected should be experienced, capable, cooperative, and willing to share ideas. Such a man will be easy to work with on an analysis.

If the man selected has never worked on a JSA, the supervisor should thoroughly explain the purpose of the analysis and show him a copy of a completed JSA. The man must be reassured that he is not being watched to see whether or not he works safely. He should understand that the purpose is to study the job, not the man, and that he was selected for observation because of his experience and capability.

The job should be observed for breakdown by basic steps. The supervisor should ask, "What is the first basic step of the job; what starts the job? What is the next basic step?" and so on. The steps must not be either too general or too limited.

In recording the breakdown, the supervisor should number the job steps consecutively in the first column of the JSA work sheet.

Each step should describe *what* is done, not *how* it is to be done. The wording for each step should begin with a verb or an "action" word, like "remove," "open," "weld." Description of the job step is completed by naming the item to which the action applies, for example, "remove *extinguisher*," "open *valve*," "weld *seam*."

After the supervisor has completed the breakdown, he should check it with the man he has observed. The supervisor should get his agreement on what is done (not how it is done) and on the order in which the steps are taken. It should go without saying that the supervisor should thank the man when the breakdown has been completed.

Identifying the Hazards and Potential Accidents

After the job has been broken down into its basic steps, each step is analyzed for hazards and potential accidents. The purpose is to identify *all* the hazards, whether produced by the environment or connected with the job procedure, so that each step, and thus the entire job, can be made safer and more efficient.

The supervisor should look for specific types of potential accidents. For each basic step in the job breakdown, he should ask himself these questions:

1. **Can the man strike** against, be struck by, or otherwise make injurious contact with an object?
2. **Can he be caught** in, on, or

339

between objects?

3. Can he slip or trip? Can he fall on the same level or from one level to another?

4. Can he strain himself by pushing, pulling, or lifting?

5. Does the environment present a hazardous exposure (toxic gases, vapors, mists, fumes, dusts, heat, radiation, and so on)?

Observation plus knowledge of the job should supply the answers to these questions. The job observation should be repeated as often as necessary until *all* hazards and potential accidents have been identified.

While observing each step, the supervisor should record the hazards that might result in accidents. Only two items of information are required: the type of accident and the agent involved. For example, to record the idea that a man might injure his legs or feet by dropping a fire extinguisher, all the supervisor needs to write down is "struck by extinguisher."

Each hazard or potential accident should be recorded on a separate line in the center column on the JSA work sheet. A hazard or potential accident pertaining to a particular job step should be kept parallel with that step. If a job step entails several hazards or potential accidents, they should be lettered "(a)," "(b)," "(c)," and so on.

The supervisor should check with the employee observed after the hazards and the potential accidents have been recorded. The employee's experience with the job

340

may suggest ideas that did not occur to the supervisor.

The supervisor should also check with others who have had experience with the job. By alternately observing the job and discussing its dangers with experienced men, the supervisor will soon develop a reliable list of hazards and potential accidents.

Developing Solutions

When the hazards and potential accidents associated with each job step have been identified and their causes are understood, the final step in the job safety analysis is to develop ways to eliminate the hazards and to prevent occurrence of the potential accidents. The principal solutions are:

1. Find an entirely different way to do the job.

2. Change the physical conditions that create the hazards.

3. Revise the job procedure if changing the physical conditions does not eliminate all the hazards.

4. Reduce the frequency of the job by correcting the conditions that make it necessary.

Occasionally, it is possible to find or devise an entirely different way to do the job that will eliminate the hazards. Attention should be focused on the work goal of the job. The ways in which that work goal can be accomplished should be determined and then should be analyzed for hazards to see if any one way is entirely safe. When such a study is being made, work-saving tools and equipment should be considered.

If a different and safe way to do the job cannot be found, then for each hazard and each potential accident this question should be asked: "What change in physical condition, such as a change in tools, materials, equipment, or location, will eliminate the hazard or prevent the accident?"

When a physical change to make the job safe is in order, it should be carefully studied to determine what other benefits, such as greater production or a saving in time or effort required to do the job, will also result from the change. These other benefits should be pointed out when the proposed change is presented to higher management—they will make good selling points.

If the hazards cannot be eliminated either by doing the job in a different way or by changing the physical conditions, the next effort in effecting a solution should be to investigate the possibility of making changes in job procedures.

For each hazard and each potential accident recorded on the JSA work sheet, this question should be asked: "What should the man do—or not do—to eliminate this particular hazard or prevent this particular potential accident?" Where appropriate, an additional question· "How should he do it?" should be asked. In most cases, the supervisor should be able to supply satisfactory answers to those questions from his own experience.

The answers must be specific

and concrete if a new recommended safe procedure is to be worthwhile. Such general instructions as "Be alert," "Use caution," or "Be careful," are useless. Answers should precisely state what to do and how to do it.

Here is an example of a poor recommended safety procedure: "Make certain the wrench does not slip and cause loss of balance." It is poor because it does not tell how to prevent the wrench from slipping.

Here, in contrast, is an example of a good recommended safe procedure that tells not only what to do but how to do it.

"Set the wrench securely. Test the grip of the wrench by exerting a slight pressure. Brace yourself against something immovable, or take a solid stance with feet wide apart before exerting full pressure, to prevent loss of balance if the wrench slips."

Often a repair or service job has to be done at frequent intervals because a condition needs to be corrected. For such repetitive jobs, this question should be asked: "What can be done to eliminate the *cause* of the condition that makes excessive repairs or service necessary?" If the cause cannot be eliminated, then the question "Can anything be done to minimize the effects of the condition?" should be asked.

For example, machine parts may become worn at a rapid rate and therefore require frequent replacement. Study of the problem may reveal that excessive vibration is the cause of this condition.

When the vibration is eliminated or reduced substantially, the machine parts will have longer life and the job of replacement will need to be done less often.

Reducing the frequency of a job contributes to safety only in that it limits the exposure. Every effort still should be made to eliminate hazards and to prevent potential accidents through changing physical conditions or revising job procedures or both.

The supervisor should check or test proposed changes by reobserving the job and by discussing the changes with the men who do the job. Their ideas about the hazards and proposed solutions may have considerable value. They can judge the practicality of proposed changes and perhaps suggest improvements.

Such discussions, however, are more than a way to check a JSA. They are safety contacts that promote awareness of job hazards and safe procedures.

Benefits and Uses of JSA

The major benefits of a job safety analysis come after its completion. However, benefits are also to be gained from the development work itself.

While making job safety analyses, supervisors learn more about the jobs they supervise. When employees are encouraged to participate in job safety analyses, their safety attitudes are improved and their safety knowledge is increased. As a JSA is worked out, safer and better job procedures and safer working conditions are developed.

But these important benefits are only a portion of the total benefits to be derived from the JSA program. The principal benefits come from use of the JSA in these phases of the supervisor's work:

1. Giving individual training to employees.
2. Making employee safety contacts.
3. Instructing the new man on the job.
4. Preparing for planned safety observations.
5. Giving prejob instructions on irregular jobs.
6. Reviewing job procedures after accidents occur.
7. Studying jobs for possible improvement in job methods.

When a JSA is distributed, the supervisor's first responsibility is to explain its contents to employees and, if necessary, to give them further individual training. The entire JSA must be reviewed with the men concerned so that they will know how the job is to be done—without accidents.

The JSA can furnish material for planned safety contacts. All steps of the JSA should be used for this purpose. The steps that present major hazards should be emphasized and reviewed again and again in safety contacts.

New men on the job must be trained in the basic job steps. They must be taught to recognize the hazards associated with each job step and must learn the necessary precautions. There is no better guide for this training than a well-prepared JSA.

Occasionally, the supervisor should observe his men as they perform jobs for which job safety analyses have been developed. The purpose of these observations is to determine whether or not the men are doing the jobs in accordance with the safe job procedures. Before making such observations, the supervisor should prepare himself by reviewing the JSA in question so that he will have firmly in mind the key points that should be part of his observations.

Many jobs, such as certain repair or service jobs, are done infrequently or on an irregular basis. The men who do them will benefit from prejob instruction that reminds them of the important hazards and the necessary precautions. Using the JSA for the particular job, the supervisor should give this instruction at the time he makes the job assignment.

Whenever an accident occurs on a job covered by a job safety analysis, the JSA should be reviewed to determine whether or not it needs revision. If the JSA is revised, all employees concerned with the job should be informed of the changes and instructed in any new procedures.

When an accident results from failure to follow JSA procedures, the facts should be discussed with all the men who do the job.

It should be made clear that the accident would not have occurred had the JSA procedures been followed.

All supervisors are concerned with improving job methods to increase safety, reduce costs, and step up production. The job safety analysis is an excellent starting point for questioning the established way of doing a job. And study of the JSA may well suggest definite ideas for improvement of job methods.

E

Protective coloring for commercial vehicles

Serious rear-end collisions are becoming increasingly numerous, particularly on the open road at night and in bad weather. Vehicles that have stopped or slowed on the traveled portion of the roadway are most frequently struck. Heavy trucks, especially, are the victims of this type of accident because soft shoulders often prevent them from getting off the highway when making emergency stops. Also, heavy vehicles are frequently obliged to travel slower than other traffic on certain highways and particular terrain. Motorists who drive into the rear of such stopped or slowed vehicles generally report that they did not see them, or that they *did not see them soon enough.*

The coloring of a vehicle, particularly the rear-end, can have an important effect upon its visibility and will generally aid in judging its size, distance, and relative speed. Reflective coloring, therefore, can be of material help in preventing accidents.

Although there is relatively little scientific study about use of color on motor vehicles, members of the National Safety Council, paint manufacturers, and others have offered opinions on the subject of reflective paint and coloring which are summarized in the next paragraph. Brochures covering various aspects and qualities of paint are available from the leading paint manufacturers.

For reasonably good night visibility, an object on the highway should reflect at least half of the light striking it from headlights. This means that the rear of vehicles should be painted a light color. Listed (right) are the approximate light reflection percentages of a number of standard colors:

LIGHT REFLECTION

	Per Cent
White	84.0
Cream	68.8
Ivory	66.7
Light Pink	66.5
Yellow	57.0
Flesh	51.6
Buff	51.5
Light Gray	51.5
Light Green	45.2
Aluminum Gray	41.0
Light Blue	36.4
Sage Green	36.3
Brown	27.5
Dark Red	13.8
Dark Green	9.2
Dark Blue	8.4

SOURCE: Munsell Color Company, Inc., using photometer and light reflected at 45 degrees.

The character of the reflection is also important. A dull surface giving a diffused reflection seems to be most desirable for large areas, because a glossy finish or aluminum paint may, at the proper angle, reflect back enough light to cause glare from the following driver's own headlights. Glossy surfaces also have the disadvantage of directing the greater part of the reflected light away from the following vehicle if the surface is at too great an angle to the headlight beam. This condition occurs on curves and at the crests of hills. Directional reflection has the advantage, however, of giving a more intense light; hence it may be used to make small or irregular surfaces seem to flash or sparkle.

Color Combinations

Another factor of visibility is color combination. It is quite possible that the best color combination may be seen further away under even less intensity of light. Therefore, the following table is important. It gives the best combinations in order of the greatest visibility:

1. Black letters on yellow background
2. Black letters on white background
3. Yellow letters on black background
4. White letters on black background
5. Blue letters on white background
6. White letters on blue background
7. White letters on green background
8. Green letters on white background
9. Red letters on white background
10. White letters on red background
11. Red letters on green background
12. Green letters on red background

Standard colors used for this test were: vermilion red, cadmium yellow, Paris green and French blue. The tests were conducted by *Le Courier de Livre,* Paris, France.

A light-colored vehicle is at a disadvantage in the winter months because it does not afford contrast with areas covered by snow. Similarly, a dark-colored vehicle, or one that blends with foliage, offers little contrast to the surrounding countryside during summer months. For this reason, part of the vehicle should be painted a dark color in some design which will make a contrast with light colored surroundings. It would appear that the two-tone color combinations of many passenger cars not only adds to their beauty but aids in their visibility to the other driver.

The most effective color combination for the rear end of a vehicle would therefore seem to be white (or yellow) and black. The background should be of the light color and diagonal stripes of black against this background. Since the top part of the truck must be seen more frequently against a dark sky than against snowbanks, the stripes need not extend clear to the top but should cover at least the lowest third of the rear end. Since the black stripes are of value only when there is snow or fog, which is not too often, they should cover not more than a third of the total area; that is, the light stripes are most effective if they are twice the width of the black ones.

To ensure visibility, the black stripes should not be less than six inches broad, and to be sure that they will be recognized as stripes, they should not be more than a foot broad. This leaves from one foot to two feet as the width of the light stripes. The stripes should be at a 45 degree diagonal because that is less likely to be confused with vertical or horizontal objects on the roadside, and is, furthermore, an accepted warning indication. The stripe can run from the upper right to the lower left or from the upper left to the lower right. (See photo on page 345.)

Red, although generally denoting danger, is not a suitable color for improving night visibility because the shades of red which usually mean danger reflect far too

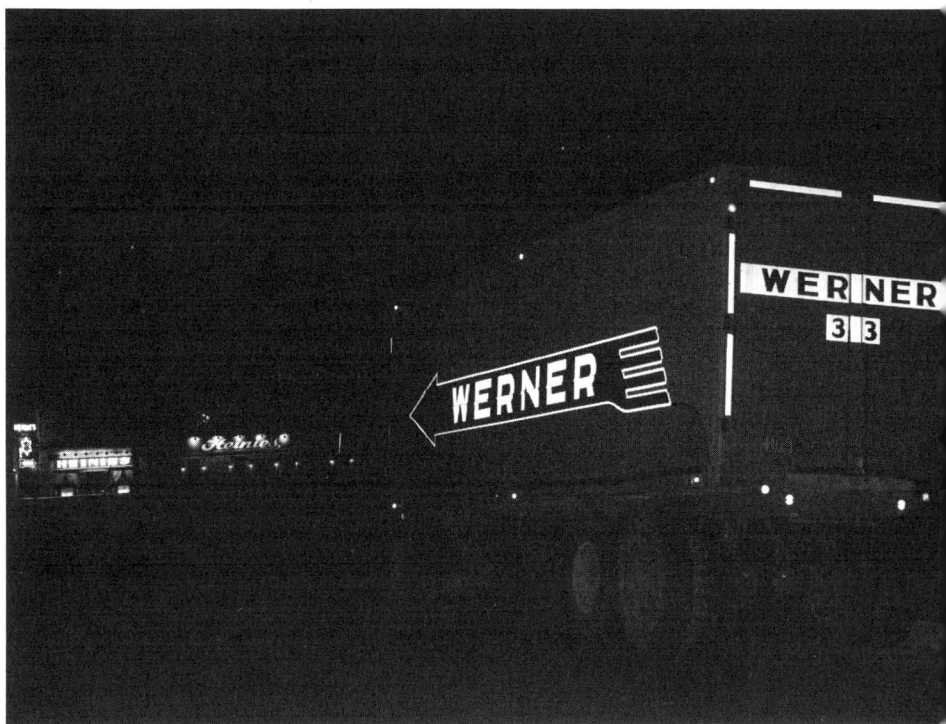

'HIGHLIGHT' COLORING helps night visibility.

little light to cause the vehicle to "loom up" in the dark. The theory that red light penetrates fog and mist has no significance in connection with automobile coloring because white reflects as much red light as any red shade, in addition to reflecting light of other colors.

The Ward La France Truck Corporation, Elmira Heights, N.Y., is experimenting with vehicle colors in order to find the ones that offer the highest visibility both during the day and at night. Its studies indicate that red, the traditional color for fire apparatus, is among the least visible colors. The safest, most visible colors range from greenish yellow to yellow.

Therefore, this company has adopted lime yellow for its fire apparatus. Because this color is more visible, motorists and pedestrians can recognize fire apparatus earlier and take prompt and proper evasive action.

An additional advantage—once at the scene of the emergency, the fire or rescue vehicle serves to alert oncoming traffic.

'Highlight' Coloring

Wheels, chassis, and other irregularly shaped underparts may be painted aluminum which gives sharp, bright reflections on small areas and thus improves visibility.

Where color schemes are important for advertising, they should be so arranged that the background colors are light and the lettering or striping is dark. The name of the company painted in large block letters across the back of the truck might well serve the same purpose as diagonal striping.

Reflector buttons give highly efficient "highlight" spotting. Several motor carriers using a product called "Scotchlite" have reported very satisfactory results. This material is available in colors and has a very high reflection value, especially at night. Name signs can be effectively outlined with this. (Some states issue license plates coated with this material.)

Housekeeping

The best selection and use of color combinations can be rendered useless, however, if road film and dirt are allowed to accumulate and "gray" the vehicle. Frequent cleaning, especially during periods of inclement weather, will help to restore the light-reflective qualities of the vehicle surfaces. Furthermore, it is as important to see as it is to be seen; therefore, windshields, windows and the surfaces of all lighting devices should be cleaned as often as is necessary to guarantee their utmost utility in preventing vehicle accidents.

F

Brakes and braking distances

The most important safety feature of any motor vehicle is its braking system—its ability to stop and thereby avoid a collision or accident. This appendix describes in general terms how brakes stop a vehicle, why some stops are longer than others, what "good" brakes are, and finally reports on actual braking distances.

How Brakes Stop a Vehicle

A moving vehicle possesses kinetic (moving) energy which must be dissipated before it can stop. Occasionally this is done by crushing and bending metal in a collision—more usually it is done by applying the brakes.

Braking depends on two friction points at which kinetic energy is dissipated. These are (1) the area of contact between the brake shoes and the brake drums, and (2) the area of contact between the tires and the road surface. As the brake shoes press harder and harder against the brake drums, more and more energy is used up by generating heat and wearing the shoes, and the wheel turns slower and slower. If the pressure is great enough, the wheel may stop turning before the vehicle stops, and the tire will then start to slide on the roadway. This is called "locking the wheels," or "making a locked-wheel stop."

'LOCKED-WHEEL STOPS'
Once the wheel starts to slide, additional pressure on the brake shoes does not affect the rate of stopping. If the roadway surface is very slippery (glare ice, for instance), very little pressure on the shoes will be required to lock the wheels. If the surface has very good gripping ability (the sharp-edged metal grids used on inspection station brake testers, for instance), it may be nearly impos-

349

LOCKED WHEEL STOP. Friction between tire and road determines stopping distance.

sible to lock the wheels.

If the wheels lock, the friction between the tire and the road determines the length of the stop. There is a constant relation between the weight and the retarding force. Thus a heavy vehicle produces a greater retarding force than a lighter one. This keeps constant the stopping distance due to friction.

This gripping ability of the road surface is usually called the "coefficient of friction." It is measured by the amount of drag (or retarding force) it puts on the vehicle, and is expressed as a proportion of the vehicle's weight. A heavy vehicle bears down harder than a light one, and the drag is correspondingly greater. A road with a coefficient of friction of 0.50 (or 50 per cent) will produce a drag of 1,500 pounds on a vehicle

weighing 3,000 pounds, but the same road will produce a drag of 2,500 pounds on a vehicle weighing 5,000 pounds (providing wheels lock in both cases).

IF WHEELS DON'T LOCK

If the wheels do not lock, then the friction between the shoes and the drum determine the stop. Thus it would be quite useless to test brakes on ice—for the poorest brakes would lock the wheels and the stopping distance would be determined by the gripping power of the ice.

That is why it is equally foolish to say that a vehicle would stop in a specific number of feet, without first knowing the gripping power of the road surface, and a number of other factors.

When the wheels do not lock and slide, friction in the brakes

350

absorbs all the energy of the moving vehicle—an important difference from the locked-wheel stop. Thus, the pressure between the sliding brake surfaces has nothing to do with the weight of the vehicle.

Each individual brake may produce a different drag, but added together they represent the total retarding force on the vehicle. This total drag depends on the number of brakes, the size of the lining surfaces, the kind of lining, and the force applied to the shoes to push against the drums.

Total drag can be spoken of as a percentage of the weight of the vehicle. Since it depends in the final analysis on the driver who controls the application of the brake, the percentage will change from zero (when the brake is not applied) to a maximum when the driver is fully applying the brake.

This maximum will change *as a percentage* as the weight of the vehicle changes. Thus, if the maximum drag that can be developed by a particular set of brakes and a particular driver is 2,000 pounds and the vehicle weighs 4,000 pounds, the total braking effort is 50 per cent. It would be impossible to lock the wheels on a road surface with a coefficient of friction over 0.50. If the weight of this vehicle is increased to 8,000 pounds, however, the braking effort will not increase beyond the former 2,000 pounds and the percentage of braking effort will fall to 25 per cent. It would then be impossible to lock the wheels on a

road with a coefficient of more than 0.25.

Factors That Affect Stopping

A number of factors, other than the brakes themselves, affect stopping—the coefficient of friction between tires and road, the speed of the vehicle, the slope of the road, and the method that brakes are applied.

COEFFICIENT OF FRICTION

The coefficient of friction is low for slippery surfaces, being 0.10 or even 0.05 on glare ice. Packed snow may be as low or 0.20. A gravel road may be 0.65, while the best road surfaces may range up to 0.80 or even approach 0.90.

Many factors affect the coefficient of friction. Major ones are:

1. Water on the surface is the most important factor. On cement concrete (particularly with oil drippings on the surface) or on many bituminous surfaces, water may increase braking distances by one-third or more, particularly at high speeds. On gravel or cinders, water may sometimes shorten stopping distances.

2. Speed is another important factor. At 40 or 50 mph, some pavements (especially when wet) have only half the coefficient of friction which they have at ten miles per hour. Speeds affect the gripping ability of gravel, cinders, snow, ice, or muddy pavements very little, however.

3. Tires do not have as much effect as one might think. Smooth treads decrease gripping ability slightly on ordinary pavements, with the greatest decrease on wet surfaces. Snow tires reduce stopping distances on ice or snow by slightly over 10 per cent.

4. Chains on ice or snow will roughly double the coefficient of friction. There is a difference between various kinds of chains, however, with reinforced chains being the best.

5. Temperature has a slight effect on the gripping ability of dry road surfaces, but this is not important except when bituminous surfaces begin to melt and bleed, thereby reducing the coefficient of friction. On snow or ice, however, temperature has an extremely important effect. Stopping distance tests from 20 mph on glare ice, for example, have shown an average braking distance of 120 feet at temperatures near zero, increasing to an average of 225 feet near 32° F. At near-freezing temperatures, the ice is coated with a film of water.

6. Foreign material on the surface may change the coefficient. Loose gravel rolls on a hard surface and halves the gripping ability. Dirt on the pavement may have no effect when dry, but at the first sprinkle of rain, it may act like a film of soap on the road. Oil drippings on concrete pavements, when they are first wet, may make the pavement more slippery than many wet asphalt pavements. On the other hand, dirt or cinders are spread on ice to increase the coefficient of friction.

7. Texture of the pavement surface is important. Gritty cement concrete, made with sharp-edged aggregate, or given a "broomed" finish, is much better than a very smooth concrete. The same is true for bituminous pavements. It is unfortunate that the texture of pavements changes with age and wear. Traffic gradually polishes the sharp edges, and also adds oil drippings to reduce the coefficient, as noted above.

EFFECT OF SPEED

The most important factor when stopping a vehicle is the effect of increased speed. The principle involved is a fundamental of physics that says that the kinetic energy of a moving body is in proportion to the square of its speed. Since in braking a motor vehicle the problem is to dissipate the energy of the moving vehicle, a higher speed means more energy to dissipate and hence longer stops. Since this energy is in proportion to the square of the speed, however, the braking distance also is in proportion to the square of the speed—twice the speed means four times as far to stop, and three times the speed means nine times as far to stop.

This is a theoretical relationship. Actual tests at high speeds have shown that braking distances for average cars were even greater than this would indicate. Thus, while a calculated distance for 90-mph stop was slightly over 400 feet, the actual stop was substantially over 500 feet. The difference probably represents a loss of efficiency for the brakes over the long period of full application.

SLOPE OF THE ROAD

If the vehicle is going downhill, braking distances are increased (until they reach the slope represented by the braking effort as a percentage of the weight of the car, in which case the car will not stop at all). Stopping distances are reduced if the car is going uphill.

For practical purposes, the percentage grade may be added to the percentage braking effort or coefficient of friction for an up-grade and subtracted for a slope down to get the resultant stopping effort on the vehicle. For example, if a car can stop on the level in 25 feet from 20 mph, it has a braking effort of 53.5 per cent of its weight. Going down a 10 per cent grade subtracts 10 per cent from this braking effort which gives 43.5 per cent. With this new figure the braking distance increases to about 31 feet.

APPLYING THE BRAKES

So far the stopping of a vehicle has been considered simply as though the brakes locked the wheels or not. Actually, the wheels will not all work exactly together, and one may slide while the others do not, or one may slide before the others. It is usually stated that the best and quickest stop is made when the wheels are all at the point of impending skid. The various coefficients are believed to be highest at this point.

The conventional brake application is made by the driver who pushes on a foot pedal and exerts pressure on the brake shoes through hydraulic lines. A heavy man can exert more pressure than a slight woman, and hence can create more retarding force.

On buses and trucks, and on some passenger cars, some form of power brakes is used. Some use engine vacuum, some compressed air, and some electricity—but all depend finally on brake shoes pressing against a drum. The basic principles are not changed. It is important to note, however, that on big vehicles there frequently is a time lag between movement of the brake pedal and application of the brakes which adds considerably to their total stopping distance.

What Are 'Good' Brakes?

There are several ways of judging the quality of brakes (1) in relation to legal requirements; (2) in comparison with the average for other vehicles; or (3) in terms of the greatest possible safety.

LEGALLY ACCEPTABLE BRAKES

Most state laws set definite standards which brakes must meet in order that vehicles may be legally operated on the public highways. These standards may be in terms of a rate of deceleration or in feet to stop from a given speed, usually 20 mph.

The best current thinking on the subject is contained in the 1962 Revision of the "Uniform Vehicle Code," Chapter 12, Sections 12–302 to 12–305, inclusive.

353

Excerpts from Uniform Vehicle Code
1962 Rev., Chapter 12

Sec. 12–302—Performance Ability of Brakes

(a) Every motor vehicle and combination of vehicles, at all times and under all conditions of loading, upon application of the service brake, shall be capable of:

   1. Developing a braking force that is not less than the percentage of its gross weight tabulated herein for its classification,

   2. Decelerating to a stop from not more than 20 miles per hour at not less than the feet per second tabulated herein for its classification, and

   3. Stopping from a speed of 20 miles per hour in not more than the distance tabulated herein for its classification, such distance to be measured from the point at which movement of the service brake pedal or control begins. [See the table on page 356.]

(b) Tests for deceleration and stopping distance shall be made on a substantially level (not to exceed plus or minus one per cent grade), dry, smooth, hard surface that is free from loose material. (SECTION REVISED, TABLE REVISED AND AMPLIFIED, 1962; TABLE REVISED, 1968.)*

* (a) There is a definite mathematical relationship between the figures in columns 2 and 3. If the decelerations set forth in column 3 are divided by 32.3 feet per second per second, the column 2 figures will be obtained. (For example, 17 divided by 32.2 gives 52.8 per cent. Column 2 is included in the tabulation because certain brake-testing devices utilize this factor.

(b) The decelerations as in column 3 are an indication of the effectiveness of the basic brakes, and as measured in practical brake testing are the maximum braking decelerations attained at some time during the stop.

This deceleration as measured in brake tests cannot be used to compute the values in column 4 because it is not sustained at the same rate over the entire period of the stop. The deceleration increases from zero to a maximum during a period of brake system application and brake force build-up. Also, other factors may cause the deceleration to decrease after reaching a maximum. The added distance which results because a maximum deceleration is not sustained is included in the figures in column 4 but is not indicated by the usual brake-testing devices for checking deceleration.

(c) The distances in column 4 and the deceleration in column 3 are not directly related. "Brake system application and braking distance in feet" (column 4) is a definite measure of the overall effectiveness of the braking system, being the distance traveled between the point at which the driver starts to move the braking controls and the point at which the vehicle comes to rest. It includes distance traveled while the brakes are being applied and the distance traveled while the brakes are retarding the vehicle.

(d) The distance traveled during the period of brake system application and brake force build-up varies with vehicle type, being negligible for many passenger cars and greatest for combinations of commercial vehicles. This fact accounts for the variation from 25 to 50 feet in the numerical values in column 4 for the various classes of vehicles.

(e) The deceleration requirement in column 3 is the same for all classifications of vehicles except for passenger vehicles, not including buses, because brakes on vehicles in the second, third, and fourth classifications are all capable with reasonable maintenance of producing the designated deceleration as measured by brake-testing devices. A higher deceleration requirement is warranted for passenger cars in view of Bureau of Public Roads test data.

Sec. 12–303—Maintenance of Brakes

All brakes shall be maintained in good working order and shall be so adjusted as to operate as equally as practicable with respect to the wheels on opposite sides of the vehicle.

Sec. 12–304—Hydraulic Brake Fluid

(a) The term "hydraulic brake fluid" as used in this section shall mean the liquid medium through which force is transmitted to the brakes in the hydraulic brake system of a vehicle.

(b) Hydraulic brake fluid shall be distributed and serviced with due regard for the safety of the occupants of the vehicle and the public.

(c) The (department or official) shall, after public hearing following due notice, adopt and enforce regulations for the administration of this section and shall adopt and publish standards and specifications for hydraulic brake fluid which shall correlate with, and so far as practicable conform to, the then current standards and specifications of the Society of Automotive Engineers applicable to such fluid.

(d) No person shall distribute, have for sale, offer for sale, or sell any hydraulic brake fluid unless it complies with the requirements of this section. No person shall service any vehicle with brake fluid unless it complies with the requirements of this section.** (REVISED, 1962; SECTION RENUMBERED, 1968.)

(e) Subsections (c) and (d) shall not apply to petroleum base fluids used in vehicles with brake systems designed to use them. (NEW, 1971.)   *Footnote starts on next page.*

PERFORMANCE ABILITY OF BRAKES

	Classification of Vehicles	*Braking force as a percentage of gross vehicle or combination weight*	*Deceleration in feet per second per second*	*Brake system application and braking distance in feet from an initial speed of 20 m.p.h.*
	1	*2*	*3*	*4*
A	**Passenger vehicles** with a seating capacity of 10 people or less including driver, not having a manufacturer's gross vehicle weight rating	52.8	17	25
B	**Single-unit vehicles** with a manufacturer's gross vehicle weight rating of 10,000 pounds or less	43.5	14	30
C-1	**Single-unit vehicles** with a manufacturer's gross weight rating of more than 10,000 pounds	43.5	14	40
C-2	**Combination** of a two-axle˝ towing vehicle and a trailer with a gross trailer weight of 3,000 pounds or less	43.5	14	40
C-3	**Buses,** regardless of the number of axles, not having a manufacturer's gross weight rating	43.5	14	40
C-4	**All combinations** of vehicles in driveaway-towaway operations	43.5	14	40
D	**All other** vehicles and combinations of vehicles	43.5	14	50

** Subsection (c) requires the adoption of brake fluid specifications based on current SAE standards if such conformance with those standards is practicable. In connection with this provision, it should be noted that a federal motor vehicle safety standard establishing standards for hydraulic brake fluid is in effect under the National Traffic and Motor Vehicle Safety Act of 1966. See Motor Vehicle Safety Standard No. 116, as added to 49 *Code of Federal Regulations* Part 371 by 34 *Federal Register* 113–15 (Jan. 4, 1969). Previously, this Standard appeared in 15 *Code of Federal Regulations* Part 6, and was originally issued under a 1962 Act of Congress. See 15 USC §§ 1301–1303, 76 Stat. 437 (1962), which was repealed in 1966 by § 117 of the National Traffic and Motor Vehicle Safety Act, 15 USCA § 1405 (Supp. 1967). However, the 1966 Act continued the brake fluid standards issued under the 1962 Act and gave them the same effect as if they had been issued under the 1966 Act.

As previously noted, when a federal motor vehicle safety standard is in effect, a state may not establish or continue in effect a standard "which is not identical to the federal standard" as to the "same aspect of performance" of the equipment—in this instance, brake fluid. 15 USCA § 1392(d). See footnotes 1 and 4, *supra,* in this chapter. For these reasons and in the interest of consistency and effectiveness of action by the states, current SAE and federal standards should be considered in the administrative formulation of appropriate brake fluid standards.

It is also recommended that consideration be given to requiring, in the regulations, an appropriate label on any container of brake fluid indicating the pertinent SAE and federal standards which have been met or exceeded. In this connection, consideration should also be given to duplicating any labeling requirement that might be specified in future federal motor vehicle safety standards.

In addition, the auxiliary brake must be able to hold the vehicle or combination of vehicles stationary under any condition of loading on any up or down grade upon which it is operated. The brake shoes in or on the wheel drums may be used for both the service brake and the hand brake.

The longer distances allowed for heavier vehicles reflect actual road tests, which have shown that while the same or nearly the same rate of deceleration could be developed, the factor of brake lag made the total stopping distance greater.

AVERAGE BRAKES

In 1948 and 1949, the U.S. Bureau of Public Roads tested more than 1,200 vehicles selected from everyday traffic. These tests showed an average stopping distance of 21 feet (from 20 mph) for hydraulic brake passenger cars. They also showed that 85 per cent of such vehicles could stop in 25 feet or less. Table F-2 reports findings of the Bureau for passenger cars and commercial vehicles, at speeds from 20 mph up, showing both the *average* performance and the performance achieved by 85 per cent of the vehicles checked.

WHAT ARE SAFE BRAKES?

With present speeds and traffic volumes what they are, the motor-vehicle owner must not think about the stopping ability of his vehicle

357

COMPARISON OF MEASURES OF BRAKING PERFORMANCE

TABLE F-1

Braking Effort (as per cent of car weight) or Deceleration (as per cent of acceleration of gravity—32.2 ft per sec²)	Deceleration		Stopping (from 20 mph—29.3 feet per sec)		Quality of Braking (general terms—passenger cars only)	Maximum Slope (on which vehicle will stand)		Coefficient of Friction (per cent)
	(feet per second per second)	(miles per hour per second)	Braking Distance (in feet)	Time (seconds)		Angle from Horizontal (deg.)	Per Cent Grade (feet per 100 feet)	
110.0	35.4	24.2	12.2	0.83	Dangerous	48	110.0	110.0
100.0	32.2	22.0	13.4	0.91	Violent	45	100.0	100.0
90.0	29.0	19.8	14.9	1.01	Uncomfortable	42	90.0	90.0
80.0	25.8	17.6	16.7	1.14	EXCEPTIONAL	39	80.0	80.0
75.0	24.2	16.5	17.8	1.22	EXCELLENT	37	75.0	75.0
70.0	22.6	15.4	19.1	1.30	GOOD	35	70.0	70.0
66.9	21.5	14.7	20.0	1.36	GOOD	34	66.9	66.9
60.0	19.3	13.2	22.3	1.52	AVERAGE	31	60.0	60.0
53.5	17.2	11.8	25.0	1.70	FAIR	28	53.5	53.5
50.0	16.1	11.0	26.8	1.82	UNLAWFUL	27	50.0	50.0
44.6	14.3	9.8	30.0	2.05	UNLAWFUL	24	44.6	44.6
40.0	12.9	8.8	33.5	2.28	Dangerous	22	40.0	40.0
30.0	9.7	6.6	44.6	3.04	Dangerous	17	30.0	30.0
20.0	6.4	4.4	67.0	4.56	Dangerous	11	20.0	20.0
10.0	3.2	2.2	134.0	9.12	Dangerous	6	10.0	10.0
5.0	1.6	1.1	268.0	18.25	Dangerous	3	5.0	5.0

VEHICLE STOPPING DISTANCES

(Passenger cars and commercial vehicles operated in everyday traffic, for various speeds—in feet)

Performance Level and Vehicle Type	Vehicle Stopping Distances From Speeds of—							
	20 mph	30 mph	40 mph	50 mph	60 mph	70 mph	80 mph	90 mph
Average Performance:								
Passenger cars (hydraulic brakes)	21	42	76	122	191	289	397	542
2-axle trucks	35	81	147	224				
3- and 4-axle combinations	49	113	206	314				
5- and 6-axle combinations	59	124	218	342				
85-Percentile Performance:								
Passenger cars (hydraulic brakes)	25	55	108	188	300	453	650	900
2-axle trucks	45	107	207	350				
3- and 4-axle combinations	57	131	262	445				
5- and 6-axle combinations	67	141	255	416				

SOURCE: U.S. Bureau of Public Roads

either in terms of the law or with respect to average performance, but rather as a matter of safety. Modern motor vehicles should be able to make good use of the gripping ability of pavements. Since ordinary pavements have co-efficients of friction of 70 per cent or more, brakes should be able to give a drag equal to 70 per cent of the weight of the vehicle. This is the basis on which the general terms describing braking performance in Table F-1 have been developed.

Brakes are rated as fair when they will just barely pass the "Uniform Code" requirements.

Brakes can be built which will give as much as 110 per cent of the vehicle's weight in stopping effort. There is little advantage in such powerful brakes, however, because tires and pavements will not match them. Furthermore, on pavements which do have a very high coefficient of friction, such strong brakes may stop the vehicle with dangerous suddenness. Passengers slide off the seats and in lunging forward, sometimes injure themselves; children, in particular, may be hurt because their legs are too short to brace against the foot rests. Quick stops will also seriously shift loads in trucks. This is particularly true of liquids in tanks, furniture, lumber, pipes, and steel beams.

If the brakes lock only the

STOPPING DISTANCES

Miles per Hour	Feet per Second	Driver Reaction Distance¹	Passenger Cars Vehicle Braking Distance²	Passenger Cars Total Stopping Distance³	Light 2-Axle Trucks Vehicle Braking Distance²	Light 2-Axle Trucks Total Stopping Distance³	Heavy 2-Axle Trucks Vehicle Braking Distance²	Heavy 2-Axle Trucks Total Stopping Distance³	3-Axle Trucks and Combinations Vehicle Braking Distance²	3-Axle Trucks and Combinations Total Stopping Distance³
10	15	11	6	17	7	18	10	21	13	24
15	22	17	14	31	17	34	22	39	29	46
20	29	22	25	47	30	52	40	62	50	72
25	37	28	39	67	46	74	64	92	80	108
30	44	33	55	88	67	100	92	125	115	148
35	51	39	78	117	92	131	125	164	160	199
40	59	44	105	149	125	169	165	209	205	249
45	66	50	136	186	165	215	210	260	260	310
50	73	55	188	243	225	280	255	310	320	375
55	81	61	230	291	275	336	310	371	390	451
60	88	66	300	366	360	426	370	436	465	531
65	95	72	380	452						
70	103	77	455	532						

¹ Driver reaction distance based on reaction time of ¾ second, typical for most drivers under most traffic conditions.

² Vehicle braking distance based on provisions of the Uniform Vehicle Code for 20 mph, adjusted where necessary at higher speeds to conform to studies of the U.S. Bureau of Public Roads.

³ If perception time is determined to be an appreciable factor for a particular situation, the distance traveled during this time should be added to the total stopping distance. After estimating perception time, the corresponding distance may be determined by reference to the second column which shows the feet traveled per second at the original speed.

NOTE: These tables developed for educational rather than legal or engineering purposes.

front wheels so that they slide on the pavement, the possibility of steering to avoid an accident is lost because the vehicle slides straight ahead. If the rear wheels only are locked, however, the vehicle tends to turn end for end in a flat spin. Worse than this is the situation in which one side of the car, due to differences in the pavement or in the brakes, has a greater drag than the other. The car has a tendency to slide around toward whichever side has the greater drag. To prevent dangerous pivoting, brakes must be approximately equal on both sides of the vehicle. The stronger the brakes are, the more important is their equalization. The total braking effort on one side of the car should not be permitted to exceed that on the other side by more than 30 per cent, 10 per cent is preferable, and more than 50 per cent difference presents a distinct hazard.

Brakes may be rated as excellent if they give a total drag up to about 80 per cent of the car's weight, which means a stopping distance of 17 or 18 feet from 20 mph. Beyond that, the hazards of quick stopping and loss of steering ability offset the advantages of stronger brakes.

Cars with only two-wheel brakes, or trucks with brakeless trailers, simply cannot have stopping performance satisfactory for high-speed traffic. From the safety standpoint, such vehicles are always poor. Because of the economic disturbances that would oc- cur if such vehicles were barred from the highways, laws (at least for a few years) must permit them to remain until they are practically worn out, but this does not reduce their danger, particularly when they are driven at speeds in excess of 25 mph.

Driver Perception Time

Perception time is the time it takes the driver to perceive a dangerous situation after it could have been perceived. If a driver is intently watching the stop light of the car ahead and it comes on bright red he will perceive it almost instantly and, for practical purposes, this perception time is zero. If, however, he is looking at scenery off to the side of the road when the stop light comes on, and only two seconds later, as he looks ahead again, he sees the light, his perception time is two seconds.

Perception time varies tremendously with circumstances. It is very closely connected to attention. Alert drivers have shorter perception times than those who let their attention wander. A driver who is usually quick to perceive may, if distracted by something especially interesting to him, experience a dangerously long perception time. It is not practical, therefore, to embody the distance traveled during perception time in tables of stopping distances of vehicles from various speeds. Table F-3 includes distances traveled during an average reaction time (¾ of a second) when stopping from various speeds. These figures provide some idea of how much distance might have to be added for perception time to the total stopping distances shown in the tables.

Driver Reaction Time

So far, only the *slowing* distance has been considered, and has been referred to as the *braking* distance. It is the distance required for the vehicle to stop from the time the brake is applied. Unfortunately, no driver can apply the brake instantly upon seeing a hazard; time is required for him to see or hear, to think and to act. This "reaction" time varies greatly in different individuals, and for the same individual under different conditions but most of the reactions in driving require between one-half second and one second. A figure of three-fourths second is commonly used. The distance traveled—reaction distance—must be added to the braking distance to give total stopping distance.

Stopping Distance Charts

It is quite impossible to develop any simple table or chart that will tell how far it will take a vehicle to stop. So many factors enter into any particular stop that the chart could not possibly fit all possible combinations.

A stopping distance chart serves a useful purpose only as an educational tool to help explain the general problems of speed and stopping distance to drivers. As such, a chart usually shows average

362

figures. Such a chart is of no value to an engineer or a police officer trying to study a particular accident, for the chance that a particular case would be *average* in all aspects is so remote as to be not worthy of a second thought.

The generally accepted tables of average reaction, braking and total stopping distances agreed upon by several national organizations is shown as Table F-3 for passenger cars, light 2-axle trucks, heavy 2-axle trucks, and 3-axle trucks and combinations respectively. Note that this is not under any circumstances to be taken as indicating stopping distances for a specific vehicle under specific conditions.

Further Data

For more information on the performance of brakes on vehicles in actual use, see *Braking Performance of Motor Vehicles,* a report of a comprehensive brake testing project of the U.S. Bureau of Public Roads, available from the Superintendent of Documents, U.S. Government Printing Office, Washington, D.C. 20402.

Model legislation is contained in the Uniform Vehicle Code, available from the National Committee on Uniform Traffic Laws and Ordinances, 1319 18th Street NW., Washington 6, D.C.

The mathematical formulas for calculating deceleration, stopping distances, stopping time, and kinetic energy may be found in most any physics textbook or engineering handbook.

G

The driver and preventive maintenance

Preventive maintenance—the scientific care that guarantees top dependability and maximum life to all vehicles—requires carefully planned inspections by the maintenance department at regular mileage or time intervals, followed by immediate attention to all reported defects. These inspections combine well-balanced checking procedures with cleaning, tightening, lubricating, and adjusting of parts and units.

Actually, preventive maintenance is the best known, simplest, and most economical means of protecting the original investment in a fleet.

Preventive maintenance depends for its success upon a high degree of cooperation between the driver and the mechanic. Although the mechanic does the work, he depends on the driver to supply him with the information he needs. Because the driver is on the road with the vehicle for a number of hours each day, he alone is in a position to observe the vehicle's performance under all conditions.

By observing these rules, a driver can contribute greatly to the success of the preventive maintenance program.

1. Avoid abusing vehicle in any way.

2. Know the vehicle well enough to make an intelligent vehicle condition report, but do not attempt to diagnose the trouble, just describe accurately what you hear, see, smell, or feel. If you only diagnose the trouble and then you are wrong, it will simply confuse the mechanics.

3. Handle all road failures strictly in accordance with company policy and report them properly.

4. Make a complete inspection of your unit before your trip and do not depart until everything is in good working order. Remember, you have a long way to go before you get back and a breakdown can occur miles away from any source of help. (The next section discusses this.)

5. Try to get along well with your mechanics. A kind word or a pat on the back will help a lot.

6. Never make derogatory remarks about company equipment.

Pretrip Inspection

The driver is always responsible for knowing the mechanical condition of his vehicle. While the maintenance department is responsible for giving the driver a vehicle that is in top mechanical condition, it is the driver who must assure himself at the start of each trip that the vehicle assigned him is in good condition.

The following is a detailed checklist for the pretrip inspection. In practice, however, each fleet should develop its own list and train drivers in its use.

PRECRANK CHECK

1. Check oil in engine crankcase and fill as necessary.

2. Check water in radiator and fill as necessary.

3. Raise hood or cab and check all belts for slippage or excessive wear, or both. Note there are belts on fan, generator, air compressor, and water pump, and that these belts are often not all in one place.

4. Lower and secure hood or cab.

CRANK CHECK

1. Enter cab of tractor and make sure parking brakes are set.

2. Depress clutch and move gearshift lever to neutral position; then check clutch for proper release bearing clearance.

3. With clutch depressed, turn on ignition switch and start engine.

4. Check all instruments—oil, heat, ammeter, and air pressure. Always build up air pressure to full tank capacity before moving vehicle.

5. Check sound of engine and other working parts for peculiar noises.

6. After building proper air pressure, put gearshift lever in the lowest forward gear, set parking brake, and turn off ignition switch. The vehicle should then be secure. (Chock wheels if necessary.) For a diesel engine, pull on parking brake and put gear lever in reverse if it will roll forward, or if it will roll backward, put gearshift lever in lowest forward gear.

7. Check BMCS safety equipment. Required are 3 flare pots (or equivalent), three fusees (or equivalent), two red flags, spare fuses, one fire extinguisher, and tire chains if weather requires them.

8. Adjust seat for proper position.

9. Adjust mirrors for proper vision.

10. Adjust windows for proper ventilation.

11. Check steering wheel. More than 1/4 turn before wheels respond indicates excessive free play.

12. Check accelerator and brake pedals for looseness.

13. Check horn, windshield wipers, heaters, and defroster.

364

LIGHT CHECK

1. Turn on headlights, clearance lights, marker lights, and right-hand turn signal. (On some tractors, the turn signals are connected with the ignition switch and will not work unless it is on.)

2. Check headlights.

3. Reach in tractor, depress head-light beam switch and recheck headlights.

4. Push headlight switch halfway in and check parking lights.

5. As you check headlights, clearance lights, stop lights, tail lights, turn signals, and reflectors, wipe away as much dirt as you can reach with a clean rag. Note any fresh damage to unit, and report same.

6. Check cab lights on tractor.

7. Check clearance and marker lights on right side of trailer. Also check and wipe reflectors on right side, including rear of cab and center of trailer.

8. Check clearance, marker and tail lights and right hand turn signal on rear of trailer. Wipe dirt off all you can reach.

9. Turn off clearance lights, marker light, and parking lights.

10. Check left-hand turn signal on tractor and trailer and wipe off.

11. Check stop lights on tractor and trailer (using a brake tie-down, trailer brake valve, or by enlisting help).

12. Cut off all switches.

GENERAL CHECK

1. Clean windshield and all mirrors.

2. Check right front tractor tire for correct pressure, cuts and bruises, and valve cap.

3. Check for loose wheel nuts and for worn wheel bushings by shaking top of wheel. (This is not too effective, but may reveal a bad situation.)

4. Check front springs, U-bolts, steering knuckles, drag links, and flexible air lines that feed brake chambers.

5. Check under tractor for oil, water, fuel, and air leaks.

6. Check right rear tractor tires for correct pressure, cuts and bruises and rocks between the wheels.

7. Check wheel nuts, axle studs, and valve caps.

8. Check for leaks around fuel tanks and note the amount of fuel in tanks. (Report if low.)

9. Check fifth wheel assembly for looseness or damage.

10. Check rear axle springs, shackles, and U-bolts on both sides.

11. Check flexible air lines between tractor and trailer for leaks or excessive wear.

12. Bleed air tanks on tractor until all visible moisture is removed.

13. Be sure trailer support crank handle is in secure position. Push handle in.

14. Check for any fresh damage to underside of trailer.

15. Check spare tires for condition, proper inflation, and valve caps. If locked, do you have key?

16. Check suspension system on trailer axles (spring, U-bolts, and shackles). If trailer has a gravity suspension system, check gear

365

boxes, torque rods, and suspension brackets.

17. Check trailer brake adjustment on all axles of trailers.

18. Bleed air tanks on trailers if necessary.

19. Check all trailer tires on right side for correct pressure, cuts and bruises, and rocks between the wheels.

20. Check wheel nuts, axle studs, and valve caps on right side. Check to see if trailer doors are secure and check seal. If trailer has open top, be sure canvas cover is secure.

21. Check all trailer tires on left side for correct pressure, cuts and bruises, and rocks between the wheels.

22. Check wheel nuts, axle studs, and valve caps on left side.

23. Check left rear tractor tires for correct pressure, cuts and bruises, and rocks between the wheels.

24. Check wheel nuts, axle stud and valve caps on left side.

25. Check left front tractor tire for correct pressure, cuts and bruises, and valve cap.

26. Check for loose wheel nuts and for worn bushing by shaking at the top of wheel.

27. Check exhaust system for leaks or looseness.

BRAKE AND COUPLING CHECK

1. Bleed air pressure below 50 psi by applying brakes several times. Trailer brakes should be set up at this point.

2. Restart engine and pump up air.

See that trailer brakes release.

3. Locate trailer brake valve lever and open. This applies brakes to trailer only.

4. With trailer brake valve lever open, put gearshift lever in lowest forward gear (see vehicle gearshift diagram). Release parking brake on tractor, and by gently releasing clutch, check coupling between tractor and trailer. This will also check trailer brakes.

5. After checking coupling between tractor and trailer, release trailer brakes by closing trailer brake valve lever. Then release clutch pedal gently. With vehicle in motion, check foot brakes.

6. Pull on tractor parking brakes while stopped and then, by releasing clutch gently, check its holding power. (Do not use lowest gear.)

7. Secure vehicle.

8. Check defect report, noting all defects. (Fill out report even if none is found.) Turn in report to proper official.

The driver should be given two clean wiping rags for use during this inspection: one for oil and grease cleanup and the other for wiping windshield and lights.

The inspection procedure can be organized in progressive fashion (instead of by system, as shown here) to save making successive trips around the unit. For instance, by using a brake tie-down, the one-minute air check can be made while checking lights and wheels, and thus show up any audible leaks.

H

Skill drills and test courses

Skill drills and test courses are used to train new drivers as well as to test the skills of trained drivers.

This course is based on the National Truck Roadeo of the American Trucking Associations, Inc. 1616 "P" Street, N.W., Washington, D.C. 20036. Copies of the book, *The Company Roadeo,* may be ordered from its Department of Safety.

The Roadeo is designed to determine, through a series of challenging competitive events, the contestant's knowledge of safety, courtesy, efficiency, first aid, and driving skill. In addition to being a testing and training device, the Roadeo serves as a community goodwill project and promotes better employee relations.

Preliminary tests consist of a written examination on the trucking industry, safe driving rules, first aid, and fire fighting. The contestant is then given a personal interview to judge his attitude, general appearance and self expression. Following the interview, an equipment defects test is administered to grade his ability to properly conduct a pretrip inspection of his vehicle. Lastly, he competes in the field test course, which is a series of driving problems simulating everyday operating conditions.

Some of these skill tests in a typical Roadeo are described below. They can be changed to suit the training situation, and additional problems may be added.

A general layout of a test course is shown on the next page. Dimensions can be adjusted to fit the size and type of vehicle that is being driven.

Parallel Parking

The object of this test is to determine the driver's ability to park parallel to a simulated curb as in making a curbside street delivery, or in moving the unit off to the side of the road.

367

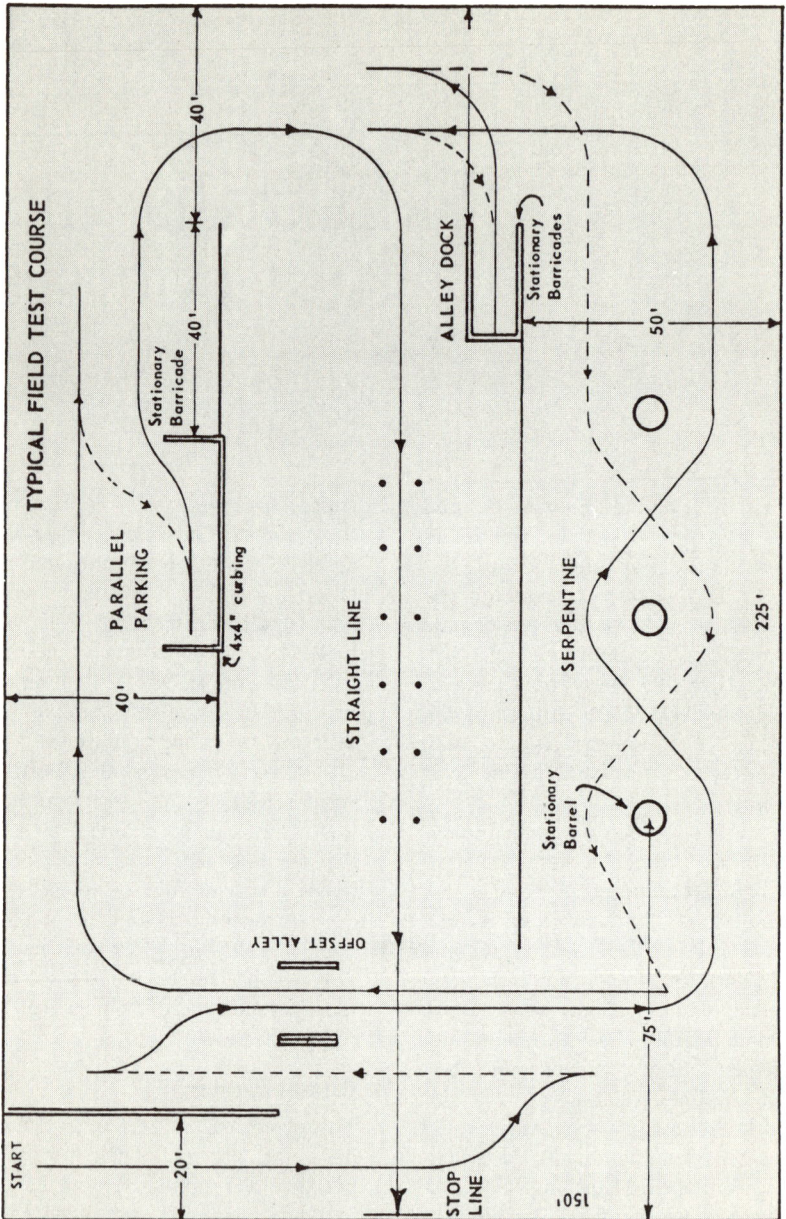

A TYPICAL FIELD TEST COURSE. Dimensions indicate placement of problem to accommodate largest class of vehicles. Scale of plan is about 1 inch = 35 feet.

Alley Dock

This test determines the driver's ability to back his vehicle into a narrow space and stop with the rear of the vehicle within a specified distance under conditions simulating backing into a dock or shipping platform between two other vehicles in a street or yard area of limited width.

Offset Alley

This test determines the driver's ability to maneuver, judge distances at all points on the vehicle, and to control his speed while maneuvering in a continuous forward motion through a confined space, simulating the avoidance of parked vehicles and maneuvering through narrow alleys.

Forward Serpentine

In this test, the driver's ability to maneuver his vehicle in and out of tight places in forward movement is tested. It is designed to simulate conditions which might be encountered when: disabled or wrecked vehicles partially block a highway; in negotiating detours; moving in heavy traffic; or in similar situations. In the skill drill, the driver must drive around drums or barrels arranged somewhat like a slalom run for skiers.

Backward Serpentine

This test is similar to the above, except that vehicle movement is backward. It is designed to test the driver's ability to back his vehicle into narrow parking places.

Straight Line

This test challenges the ability of the driver to accurately judge the position of the right wheels of his vehicle and to steer the vehicle in a straight line. It simulates conditions in which the driver must keep as far to the right as possible as on narrow streets and highways when meeting on-coming traffic. It helps him to gauge distances on the right-hand side of the pavement to avoid running off onto a highway shoulder with the resultant danger of loss of control, tire abuse, and the "dusting" of the following traffic.

Stop Line

Here the driver's ability to judge the position of his front bumper with respect to a fixed line is challenged. This problem simulates the conditions encountered in stopping at a marked crosswalk, or a situation in which it is advantageous for the driver to pull as far forward as possible in close quarters without hitting a stationary object or vehicle.

369

I

Carbon monoxide dangers

Carbon monoxide, a gas composed of one atom each of carbon and oxygen (CO), is formed by incomplete combustion of oil or gasoline (or other carbonaceous materials) and is found in exhaust gases from internal combustion engines. It is a dangerous gas because, when breathed, it combines with the hemoglobin of blood (found in the red corpuscles) and crowds out the oxygen that must be carried to body tissues. Lack of oxygen (anoxia) first affects the brain and the nervous system, and then finally poisons the entire body.

Carbon monoxide gas is non-irritating, colorless, and tasteless, and has no odor except in very high concentrations. It must not be confused with carbon dioxide, CO_2 (used to make dry ice and to put the bubbles in soda water), which will suffocate, but not combine with hemoglobin in the subtle way that CO does.

Carbon monoxide is also flammable and is a serious fire and explosion hazard in concentrations higher than those that can kill. (Explosive limits in air are from 12.5 to 74.2 per cent, by volume.)

Because its specific gravity is so close to that of air (0.967: 1.000), CO mixes readily with air. Once it is breathed into the lungs, however, CO is picked up and retained by the blood in preference to oxygen. The affinity of hemoglobin for CO is about 300 times that for oxygen.

If the victim of carbon monoxide poisoning can be given fresh air or oxygen in time—before too much brain or nervous system damage can occur—the hemoglobin will slowly free itself of CO and then resume its normal function.

Symptoms
Symptoms depend on the per cent saturation of hemoglobin with CO.

370

This saturation depends on the victim's degree of activity, the duration of his exposure, the air temperature, his health, and his metabolic efficiency.

Even over a prolonged period, hemoglobin can only absorb a proportion of the CO in the atmosphere. For example, if the ratio is 100 parts CO to one million parts of air (100 ppm), the hemoglobin can only hold 17 per cent CO and 83 per cent oxygen. At this concentration, there are no visible symptoms of poisoning. However, disturbances of coordination, judgment, psychomotor reactions, and visual acuity appear. This is why a leaky exhaust system that permits even the slightest amount of CO to leak into the cab is so dangerous.

If the ratio is 200 ppm, hemoglobin will hold up to about 20 per cent CO. Symptoms of mild poisoning will now appear in a few hours.

At 1,000 ppm, 60 per cent will be held and a person will drop unconscious in about two hours.

If the CO concentration goes up to 10,000 ppm (1.0 per cent), hemoglobin will hold 90 per cent CO. This produces death in just a few minutes. The relative effects of various concentrations and exposures are charted in the accompanying illustration.

The first symptoms of CO poisoning are:

a. Shortness of breath,
b. Headache,
c. Dizziness,

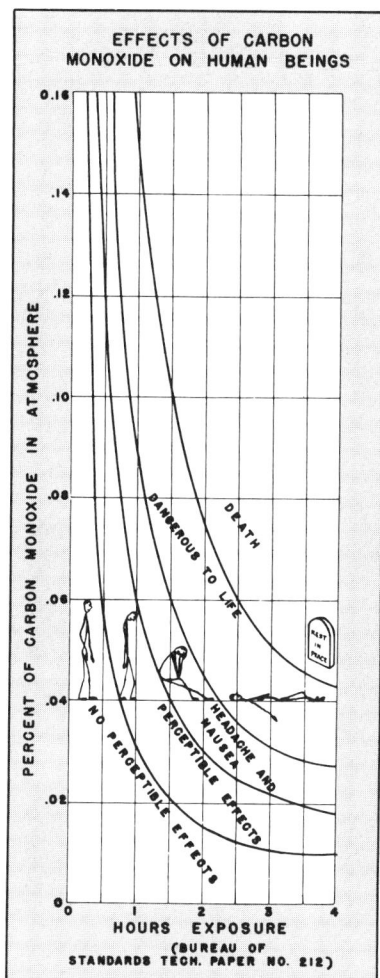

EFFECTS OF CARBON MONOXIDE ON HUMAN BEINGS

CARBON MONOXIDE EFFECTS. How concentration and exposure affect human beings.

d. Muscular weakness, and
e. Nausea.

The compound that CO and hemoglobin form (carboxy-hemoglobin) has a bright cherry-red color. This sometimes gives a red-

371

dish color to the lips, eyelids, ears, and skin of asphyxiated victims. A list of symptoms follows:

SYMPTOMS OF CO POISONING

MILD POISONING

Sensation of tightness across forehead.
Headache.
Nausea.
Dizziness.
Abdominal pains.
Change in disposition, evidenced by irritability, loss of memory, and loss of accuracy.
Occasional hallucinations.
Insomnia.

SEVERE POISONING

Unconsciousness.
Convulsions.
Lockjaw.
Needless movement of arms and legs.
Uncoordinated attempts to crawl or walk.
Aimless talk and muttering.
Accelerated breathing.
Discoloration of skin, usually too bright red.

VERY SEVERE POISONING

Profound coma.
Body chills.
Complete quiescence.
Slow and weak breathing, broken by gasps or no breathing at all.
Pulse rapid and thready.
Uncontrolled urination and defication.
Reflexes gone or hard to stimulate.

THESE SYMPTOMS represent extensive clinical experience and all may not be encountered in every case of poisoning. Those printed in bold face type are the most commonly encountered.

Aftereffects

Occasionally there are also memory disturbances; visual, speech, and hearing disturbances; and even psychosis (losing contact with reality), neuritis (degeneration of the nerves), and paralysis (loss of ability to move). These only result after severe gassing or after the victim has recovered from prolonged unconsciousness.

Usually CO poisoning is followed by an increase in the red cell count. Occasionally, however, anemia (lack of red cells) results. Many authorities believe that if anemia follows CO gassing, it results *not* from the CO, but rather from other vapors (such as benzene or unburned gasoline) or from already existing bodily condition that the lack of oxygen (anoxia) aggravates.

If a recovered victim develops pneumonia, this is probably due to saliva, infected mucus, vomitus, or other foreign material that entered his respiratory tract when he was unconscious.

The slowing of circulation and respiration that follows gassing contributes to the development of pneumonia.

Infrequently, heart ailments follow CO gassing. This may be due to weakness of the heart muscle created by the period of anoxia. Many authorities feel, on the other hand, that anoxia may merely aggravate a preexisting weakness.

Protection

Prevention of CO poisoning depends on three variables, listed in order of effectiveness.

1. Prevent the formation of the gas either by not creating it in the first place, or by changing it to an innocuous compound once it is formed.
2. Ventilate sufficiently to keep concentrations low, and
3. Have personnel wear protective equipment.

Unless special catalytic afterburners and unleaded gasoline are used, carbon monoxide cannot be eliminated from the exhaust of internal combustion engines. CO can be kept from inside the driving area by keeping vehicles well maintained and by keeping exhaust systems in good repair. In garages, the most practical method is to carry away exhaust gases.

Time-weighted average CO concentrations should never exceed 50 ppm for an 8-hour exposure, or 400 ppm for a 1-hour exposure. In both cases, the atmosphere must contain at least 19 per cent oxygen, by volume. (Air usually contains 20.8 per cent oxygen.)

These are maximum levels. Exhaust systems should be designed to keep levels even lower. Local exhausts that remove combustion gases at the source are preferred, but general ventilation will also control the CO level.

Garage air should be sampled periodically to make sure CO levels do not exceed safe limits. Commercially available portable testing devices utilizing National Bureau of Standards Colorometer Gel are

convenient to use. It is very important that air samples be truly representative of the air that workmen actually breathe all day.

If concentrations exceed these maximums and cannot be reduced, persons must be protected by personal protective equipment. The U.S. Bureau of Mines has approved only three types (for CO use):

1. Self-contained breathing apparatus and hose masks with blowers located in an uncontaminated atmosphere are approved where there is also an oxygen deficiency.
2. Type D masks (specific for CO) and Type N masks (universal) are not approved for concentrations exceeding 2 per cent (20,000 ppm).

The hose mask and blower combination is suited for work in a contaminated atmosphere. Self-contained breathing apparatus is, at best, useful for two hours, and is only used for rescue work. The gas mask is used only for escape.

Mask canisters have a limited operating life. A record of the time each canister is used should be kept with the canister. Some devices will measure the intake volume on each canister and indicate its expected life.

Education and Supervision
Proper education of employees and good supervision are important to protecting personnel from CO poisoning. Before anyone works in an area of probable contamination, he should understand the risk, know CO poisoning symptoms, and

know what to do if he or a buddy is overcome.

He should know how to give first aid and how to use the respiratory devices.

Only experienced supervisors should be in charge of men working in CO-contaminated areas. Supervisors, in turn, must be well supervised.

First Aid

The following first-aid procedures are recommended.

1. The patient should be removed immediately from the contaminated area to an area free from the gas and comfortably warm.

2. If breathing has stopped, or is weak, or consists only of occasional gasps, artificial respiration should be administered until normal breathing is resumed.

3. A physician should be called as soon as possible.

4. Regardless of the apparent severity of the exposure, oxygen should be administered as soon as possible, with artificial respiration if it is necessary. Pure oxygen (O_2) is preferred, but if a CO_2/O_2 mixture is used, it should be administered only by someone especially trained in its use.

5. It is extremely important to keep the patient warm and out of drafts. Blankets may be used to maintain body temperature. External heat sources such as hot water bottles or heating pads should be used with extreme caution. Very severe burns and blisters can be produced on an unconscious body by heat sources that seem quite cool to the person applying them.

6. The victim should be kept at rest, lying down, to prevent a strain on his heart. As an aid to circulation, his body can be inclined, head down, at a slight angle. He should be treated as a convalescent and given plenty of time to rest and recuperate.

7. The aftereffects of CO poisoning should be treated symptomatically by a physician. They may be serious enough to warrant hospitalization.

Industrial medical facilities near garages, terminals, and other areas where there is danger of CO poisoning should be equipped to test blood samples. Often, the serious results of CO poisoning can be anticipated and prevented if CO concentration in the blood is known. Spectroscopic, colorimetric, or the pyrotannic method is used.

J

Occupational Safety and Health Act (OSHAct)

The Occupational Safety and Health Act (OSHAct) was signed by the President of the United States on December 29, 1970, and became effective on April 28, 1971. OSHAct requires employers to provide safe places of employment, free from health hazards. It is estimated that over 4,000,000 establishments and more than 57,000,000 workers are covered by OSHAct. The OSHA poster, which must be prominently displayed in places of employment, is shown on the next page.

Administration of OSHAct is the responsibility of the Department of Labor. The provisions of OSHAct are carried out by the regional offices, which maintain area offices in the states under their jurisdiction (see Exhibit J-1).

Commercial vehicle fleets must keep the following OSHA records at each terminal or operat-ing base, or other authorized location. Instructions are printed on the back of each form.

• Log for Calendar Year (Form 100)—Log every injury or illness within six days of occurrence.

• Supplementary Record (Form 101)—Make a report of each injury or illness, available for inspection within six days. Workmen's Compensation or similar reports can be used if they provide the same information required on Form 101. (See pp. 87–88.)

• Annual Summary (Form 102) —Certified summary must be posted at each terminal or operating base by February 1st and remain in place for 30 days.

Record-keeping requirements, pertinent forms, and posters may be obtained from the offices of the Bureau of Labor Statistics (see Exhibit J-1).

375

SAFETY AND HEALTH PROTECTION ON THE JOB

The Williams-Steiger Occupational Safety and Health Act of 1970 provides job safety and health protection for workers. The purpose of the Federal law is to assure safe and healthful working conditions throughout the Nation.

The U.S. Department of Labor has primary responsibility for administering the Act. The Department issues job safety and health standards, and employers and employees are required to comply with these standards.

BY LAW: SAFETY ON THE JOB IS EVERYBODY'S RESPONSIBILITY!

EMPLOYERS: The Williams-Steiger Act requires that each employer furnish his employees a place of employment free from recognized hazards that might cause serious injury or death; and the Act further requires that employers comply with the specific safety and health standards issued by the Department of Labor.

EMPLOYEES: The Williams-Steiger Act also requires that each employee comply with safety and health standards, rules, regulations, and orders issued under the Act and applicable to his conduct.

COMPLIANCE WITH SAFETY AND HEALTH REQUIREMENTS

To ensure compliance with safety and health requirements, the U.S. Department of Labor conducts periodic job-site inspections. The inspections are conducted by trained safety and health compliance officers. The law requires that an authorized representative of the employer and a representative of the workers be given an opportunity to accompany the inspector for the purpose of aiding the inspection. Workers also have the right to notify the Department of Labor and request an inspection if they believe that unsafe and unhealthful conditions exist at their worksite. In addition, employees have the right to bring unsafe conditions to the attention of the safety and health compliance officer making the inspection. If upon inspection the Department of Labor believes that the Act has been violated, a citation of violation and a proposed penalty is issued to the employer.

Citations of violation issued by the Department of Labor must be prominently displayed at or near the place of violation.

The Act provides for mandatory penalties of up to $1,000 for each serious violation and for optional penalties of up to $1,000 for each non-serious violation. Penalties of up to $1,000 are required for each day during which an employer fails to correct a violation within the period set in the citation. Also, any employer who willfully or repeatedly violates the Act is to be assessed civil penalties of not more than $10,000 for each violation.

Criminal penalties are also provided for in the Act. Any willful violation resulting in death of an employee, upon conviction, is punishable by a fine of not more than $10,000 or by imprisonment for not more than six months, or by both. Conviction of an employer after a first conviction doubles these maximum penalties.

The Act provides that employees may not be discharged or discriminated against in any way for filing safety and health complaints or otherwise exercising their rights under the Act.

For assistance and information, including copies of the Act and of specific safety and health standards, contact the employer or the nearest office of the Department of Labor.

J D Hodgson
Secretary of Labor

FULL-SIZE OSHA POSTER (15½ in. high) must be displayed in every establishment.

EXHIBIT J-1

OCCUPATIONAL SAFETY AND HEALTH ADMINISTRATION
BUREAU OF LABOR STATISTICS REGIONAL OFFICES

Region 1—Boston
Connecticut
Maine
Massachusetts
New Hampshire
Rhode Island
Vermont

OSHA
John F. Kennedy Federal Bldg.
Government Center 1700-C
Boston, Massachusetts 02203
Area code 617

BLS
Regional Director
1603-A Federal Office Building
Boston, Massachusetts 02203
Area code 617

Region 2—New York
New Jersey
New York
Puerto Rico
Virgin Islands

OSHA
Astor Plaza
1515 Broadway
New York, New York 10036
Area code 212

BLS
Regional Director
341 Ninth Avenue
New York, New York 10001
Area code 212

Region 3—Philadelphia
Delaware
District of Columbia
Maryland
Pennsylvania
Virginia
West Virginia

OSHA
Penn Square Building
Room 410
Juniper and Filbert Streets
Philadelphia, Pa. 19107
Area code 215

BLS
Regional Director
Penn Square Building, Room 406
1317 Filbert Street
Philadelphia, Pennsylvania 19107
Area code 215

Region 4—Atlanta
Alabama
Florida
Georgia
Kentucky
Mississippi
North Carolina
South Carolina
Tennessee

OSHA
Room 311
1371 Peachtree St., NE.
Atlanta, Georgia 30309
Area code 404

BLS
Regional Director
1317 Peachtree Street, NE.
Atlanta, Georgia 30309
Area code 404

Region 5—Chicago
Illinois
Indiana
Michigan
Minnesota
Ohio
Wisconsin

OSHA
300 South Wacker Dr.
Chicago, Illinois 60606
Area code 312

BLS
Regional Director
300 South Wacker Dr.
Chicago, Illinois 60606
Area code 312

Region 6—Dallas
Arkansas
Louisiana
Oklahoma
Texas
New Mexico

OSHA
Texaco Building
1512 Commerce Street
Dallas, Texas 75201
Area code 214

BLS
Regional Director
1100 Commerce St.
Dallas, Texas 75202
Area code 214

Region 7—Kansas City
Iowa
Kansas
Missouri
Nebraska

OSHA
Waltower Building
823 Walnut Street
Kansas City, Missouri 64106
Area code 816

Region 8—Denver
Colorado
Montana
North Dakota
South Dakota
Utah
Wyoming

OSHA
Federal Building
1961 Stout Street
Box 3588
Denver, Colorado 80202
Area code 303

BLS
Regional Director
Federal Office Building
911 Walnut Street
Kansas City, Missouri 64106
Area code 816

378

EXHIBIT J-1—Concluded

Region 9—San Francisco
Arizona
California
Hawaii
Nevada

OSHA
10353 Federal Building
450 Golden Gate Avenue
Box 36017
San Francisco, California 94102
Area code 415

Region 10—Seattle
Alaska
Idaho
Oregon
Washington

OSHA
1804 Smith Tower Bldg.
506 Second Avenue
Seattle, Washington 98104
Area code 206

BLS
Regions 9 and 10—San Francisco and Seattle
Regional Director
450 Golden Gate Avenue
Box 36017
San Francisco, California 94102
Area code 415

K

Bureau of Motor Carrier Safety

New Driver Qualifications

On January 1, 1971, the Department of Transportation required that, before driving a commercial motor vehicle, new drivers must successfully complete a prescribed road test and written examination, and must be issued certificates of such completion. Information on such tests, files and records, and exemptions is contained in Part 391 of the *Motor Carrier Safety Regulations*.

For a determination as to whether your drivers and vehicles operate under federal safety regulations, contact the Bureau of Motor Carrier Safety, Federal Highway Administration, Department of Transportation, Washington, D.C. 20591, or its local representative for your area. (See Exhibit K-1 for regional offices.)

To assist in the administration of these tests and other required documents, the National Safety Council has prepared a unique, copyrighted set of all required driver forms. These are available through the NSC Order Department and include: employment application; physical examination, with certificate—in triplicate; road test with two certificates—in duplicate; written examination with answers; certificate of violations; annual review of driving record; previous employer inquiry; and state agency inquiry.

Pretrip Checklists for Truck and Bus Drivers

The Bureau of Motor Carrier Safety has prepared pretrip checklists designed to provide a safe, sequential, and time-saving proced-

FASTEN THAT SAFETY BELT! "A motor vehicle which has a seat belt assembly installed at the driver's seat shall not be driven unless the driver has properly restrained himself with the seat belt assembly." U.S. Dept. of Transportation, *Motor Carrier Safety Regulations,* Title 49, § 392.16.

ure for trucks and buses. These checklists include the federal regulatory pretrip check requirements. Copies of these checklists may be obtained from the Bureau of Motor Carrier Safety, Federal Highway Administration, Department of Transportation, Washington, D.C. 20591.

The checklists contain the information shown in Exhibits K-2 and K-3 of this Appendix.

Driver Qualification File

If your motor fleet is subject to federal Bureau of Motor Carrier Safety Regulations, the information shown in Exhibit K-4 must be maintained for your drivers, pursuant to Section 391.51 of the Regulations.

For information from the Bureau peculiar to specific regions of the U.S., Mexico, and Canada, see Exhibit K-1.

381

EXHIBIT K-1
U.S. DEPARTMENT OF TRANSPORTATION
Federal Highway Administration
Bureau of Motor Carrier Safety
Regional Offices

Region 1
4 Normanskill Boulevard
Delmar, New York 12054
Phone: 518—472-7866

Connecticut
Maine
Massachusetts
New Hampshire
New Jersey
New York
Rhode Island
Vermont

That part of Canada east of Highways 19 and 8 from Port Burwell to Goderich; thence a straight line running north through Tobermory and Sudbury, and thence due north to the Canadian Border.

Region 2 [Reserved.]

Region 3
31 Hopkins Plaza
Baltimore, Maryland 21201
Phone: 301—962-4572

Delaware
District of Columbia
Maryland
Pennsylvania
Virginia
West Virginia

Region 4
1720 Peachtree Road, NW.
Atlanta, Georgia 30309
Phone: 404—526-5049

Alabama
Florida
Georgia
Kentucky
Mississippi
North Carolina
South Carolina
Tennessee

Region 5
18209 South Dixie Highway
Homewood, Illinois 60430
Phone: 312—799-6300

Illinois
Indiana
Michigan
Minnesota
Ohio
Wisconsin

That part of Canada west of Highways 19 and 8 from Port Burwell to Goderich; thence a straight line running north through Tobermory and Sudbury, and thence due north to the Canadian border, and east of the boundary between the Provinces of Ontario and Manitoba to Hudson Bay and thence a straight line due north to the Canadian border.

Region 6
819 Taylor Street
Fort Worth, Texas 76102
Phone: 817—334-3225

Arkansas
Louisiana
New Mexico
Oklahoma
Texas

All Mexico except the States of Baja California and Sonora, and the territory of Baja California Sur.

Region 7
P. O. Box 7186
Country Club Station
Kansas City, Missouri 64113
Phone: 816—361-7898

Iowa
Kansas
Missouri
Nebraska

EXHIBIT K-1—Concluded

Regional Offices

Region 8
Room 242, Building 40
Denver Federal Center
Denver, Colorado 80225
Phone: 303—233-2330

    Colorado
    Montana
    North Dakota
    South Dakota
    Utah
    Wyoming

That part of Canada west of the boundary between the Provinces of Ontario and Manitoba to Hudson Bay and thence a straight line due north to the Canadian border, and east of Highway 95 from Kingsgate to Blaeberry and thence a straight line due north to the Canadian border.

Region 9
450 Golden Gate Avenue
San Francisco, California 94102
Phone: 415—556-3951

    Arizona
    California
    Hawaii
    Nevada

The States of Baja California, and Sonora, Mexico, and the Territory of Baja California Sur, Mexico.

Region 10
222 Southwest Morrison Street
Portland, Oregon 97204
Phone: 503—226-3793

    Alaska
    Idaho
    Oregon
    Washington

That part of Canada west of Highway 95 from Kingsgate to Blaeberry and thence a straight line due north to the Canadian border, and all of the Province of British Columbia.

EXHIBIT K-2
BUS DRIVERS' PRETRIP CHECKLIST

INSIDE

[ ] Parking Brake

Start Engine

[ ] Oil Pressure (Light or Gauge)

[ ] Air Pressure (Gauge)

[ ] Low Air Warning
(Air pressure below 40 psi check on pressure build-up. Air pressure above 60 psi deplete air until warning device works.)

[ ] Windshield Wiper & Washer

[ ] Heater—Defroster

[ ] Mirrors

[ ] Instrument Panel
(Telltale Lights or Buzzers)

[ ] Horn

[ ] Standee Line or Bar & Sign

[ ] Emergency Door—Light & Sign
(If Equipped)

[ ] Apply Rear Wheel Brakes in Emergency (Driver Manual Control)

[ ] Windows—Emergency Exit Sign

[ ] Steering Wheel—Play

[ ] Warning Devices, Fire Extinguisher, First Aid Kit, Axe

[ ] Turn on all Lights including 4-way Flasher

OUTSIDE

Front

[ ] Headlights

[ ] Clearance Lights

[ ] Identification Lights

[ ] Turn Signals & 4-way Flashers

[ ] Tires

Left Side

[ ] Sidemarker Lights

[ ] Reflectors

[ ] Wheels (Lugs)

Rear

[ ] Tail Lights

[ ] Stop Lights

[ ] Turn Signal Lights

[ ] Clearance Lights

[ ] Identification Lights

[ ] Reflectors

[ ] Tires

Right Side

[ ] Side Marker Lights

[ ] Reflectors

[ ] Entrance Door

[ ] Wheels (Lugs)

INSIDE

Stop Engine

[ ] Apply Service Brakes—Air loss should not exceed 3 psi per minute

EXHIBIT K-3
TRUCK DRIVERS' PRETRIP CHECKLIST

INSIDE

[　] Parking Brake (Apply)

Start Engine

[　] Oil Pressure (Light or Gauge)

[　] Air Pressure or Vacuum (Gauge)

[　] Low Air or Vacuum Warning Device (Air pressure below 40 psi check on pressure build-up. Air pressure above 60 psi deplete air until warning device works) (Vacuum below 8 inches Hg. check on build-up. Above 8 inches Hg. deplete vacuum until device works)

[　] Instrument Panel (Telltale lights or buzzers)

[　] Horn

[　] Windshield Wiper and Washer

[　] Heater—Defroster

[　] Mirrors

[　] Steering Wheel (Excess play)

[　] Apply Trailer Brakes in Emergency

[　] Turn on all Lights including 4-way Flasher

[　] Fire Extinguisher and Warning Devices

OUTSIDE

Front

[　] Headlights

[　] Clearance Lights

[　] Identification Lights

[　] Turn Signals and 4-way Flasher

[　] Tires and Wheels (Lugs)

Left Side

[　] Fuel Tank and Cap

[　] Sidemarker Lights

[　] Reflectors

[　] Tires and Wheels (Lugs)

[　] Cargo Tie-downs/or Doors

Rear

[　] Tail Lights

[　] Stop Lights

[　] Turn Signals and 4-way Flasher

[　] Clearance Lights

[　] Identification Lights

[　] Reflectors

[　] Tires and Wheels (Lugs)

[　] Rear End Protection (Bumper)

[　] Cargo Tie-downs/or Doors

Right Side

[　] Fuel Tank and Cap

[　] Sidemarker Lights

[　] Reflectors

[　] Tires and Wheels (Lugs)

[　] Cargo Tie-downs/or Doors

On Combinations

[　] Hoses and Couplers

[　] Electrical Connector

[　] Couplings (Fifth wheel, tow bar, safety chains, locking devices)

On Vehicles Transporting Hazardous Materials

[　] Marking or Placards

[　] Proper Shipping Papers

INSIDE

Stop Engine

[　] Release Trailer Emergency Brakes

[　] Apply service Brakes—Air loss should not exceed—
3 psi per minute on single vehicles
4 psi per minute on combinations

FASTEN SEAT BELT

Courtesy U.S. Department of Transportation, Federal Highway Administration

385

EXHIBIT K-4
DRIVER QUALIFICATION FILES
BUREAU OF MOTOR CARRIER SAFETY REGULATIONS
(Section 391.51)

(a) Each motor carrier shall maintain a driver qualification file for each driver it employs. A driver's qualification file may be combined with his personal file.

	(b) Regularly employed driver for continuous period beginning before January 1, 1971.	(c) Regularly employed driver not regularly employed for continuous period beginning before January 1, 1971.	(d) Intermittent, casual, or occasional driver employed under rules in Section 391.63.	(e) Driver furnished by another motor carrier and employed under rules in Section 391.65.
1. Medical examiner's certificate or legible photographic copy.	Required	Required	Required	Required
2. Waiver of physical disqualification under Section 391.49.	Required	Required		
3. Certificate of violations of motor vehicle laws required by Section 391.27.	Required	Required		
4. Annual review of driving record, pursuant to Section 391.25, dated and signed by person making review.	Required	Required		
5. Any other material relating to driver's qualifications or ability to safely drive a motor vehicle.	Required	Required		
6. Driver's employment application required by Section 391.21.		Required		
7. Responses of State agencies to inquiries on driver's record required by Section 391.23.		Required		

8. Certificate of road test required by Section 391.31 (e), or equivalent pursuant to Section 391.33.	Required	Required	
9. Certificate of written examination required by Section 391.35, or equivalent pursuant to Section 391.37.	Required	Required	
10. Driver's name, social security number, and identification number, type and issuing State of motor vehicle operator's license.		Required	
11. Certificate from motor carrier that regularly employs driver stating driver is fully qualified to drive a motor vehicle under federal safety regulations.			Required

(f) Except as provided in paragraph (g) of this section, each driver's qualification file shall be kept at the motor carrier's principal place of business for as long as a driver is employed by that motor carrier and for three years, thereafter.

(g) Upon a request in writing to, and with the approval of, the Director, BMCS, a motor carrier may keep one or more of its drivers' qualification files or parts of files at a regional or terminal office that the Director, BMCS, approves.

L

Sources of information on chemical safety

In order to keep abreast of current developments in chemical safety, many sources of information must be consulted. Books and printed matter quickly become outdated. Therefore, several practical sources of information are recommended to encourage wider use of a broad base approach. It is recognized that the following is incomplete, but may serve as a guide to other sources.

Emergency response systems are indicated by an asterisk (*). All other listings are non-emergency.

Compiled by H. H. Fawcett,
National Research Council
Washington, D.C.

ASSOCIATION OF AMERICAN RAILROADS

Director & Chief Inspector
Bureau of Explosives—Room 620
Association of American Railroads
American Railroads Building
Washington, D.C. 20036   Area Code 202/293–4048*

AMERICAN CHEMICAL SOCIETY

The 174 local sections of the American Chemical Society are interested in assisting in chemical safety wherever practical and should be considered as a source of scientific expertise. For the names and addresses of the officers of the local sections, write to:

American Chemical Society
Local Sections Operations
1155 Sixteenth Street, N.W.   Area Code 202/RE7–3337, Ext.
Washington, D.C. 20036   465

The Committee on Chemical Safety of the A.C.S. will also assist whenever possible. Mr. Earl Klinefelter is the staff liaison to the committee. The address and telephone number is the same as listed above.

DEPARTMENT OF COMMERCE—BUREAU OF STANDARDS

National Bureau of Standards   Information & Data Section, Fire
Washington, D.C. 20234   Technology Division
                                    301/921–3246

Office of Flammable Fabrics   Area Code 301/921–3116

Fire Services Section   Area Code 301/921–3175

Chief, Fire Research Section
Building Research Division   Area Code 301/921–3461

DEPARTMENT OF HEALTH, EDUCATION, AND WELFARE

Food and Drug Administration and Public Health Service

Bureau of Radiological Health
5600 Fishers Lane
Rockville, Maryland 20852   Area Code 301/443–4690

Division of Electronic Products   Area Code 301/443–4016

Office of Information   Area Code 301/443–3434

Division of Hazardous Substances & Poison Control
Bureau of Product Safety
5600 Fishers Lane
Rockville, Maryland 20852   Area Code 202/496–7606

Poison Control Center, National
  Clearinghouse
5401 Westbard Avenue
Bethesda, Maryland 20016   Area Code 202/496–7616

389

Toxicology Information Program
National Library of Medicine   Area Code 301/496–3147
8600 Rockville Pike
Bethesda, Maryland 20014   Area Code 301/496–1131

DEPARTMENT OF THE INTERIOR—BUREAU OF MINES

Coordinator of Explosives Research
Interior Building Room 3529
18th and C Streets, N.W.
Washington, D.C.   Area Code 202/343–3500

Pittsburgh Mining and Safety
  Research Center
4800 Forbes Avenue
Pittsburgh, Pennsylvania 15213   Area Code 412/621–4500 Ext. 260

DEPARTMENT OF LABOR

Information Services
Occupational Safety & Health
  Administration
1726 M Street, N.W.
Washington, D.C. 20210   Area Code 202/961–3914

MANUFACTURING CHEMISTS' ASSOCIATION

M.C.A. CHEMTREC (Chemical Transportation Emergency Center) is designed to provide immediate emergency-type information regarding hazardous chemicals in transportation, on a 24-hour basis.

Manufacturing Chemists Association
1825 Connecticut Ave., N.W.   Toll free number*
Washington, D.C. 20009   Area Code 800/424–9300

The Safety and Fire Protection Committee of the M.C.A. develops useful information on the safety and fire aspects of chemicals. Contact:

Manufacturing Chemists Association
1825 Connecticut Ave., N.W.   Area Code 202/HU3–6126 Ext.
Washington, D.C. 20009   242

Approximately 100 data sheets, plus chemical information cards and water transport information cards are available.

NATIONAL AGRICULTURAL CHEMICALS ASSOCIATION

National Agricultural Chemicals
Association
1155 Fifteenth St., N.W.
Washington, D.C. 20005   Area Code 202/296–1585
(Class B agricultural poisons)
Emergency Calls (24-hour re-
sponse)   *Area Code 513/961–4300**

NATIONAL ACADEMY OF SCIENCES–NATIONAL RESEARCH COUNCIL

NAS-NRC-NAE
2101 Constitution Avenue, N.W.
Washington, D.C. 20418

Committee on Fire Research
(Colonel R. Cliffe, Director)   Area Code 202/961–1486

Committee on Hazardous Ma-
terials
(H. H. Fawcett, Technical
Secretary)   Area Code 202/961–1579

NATIONAL FIRE PROTECTION ASSOCIATION

The numerous publications of the NFPA include a *Fire Protection Guide on Hazardous Materials,* Third Edition (1969), which includes Standards 325A, 325M, 49, 491M and 704M. For availability of this book, plus other services and advice, contact

The National Fire Protection Association
60 Batterymarch Street
Boston, Massachusetts 02110   Area Code 617/482–8755

FEDERAL FIRE COUNCIL

The Federal Fire Council coordinates fire prevention efforts for the Federal government, but will also service non-governmental requests whenever possible. The Fire Council Library (now at the Bureau of Standards, FRASIC collection) is an excellent source of reports and other publications.

Staff Director, Federal Fire
Council
7th and D Streets, S.W.
Washington, D.C. 20407   Area Code 202/962–6228

NATIONAL SAFETY COUNCIL

The Industrial Department of the NSC includes:

(a) Chemical Section

(b) Research and Development Section

(c) Public Employee Section, Fire Division

(d) Occupational Health Nursing

(e) Industrial Hygiene

Each has a staff representative who may be reached:

c/o The National Safety Council

425 N. Michigan Avenue
Chicago, Illinois 60611

Area Code 312/527–4800
(ask for services desired)

In addition, the NSC Library has extensive collections of literature on chemicals and other materials, and will assist in locating desired data.

NEW YORK STATE

Division of Fire Safety
155 Washington Avenue
Albany, New York 12210
NOTE: Radio contact by
   KDX 409 on 45.88 mHz or
   KLG 647 on 45.5 mHz.

Area Code 518/474–6746

Information on fire aspects of chemicals in emergencies is available on a 24-hour basis.

OFFICE OF CONSUMER AFFAIRS

Office of Consumer Affairs
Executive Office of the President
New Executive Office Building
Washington, D.C. 20506

Area Code 202/395–3682

Director for Industry Relations.

Area Code 202/395–3320

UNDERWRITERS' LABORATORY, INC.

Underwriters' Laboratory, Inc.
207 E. Ohio Street
Chicago, Illinois 60611

Area Code 312/642–6969

Underwriters' Laboratory has extensive "chemical" files, acquired during evaluation and labeling. Ask for specific services desired.

392

CANADIAN CHEMICAL PRODUCERS' ASSOCIATION

The Transportation Emergency Assistance Plan (TEAP) is an industry-wide program of the Canadian Chemical Producers' Association (CCPA). It enlists the cooperation of its members and co-ordinates their efforts to provide technical advice and assistance to police, fire, and civil protection authorities in the event of highway, rail, and marine accidents involving chemical products. Further information may be obtained from:

The Canadian Chemical Pro-
   ducers' Association
Suite 2121 Tower "A"
Place de Ville
Ottawa, Canada   Area Code 613/237–6215

INDUSTRIAL HEALTH FOUNDATION

This group, whose membership includes over 400 companies and other groups, abstracts, researches, and coordinates knowledge on industrial health and safety problems. For information on services (including excellent monthly abstracts and other services) contact:

Industrial Health Foundation
5231 Centre Avenue
Pittsburgh, Pennsylvania 15232   Area Code 412/687–2100

INTERNATIONAL LABOUR ORGANIZATION, GENEVA, SWITZERLAND

This group, founded under the League of Nations in 1920, is part of the United Nations, and has 121 national members. The Health and Safety Center abstracts and re-distributes 30,000 documents of world literature and prepares 2,500 cards under the *CIS* system per year. For service details contact:

U.S. National Center Director
International Labour Office
666 11th Street, N.W.
Washington, D.C. 2001   Area Code 202/638–5656

or write directly to:

International Occupational
   Safety Health Informa-
   tion Centre
International Labour Office
1211 Geneva 22,
Switzerland

393

AMERICAN MEDICAL ASSOCIATION

American Medical Association
Office of Occupational & Environmental Health
535 N. Dearborn Street
Chicago, Illinois 60610   Area Code 312/527–1500, Ext. 481

NATIONAL INSTITUTE FOR OCCUPATIONAL SAFETY AND HEALTH (NIOSH)

Scientific Reference Branch
National Institute for Occupational Safety & Health
1014 Broadway
Cincinnati, Ohio 45202   Area Code 513/684–2693

OAK RIDGE NATIONAL LABORATORY

Nuclear Safety Information
Oak Ridge National Laboratory
P.O. Box Y   Area Code 615/483–8611
Oak Ridge, Tennessee 37830   Ext. 3–5453

Toxicology Information Re-
sponse Center
Oak Ridge National Laboratory
P.O. Box Y   Area Code 615/483–8611
Oak Ridge, Tennessee 37830   Ext. 3–5533, 3–7422

ENVIRONMENTAL PROTECTION AGENCY

WATER: Oil and Hazardous
       Materials
       EPA Crystal Mall
       Bldg. 2, Room 512
       Arlington, Virginia
       22202   Area Code 703/557–7663

AIR: U.S. Environmental
       Protection Agency
       Air Pollution Control Office
       Research Triangle Park
       North Carolina   Area Code 919/549–8411
       27701   Ext. 2251

394

Office of Air Programs
EPA Park Lawn Bldg.,
Room 1759
5600 Fishers Lane
Rockville, Maryland
20852   Area Code 301/443–4120

INSTITUTE OF MAKERS OF EXPLOSIVES

Institute of Makers of Explosives
420 Lexington Avenue
New York, New York 10017   Area Code 212/689–3237

General References

"Safety and Accident Prevention in Chemical Operations," Ed. by Fawcett and Wood, Interscience Div., John Wiley & Sons, New York, N.Y., 1965, 617 pages.

"The Literature of Chemical Safety," by H. H. Fawcett, in two parts, Part I, page A815 (Oct.); Part II, page A897 (Nov.), Journal of Chemical Education, Vol. *42, 1965.*

"References to Representatives Sources of Information on Chemicals," by H. H. Fawcett, March 1967 (published as revised edition of National Safety Council Data Sheet, "Chemical Safety References," No. 486).

Publications of the Manufacturing Chemists' Association, 1825 Connecticut Avenue, N.W., Washington, D.C. 20009 (free index available).

Publications of the National Safety Council, 425 N. Michigan Avenue, Chicago, Ill. 60611 (free index available). Also recommended is Chemical Section Monthly Safety Newsletter, published by NSC.

Publications of the Compressed Gas Association, 500 Fifth Avenue, New York, N.Y. 10036 (free index available).

Publications of the Industrial Health Foundation, 5231 Centre Ave., Pittsburgh, Pa. 15232.

Publications of the American Industrial Hygiene Association, 210 Haddon Ave., Westmont, N.J. 08108.

Nuclear Safety Information Center, Oak Ridge National Laboratory, P.O. Box Y, Oak Ridge, Tenn. 37831.

COSATI Directory of Federally Supported Information Analysis Centers,

January 1970, Committee on Scientific and Technical Information, Federal Council for Science and Technology, 71 pages, available as PB 189300 from National Technical Information Service, 5285 Port Royal Road, Springfield, Va. 22151, $3.00 (hardback) or $.65 (microfiche). This directory of 119 Federally-supported information analysis centers is descriptive, containing information on mission, scope, and services provided by the listed centers.

Publication and services of the Environment Information Center, Inc., 124 East 39th St., New York, N.Y. 10016. Tele. 212–685-0955

Bibliography

American National Standards Institute, 1430 Broadway, New York, N.Y. 10018, *Safety Standard for Powered Industrial Trucks.*

―――. *Manual on Uniform Traffic Control Devices for Streets and Highways.*

―――. *Method of Recording and Measuring Motor Vehicle Fleet and Passenger Accident Experience.*

―――. *Method of Recording and Measuring Work Injury Experience.*

American Trucking Association, Inc., Washington, D.C., *Motor Carrier Machinery Handling Guide.*

Association of American Railroads, Chicago, Ill., *Suggested Methods for Loading, Blocking and Bracing of Freight in Closed Trailers for Trailer on Flat Car Service* (Revised 1965).

Baker, J. S., *Traffic Accident Investigator's Manual for Police,* Northwestern University, Evanston, Ill. (1965).

Burton, H. *The School Bus,* Belknap Educational Enterprises, Inc., Nashville, Tenn.

Institute of Public Safety, Pennsylvania State University, University Park, Pa., *Motor Fleet Safety Supervision, Principles and Practice* (1972).

National Conference on School Transportation, Florida State Department of Education, Tallahassee, Fla., *Standards for School Bus Operation* (Revised 1970).

National Safety Council, 425 N. Michigan Ave., Chicago, Ill. 60611:

Accident Facts, Stock No. 021.52. (Issued annually.)

Accident Prevention Manual for Industrial Operations, Stock No. 121.36.

Fleet Accident Rates, Stock No. 229.26.

Fundamentals of Industrial Hygiene, Stock No. 151.12.

Getting Started, Stock No. 229.71.

How To Make a Safety Speech, Stock No. 029.02.

Manual on Classification of Motor Vehicle Traffic Accidents, Stock No. 329.34.

Million Mile Club, Stock No. 298.06

Motor Fleet Catalog, Stock No. 2318–127.

National Directory of Safety Films, Stock No. 029.12.

National Fleet Safety Contest Rules, Stock No. 0612–44.

National Safety Council Catalog-Poster Directory, Stock No. 2318–197.

National Safety News, Stock No. 111.01. (Monthly.)

OSHA Standards Checklist (in 16 volumes), Stock No. 115.01.

Professional Way—Defensive Driving, Stock No. 298.60.

Safe Driver Award Rules, Stock No. 229.65.

School Transportation: A Guide for Supervisors, Stock No. 221.32.

Small Fleet Guide, Stock No. 221.34.

Successful Supervision, Stock No. 221.33.

Supervisors Guide to Human Relations, Stock No. 151.09.

Supervisors Safety Manual, Stock No. 151.05–3.

Talk Topics: Motor Fleet Book 1, Stock No. 229.56.

Traffic Safety, Stock No. 311.01. (Monthly.)

Vehicle Damage Scale for Traffic Accident Investigators, Stock No. 329.31.

National Fire Protection Association, 60 Batterymarch St., Boston, Mass. 02110. *Fire Protection Handbook*, 13th ed.

———. *National Fire Codes*. (10 volumes.)

Nichols, James L. *Drug Use and Highway Safety: A Review of the Literature*, Wisconsin State University, July, 1971.

Presnall, Lewis F. *What About Drugs and Employees?* Advertising and Public Relations Department, Kemper Insurance Group, Long Grove, Ill.

State of Illinois, Governor's Traffic Safety Coordinating Committee. *Effects of Drugs on Driving*, September, 1971.

Transportation Safety Association of Ontario and Industrial Accident Prevention Associations, Toronto 1, Ontario, *Operator's Manual, The Safe Use of Industrial Power Trucks.*

U.S. Department of Labor. Occupational Safety and Health Standards. Part 1910, Chapter XVII, "Title 29—Labor," *Code of Federal Regulations.* For sale by Superintendent of Documents, U.S. Government Printing Office, Washington, D.C. 20402.

U.S. Department of Transportation. *Alcohol Safety Countermeasures Program*, National Highway Safety Bureau, June, 1970.

———. *Motor Carrier Safety Regulations*, Federal Highway Administration, Bureau of Motor Carrier Safety. Available as Stock No. 5004–0006 from Superintendent of Documents, U.S. Government Printing Office, Washington, D.C. 20402.

Index

400

Clothing hazards, 81, 82
Coefficient of friction
  braking, 350–352
  chains, 352
  tires, 351
Collision prevention, 137
  rear-end, 344
  six positions, 137
Coloring, protective, 16, 105, 344–348
  "highway yellow" paint, 201
  two-tone combinations, 345–347
  visibility, night, 344–345
Commentary driving, 131–132
Committees
  accident investigation, 79–80
  accident review, 74, 178–185, 272–273
  safety, 25, 30, 188, 239–240
Communication, supervision of, 165
Consumer affairs, U.S. Office of, 392
Contests, safety, 5, 213–214
  American Transit Association, 26
  National Fleet, 64–65, 166, 250–251, 269–270
  see also Awards
Cornell Aeronautical Laboratories, Inc., 22
Costs, accident; see Accident costs
  hiring; see Drivers, cost
Coupling check, 366
Courtesy cards, 47–48
Courtesy driving, 249
  in driver selection, 105
Court action, 39
Crank check, 364
Creepers, garage, 201

Dashboard sticker, 47–48
Decisions, written, 184
  policy, 12, 240
Defensive driving, 135–136
  course, 129, 131, 144
Detonators, brake, 138
Discrimination, job, 108, 124–125
Dispatchers, 155, 161–162
  ambulance, 275–278
Diagram, accident, 57–59
Dock boards, 202
Drinkers, problem, 174
  see also Alcohol
Drivers
  age, 108, 271

Drivers (*Continued*)
  attitudes, 99–101, 105, 110, 218, 283, 304–306
  bus, 234
  cost of hiring, 34, 106
  daily report form, 232
  education, 109, 304–306
  fines, 104, 159
  handbook, 303
  Improvement Program, 134, 304
    see also Defensive driving course
  inspection, 105, 286–289
    report, 231
  motivation, 36, 166
  performance; see Performance, driver
  preventive maintenance by, 127, 230–232, 363–366
  profile of, 103
  reaction time, 139, 362
  responsibilities, 99–101
  selection, 76, 99–125, 282–283
    procedure, 110
    qualifications, 380–381, 386–387
    see also Applicants, job
  sex of, 108
  supervision, 36, 154–167, 304
    school bus, 300–301
  testing; see Testing
  training; see Training
  truck, 234
Driving
  alcohol and, 168, 169
  awards; see Awards
  commentary, 131–132
  defensive; see Defensive driving
  discourteous, 105
  drugs and, 168–169, 170–171
  emergency, 262, 265–267, 284–286, 289
  errors, 155–161, 184
  evaluation, 100
  experience, previous, 103–104
  maneuvers, basic, 140
  natural ability, 104, 107–110
  ranges, 104, 132
  records; see Records
  roadeos; see Roadeos
  seeing habits, 137
  skill, 104–105
  stop-and-go, 271
  traffic, 104, 140
Drugs, use of, 123, 168–177, 269
  abuse, 170

401

NOTE: The information and recommendations contained in this Manual have been compiled from sources believed to be reliable and to represent the best current opinion on the subject. No warranty, guarantee, or representation is made by the National Safety Council as to the absolute correctness or sufficiency of any representation contained in this and other publications, and the National Safety Council assumes no responsibility in connection therewith. Nor can it be assumed that all acceptable safety measures are contained in this (and other publications), or that other or additional measures may not be required under particular or exceptional conditions or circumstances.